SEXUAL SABOTAGE

SEXUAL SABOTAGE

JUDITH A. REISMAN, PHD

HOW ONE MAD SCIENTIST UNLEASHED A PLAGUE OF CORRUPTION AND CONTAGION ON AMERICA

WND Books

SEXUAL SABOTAGE

WND Books

Published by WorldNetDaily

Washington, D.C.

Written by Judith A. Reisman Ph.D.
Jacket design by Mark Karis
Interior design by Neuwirth & Associates, Inc.

WND Books are distributed to the trade by:
Midpoint Trade Books
27 West 20th Street, Suite 1102
New York, NY 10011

WND Books are available at special discounts for bulk purchases. WND Books, Inc. also publishes books in electronic formats. For more information call (541) 474-1776 or visit www.wndbooks.com.

ISBN 13 Digit: 978-1-935071-85-3

Library of Congress information available

Printed in the United States of America

10 9 8 7 6 5 4 3 2 1

CONTENTS

IN PRAISE AND GRATITUDE

To our moral and honorable Judeo-Christian "Greatest Generation" to redress their libeled historical record.

And to United States Supreme Court Justice Antonin Scalia who assured me decades ago that authoritative evidence might reverse our scientifically fraudulent sex laws.

Mother's Flag

ACKNOWLEDGEMENTS

MY ABIDING GRATITUDE TO my longtime friends Elizabeth and Joseph Farah of WorldNetDaily for their resolute belief in my work and for shepherding this book through to fruition despite its many bizarre trials and tribulations.

Thanks particularly to David Kupelian for his consistent encouragement, to my WND Editor Megan Byrd for her kindly, professional, unruffled resolve, and to Katie Clark Vecchio for reducing my behemoth manuscript into a readable size.

I am especially grateful to the excellent WND team that made it possible for one more politically incorrect book to reach the great American public, and to my diverse and loyal readers who have informed, encouraged, and supported me for these many years.

And finally, of course, to my generous, cherished family, all of whom have succored me through good times and bad. I owe them my balance and my joy.

[CHAPTER 1]

Hate America: Libeling the World War II Generation

> [T]his generation . . . left their ranches in Sully County, South Dakota, their jobs on the main street of Americus, Georgia, they gave up their place on the assembly lines in Detroit and in the ranks of Wall Street, they quit school or went from cap and gown directly into uniform. They answered the call to help save the world from the two most powerful and ruthless military machines ever assembled.[1]
>
> —Tom Brokaw, *The Greatest Generation* (1998)

AFTER WORLD WAR II, it would take roughly fifteen years for hedonistic "hate America" saboteurs to seduce the children of the "Greatest Generation:"

> Picture a thirteen-year-old boy . . . wearing his Walkman headphones or watching MTV. He enjoys the liberties hard won over the centuries by the alliance of philosophic genius and political heroism, consecrated by the blood of martyrs; he is provided with comfort and leisure by the most productive economy ever known to mankind; science has penetrated the secrets of nature in order to provide him with the marvelous, lifelike electronic sound and imagery production he is enjoying . . . life is made into a nonstop, commercially prepackaged masturbational fantasy . . . the new American life-style has become a Disneyland version of the Weimar Republic for the whole family.
>
> —Allan Bloom, *The Closing of the American Mind* (1987)[2]

"Mother's Flags" hung in the windows of most homes in my neighborhood in 1942. Walking past them, I knew that when a blue star was replaced with a gold one, another son or daughter had died to protect me and my country.[3] My gratitude and sense of obligation began then, as 416,800 soldiers died, sixteen million fought under arms, and millions of stateside Americans shouldered the burdens of war.[4] Little did we know that, having survived the enemy forces in Europe, Africa, Asia, and the Pacific Ocean, our heroes would come home only to be sabotaged, betrayed by a cult of American draft dodgers lounging on the grassy slopes of Indiana University.

There, strolling along the tree covered green campus and the undisturbed wilderness of Dunn's Woods, Alfred C. Kinsey, a zoologist, studied gall wasps, taught classes, conducted "sexual research," and, in 1948 and 1953, published reports that defamed our heroes, their families, and everything they fought and died for. With a cadre of devoted followers, this "scientist" lied about our forebears and slandered the World War II generation as promiscuous, adulterous, homosexual, and even bestial. Abundant evidence proves that these sexual perversions reflected the activities and character of the Indiana University professors—not of our accused World War II fighting men and women. Nonetheless, this false "statistical survey" of the morals of World War II Americans would be believed and relied upon for generations to come. *Indeed, it continues to seduce our nation, even today.*

In 1948, when Kinsey's first book was published, I was thirteen years old and wholly unaware that my freedom and safety were a legacy granted me largely by unknown women bred as independent ladies and unknown men bred with "religion and the spirit of a gentleman." Little did we know, in 1948, that the nation's character would be transformed from Tom Sawyer and Becky Thatcher to that of the tortured youth of the 1948 pornographic novel, *Amboy Dukes*. We were still being lifted aloft to higher things by the virtues of the founders' generation reflected in our own World War II parents.

In 1948, my parents, like most people on our street, never locked the car or our front door. The paint spray can was not invented until 1949, and graffiti did not mar shops and signs, even on the tough side of town. Stores did not have wrought-iron bars protecting their windows. Burglar alarms were rare indeed.

In 1948, I walked the mile from my house to Bancroft Junior High

School in Los Angeles. My fellow students discussed weekend plans—parties, dances, and church and synagogue events—and we commiserated with several movie stars' children, whose parents were divorced.

On Saturdays, I often took the trolley from Hollywood to the beach, where I spread my towel on the sand, searched my lunch bag for an apple, and lolled about reading my book, swimming, and finding seashells. Catching the last streetcar back to L.A., I sauntered home after dark. Some Saturdays I might have tarried on Hollywood Boulevard, peeking in the shops, enjoying an ice cream cone before I moseyed home in the evening.

In 1948, as my friends and I meandered through beaches, parks, and streets, we had no idea of the "sex, drugs, and rock 'n' roll" that would soon assault us. Like me, Elvis was thirteen, and John Lennon was only eight years old. Few kids smoked cigarettes or drank alcohol. Drugs? A very sophisticated friend once asked me if I'd like to smoke marijuana. "What is it?" I asked. When she told me, I was stunned. "Why would I ever want to do *that*?" I chalked up this strangeness to the fact that her father was a film director. Again, we all knew about "movie people."

Though very few kids had cars in the late 1940s and early 1950s, one nice sixteen-year-old boy rode a motorcycle and occasionally picked me up after classes at Fairfax High School. Of course, he never tried to kiss me. The phrase "sweet sixteen and never been kissed" still applied to most girls I knew. We never heard of "date rape."

In 1948, my parents did not worry much about my safety. They knew I didn't take rides from strangers and I was a "good girl." Even our liberal crowd was not a *sexually* liberal crowd. Child molesters were considered rare indeed, and though some of those queer fellows lurked about in movie theaters, parents still usually felt their children's independence and freedom outweighed the rare possibility of harm.

This was the common reality in 1948. Americans of all races and religions and from most socioeconomic backgrounds tended to share similar morals. In fact, most single men were quite likely to be virgins as adults, including *Playboy's* Hugh Hefner and liberal CBS newscaster Andy Rooney. Drafted in 1941, Rooney recalled his Colgate college football team, saying that none of his friends there had smoked and "we didn't say 's—t' or 'f—k,' and we didn't sleep with our girlfriends. Sex was only a rumor to us."[5]

Former NBC anchorman Tom Brokaw wrote what is perhaps the

most celebrated study of World War II Americans in his 1998 book, *The Greatest Generation*. Through stories, private letters, poems, pictures, and diaries, he documented and summarized their values and ethical character. Brokaw wrote that their morals were as important for victory as were "tanks and planes and ships and guns." He thought it would be wonderful to have a "statistical survey of America's strengths." Indeed, such research would have been valuable.

For tragically, the world would soon view a false "statistical survey" of World War II Americans defining this generation's moral and ethical character. While our fathers and grandfathers fought World War II, and while our mothers and grandmothers both overseas and on the home front bore the burdens of war, Alfred C. Kinsey did not. Instead, when America entered the war December 7, 1941, the forty-one-year-old zoologist[6] was an Indiana University teacher "researching" human sexuality. Wrapping himself in the mantle of "science," Kinsey, a secret sexual psychopath, would project his own sexual demons onto the men and women appreciably called the *Greatest* Generation, the Americans who saved the world from Hitler's national socialism.

Riding on the financial support and seemingly impeccable credentials of the Rockefeller Foundation, the National Research Council, and Indiana University, Kinsey published his distorted data in *Sexual Behavior in the Human Male* in 1948 and *Sexual Behavior in the Human Female* in 1953 and, as his fans say, the world was never the same. With a Madison Avenue advertising blitz, these two reports were aggressively marketed and gained credibility as Kinsey focused the western world on the imagined mote in the eye of his fellow citizens, rather than on the beam in his own.

The men who came home after World War II surely would have agreed with 1960s pop singers Paul Simon and Art Garfunkel: "Gee, but it's great to be back home. Home is where I want to be." But while these heroes were trying to resume their lives, they were being sabotaged by a subversive barrage, a twisted campaign that informed the world that American men were sexually deviant. Under this assault, they surely would also have agreed with other Simon and Garfunkel lyrics: "Everywhere I go, I get slandered, libeled. I hear words I never heard in the Bible. . . ."

"Kinsey not only studied sexuality," wrote one of his admirers, "he helped create it . . . in such a way that it is difficult for us to recognize what pre-1950s sexuality looked like."[7] True. But while Kinsey's *narrative* described "a period of sexual repression," his *statistics* claimed that the generation was sexually immoral, promiscuous, and deviant.[8] Why the contradiction? As one who was there, I witnessed firsthand his sexual slander of heroic Americans. And, as one of the elders now, I have researched Alfred Kinsey for thirty-five years, finding that he and his cult libeled our World War II warrior generation in order to validate his own cowardly perversions by creating a "sexual revolution."

Sadly, he succeeded. Morris Ernst, Kinsey's American Civil Liberties Union (ACLU), lawyer, explained that Kinsey could collapse Victorian morality by libeling World War II fathers. Since "the whole of our laws and customs in sexual matters is to protect the family [and] the base of the family is the father [Kinsey would prove] 'is quite different from anything the general public had supposed.'"[9] Thus, slandering "father" could gut the laws and customs that protected mothers, children, and the family. And it did.

No match for Kinsey's media blitzkrieg, the war generation's humble reticence to "talk about what happened" gave Kinsey & Company carte blanche. Domestic propagandists launched a stealth attack on their own homeland by defaming our heroes as hypocritical perverts, while our fighting men, still in shock from combat, tried to rebuild their lives. War-weary, America was bombarded with the highly publicized tale that Kinsey sold as reality. In believing the lies about the World War II generation's sexual character, our culture would see the hijacking of the hard-earned sexual laws and customs that protected the family, children, and civility. Alfred Kinsey decisively influenced and grievously damaged my society—and tarnished the legacy of the generation that saved the world. And as our society takes this slander for granted and allows the damage to spiral, Kinsey's co-conspirators continue to terrorize our nation. This is why I track the Kinsey lobby. Our children deserve better. Our Greatest Generation deserves better.

In 2005, sixty years after the end of World War II, I watched the documentary, *The League of Grateful Sons*. In one scene, several elderly former marines stand at attention beside an Iwo Jima graveyard epitaph: "*When You Go Home, Tell Them For Us . . . For Your Tomorrows, We Gave Our Today. Semper Fi.*" The narrator explains that, for "half a century they were silent."[10] Finally, sighs an aged veteran, our "real history is being transferred to the younger generation."

That is my passion, to transfer the *real* history about the "Greatest Generation" to their heirs and to expose the libel of our finest Americans. It is vital that we clear the reputations of our parents, grandparents, and great-grandparents. The younger generation must know that their ancestors have been betrayed and defamed—and understand *why* and *by whom*. It is up to us to set the historical record straight.

Who Were We, Before Kinsey?

Although black slavery ended with the Civil War in 1865, women continued to live largely under patriarchal control for another fifty-five years. Indeed, in the 1860s and early 1870s, a new national scandal thrived: Traffic in *white female* sex slaves flourished in scores of big cities. New York was the "center of commercialized sex in the United States." Child and adult brothels were everywhere. Catering to "heterosexual and homosexual pleasures," commercial sex pictures and prices were posted "in hotels, shops, and saloons throughout the city," using alcohol and sex devices to "tempt the crowds."[11]

Catapulted by the Young Men's Christian Association (YMCA), on March 3,1873, New Yorkers passed an antiobscenity statute to try and control the spread of venereal disease and crime.[12] When he moved from Connecticut to New York, social reformer and crusader, Anthony Comstock, was horror-struck by the visible public traffic in sex. In 1868, he organized a public "suppression of vice" that resulted in massive arrests and a successful cleanup of New York City that spread nationwide over the next four decades.[13]

Markedly casual toward victims of the white slave traffic, sexually liberated psychiatrists, and psychologist-educators actively marketed the sexual freedom advocated by Clark University president G. Stanley Hall, his Viennese visitor, Dr. Sigmund Freud, and their colleagues. Thus—just as it does today—the battle raged between "repressed," pious, Americans and the "liberated" licentious academic elites. By 1910, men increasingly joined the organized women's movement to end the white slave traffic. In 1917, America entered World War I, a conflict joyfully ended in 1918. By the 1920s, even New Yorkers increasingly lived in a relatively sexually restrained and, thus, safe and sane environment. This was the culture in which our future World War II heroes were born and raised. But the battle for America's character still raged.

Stepping boldly into the fray, in the late 1920s, the Catholic Church began a campaign against Hollywood's brazen nudity and sadistic pornographic film indecency. As a result, with theaters half-empty, Hollywood studios were forced to hire writers and produce films that "fit" the moral values of average Americans. This meant hiring brilliant, often very moral writers to produce fluffy, witty, or charming dialogue and good drama that did not run afoul of the new Motion Picture Production Code, popularly known as the "Hays Code" for its creator, Will Hays. Under these highly moral guidelines, Hollywood entered its "golden era" from 1934 until the 1960s.[14]

So, while F. Scott Fitzgerald described Big City flappers "kissing, smoking, drinking, partying," average folks loved Norman Rockwell's small town Americana illustrations of naïve youths who fished, skipped school, graduated, dated, and married—though artistic elites ridiculed these images. Even in the wild world he described, Fitzgerald exposed the modesty of the times when he said that parents worried about their daughters "kissing" their beaux. "Kissed!" laughed contemporary historian Gertrude Himmelfarb. "Bloomsbury," she said of the elitist English blueblood-wanabees, "would have been amused by so quaint a notion of liberation."[15]

Like Fitzgerald and Rockwell, playwright Thornton Wilder lived among and wrote about Americans in *Our Town*. In his classic 1938 play about Grover's Corners, a boy and girl grow up as friends, fall in love, marry (naturally as virgins), work, have children, age, and die.[16]

Commending the common decency of most of the townsfolk, *Our Town* did not idealize the fictional town or the people who live there. The play described the basic decency and morality of a typically religious, conservative America, though it did not "point fingers, stereotype others, and otherwise divide people from one another."[17] Most Americans, white and black, in fact, tended to fit Wilder's description.[18]

With the Great Depression, however, between 1929 and 1932, the average American family income dropped 40 percent, from $2,300 to $1,500 annually,[19] as people lost their jobs, farms, and businesses. While many also lost hope, poverty-ridden and desperate Americans—on soup lines and bread lines—held true to their religious and moral values. "[S]urvival became the keyword . . . . [while] Democracies such as Italy and Germany eventually fell to dictatorships."[20]

By 1934, however, while Hitler's corporate, leftist *National Socialist German Labor Party* [Nazi] secretly geared for war,[21] America enjoyed an economic upturn that brought jobs to her thirteen million unemployed. Meanwhile, Berlin was the international center of the sexual decadence that nurtured Hitler's National Socialism. Later I will address Hitler and his comrades' sexual deviance, but for now note that the Nazis advocated a bogus platform of "family values." Here at home, the United States did *not* return to the big-city decadence of the late 1800s or of the Bloomsbury effete. By 1939, men who had been on soup lines worked in war factories. A couple of years later, they fought overseas to defend the values that had sustained them during the Great Depression. In fact, between 1941 and 1945, 416,800 U.S. soldiers would die to preserve those values.[22]

Joseph Heller, who wrote the classic World War II novel, *Catch-22*, grew up in a small Coney Island flat. Heller says he and his friends didn't know they were poor. Like most people, he lived with his family until he joined the service and, like my own father, mother, aunts, and uncles, he brought his paycheck home to his mother until he enlisted. Women and children walked about most small and large cities, day and night, alone and "without fear, without harm," says the observant war reporter and novelist. His New York neighborhood was poor but "safe, insular, and secure":

> In the nineteen years I lived on that street before going into the army . . . I never heard of a rape, an assault or an armed robbery in our neighborhood. . . . There was just about no fear of violence. . . . And there was practically no crime. . . . Both inside and outside the house we were safe. There were no kidnappings or burglaries, and always in decent weather there were scores of kids on the street to play with.[23]

Divorce was rare and nearly everyone had married parents. Some, like Heller and his sister and brother, were raised by a widowed mother; unwed mothers were rare and, therefore, seldom seen, as disdain for "illicit" sex crossed class, race, and education lines. Indeed, Heller and his cronies joined the military as virgins. He adds "with pride" that his married pilot buddies never "exhibited even the slightest interest in sex with another woman, not on rest leaves in Rome and not in Sicily, Cairo, or Alexandria."[24]

"Sex without love" still "seemed utterly unethical" to college men,[25] complained Dutch sexual libertarian sex and law researchers, Phyllis and Eberhard Kronhausen, PhD, in 1960. Rich or poor, all races and religions tended to share the sexual morality, the value of male and female chastity belittled by the Kronhausens', reported by Fitzgerald, and celebrated by Rockwell, Wilder, and Heller. And while the sophisticated elite ridiculed America as sentimental and unreal, America *did* largely resemble Norman Rockwell's paintings.

The Greatest Generation: God, Country, Family

Born in 1940, retired NBC news anchorman Tom Brokaw confirms Wilder's fiction and Heller's nostalgia in his landmark 1998 book, *The Greatest Generation*. Brokaw interviewed World War II Americans and published their intimate records, revealing their hearts and souls, the "values bred into the young men and women" who came of age as war broke out. "[R]esponsibility and a commitment to honesty," said Brokaw, ". . . . are the connective cords of their lives."[26] There were certainly exceptions, but this was the rule.

American history is unambiguous about what Brokaw calls "faith in God" as a singular mark of this generation. Since the Revolutionary and even the Civil Wars, the beliefs and valor of American warriors certainly shaped the World War I and World War II American character. To understand the heroes of the generation, we need to understand their beliefs in God. For, despite the current fashion of covering up our religious heritage; masking truth by bearing false witness about American faith defiles both historical accuracy and the American people.

Always wary of "temptation," our founders labored to rear generations cut from the sturdy, unpretentious, and demanding cloth of Scripture. As a result, the World War II generation was *trained* to honor God, country, and family—and was thus trained to build a secure life for their children and, indeed, for us all. "Faith in God was . . . part of the lives of the WWII generation," Brokaw wrote. "They stayed true to their values of personal responsibility, duty, honor, and faith. . . . [Those] outside their families reminded them of the ethos of their family and community."[27]

Most World War II Americans embodied the "strict standards of my mother and father," wrote Brokaw, "the parents of my friends, my teachers, my coaches, my ministers." Even local businessmen would remind him, "that's not how you were raised."[28] After the bombing of Pearl Harbor on December 7, 1941, Brokaw found those "strict standards" at work. Those who could not serve in the military did everything in their power to help at home. One World War II reporter recalls:

> Men and women alike exuded a patriotic fervor unmatched in history up to that time in the USA. Families saved the lard from cooking and took it to the markets where it was recycled. Ration books were ever-present, containing tokens allowing for monthly gasoline and food allowances. Extras were nonexistent. Only the bare necessities for life were used.[29]

Eager to free their men for combat, women served in the Army Nurse Corps, Navy Nurse Corps, and as WACS (Women's Army Corps), WAVES (Women Accepted for Volunteer Emergency Service), and WASPS (Women Airforce Service Pilots). Six million "Rosie the Riveters" built tanks, ships, planes, guns, jeeps, and machines needed for war.[30] Certainly, some women delighted in and some exploited their freedom, dancing and partying. However, millions more hurried home to shop, cook, and clean, to comfort, teach, and pray with their children, and often to care for aging parents. Millions wrote to their husbands and sweethearts every night. Most working moms relied on family, friends, and neighbors for childcare with less than a million children in government care centers at the war's end.[31]

Our Mothers' War recorded the perspectives of women typical of the time. Young brides reassured husbands of fidelity, no matter the war wounds. A wife moaned that, after Pearl Harbor, her husband awoke at "about five," looked in her eyes and said, "Listen, dear, I have to join up, now."[32] Women habitually downplayed shortages and rationing. "Possibly you have been reading of the severe cold and fuel shortage. We are very comfortable, have not had to shut off any rooms."[33] Scores had their babies alone. "Melisse," wrote that the "greatest hardship, of course, for those who were left at home" is the fear for their beloved's safety.[34] Mary

King, a Rhode Island mother "got the worst news possible about her son, [killed] in the last months of the war."[35] Unaware of her husband Frank's death, Natalie wrote to him, "Oh God, I think I'll go nuts. I see you everywhere. . . . Everyplace. . . . I'm so worried about you."[36]

On June 6, 1944, a million American soldiers aboard four thousand ships began landing on the Normandy beaches. After ten weeks of combat, American forces had driven the Germans from almost all of France. D-Day was the beginning of the end of the Third Reich, as the valorous Allied invasion of Europe defeated the Germans, who unconditionally surrendered by May 1945.[37]

Brokaw's own "wake up" call came in 1984, while filming an NBC documentary about the fortieth anniversary of D-Day. Recalling his trip to Normandy Beach in France, he said, "I had come to understand what this generation of Americans meant to history. *It is, I believe, the Greatest Generation any society has ever produced*"[38] (emphasis added).

Like our founders, the Greatest Generation did not glorify war, but rose to the occasion and became heroes and heroines. Robin, a regular G.I. Joe, wrote about his D-Day experience at Normandy; his poem, "Longest Day," includes this telling excerpt:

Do not call me hero,
Each night I stop and pray,
For all the friends I knew and lost,
I survived my longest day.
Do not call me hero,
In the years that pass,
For all the real true heroes,
Have crosses, lined up on the grass.

The *New York Times Book Review* described Brokaw's *Greatest Generation* as a "tribute to the members of the World War II generation to whom we Americans and the world owe so much."[39] *Biography Magazine* wrote that we owed the Americans of the '40s our freedom, our very lives.

The *Times* added, "We who followed this generation have lived in the midst of greatness." *The Daily Press* of Newport News, Virginia, wrote that the Greatest Generation was made up of "brave men and women who quite literally saved our skins." And documentarian Ken Burns extolled: "A generation of remarkable Americans—our better angels."[40] Indeed.

But after the war, our weary warriors didn't know what hit them. Alfred Kinsey claimed to have studied them when he reported that *nearly all* American men—our "better angels"—were actually sex offenders, though he also claimed that *no* women or children were harmed by rape or incest. Kinsey's saboteurs claimed that most pregnant single women—many our soldiers' sweethearts, who worked so hard to support the war effort—had supposedly aborted their babies en masse. He alleged that half of women and a vast majority of men had engaged in premarital sexual intercourse, most without regret. According to Kinsey, the men were not only promiscuous; most, he said, had supposedly used prostitutes, about a quarter had engaged in homosexual acts and, horrifyingly, a significant number of our fighting men who came from farms had actually committed sex acts with animals.

These are the boys who married their sweethearts in droves, to enjoy precious days or weeks before they went off to defend their ethical heritage. Contrast Kinsey's image of our war generation with the recollections of Tracy Sugarman in *My War: A Love Story in Letters and Drawings*, in which he reminisced about his relationship with June, his college love:

> How young and innocent most of us were. . . . For most of us in the 40s who were in love, romance and fantasy were the best we could manage . . . it was still hell having to wait to make it "legal."[41]

Tracy and June married so they could have a few "legal" months together before he joined the Navy and shipped out. The pledge of their love shimmers through every snippet from his letters:

> There's such a hell of a lot I want to show you and tell you. . . . Nope—distance doesn't make my heart grow fonder—it just lets me see what I've been looking at all along! And it's a lovely thing, a wonderful adorable wife . . . you've given me enough luck and happiness to keep me intact for a dozen wars! . . . I love you, Junie—with all my heart and soul and might. God bless you, wife. Your adoring happy husband.[42]

The Sugarmans were joyfully, faithfully married for over fifty years.

James Dowling wrote from a German POW camp to his girlfriend, Dorothy:

> Dearest Dorothy, I am all right, sweetheart. . . . Don't worry about me. We'll get married as soon as I get home again. I love you and miss you terribly, sweetheart, and wish that I could be with you soon. I have lots to tell you when I get back.[43]

Brokaw says James and Dorothy Dowling still have that love note.

Not "sexy" not "hot" but "sweetheart," "darling," "dearest," "honey," "wife." Chastity before marriage and faithfulness within it—this is what sexuality looked like, according to many typical World War II men. Disciplined by their military training and sacrifices, our World War II generation married in record numbers. This was their ethic. In the hell of war, of course, people did not always live up to this moral code, but it was always their ideal.

The marital picture Kinsey painted, however, is a lesson in contradiction. In Kinsey's world, almost half of all men and a quarter of women committed adultery ("extramarital sex" in Kinsey's parlance) before they were forty years old. Worse, he claimed that a quarter of *wives* had aborted their babies (without complications). Does this *really* sound like the Americans who "saved our skins"—the men of honor who fought for our country and the women who devoted their lives to their families and the war effort?

Marine battalion commander Lt. Col. John A. Butler's last words in letters to his wife and son typify the best of our men's values.

> Babe, I am leaving you with four small children . . . the living testimonials of this love. . . . I have great faith in them, babe, because I have faith in you. . . . It is so . . . important that they know, love and serve God and respect the integral dignity of all men. It is goodbye for a little while only, babe. I always loved you. Yours forever, Johnny.[44]

Ladies and Gentlemen

On public transport, most males automatically gave up their seats to the elderly, women, and children, and men and older boys commonly held open the door for women, old folks, and children. They would commonly offer to carry a girl's parcels or books, should she wish. Before seating themselves, men commonly held the chair for ladies to be seated, and waited to eat until the ladies had begun. Men asked permission to smoke and were especially careful to use "decent" language in the company of women and girls, who were called "ladies" and "young ladies." And a gentleman always defended ladies in any encounter. Patriarchy had many drawbacks if one's male intimate was alcoholic, violent or a slough, but the flip side was the male view of men as obligated, respectful, and of service to the female "weaker" sex.

In *The Compleat Gentleman*, Brad Minor, the former literary editor of *National Review* discussed American chivalry and gallantry: "I'll say plainly that the American republic . . . was founded by gentlemen and depends upon their gentlemanly ideals for both its prosperity and its posterity. Our republic, in fact, is the gentleman writ large . . . it's all about balance and restraint."[45] Minor supports this concept in his discussion of the *Titanic* survival rates; when even the wealthiest gentlemen gave their lives to secure the safety of women and children of all classes. Despite the claims of the feature film, *Titanic*, "Upper and-middle-class men," Minor wrote, "had the lowest rate of survival on the *Titanic*."[46]

On the other hand, men who are not reared to be courteous, to be gentlemen in service of ladies and children, often sink to the level of scoundrels. To paraphrase Voltaire, a belief in and fear of God are especially important for those in authority. *They* must fear a Higher Authority, who sees all that they do and who will mete out eternal punishment. Otherwise, they may do whatever evil pleases them. Voltaire also warned, "Those who can make you believe absurdities can make you commit atrocities."[47] In 1948, Kinsey, the antithesis of a gentleman, caused millions to believe absurdities about the sexual morality of the Greatest Generation. Predictably, restraint slackened and sexual atrocities followed—and have skyrocketed.

But as "our boys" recovered from the ravages of World War II, the ethos of family and community supported faith, fidelity, personal responsibility, honor, and children's innocence. In a sign of Comstockian success, New York City's Central Park welcomed couples and families who were unafraid and unaware of the misery and crime that had blighted the city a few decades earlier. In 1948, the safer, saner, softer, and *superior* society was visible to the naked eye. Cities that had once been vice-ridden saw women and children enjoying the freedom to casually roam streets, paths, and beaches. These venues were created because America's character supported public areas where men, women, and children—alone or otherwise—could safely wander, day *or* night. Today, however, these once-congenial places of public recreation are again vandalized centers of crime and cruelty, unsafe after dusk. The comparison is stark.

The sex industry had been thwarted—and vice squads contained its re-emergence—but elitist revolutionists often attacked our founders' beliefs in favor of lifestyles they fancied as licentious European cosmopolitanism. Building on the legacy of America's rugged provincialism and religious belief, World Wars I and II revived our national honor and stoked our confidence. Our refreshed patriotism made America great and kept us so for decades.

This really was who we were before, during, and after World War II. This is the generation that I knew as a child. This was America—an extraordinary nation that came of age during the Great Depression and two World Wars and went on to build the greatest modern society the world has ever known. And these are the men and women, our fathers and mothers and grandsires, our heroes and heroines, whom Kinsey claimed to truthfully reveal in *Sexual Behavior in the Human Male* (1948) and *Sexual Behavior in the Human Female* (1953), the generation that was sabotaged by a deviant pseudo scientist who libeled our legacy and screwed our society.

[CHAPTER 2]

The Kinsey Reports as Sabotage

> [I]t is probable that half or more of the boys *in an uninhibited society could reach climax by the time they were three or four years of age,* and that nearly all of them could experience such a climax three to five years before the onset of adolescence. (emphasis added)
>
> Alfred Kinsey, *Male* volume, p. 178

HOW DID THE WORLD come to see our Greatest Generation as sexual hypocrites?

Going into battle, many a soldier carried a photo of his wife or sweetheart and, with it, he carried the palpable fear of her possible abandonment. In all wars, the chastity and loyalty of women back home is critical to soldiers' morale and fighting spirit. Soldiers who doubt this fidelity begin to question the value of risking their lives to defend their wives or girlfriends—and their country. So suggestions of infidelity are an effective and universal war propaganda tool.

Alfred Kinsey took a page from the World War II playbook, capitalizing on the seeds of doubt planted by war propaganda—and copying its methods of sabotage.

On both sides of World War II, psychological warfare received huge sums of money. A 1943 *Life* magazine article revealed that the Office of War Information trained over "300 newsmen, radio and printing technicians" and others in propaganda. On the other side, "80% of Italian prisoners," the article said, "had PWB [Psychological Warfare Branch] leaflets in their possession or had read them."[48]

We now know that most soldiers—on all sides—were exposed to propaganda, including sexual propaganda. White (positive) propaganda encouraged soldiers to stay clean, strong, and to return home as healthy and honorable as when they left (despite the reality that some fighters *did* have sex abroad, amid the ever-present possibility of death). On the other hand, black (negative) propaganda was counterfeit information, made to look like helpful warnings from the soldier's country, seemingly obligated to reveal information about promiscuity at home. Such propaganda often claimed that wives and sweethearts were being unfaithful.

For the "benefit" of American GIs, Tokyo Rose and Axis Sally infamously broadcast tales of stateside betrayal.[49] Our surviving warriors confirm the historical record;[50] Axis Sally liked to tease and taunt the soldiers about their wives and sweethearts back in the States. "Hi fellows," she would say. "I'm afraid you're yearning plenty for her. But I just wonder if she isn't running around with the 4-Fs way back home."[51] Such broadcasts were hurtful, to be sure, but Allied soldiers easily saw through these enemy productions.

The most pervasive—and effective—black propaganda strategy used venereal disease "health education" campaigns. According to the extensive body of wartime literature, such as "WW2 US Medical Research Centre," venereal disease was a concern. Propagandists aimed to destroy the morale of the enemy by charging in leaflets dropped from airplanes, that wives and girlfriends are having illicit sex and being infected at home.

To increase their power, these materials regularly used credible-looking but invented "scientific" statistics. As Kinsey's oft-quoted reports would later demonstrate, people believe numbers *even if they are phony*. For example, a Nazi flyer that was dropped on English-speaking Allied soldiers, claims that of "20,000 women investigated a staggering proportion had venereal diseases, over 80% had V.D." The flyer alleged that, of infected women, 21% were prostitutes. Of the rest, 61% were "pickups," 18% were girlfriends, 17% were "girls under 20 years," and "84% were wives of men serving in the armed forces abroad."[52]

These false statistics defamed women and confused soldiers, damaging the men and their families, as this extract from a soldier's letter suggests: "Honey I don't want you to get mad when I ask you this question is there somebody else. If there is tell me."[53] In another snippet, after several paragraphs of sweet chatter to her soldier at war, a woman responds to such a suggestion: "I didn't like that remark you made about me taking guys out in your car hon . . . . That would be a dirty trick I think Henry . . . dear."[54]

During World War II seeking ways to demoralize enemy troops, the Axis and the Allies alike slandered their enemy's wives and sweethearts "back home" as sexually promiscuous. After the war Kinsey repeated this libel against American wives and sweethearts. It worked.

How did this battlefront in the war affect our postwar culture? Could it have planted seeds of doubt and roots of jealousy that caused divorce rates to spike after the war? Perhaps. A more lasting legacy may be that Alfred Kinsey was able to capitalize on the domestic effects of this damage, as Axis lies may have tweaked our view of American culture, made us more likely to receive "scientific" fiction as fact, and set us up for Kinsey's campaign. Tearing down America's dearly held ideals and faith in chastity and fidelity, it is entirely probable that world War II propaganda prepared the way for Kinsey's campaign—and provided models for his crusade. Just a few years hence, Kinsey's fraudulent publications would strongly resemble the battlefield's propagandist booklets, complete with purported scientific data.

The End of One War, the Beginning of Another

On August 15, 1945, Japan surrendered. After almost four years of war and a year of pre-war preparation, it could take years before all sixteen million soldiers staggered home. They never suspected that they would soon face another war—waged by a group of American draft-dodgers armed with their own domestic form of black propaganda.

Few veterans spoke much about their service. Laboring to remember the best and forget the worst, the repatriated warriors commonly experienced sudden, terrifying flashbacks and sleep disturbances. Post-traumatic stress, shell shock, was common. Some stammered for the rest of their lives. Trying to overcome the traumas of war, men made trips to military hospitals, sometimes frequent, often useless.

Every American city and hometown was shaken. Men and women struggled to find jobs again, earn a living, finish their educations, and restore their health, families, farms, and homes. The separations and shocks of war changed everyone, taxing even the most mature and committed. Husbands and fathers struggled to get to know their families—again or for the first time.[55] Children had grown without the control of their fathers and often resented the discipline dad needed and expected. The men worked to repair broken down homes and relationships gone rusty, or just gone after the four plus-year conflict. Divorces increased; many whirlwind marriages—by poorly matched couples trying to grasp the future before the boys shipped out—would soon collapse.

But the postwar years also brought dramatic increases in marriages and births. Having cheated death, many returning vets cherished life and got married immediately. Births jumped to the highest in our history. The population increased by twelve million between 1940 and 1947 with the unprecedented "Baby Boom" and, by 1950, youngsters under fifteen would be the largest single population group in the country.

Adding to the trauma facing returning warriors, the polio epidemic, that had begun in 1916, surged into "the 1940s and 50s when the disease crippled tens of thousands of children every summer. . . . In 1952 there were 59,000 new cases of polio. . . ."[56] It is hard for people today to imagine the terror of a veteran who came home to the specter of his children struck down by this seemingly random disease. In fact, *A Paralyzing Fear* documents families fleeing their homes after children in their neighborhoods were infected.[57]

Victorious in battle, the Greatest Generation knew who they were. Faith, loyalty, honesty, and patriotism were their defining characteristics. But overcome by the need to get back on their feet, to regain their health and sanity, they hunkered down. In doing so, they largely failed in one crucial area: to guard against domestic propagandists who would defame them—and their values—to their descendents. And so these heroic warriors could not defend themselves from a new, insidious enemy—the draft dodgers, domestic traitors, and elitists who had avoided war, who had stayed safe at home, and who would soon inflict their immorality on the rest of us. No, our heroes did not see it coming. A new war, *at home*, was about to assault the victors of World War II.

Before the "Welcome Home, Joe" banners had yellowed from the sun, a postwar twist on black propaganda punched the Greatest Generation below the belt. In January 1948, a mere three years

how did grampa avoid the draft?

the war ended, nearly every mainline American newspaper and magazine burned with headlines and quotes from a book that had hit colleges and bookstores. America's men, sons, fathers, and husbands were allegedly amoral and abnormal.

Then, with a one-two punch, Kinsey scored a knockout. In 1953, he launched *Sexual Behavior in the Human Female*, adding "scientific statistics" about American women, wives, and mothers. According to Kinsey, his survey *proved* that the men and women of our Greatest Generation were, as Ben Shapiro put it, "secret perverts and sex maniacs."[58] And worse.

"Kinsey stated it very clearly," said Charles Socarides, MD. "That all types of sexual activity—sex with the opposite sex, sex with the same sex, sex with both sexes, sex with children, sex with whips and chains, fisting sex, sex with animals—any kind of sex was normal and common."[59]

A Brief Review of Kinsey on Sexual Behavior in the Human Male

When Americans read *Sexual Behavior in the Human Male*, they invariably envisioned their own husbands and fathers—mostly hard-working, sacrificing family men whom they had presumed to be faithful and heterosexual. With far-reaching consequences, Kinsey's creepy statistics ate at the younger generation like emotional poison.[60] The Greatest Generation was slandered in the name of "science."

According to *Human Events*, Kinsey's initial report stunned the nation. It said American men were so sexually wild that 95% could be accused of some kind of sexual offense under 1940s laws, while 37% had had at least one homosexual experience,[61] and 47% of college men did so to orgasm—if they were still single by age thirty-five.[62] Since most normal American men were married by age thirty-five this allowed Kinsey to suggest "47%" of men were sometime homosexual, as though these were normal males. But there was more. The report described American men as undeniably corrupt, claiming that nearly all American men violated sex crime laws, a majority used prostitutes, many performed homosexual sodomy to orgasm, and more than a few had sex with animals.

Sexual Behavior in the Human Male made the following claims:

"UP-TO" RATINGS OF GENERAL MALE SEXUAL ACTIVITY

- 92% masturbated to orgasm (p. 499).
- 67% to 98% had premarital sex (p. 552).
- 39% at the "college level" performed premarital oral sex on a woman (p. 371).
- 68% had premarital coitus by age eighteen (p. 549–552 including Table 136).
- 69% of white males had at least one experience with a prostitute (p. 597).

MARRIAGE & ADULTERY

- 49% performed oral sex within marriage (p. 256 and 371, College Sample).
- 50% of husbands were adulterers, labeled by Kinsey as "extra-marital" acts (p. 585, 587).

HOMOSEXUALITY

- 10–37% sometimes commit homosexual acts (p. 650–651).
- 14% performed and 30% received homosexual oral sex with climax at least once (p. 373).
- Nearly 46% engaged in heterosexual and/or homosexual activities, or "reacted to" both sexes in the course of their adult lives (p. 656).

A SAMPLE OF VARVIED DEVIANT BEHAVIORS

- 11% of married individuals participate in anal sodomy at least once, (p. 383, college later tape analysis).[63]
- 22% were aroused by sadomasochistic stories (p. 677, *Female*).
- 50% responded erotically to being bitten (p. 677–8, *Female*).
- 95% are sex offenders (p. 392, *Male*).[64]
- 50% of farm boys have sex with animals, 17% to orgasm (p. 671, *Male*).

Although bestiality is *not* natural behavior, Kinsey argued that *even this* was normal for humans, writing:

> With most males, animal contacts represent a passing Chapter in the sexual history. They are replaced by coitus with human females as soon

as that is available . . . . [Men] who have risen to positions of importance in the business, academic, or political world in some large urban center . . . have lived for years in constant fear that their early [animal contacts] will be discovered [whereas] such activities are biologically and psychologically part of the normal mammalian picture. . . .[65]

A Brief Review of Kinsey's Sexual Behavior in the Human Female

American women and girls were targeted by the K-Bomb. Just as the first report took on personal significance, people unconsciously envisioned their own mothers and wives when they read Kinsey's *Sexual Behavior in the Human Female.*

Having survived the misogynistic defamation of the war's black propaganda, sweethearts, wives, and mothers were again maligned as promiscuous, unfaithful, and bi/homosexual. On the one hand, Kinsey claimed our women were so sexually ignorant they thought they could become pregnant through kissing and did not know what an orgasm is. But as *Life* magazine reported in their deferential and zealous report, the Kinsey team also said that half of our women had relations before marriage and that after marriage, "40% of women have been or will be unfaithful."[66] Though these two claims reveal a gaping contradiction, scientists and the media were conditioned not to notice.

In *Sexual Behavior in the Human Female*, Kinsey *claimed* the following, although his "data" fluctuated rather widely:

GENERAL FEMALE SEXUAL ACTIVITY

- 62% reported they had masturbated (p. 142).
- 50% had premarital sex; 66–77% of these had no regrets, (p. 286, 332).
- 16 to 43% to 62% performed oral sex on a man before marriage (p. 258).

MARRIAGE & ADULTERY

- 0% cite anal sodomy despite Kinsey Institute's alleged 11% male cite above.[67]

- 49% performed oral sex in marriage (p. 361).
- 26% committed adultery, called "extramarital coitus," by age 40 (p. 416).
- 25% commit adultery and 17% more, Kinsey reported in "The Model Penal Code," "wanted or would consider" committing adultery.[68]
- 63% to 85% of coitus resulted in orgasm (year one to twenty) of marriage (p. 375).

HOMOSEXUALITY

- 28% had a homosexual experience for over three years (p. 458).
- A very small portion had exclusively homosexual histories over time (p. 458–9).
- The bogus "Kinsey Scale" rates the average human as bisexual (p. 470).

SADOMASOCHISM

- 12% reported an erotic response to a sadomasochistic story (p. 677).
- 55% reported responding erotically to being bitten (p. 678).

ABORTION REPORTED BY KINSEY CO-AUTHORS

- 20 to 25% of wives deliberately aborted (no complications) (p. 102, Gebhard in Weinberg).[69]
- "90 to 95% of pre-marital pregnancies are aborted" Dr. Mary Calderone claimed Kinsey found (Roe *v.* Wade).[70]

VENEREAL DISEASE, RAPE

- 1,753 females had premarital sex but "only 44 females" ever had a venereal disease (p. 327).
- Of 4,441 women interviewed, none were ever harmed by rape.[71]
- *Kinsey reported one possible rape of a child and no rapes of women or boys.*[72]

The *Female* volume included no data on normal mothers or births within marriage. Examining hundreds of charts and narratives in this volume, we can patch together three cryptic citations describing 476 single mothers, 333 premarital pregnancies. "Among 16 females we have a record of 18 pregnancies resulting from the extra-marital coitus."[73] Kinsey provided no data, though, on whether these babies were aborted or how these pregnancies affected the mothers' lives—even sexually. As a "taxonomic classification," babies or children in both the *Male* and *Female* reports appear only as sexual subjects—objects and sex "partners" for adults and older children.[74]

A Brief Review of Kinsey on Sexual Behavior in Boys

In *Paedophiles in Society,* Professor Goode states that the evidence from his books proved that "his work was based on the rape of children." Kinsey says "the only 'abnormal' sex is no sex; that the 'human animal' needs orgasms; and that the earlier boys and girls have orgasms, the better for them." Both his books stand on these claims, backed by "copious data" some gotten from adult recall but according to Gebhard most from men:

> . . . manipulating' children, aged from birth to adolescence. Under both national and international legislation, this is (and was at the time) child sexual abuse. Where it involves penetration, as it clearly did in some cases, it is (and was at the time) rape.[75]

At minimum, Kinsey's disturbing allegations and conclusions are illogical, contradicting the conservative nature of our World War II generation. Worse, Kinsey's "work" regarding the sexuality of teenagers, pre-adolescent children, and infants is horrifying. *Sexual Behavior in the Human Male* and *Sexual Behavior in the Human Female* provide abundant evidence of *child sexual torture by Kinsey's "researchers,"* who engaged in brutal, sexual experiments on children. This "work" is critically important to the effects of the Kinsey reports on our society, our laws, and the Kinsey lobby today.

In the *Male* book, Table 30 reports data on 214 male children, the youngest only *one year old.* The column "ORGASM: Data from Other Subjects," reveals the age range of these children: one to fourteen years, with twelve-month-old infants supposedly reaching orgasm through sex "play"; many of these "orgasmic" children were toddlers and preschoolers.

TABLE 30. PRE-ADOLESCENT EROTICISM AND ORGASM

AGE	FIRST PRE-ADOLESCENT EROTIC AROUSAL AND ORGASM NUMBER OF CASES						
	EROTIC AROUSAL			ORGASM			
	In Any Sex Play	In Hetero-sexual Play	In Homo-sexual Play	Date from Present Study	Date from Other Subjects	Total Cases	% of Total
1					12	12	2.5
2					8	8	1.6
3				2	7	9	1.8
4	10	9	2		12	12	2.5
5	30	23	8	5	9	14	2.9
6	26	21	8	15	19	34	7.0
7	32	29	6	21	17	38	7.8
8	38	29	12	27	21	48	9.9
9	38	37	3	24	26	50	10.3
10	83	71	17	56	25	82	16.8
11	72	67	13	54	22	76	15.6
12	92	84	13	51	23	74	15.2
13	37	37	3	15	9	24	4.9
14	10	10		3	3	6	1.2
15	3	2	1				
Total	471	419	86	273	214	487	100.0
Mean Age Median Age	10.28 9.75	10.41 9.87	9.62 9.26	10.40 9.77	8.51 8.10	9.57 9.23	

"Of the 214 cases so reported, all but 14 were subsequently observed in orgasm (see Table 31)."

According to this table, these children's first orgasm experience *was observed*. But how did they *arrange* this first "observed" pseudo-scientific sexual experience? Table 30 neatly chronicles what Kinsey called heterosexual and homosexual "play" that resulted in the data for this chart—children's *first* arousal and "orgasm." Kinsey asserted, "Of the 214 cases . . . all but 14 were subsequently observed in orgasm." Observed?! Who "subsequently observed" (defined as "occurring or coming later or after") these infants and boys being—yes—sexually tortured, timed, and recorded? Who, of Kinsey's team, did this under his direction? The youngest boy tested to "climax" is "2 mon." old (see Table 31).

TABLE 31. AGES OF PRE-ADOLESCENT ORGASM

AGE WHEN OBSERVED	PRE-ADOLESCENT EXPERIENCE IN ORGASM					
	Total Population	Cases Not Reaching Climax	Cases Reaching Climax	Cumulated Population	Cumulated Cases to Climax	Percent of Each Age Reaching Climax
2 mon.	1	1	0			
3	2	2	0			
4	1	1	0			
5	2	1	1			
8	2	1	1			
9	1	1	0			
10	4	1	3			
11	3	1	2			
12	12	10	2			
Up to 1 yr.	28	19	9	28	9	32.1
Up to 2 yr.	22	11	11	50	20	
Up to 3 yr.	9	2	7	59	27	
Up to 4 yr.	12	5	7	71	34	57.1
Up to 5 yr.	6	3	3	77	37	
Up to 6 yr.	12	5	7	89	44	
Up to 7 yr.	17	8	9	106	53	
Up to 8 yr.	26	12	14	132	67	63.4
Up to 9 yr.	29	10	19	161	86	
Up to 10 yr.	28	6	22	189	108	
Up to 11 yr.	34	9	25	223	133	
Up to 12 yr.	46	7	39	269	172	80.0
Up to 13 yr.	35	7	28	304	200	
Up to 14 yr.	11	5	6	315	206	
Up to 15 yr.	2	2	0	317	206	
Total	317	111	206	317	206	65.0

Based on actual observation of 317 males.

"Based on actual observation of 317 males," this chart in the *Male* book includes boys from *two months* to fifteen years of age, with data as to whether these "cases" did or did not reach "climax."[76] Each age category included children tested for "orgasm." According to these data, only eighteen out of 214 boys (Table 30) and "up to" 7 out of 317 boys (Table 31) would have reached hormonal maturity (at least thirteen years of age) when they were given their "first" orgasm by Kinsey's team. Kinsey further asserts here that "orgasm" "*was observed*" in a male infant of five months.

Notably, *in thousands of pages*, Kinsey *never* uses emotional, human terms such as "infant," "baby," "child," "tot," "toddler" for these boys.

For this allegedly scientific Table 32, Kinsey's "researchers" observed 1,888 boys ("from five months of age to adolescence") and timed them with a "second hand or stopwatch" while they were being "erotically stimulated" in order to determine the "duration of stimulation before climax."[77]

TABLE 32. SPEED OF PRE-ADOLESCENT ORGASM

Time	Cases Timed	Percent of Population	Cumulated Percent
Up to 10 sec.	12	6.4	6.4
10 sec. to 1 min.	46	24.5	30.9
1 to 2 min.	40	21.3	52.2
2 to 3 min.	23	12.2	64.4
3 to 5 min.	33	17.5	81.9
5 to 10 min.	23	12.2	94.1
Over 10 min.	11	5.9	100.0
Total	188	100.0	
Mean time to climax: 3.02 minutes Median time to climax: 1.91 minutes			

Youngest boy "observed" is "five months" and the "stimulation" and "Mean time to climax" of 188 boys is timed with "a second hand or stop watch."

Make no mistake: Each "case" represents a helpless child who was criminally stimulated, observed, and timed by sex offenders for Kinsey! This table lists 188 children who were stimulated by pederast employees who observed children's reactions, timed them, and followed this abuse by keeping copious pederastic interpretive notes. The abusers could definitely have been Kinsey, Pomeroy, Martin, Gebhard, and/or others hired for their team. In an audio-taped interview, Paul Gebhard later acknowledged that they asked child rapists to get data on child orgasm, use stopwatches "take notes . . . . time it and report back to us. . ."

GEBHARD: When we interview pedophiles, we would ask them, "How many children have you had it with? What were their ages? Do you think they came to climax or not? . . . Are you sure it really was climax or not?"

INTERVIEWER: So, do pedophiles normally go around with stop watches?

GEBHARD: *Ah, they do if we tell them we're interested in it. . . .*[78]

TABLE 33. MULTIPLE ORGASM IN PRE-ADOLESCENT MALES

No. of Orgasms	Cases Observed	Percent of Population	Cumulated Percent	Time Between Orgasms	Cases Timed	Percent of Population	Cumulated Percent
1	81	44.5	100.0	Up to 10 sec.	3	4.7	4.7
2	17	9.3	55.5	11 to 60 sec.	15	23.5	28.2
3	18	9.9	46.2	Up to 2 min.	8	12.5	40.7
4	10	5.5	36.3	Up to 3 min.	10	15.6	56.3
5	14	7.7	30.8	Up to 5 min.	7	10.9	67.2
6–10	30	16.5	23.1	Up to 10 min.	11	17.2	84.4
11–15	9	4.9	6.6	Up to 20 min.	7	10.9	95.3
16–20	2	1.1	1.7	Up to 30 min.	1	1.6	96.9
21+	1	0.6	0.6	Over 30 min.	2	3.1	100.0
Total	182	100.0	100.0	Total	64	100.0	100.0
Mean No. of Orgasms: 3.72 Median No. of Orgasms: 2.62				Mean Time Lapse: 6.28 minutes Median Time Lapse: 2.25 minutes			

Pedophile "Orgasm" Torture of 246 Little Boys

Table 33 claims to present the number of "orgasms" among 182 pre-adolescent boys and the purported time between "orgasms" for sixty-four more boys. "The most remarkable aspect of the pre-adolescent population is its capacity to achieve repeated orgasm in limited periods of time," the Kinsey team claimed: "This capacity definitely exceeds the ability of teen-age boys who, in turn, are much more capable than any older males." Kinsey concluded: "It is certain that a higher proportion of the boys could have had multiple orgasm [*sic*] if the situation had offered. Even the youngest males, as young as 5 months in age, are capable of such repeated reactions."[79]

Kinsey described this table as including "typical cases." The youngest was five months old. According to Kinsey, "The maximum observed was 26 climaxes in 24 hours [in a four-year-old and a thirteen-year-old],

TABLE 34. EXAMPLES OF MULTIPLE ORGASM IN PRE-ADOLESCENT MALES

SOME INSTANCES OF HIGHER FREQUENCIES

Age	No. of Orgasms	Time Involved	Age	No. of Orgasms	Time Involved
5 mon.	3	?	11 yr.	11	1 hr.
11 mon.	10	1 hr.	11 yr.	19	1 hr.
11 mon.	14	38 min.	12 yr.	7	3 hr.
2 yr.	7	9 min.	12 yr.	3	3 min.
	11	65 min.		9	2 hr.
2½ yr.	4	2 min.	12 yr.	12	2 hr.
4 yr.	6	5 min.	12 yr.	15	1 hr.
4 yr.	17	10 hr.	13 yr.	7	24 min.
4 yr.	26	24 hr.	13 yr.	8	2½ hr.
7 yr.	7	3 hr.	13 yr.	9	8 hr.
8 yr.	8	2 hr.		3	70 sec.
9 yr.	7	68 min.	13 yr.	11	8 hr.
10 yr.	9	52 min.		26	24 hr.
10 yr.	14	24 hr.	14 yr.	11	4 hr.

Pedophile Orgasm Torture of 30 Boys Up to 24 Hours around the Clock, The Youngest 5 Months, Suggesting Other Victim as "Some Instances of Higher Frequencies."

and Kinsey says "still more might have been possible in the same period of time."[80] This, of course, is a round-the-clock sexual experiment, requiring twenty-four hours of sexual assaults by a team of sex criminals on both children. Kinsey adds, "Some instances of higher frequencies." Why exclude some of the children in this table?

Redefining Orgasm in Boys

"At an early point in the development of our research," Pomeroy said, Kinsey began finding ways to experiment and to watch sex.[81] So Kinsey collected "data" from various sources—his sabotage team, subjects' parents, nursery school teachers, a pedophile group he was working with, and at least two (now) known serial pederasts.

One these was a German Nazi serial pedophile, Dr. Fritz von Balluseck, a lawyer and a member of Hitler's World War II Gestapo (secret police). Von Balluseck contributed both his past and contemporaneous records of sex crimes against children, circa 1936–1956, to Kinsey's research database.[82] In correspondence, Kinsey warned von Balluseck to "be careful," not to get caught by the police as he assaulted both boys and girls. Paul Gebhard was one of several in Kinsey's inner circle who knew about Kinsey's collaboration with a possible child sex killer Von Balluseck.[83] In 1998, the Yorkshire Television investigators found criminal trial records and scores of headlines about Kinsey throughout Germany.

One other named Kinsey pedophile was Rex King, an American serial child rapist also known as "Mr. Braun," "Mr. Green," and "Mr. X." The "king" of child molesters is on record as raping *at least eight hundred children*, the youngest *two months of age*. Kinsey met King in about 1943 when King demonstrated his instant-orgasm ability for Kinsey and Pomeroy.[84] Kinsey's mentor, the famous sexologist, Robert Dickenson, MD, had "trained" King to keep child sex-abuse records. Kinsey suggested King use a stopwatch to record his victims' "orgasms." King collaborated with Kinsey and, together, they constructed definitions of "six kinds of orgasm" in boys, including so-called older males (*all under thirteen years*). Kinsey reprinted these definitions (p. 160–161, *Male*), which he and King used to categorize 196 little boys' so-called "orgasmic" responses. Kinsey, a longtime psychopathic sadomasochist, *would* see a child's *pain* as a sign of *orgasm*. For King and Kinsey's complete definitions, refer to the original; in the interest of discretion, the following descriptions *exclude* many of Kinsey's most alarming, graphic quotes:

1. "Reactions primarily genital" (22% of the pre-adolescent cases).
2. "Some body tension" (45% of the pre-adolescent males). These reactions included rigidity of the body and twitching of mouth or extremities . . . spasms.
3. "Extreme tension with convulsion" (17% of pre-adolescent boys).

The following are Kinsey's words, as witness or participant:

This "orgasm" often involved several minutes of recurrent spasm with rigidity, spasmodic twitching, knotted muscles, pointed toes, contracted abdominal muscles, stiff shoulders and neck, sudden heaving or jerking, violent convulsions of the whole body, grasping hands, mouth distortions, and sometimes synchronous genital throbs or violent jerking; gasping, heavy breathing, or holding of breath; eyes staring or tightly closed and, *"groaning, sobbing, or more violent cries, sometimes with an abundance of tears (especially among younger children)"* [emphasis added].

Following this, said Kinsey, boys are "often capable of participating in a second or further experience."

4. "Type 1 or 2" with hysteria (5% of pre-adolescents).

This includes "hysterical laughing, talking, or sadistic or masochistic reactions and rapid motions. . . . culminating in" frenzied movements.

5. "As in any of the above" but culminating in extreme trembling or complete collapse (3% of pre-adolescent males).

This "orgasm" culminates in the boy's "extreme trembling, collapse, loss of color, and sometimes fainting. . . ." King, Kinsey, et al., note that "Such complete collapse is more common and better known among females" but that, in these children, this reaction "Sometimes happens only in the boy's first experience."

6. "Pained or frightened" (About 8% of younger boys and a smaller percentage of older boys "continue these reactions throughout life").

"Before the arrival of actual orgasm," these boys became hysterical, evinced by their hypersensitive genitalia, they "suffer excruciating pain and may scream if" the abuse continues and "the penis even touched." They will "fight away from the partner and may make violent attempts to avoid climax, although they derive definite pleasure from the situation." Kinsey reported that, "Such individuals quickly return to complete the experience, or to have a second experience if the first was complete."[85]

Even older children would have lacked the language to express their pain, bewilderment, and trauma at being tortured to what King and Kinsey called "orgasm," sometimes around the clock! So, King, Kinsey, and other pederast experimenters *expressed it for them*, *redefining* as orgasm the terror and physical pain of small, prepubescent boys—their hysterical trembling and convulsions, violent cries, sobbing, collapse, fainting, loss of color, desperate attempts to avoid "climax," screaming, and fighting to get away. Thus, Kinsey and his other pedophiles *define their victims' agony as ecstasy, name it "orgasm,"* and use this new definition to help ambush American, and global western, culture. These records are blatant evidence of the child sexual abuse of 196 to perhaps over 2,000 small boys (discussed further shortly) by Kinsey's adult team of sex criminals, rapists, and sodomizers.

A Brief Review of Kinsey on Sexual Behavior in Girls

GIRL "MASTURBATION" DATA (FEMALE, PP. 177 & 180)

Age	Percentage (Table 21, p. 177)	"Orgasm" (Table 25, p. 180)
3	1% (of 5,913)	0% (of 5,913)
5	4% (of 5,866)	2% (of 5,866)
7	7% (of 5,841)	4% (of 5,838)
10	13% (of 5,808)	8% (of 5,802)
12	19% (of 5,784)	12% (of 5,778)

Kinsey's Unverified Girl Masturbation Data

Despite his preference for little boys as unverified orgasm subjects, little girls did not escape Kinsey's "research." In *Sexual Behavior in the Human Female*, for example, Kinsey provides unverified "data" on fifty-nine girls up to age three as well as 235 girls up to age five and so on, who supposedly masturbated with half of these to "orgasm." Though this implies that they did it to themselves, Kinsey's "scientifically trained observers" or "adult partners" could be responsible. The *Female* volume states (p. 127) that pre-adolescent girls may have attained "orgasm" from masturbation or from "socio-sexual contacts"—Kinsey code for adults violently assaulting the children.

Chapter four of the *Female* volume contains Kinsey's "tests" of purported female child sexuality; we know that, just as they timed boys to "orgasm" with stopwatches, Kinsey's "researchers" similarly timed and "observed" "147 females ranging in age from 2 to 15 years."[86] From "any source" suggests that the 117 little girls up to age five Kinsey includes here were outsourced to pedophiles as were much if not all of these unverified girl data. Kinsey excludes "data" about "tests" of "speed to orgasm" for these girls. After counting the "orgasms" and the time spent pausing for breath of one little three-year old girl allegedly "masturbating,"[87] Kinsey concluded, "We have similar records of observations made by some of our other subjects on a total of 7 pre-adolescent girls and 27 pre-adolescent boys under four years of age (see our 1948 study: 175–181)."[88] These records are blatant evidence of the child sexual abuse of 145 young girls by Kinsey's adult team of sex criminals.

TABLE 10. ACCUMULATIVE INCIDENCE: PRE-ADOLESCENT "ORGASM" FROM ANY SOURCE (P.127)

Age	% of Total Sample	Cases
3	–	5,908
5	2	5,862
7	4	5,835
9	6	5,772
11	9	4,577

"Sin," "Sex," or "Soap"?

Kinsey, the biologist, neglected to report that little girls' "masturbation" is commonly a reaction to sexual molestation, parasites, or vaginitis. "Between 10% and 40% of *children* have *pinworms* at any given time,"[89] that causes severe vaginal itching. "Vaginitis. . . bacteria, protozoa, fungi, hormonal changes, contact with irritants, and true allergic reactions," medicines, antibiotics, etc., cause an impaired vaginal pH.[90] While "repressed" societies might have called the poor child sexually sinful, a Kinseyfied culture humiliates the child by calling the child sexually precocious. Both responses damage the child by neglecting the actual physiological cause of her distress.

Kinsey's Conclusions

Prior to Kinsey, the world understood that sexual maturation meant *puberty*—"when sex glands become functional . . . when a person is first capable of sexual reproduction of offspring," according to standard dictionary definitions. Kinsey was a biologist, a zoologist. But his sexual interest caused him to rev up the natural, biological timetable considerably. In complete repudiation of the physiological realities of slow, progressive, and normal human development, Kinsey eroticized toddlers and young children and exposed them to sexual stimuli.

According to his reports, *all* infants and children—100 percent of them—are potentially orgasmic. Orgasm "occurs among pre-adolescent girls," Kinsey said, and it is "not at all rare among pre-adolescent boys." In other words, Kinsey claimed, most children can experience orgasm. Thus, *all of us are sexual from birth*. We are all, according to the human sexuality cliché, "sexual beings."

Building on this premise, Kinsey asserted that our culture restricted and inhibited child orgasms to children's detriment. If infants and children are not having orgasms, Kinsey said, they are being psychologically harmed by foolish adult puritanical inhibitions:

> [T]he positive record on . . . boys who [had] the opportunity makes it certain that many infant males and younger boys are capable of orgasm (p. 178, *Male*).

FIGURE 1

WHAT DID KINSEY SAY ABOUT CHILD SEX ABUSE

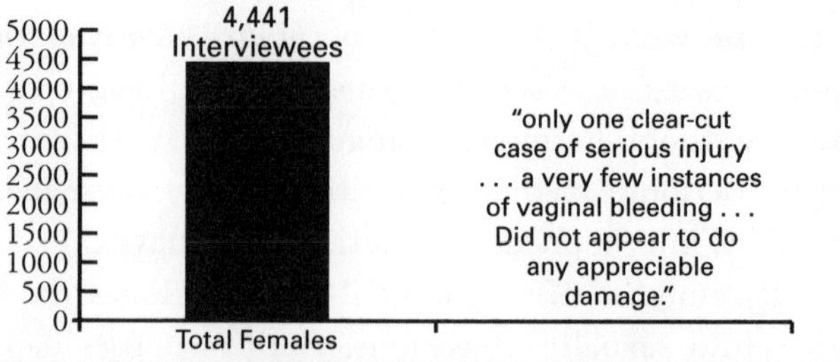

Out of 4,441 Females "only one" case of "serious injury."

Source: *Female*, p 122, No Harm to Children From Sexual "Contacts" With Adults

While Kinsey included scores of arcane tables on male and female sexuality, he offered *no* tables specific to child molestation or incest. Instead, he identified what he euphemistically called "adult partners" of 609 girls. Of these, 140 (23%) were victimized (my term) by relatives and 32% by family friends, friends' brothers, or someone else.

Of 5,940 white, non-prison females allegedly interviewed, Kinsey said 1,075—18%—had been sexually approached by adults as children[91] while twenty-three girls, or 2% of his 1,039 "Adult Contacts," were victims of incest. In any event, he said in cases of incest, little girls "actively sought repetitions of their experience."[92] Of his 4,441 women interviewed (figure one), there was "only one clear-cut case of serious injury done to the child, and a very few instances of vaginal bleeding which, however, did not appear to do any appreciable damage" (p. 122, *Female*). Outrageously, the reports claimed that 0.06939% statistically *no* women or children experienced harm from rape or incest![93] No one challenged this mad claim.

Presented as scientific "research," Kinsey's unverified black propaganda feigned concern over the sexual health of the American people. Kinsey admonished readers to have orgasms as often as possible, any way they could get them. For health, he urged early masturbation, all but mandating childhood masturbation as early as possible if a child was to be "normal." In *Sexual Behavior in the Human Male*, Kinsey advocated his personal model as "superior" to making love: a "quick" masturbatory orgasm. (His poor wife!) Further, Kinsey claimed that promiscuity was harmless, without consequences of venereal disease, illegitimacy, or anything else. And worst, his data and "orgasmic" narrative claimed that rape, incest, and pedophilia/pederasty were also harmless.

But Kinsey's data were obviously fraudulent. Just as World War II saboteurs cooked up "scientific statistics" about enemy soldiers' women, Kinsey cooked up "scientific statistics" about American women and children, black propaganda, pretending to be helpful, pretending to offer hints on better sexual lives, pretending to be honest, open, without secrets. But Kinsey's "statistics" were lies. Just like the black propagandists, he deceived Americans—and for the same purpose: To demoralize us. To sabotage American morale, trust, and confidence. To validate and legitimize his own perversions so that he could liberate our "repressed" society for his "sexual revolution."

[CHAPTER 3]

Kinsey's Orgy-Porgy Attic

> [T]welve pairs of hands beating as one; as one, twelve buttocks slabbily resounding . . . the coming. . . . "Orgy-porgy," it sang, while the tom-toms continued to beat their feverish tattoo. . . . *"Orgy-porgy gives release."*
>
> Aldous Huxley, *Brave New World*, Chapter 5

SOMETHING WENT AWRY IN the life, mind, body, and soul of young Alfred Kinsey. Kinsey became a boy with a closeted secret life as a violently masochistic masturbation addict. He became a man whose sexual addictions, self-hatred, and contempt for women shaped his sex "research" and his legacy. Indeed, *sex addictions shaped everything Kinsey thought, said, wrote, did, and hid.* In 1901, the seven-year-old Kinsey joined some children in his Hoboken neighborhood, meeting in one of their basements. According to biographer James Jones, about six kids played "you show me and I'll show you." The children "look[ed] at one another, poke[d] straws in various apertures, stuff like that, and that made him feel very peculiar and rather guilty."[94] Kinsey's colleague and co-author, Paul Gebhard, said Kinsey dubbed these cellar trysts "homosexual." Kinsey later wrote that child sex activity dramatically shapes adult sexuality. Jones concluded, "Kinsey's theories suggest that he traced his own adult sexual interests" (homosexual and sado-masochistic) to that Hoboken basement.

Though he was quite ill and confined to bed for months at a time, his father willingly supported and encouraged his boyhood interests in zoology and music. When he was ten, Kinsey and his family moved to a suburb where they lived in a five-bedroom corner home for ten years. His father encouraged his interest in nature and even built a glass conservatory behind the house for the boy's plant specimens. But Kinsey apparently spent time in his own private world, in the elegantly designed French mansard attic. Hidden behind its graceful window treatment, a shameful treasure later revealed his twisted life.

Years later, Bill Gury, a later resident of the Kinsey home, happened to meet Alfred's brother, Robert Kinsey. Alfred's brother directed Gury to a "private space" in the attic, where his "crazy brother" had long ago hidden "treasures of some sort." Indeed, in the attic hideaway, Gury found a box that had lain locked away. It held a strange, hand-sewn brush, which, Gury said, was "just a little bit bigger than you would envision a tooth brush, with holes drilled at one end. . . ."[95] According to Jones, Kinsey "hid from his family and the world the instrument he used to seek both sexual pleasure and physical pain."[96] This torture chest, reported Jones, was the future sexologist's sadosexual cache, his masturbatory starter kit. After the youthful aperture-poking in the Hoboken basement, Kinsey's private methods of self-abuse became more sophisticated in what Jones documented as a permanent pattern of increasingly barbaric sexual self-torture.

Cagily candid, Jones reveals that Kinsey's sexually disordered behavior was entrenched in his youth.[97] "By late adolescence, if not before," Jones concluded, "Kinsey's behavior was clearly pathological, satisfying every criterion of sexual perversion."[98] Disclosing some of Kinsey's boyhood psychopathologies, Jones concluded that, during urination and long after each self-torture experience, Kinsey experienced "exquisite pain." (What normal man would find such pain "exquisite"?)

Using increasingly torturous instruments, Kinsey waged a lifelong war on his reproductive organs. Each incident further dulled his agony, increasing his need for more effective (larger and more traumatizing) paraphernalia—just as any addict requires more and stronger doses of their drugs of choice. By age thirteen, Kinsey was a sex addict, foreshadowing today's growing multitude of youthful Internet pornography addicts.

Obsessive masturbation is a typical sign of sex addiction and early sexual abuse. Can we deduce that someone had abused Kinsey—paired pain with pleasure and showed him how to torture himself sexually?

His behavior certainly points to early sadistic sexual abuse. Who would have perverted Alfred Kinsey when he was young?

Using his parents as excuses for Kinsey's deviancies, his biographers have painted his father as a tyrannical villain and his mother as a thrifty doormat. But no evidence indicates that Alfred's parents severely punished him or exposed him to domestic violence, adultery, or incest. Kinsey's father was authoritarian, apparently condemned tobacco, alcohol, and masturbation, and was reticent to show parental affection, but he was, based on Kinsey's many friendly biographers, in fact, *less* strict than many fathers of the time. And at a time when fewer than 10 percent of American children attended high school,[99] Alfred was one of the priveledged few and never missed a day. His parents even helped him attain a college education, an opportunity, said Kinsey, achieved by less than 1 percent of the population of his day. No, it does not appear to have been his father, but someone or something else that distorted Kinsey.

Unusually attractive—tall, blond, educated, athletic, and musical—Kinsey is on record as desperately "shy" around girls. Wardell Pomeroy, Kinsey's handsome young protégé, co-author, and sometimes lover, wrote that "Young Al" was known as "the boy who never had a girl."[100] This is another common trait of abused boys. With a clear preference for the company of other boys, Kinsey sought them out. He joined the Boy Scouts of America quite late, at age seventeen according to most biographers, and proudly became an Eagle Scout. But did he truly have an altruistic interest in young camp companions?

Pomeroy revealed part of a letter Kinsey wrote to a Scouting friend: "We did have good times together, and you must understand from that Scout troop I began to learn some of the things that made it possible for me to do some of the research that we are now engaged in."[101] Kinsey often described how one Scout sought his help in curing habitual masturbation. The 2005 film, *Kinsey*, showed Alfred (played by Liam Neeson) with a Boy Scout, praying that the lad would receive the strength to stop.[102] The filmmaker revealed, however, that it was not just a friend who was plagued by masturbation, but Kinsey himself, now guilt ridden.[103] "Kinsey prayed, asking God to forgive him and to give him the strength not to sin again," Jones stated. "Neither prayer nor cold showers enabled him to stop masturbating. As a result, Kinsey was consumed by guilt" and hated God.[104]

Kinsey shows no attraction whatsoever to girls but was very interested in young boys. Regardless of his lack of faith, "into college and beyond,"[105] Alfred continued to teach children's Sunday school and to counsel boys at the Young Men's Christian Association (YMCA), the local Bethany Methodist Episcopal Boys' Club, and at Camp Wyanoke in New Hampshire.[106] A Scout leader into his twenties, he secretly showed campers his "nature library" (likely code for nudist or otherwise erotic pictures). Ample evidence suggests that Kinsey shared his sexual habits with this circle of younger campers, and Jones confirms that Kinsey was engaged in questionable activity with the boys he took on nature hikes and slept with in tents.[107] In fact, as an adult, Kinsey claimed that, by age eighteen, he already had "contribut[ed] to sexual knowledge," in "secondary schools."[108] *What might the eighteen-year-old virginal Kinsey have contributed to the sexual knowledge of secondary school children?*

Biographers bury much of the truth to protect the Kinsey propaganda, portraying him as a normal, *objective* sex researcher.

Kinsey studied zoology and biology, and some sociology and psychology.[109] He left Stevens Institute in 1916, graduated magna cum laude from Bowdoin College in Brunswick, Maine, and went on to study at Harvard's Bussey Institute. Kinsey continued his work with young boys at the Bethany Boys' Club—sharing his exotic knowledge.[110]

When the United States entered World War I in April 1917, Kinsey's biographers say he was a strapping, all-around twenty-three-year-old outdoorsman who enjoyed camping and daring athletes to compete in hikes and races on rugged terrain, which Kinsey regularly won. Clearly his physical maladies had long since been cured. However, unlike his, well, more patriotic Harvard classmates, Kinsey avoided serving in the war, finishing college as the Roaring Twenties began.

Studying at the Bussey Institute, where Darwin reigned as the unquestioned authority,[111] the twenty-five-year-old Kinsey joined with other elitist eugenicists who sought to "improve" the human species with super men like themselves. Long before the Nazis gave eugenics a bad name, Darwinism and "the New Biology" led to grotesque abuses. In 1907 for example, Indiana enacted legislation that forced sterilizations based on eugenic "science." The trend spread nationally, as thirty states signed on and more than 50,000 Americans—who did not meet elitist standards—were sterilized by order of the State.

A few years later, eugenics helped shape Hitler's Nazi agenda, and Kinsey was a party to this thinking. As he rejected the belief that all humans are created in God's image, Kinsey's dogmatic atheism supported his eugenicist ideology. In fact, Jones says Kinsey called for mass sterilization of "perhaps a tenth of our population" to reduce "the birth rate of the lowest classes."[112] Among Kinsey's secret papers, Jones quoted Kinsey in later years calling for a "program of sterilization that was at once sweeping and terrifying."

Kinsey graduated with a Doctor of Science degree, and was disappointed that no Ivy League school wanted him. He grudgingly joined Indiana University as an assistant zoology professor. Indiana was in the forefront of the forced-sterilization movement, which fit Kinsey's philosophy perfectly.[113] Also, eugenicist Thurman Rice, MD, taught sexuality at Indiana University and was a Kinsey intimate until the young zoologist ousted him as the resident sexpert.

In 1920, at age twenty-six, Kinsey was the faculty insect expert for Indiana University. His bug work was excellent cover for his hush-hush sex orgies, or studies. Kinsey proudly explained that he saw no difference between measuring insect wings and measuring other people's sexual conduct. Affirming his inability to distinguish between insects and humans, Professor Kinsey is on record as embracing bestiality.

Mac

By age twenty-seven, Kinsey's deviant values were set in concrete and his crusade to undermine America had begun. But he required a trustworthy persona, a *front*. He needed to look like an honorable family man, just independent-minded enough to report the truth about human sexuality.

Middle-class Americans, he certainly realized, would not march off a moral cliff for a pornography-addicted, sado-masochistic, bi-homosexual pederast. In fact, he knew that Americans did not trust single men. He needed a "cover," a disguise known by homosexuals as a "beard": He needed a wife who was young, educated, but insecure and obedient.[114]

Kinsey had never dated a female. His publicists said it was his interest in gall wasps that attracted him to Clara Bracken McMillen, an insect enthusiast and chemistry major at Indiana University. Kinsey called her "Mac." After seeing each other casually at several campus events, the twenty-seven-year-old zoology professor took the young student for a walk and proposed.[115]

Married on June 3, 1921, the couple had an intolerable honeymoon. Aware that Clara had never climbed a mountain before, Alfred took her on a perilous climb of Mt. Washington—a brutal, life-threatening torrent of a mountain—during a blizzard. According to Christenson, his official biographer, Kinsey designed this honeymoon from hell to *"test"* Clara. But why? Why would the alleged sexpert—by then a supposed twenty-eight-year-old virgin—prefer to spend his wedding night wrapped in clothes, in separate sleeping bags followed by a grueling mountain scaling assent in a frigid storm? Why arrange this brutal honeymoon rather than sipping wine by the fire in a cozy cottage? This was abnormal sexual behavior. Why? Consider.

Kinsey's long history of painfully savage masturbation vetoed normal sex. Even if Kinsey had *liked* women, after traumatizing his sex organs for nearly twenty years, he would be chronically impotent, especially during his honeymoon. Biographers Jones and Gathorne-Hardy admit that Kinsey could not experience orgasm except through pain, shame, and stigma. Obviously, no *normal* woman and certainly no *normal* marriage act could possibly satisfy Kinsey's sadomasochistic needs.

Naturally, Kinsey's biographers blame Clara's *anatomy* for what they admit was Kinsey's inability to consummate their marriage for some period of time. The *Kinsey* film actually devotes several scenes to Kinsey's prowess—providing a sketch of his large organ size. As the pied piper of harmless masturbation, it was critical to ignore the evidence that *Kinsey's* anatomy had been gimped, damaged, by decades spent battering his "privates" and plunging widgets into his urethra. *But were Kinsey's impotency known, it would negate the aggressive Kinseyan claims that chronic masturbation is harmless.* Fortunately, for Kinsey, Clara was inexperienced, untried. She didn't know the difference.

Despite his early impotence, it is fair to assume that Kinsey fathered all four of Clara's children, though we also know that Kinsey actively sent men to Clara's bed, so paternity could be uncertain. Jones explains that Kinsey had to masturbate before he could perform sexually, which may have been his tawdry means to fatherhood. Certainly, once their last child arrived, Kinsey quit his spousal sexual duties.[116]

When sexual deviants marry, most do so with the initial hope that their unsuspecting spouse will cure them. Since Clara could not do so, Kinsey would have justified his anger toward her, which he expressed in well-documented acts of contempt and cruelty. We know Kinsey rejected Clara and sexually pursued male students during his wasp-hunting "field trips" from 1926 to 1929. "He seizes the opportunity to engage his students in conversations about sex," admitted the PBS series, *American Experience*, in a timeline. "He finds himself attracted to his favorite graduate student, Ralph Voris."[117]

Indiana University has hidden incriminating Kinsey letters for decades. Jones, however, revealed the unabridged professor in some student responses to Kinsey letters, which contain adolescent sex language, locker-room jokes, and excited references to pornography use. Kinsey ignored "sexual taboos . . . he was determined to flaunt them." Homer Rainwater said Kinsey went "naked if we were in a campground. He just didn't give a damn. Nor did he show any inhibitions about his bodily functions."[118] One student said he went "to the bathroom" in front of them, would casually "take a leak" in the open, ignoring any passing campers, families, and children. Professors, normal people, did not do that kind of thing. But Kinsey did.

Like most sex addicts, Kinsey was eager to talk about sex. Rainwater noted Kinsey would "talk about his wife, and what a good sex partner she was. . . . He had a pretty wife, and apparently she was very accommodating, and he talked about that to us." Then Kinsey asked Rainwater about *his* sex life,[119] and offered Clara for sex, hoping the students would learn too late that Kinsey wanted sex with *them*, not *their* wives.[120]

While Kinsey offered Clara for sex, she was actually nursing their newborn baby and mothering three other children—including their very ill son, Donald. Kinsey was thirty-two-years old when their toddler died in a diabetic coma in 1926. Though apparently grieved by Donald's death,[121] Kinsey deserted his mourning wife with their three small children and journeyed off on libidinous camping frolics.

Kinsey continued the tent sex activity of his Boy Scout days, including "nude and not nude" episodes. In a PBS TV documentary, Jones reported that a sexually explicit "photograph of Kinsey in the buff" was quite consensually well distributed. Two students engaged in "group masturbation," while trying "to keep Kinsey at arm's length."[122] Kinsey bathed in the nude with students, said one boy: "Such a mania for baths I've never seen."[123] Kinsey, nude with his young aides, was also a Peeping Tom while they showered.

Kinsey's textbook, *An Introduction to Biology*, was published in 1926. College boys felt honored if Kinsey selected them for his field gambols, and the professor, cruising for a sexual stable of young males, exploited his position of authority. He often rejected the brightest, most deserving zoology students if he suspected they might disclose or dislike his erotic moves "in the field."

Jobs were scarce, and young men were flattered when the acclaimed scientist invited them home, lured by potential advancement and the opportunity of getting into Kinsey's good graces. Seeing themselves as the chosen, perhaps as protégés, they assumed the scientist admired their *minds*. Of course, Kinsey had less lofty interests.

At the professor's normal-looking, middle-class home, Clara provided the maternal façade; but their entertainment often divided husbands and wives. One such couple was graduate student Ralph Voris and his wife, Geraldine. Voris was twenty-one years old when he arrived at Indiana University in 1925. Clara and Alfred wooed the couple with food, wine, sex talk, and advice—if not action. Voris and Kinsey were intimate by 1926, and Voris who entered college with a bachelor's degree was given a doctorate "under Kinsey's direction three years later."[124] Amazing speed! Geraldine, though, was uncomfortable with the visits, alluding to something very disturbing that happened.[125] Later letters from Alfred to Ralph (which the Kinsey Institute has since secreted away) indicate that the men shared a private relationship that excluded Geraldine.

Kinsey also "bombarded" young Osmond Breland with invitations. Osmond and his wife, Nellie, stayed at Kinsey's house at least once. According to Jones, Nellie "hated" Kinsey and never visited again.[126] Asked what she thought about her husband's erotic escapades with Kinsey, Nellie was silent but, decades later, her anger was clear. "He was a dirty old man," she said. "He really hurt us. We were just kids from Mississippi. We didn't know anything."[127] Obviously, Kinsey's homosexual assaults would have harmed his students' sense of their own masculinity—as well as their marriages—beyond calculation.

Students who balked at Kinsey's advances risked their grades and careers. If they reported the professor's sexual harassment, the school clearly did nothing. In an excerpt from a Kinsey letter to Voris, published by Pomeroy, the professor described a field trip when a student refused to *disrobe* and bathe.[128] The young man was fired, "left behind in Southern Tennessee," and Kinsey barred him from future zoological trips, thus impeding his career.[129]

Within his university cocoon, Kinsey developed a secret faculty cult among influential professors and administrators who would be his university lobby. Kinsey tested "early data on them." When he said he let "a limited number of influential faculty members" in on a project fraught with "potential academic dangers,"[130] Kinsey was not speaking of gall wasps.

In 1929, Voris was collecting his new doctorate as the Great Depression devastated the nation—indeed, the world. Starving people stood in soup lines, families lost their homes, and men jumped to their deaths from skyscrapers. Adolf Hitler became chancellor of Germany in 1933 and launched his plan of selective extermination and global domination.

Like the leaders and professors in most universities, Kinsey was unconcerned. Elitist Ivy League leaders, including those at Harvard, commonly supported Nazi doctrines.[131] Certain that he was one of the super elite, Kinsey had much in common with Hitler. Just as Kinsey's suspected homosexuality was confirmed recently by his worshipful biographers in 2001, Hitler's suspected homosexuality was "demonstrated beyond question by German historian Lothar Machtan's massively researched new book, *The Hidden Hitler*, which shows homosexuality's central role in Hitler's personal life."[132] Both closet homosexuals were also eugenicists. Both wanted "defective" humans to be sterilized—or worse—though, ironically, Kinsey himself was physically "defective." Like Hitler, Kinsey refused to employ Jews, women, blacks, or believing Christians. Entering Austria in March 1938, Hitler loudly launched his campaign to destroy Western civilization; four months later, Kinsey quietly initiated his campaign to do the same.

Long before his sex studies began, Kinsey believed he had all the answers, concluding that "the ignorance of sexual structure . . . and the prudish aversion" to sex is what causes "psychic conflict and resulting broken marriages."[133] Like doctors Joseph Mengele and Hubertus Strughold—Nazis who tortured men, women, and children in the name of "science"—the bow-tied Kinsey only needed to concoct some "science" to further his manic mission. He was not alone.

Indiana University's Stealth "Marriage Course"

Kinsey's inner circle included faculty members similarly interested in sexuality "research." Topping the list was Kinsey's friend and protector, the influential Herman Wells, an ambitious economics professor, an overweight bachelor well over age thirty-five. Based on Kinsey's statistics, Wells should be a homosexual capable of same sex orgasm.[134] If so, the facts about Wells, like the facts about Kinsey are carefully protected by Indiana University. Mr. Wells became president of Indiana University in 1938 and immediately proffered Kinsey carte blanche, eagerly supporting all of his chum's proposals.

The Kinsey lobby has convinced hundreds of millions of people that because Kinsey watched wasp mating and larvae laying, he had the proper "scholarly perspective" to teach human mating. The university's *official and oft-repeated* falsehood is that the Association of Women Students *asked* Kinsey to create a "marriage course." Allegedly surprised by the dearth of sexual materials, he decided to fill the void with his own research—setting the stage for arguably the most colossal academic fraud of all time.

Of critical importance, in 1938, Kinsey was not *responding* to students' calls for sex information; he *initiated* these calls. The evidence confirms that Wells approved Kinsey's sex plans long before the department announced that Kinsey was "asked" to initiate a marriage course (really, a sex course). I documented this "shell game" in earlier books. Even Jones, a Kinsey disciple, confirmed that the Kinsey lobby lied (and continues to lie) about Kinsey's "Marriage Course."

> The contention that Kinsey just happened to be selected to head the Marriage Course cannot be supported by fact. . . . Kinsey planned from the beginning to use the Marriage Course.[135]

Jones agreed that Kinsey's plan was to exploit "marriage" in order to *eliminate* it, to make his own pathological sexual behavior the legal, universal norm.

On campus, Kinsey badgered college girls into describing their sexual measurements and alleged masturbation techniques, every detail of any sexual relations they'd allegedly had. Kate Mueller, PhD, the university's dean of women at the time, recalled, "[He] ran into difficulties with parents and girls who objected, girls who were really scandalized, you see. . . ."[136]

Kinsey, like most psychopaths, demanded absolute subservience, insisting that Dean Mueller compel all Indiana University co-eds to answer his sex questions. (Some universities did force 100 percent of their students to submit—"for science," of course.) Mueller tried to explain to Kinsey that he could not harass girls for sex information "when they did not voluntarily want to do so." Then she saw Kinsey physically change before her eyes, growing pale, overcome with fury. "I think that the one thing that he could not endure was to be thwarted," she observed.

Terrified, Dean Mueller hoped Kinsey might leave her office quietly. Not a chance. After another outburst, he turned upon her with unmitigated wrath, snarling, she explained, that she was "unsuited for the job I had." Jones reports *something* of Kinsey's violent attack:

> "He thought I ought to give him my own history," she said with a grimace. Choking back tears, she added, "He went so far as to say I should have some treatment by a psychiatrist to correct my bad attitudes and so forth."[137]

That she choked back tears five decades later indicates the power of Kinsey's malicious attack and provides a peek at what Clara, his children, and students must have endured. With "zero tolerance" for anyone who did not swiftly bow to his sick and degrading demands, Kinsey's abusive bullying of female faculty members, his wife, and female students attested to his misogynistic disdain for women.

Obviously, Indiana University faculty and administration knew and now know much of this. But despite the potential for exposure—and great consequences—Kinsey threw caution to the wind. After all, his close friend was the university's president. And Kinsey's "intimate" knowledge of President Wells and many other university professors gave him leverage to do as he pleased. Pomeroy added some useful perspective:

> There was no question that the histories did give him unique potential power. On the Indiana campus alone, there were at least twenty

> professors with homosexual histories unknown to anyone else, not to mention the numerous extramarital experiences recorded. . . . With his intimate knowledge of the sexual lives of important people, Kinsey could have figuratively blown up the United States socially and politically.[138]

Using sexual secrets to blackmail is standard sabotage. Pomeroy may have exaggerated the number of Indiana University professors with homosexual and/or adulterous affairs. Kinsey's closest intimate at IU was its bachelor president, who, based on an interview I had with a Wells's colleague, had a known fondness for third world boys. Kinsey is on record hinting at his ability to blackmail all of his interviewees. He could have hidden or even *made up* sex sins about people he interviewed. This partially explained his obsession for collecting sexual histories, despite the fact that he threw three-quarters of them away.[139]

Thurman Rice, MD, the eugenics professor who taught a required sex hygiene class at Indiana University, was a Kinsey fan. But Kinsey's open aggression towards coeds dampened Rice's zeal, especially when Kinsey demanded female students tell him "the length of their clitorises, which indeed he had."[140] Biographer Jones noted no "scientific" problem with measuring clitoral "variations among specimens" for Kinsey "merely substituted people for gall wasps."[141] But Kinsey pointed out that a "woman could certainly get no clear estimate of her own clitoris without technical training."[142] Did Kinsey suggest that a "technically trained" person should measure co-ed clitorises for them? Did Kinsey offer to do the measuring? Or did he ask the measurement question just to give himself a deviant thrill by degrading the young women?

In the name of "science," such trusting subjects are exploited to satisfy an interviewer's pathologies. Today, we call such Machiavellian questions criminal "sexual harassment"—or worse. But Pomeroy and others waxed indignant when parents dared to complain bitterly to the university, objecting that Kinsey had crudely assaulted their daughters. Kinsey was outraged at the parents.

One University of California coed whom Kinsey interviewed, now almost eighty-one, told me she felt "verbally raped" by the interview her college sorority forced her to give to Kinsey. "Sarah" said the "researchers," Kinsey and Pomeroy, were clearly "having a jolly good time." Traumatized by Kinsey's questions and his obvious contempt for everything she had been taught to believe about premarital chastity, she told me that the interview actually destroyed her Orthodox Jewish beliefs. The interviewers made all the girls feel ignorant, backward, and old-fashioned, Sarah said, telling them that scientific "data" proved their parents' generation raised them on lies and "sexual hypocrisy." Later that day, she and her sorority sisters, all virgins, walked to the local dime store, bought "wedding rings," and that night, finally slept with their boyfriends. Sarah could not speak for the other girls but, for her, that single event pushed her into a damaging life of sexual promiscuity, abortion, and several bad marriages.[143]

The sexual revolution had begun.

But who would fund such an enterprise? Long before his first sex book was published, Kinsey personally paid at least two staffers out of his own pocket.[144] But by 1941, much of the funding for travel, salaries, and equipment came from the Rockefeller Foundation. Then, expensive film production equipment was purchased[145] and Indiana University's first (but not last) pornography productions originated in Kinsey's attic and in Kinsey's soundproofed offices on campus.[146]

The Rockefeller Saboteurs

According to propaganda expert Christopher Simpson, some of America's most reputable, tax-exempt foundations funded "secret psychological war projects" in the late 1930s to control public opinion. The Rockefeller Foundation, for example, "believed mass media . . . constituted a uniquely powerful force in modern society," and America's elite—including the Rockefellers—determined that they would use the media to impose their will "on the masses."[147] So, according to the *International Encyclopedia of the Social Sciences*, in 1938, Kinsey obtained his first benefactors, the National Research Council and the Medical Division of The Rockefeller Foundation.[148]

With the war in Europe raging, the English charged that Rockefeller's Standard Oil had re-classified their ships as Panamanian to allow them to carry oil to the Canary Islands and from there into German tankers for Nazi use. Although we were not officially at war on March 31, 1941, the U.S. State Department charged Standard Oil with "fueling enemy ships." *The Thistle* asserted that Standard Oil transferred tetraethyl lead to the Japanese government, "but no direct action was ever taken against Standard Oil" for fueling the Nazis.[149]

After Japan bombed Pearl Harbor on December 7, 1941, and the United States officially entered the war, John D. Rockefeller's Standard Oil was still sending fuel to Hitler. So outrageous were the Rockefellers' internationalist war munitions dealings that in 1942 the then-Senator Harry Truman said on the Senate floor that Standard Oil was committing "treason."

Heading a senatorial investigating committee, Truman also declared that Standard Oil "was a hostile and dangerous agency of the enemy." Even after we were in the war, Standard Oil of New Jersey continued to send war materials to Germany. Truman said, "Yes, it is treason. Period."[150]

From 1930 to 1950—including during the war—the Carnegie Institute, with the Rockefeller Foundation, financed eugenics research and "brain studies" at the Kaiser Wilhelm Institute in Germany.[151] A plan was in place to alter America's belief system, even as America naïvely viewed only Germany, Japan, and Italy as enemies.[152]

The Rockefeller Foundation's World War II activities continued its long-term pursuit of social control through eugenics. Dennis L. Cuddy, PhD, reports that one 1934 Rockefeller Foundation "progress report" asked, "Can we develop so sound and extensive a genetics that we can hope to breed, in the future, superior men?" After WWII, the Foundation continued its mind-control efforts,"[153] but, in 1941, the Rockefeller Foundation reluctantly ended its financial support of Nazi brain research at the Kaiser Wilhelm Institute in Berlin. Instead, it redirected its funding to Kinsey's sex research in Bloomington.

The Foundation made this extraordinary decision when the United States was desperately pouring every available resource into the war effort. The grant to Kinsey came through the National Research Council's Committee for Research in Problems of Sex: "In 1941, the committee awards him $1,600."[154] When the United States declared war against Germany, Japan, and Italy, Kinsey became the Rockefellers' golden boy.

Those who swallowed Kinsey's big lies had no idea that the German-based sex "reform" movement existed, let alone that he was tied to it. But Kinsey wrapped German perversion in red, white, and blue—with the help of eugenicists and the Rockefellers, whom Truman called traitors.

While the most horrific war in world history raged, and amid daily reports of the dead, wounded, and missing, Kinsey lived off the fat of the land. Despite his explosive subject matter and the open secret among Indiana University insiders of his debauched conduct with male students and his research subjects, Kinsey had a thin but well-crafted veneer of respectability. Requesting and receiving funds earmarked for sex "research," Kinsey provided glowing information about his "Marriage Course" to the Foundation, which continued its financial support. And Indiana University's board members were delighted, as their current board members also appear to be.

For those making the funding decisions, Kinsey evidently gave the answers they wanted to hear. His highly publicized but ludicrous "finding" (that human health depends upon sex early, sex often, sex in any form, and sex with anyone or anything) pleased the funders enough to keep the money flowing.

There was one doubter, though. The Foundation's top scientist, Warren Weaver, reported that "sexuality data" abounded, thanks to the German "sexual freedom" movement.[155] Therefore, he felt there was no great need for more sex research. The Foundation ignored him. Weaver also expressed outrage at Kinsey's "library of erotic literature and a collection of pictures and other 'art' objects of erotic significance," and at his use of funds for a photographer and equipment. By 1946, Weaver was clearly suspicious of Kinsey and strongly objected to financing Kinsey's "erotica" and, he suspected, pornography. Without realizing that Kinsey *was actually making obscene films*, Weaver asked why the money was given "for the specified purpose."

During my 1996 interview with W. Allen Willis, premier statistician and past president of the American Statistical Association, he recalled, "They didn't want Warren's interference. Warren was quite disgusted. He thought Kinsey was a total fraud. He didn't think that anything Kinsey said should be believed."[156] The Rockefellers promoted Weaver "up" and out of the way.

We still do not know *who* at the Rockefeller Foundation so staunchly backed Kinsey's enterprise, or what that person's or persons' agendas might have been.

Kinsey's Anglo-Saxon Boy Team

With a steady stream of Rockefeller finances, Kinsey was able to handpick his dream team. Of course, he could not hire any normal, moral personnel. Kinsey engaged in brazenly perverse, criminal behavior, and one independent-thinking whistleblower would vaporize Kinsey's revolution, and he would face disgrace and prison. Knowledge of the truth about Kinsey, biographer Jones observed, "would have been catastrophic for his career."[157] Sexual radicals are, by nature, suspect and secretive.

Pomeroy's description of who Kinsey would hire has been discussed often. No "prudes." No Jews. No blacks. No Catholics. No female interviewers. Absolutely no one with religious or ethical beliefs was allowed on his staff.[158] None were hired unless they, *their wives, and their children* gave Kinsey their erotic histories.[159] Women who passed Kinsey's bizarre sex test could serve in some clerical roles but, for the most part, he staffed his institute with handsome, young, white, insecure, and aberrant males. This included *no* seasoned doctorates—no *scientists*!

According to *The American Experience* narrator, "Kinsey himself slept with Pomeroy . . . then seduced Martin, nearly 30 years his junior." Like a movie mogul promising to turn a girl into a star in exchange for sex, Kinsey, the academic mogul, promised academic fame—and proffered draft deferments to boot. Not only did Kinsey hand out jobs in exchange for sodomy, but his *Male* book co-authorships went to Wardell Pomeroy and Clyde Martin, who both sexually serviced Kinsey. On the flipside, we can't know how many honest, skilled students Kinsey rejected and penalized due to their sexual morality. But certainly Indiana University could be charged with having failed to take corrective action for myriad of Kinsey's abuses.

Clyde Martin. Meek, winsome, poor, and very attractive, Martin was a nineteen-year-old virgin when he enrolled at Indiana University in 1937.[160] Like most of his friends, Martin planned to be a virgin on his wedding night. Obviously vulnerable, he certainly had never considered homosexual sex until 1938 when Kinsey interviewed Martin and took his sexual history. As an elderly man, Martin told the PBS *American Experience* of Kinsey's manipulations:

> [Kinsey] emphasized that I always ought to wear a condom, uh, which I remember rather shocked me. I'd never thought of uh, trying to have sex before marriage. . . . It was a very friendly sort of interview and I came away with the idea that masturbation's perfectly okay.[161]

When Martin married, he was *not* a virgin. Kinsey ruthlessly seduced the inexperienced youth and later gave him to Clara. Martin joined the professor's male harem. Kinsey first hired Martin as his gardener, making him "virtually a member of the family." Kinsey later hired him in the research laboratory in 1941.[162] Like everyone in Kinsey's inner circle, Martin kept Kinsey's secrets. Still, Kinsey sadistically singled out the lad for perverse derision. Kinsey's photographer, William Dellenback, said Martin sometimes left staff meetings figuratively "covered in blood."[163] Such humiliation naturally would twist and break the sensitive lad.

Vincent Nowlis. In 1943, Kinsey *did* hire a scientifically credentialed psychologist, the young Vincent Nowlis. But Nowlis was *not* in Kinsey's harem. Robert Yerkes, Kinsey's Rockefeller Foundation mentor, recommended Nowlis to Kinsey. To avoid antagonizing Yerkes, Kinsey let Nowlis join his team—with a draft deferment, obviously—even though Nowlis's wife Helen (another psychologist) refused to give Kinsey her history. In a hotel room during one "research" trip, Kinsey and his boys asked Nowlis "to disrobe with the clear understanding that sexual activity would follow."[164] Stunned, Nowlis resigned the next morning. If Nowlis had revealed the sexual perversions behind Kinsey's "objective" façade, Kinsey's career would have been over and his arrest likely; sodomy was illegal, and Kinsey's lies and assertion that his research served the war effort were treasonous. But Nowlis, likely protecting his career, left quietly and, in fact, became a famous psychologist. Disgusted by what he called Kinsey's "outrageous" child sex abuse protocol, Nowlis stayed silent about these crimes against children until Jones interviewed him[165] half a century thereafter?[166] *Why?*

Kinsey's cult of young, sexually aberrant aides combined business with pleasure. They were Kinsey's homosexual lovers and pornography stars, sex procurers, panderers, and predators, each with his own deviance, his own twisted agenda. Kinsey carefully chose them based on their Anglo-Saxon good looks, masculinity, atheism, sexual amorality, and sexual willingness. They shared his "faith": man as god—or, more likely, Kinsey as god. Ambition was another obvious specification; all planned to ride to fame and fortune on the Rockefeller-Kinsey coattails. And they did. Along with Martin and Nowlis, his closet cabal included:

- Wardell Pomeroy, a lower-level prison psychologist for the state of Indiana, a prize catch: handsome and moral-free. An early Kinsey lover, Pomeroy received second-author status in Kinsey's famous sex reports.
- Paul Gebhard, extremely handsome and sexually available. Gebhard had a Master's degree. His failing, however, was that he was homosexually incapable.
- Glenn Ramsey, a schoolteacher, was fired for molesting scores of adolescent boys (350 of whom were "incorporated into the [Kinsey] files.)"[167]
- Clarence Tripp, Kinsey's secret pornographer was a staff photographer in 1941.[168] A homosexual zoophile (bestiality with dogs),[169] Tripp was a child pornographer, filming boys in sex acts *for Kinsey*.
- William Dellenback, Tripp's partner, would also have been hired as a pornographer by 1941. Some records say Kinsey hired sex photographers in 1948, but although he remained very secretive about the dates, Pomeroy said they began making sex films "at an early point in the development of our research."[170]
- Samuel Steward was collecting sex stories for Kinsey in about 1944. A homosexual masochist, Steward was beaten and battered for Kinsey's pornographic movies. Steward also became a psychologist and a strongly suspected pederast, Steward, like all of Kinsey's coterie, remained silent about Kinsey's frauds and crimes against children.
- Robert Bugbee collected bugs with Kinsey as a young graduate student, then was hired to do sex lab work, resigning in 1945. Like all former Kinsey staff members, he kept silent about Kinsey's abuses until the Jones biography, perhaps because he, like many, obtained draft deferments in exchange for loyalty.
- Ralph Voris, who Kinsey nicknamed "Mr. Man" and to whom he wrote arguably erotic letters. When he died May 9, 1940, Kinsey burglarized Voris' office.

Kinsey said he selected only those not "prone to moral evaluations"[171] to work on his projects. In fact, his hires had to agree with Kinsey's pathological immorality, and to be obedient and malleable (like his wife), to share his beliefs—or be bullied into accepting them.

To create the trustworthy academic look, Kinsey's male staffers were required to *look* like sober, sensible professionals in suits and ties, with short hair. Kinsey spread the lie that all of his male aides were married, because "people who had never married were suspect to a good many Americans,"[172] and single men would have jeopardized the team's image.

Publicity photographs of Kinsey's staff and family morphed these amoral, psychopathic cult members into typical-looking, conservative 1940s Americans. But this closeted group was married in name only; everyone was a bisexual, homosexual, pedophile, pederast, or just wholly amoral. By 1940, Kinsey directed all of his team members—married and unmarried—to "experiment sexually," as he had been doing. Adultery among the staff insiders was largely an employment *obligation*.

"I felt a certain amount of pressure and so I tried homosexuality," Gebhard said in the PBS special, *The American Experience*. Clearly describing his sodomite efforts for Kinsey, he says: "And, uh, I was always impotent and humiliated, so I finally said, Kinsey you know I said, Prok, [the abbreviation of Professor Kinsey] to hell with this. . . . *No, so then he, he stopped*, he said, okay. You know, you tried."[173] Agreeably amoral, however, Gebhard was able to appease Kinsey in myriad other ways, such as obsessively committing adultery with women for Kinsey's filmmaking and voyeuristic pleasure.[174] (Still, Gebhard was denied authorship until Kinsey's *Female* volume, although he was eventually rewarded when, after Kinsey died in 1956, Gebhard became director of the Kinsey Institute.)

Kinsey had sex with his harem of assistants and with men in bars, bathhouses, and hotels in Chicago, New York, Delaware, Ohio, and elsewhere—before, during, and after World War II.[175] According to *The American Experience*, by 1939 "Kinsey travels to Chicago on several occasions to interview homosexuals. On these trips, Kinsey has sexual encounters with other men." Indeed, nearly every weekend, the addict drove the 500-mile round-trip to Chicago to "interview" homosexual men and boys.

He no longer reserved his exhibitionism for nature trips, but displayed it in his yard. According to Jones, "Kinsey's neighbors were shocked to see him work the garden clad only in a brief loin cloth that covered the bare essentials, but nothing more."[176] On Sunday mornings—as neighbors walked by, dressed for church—Kinsey and young Martin gardened side-by-side, as naked as possible. Such behavior certainly ran contrary to a conservative public image in Bloomington. But then, as now, Kinsey was untouchable. Higher-ups protected him.

While his sexual obsessions dictated unremitting self-indulgence, Kinsey was oblivious to the unprecedented human suffering of World War II in the mid-1940s and later. Instead, he romped around having sex with young men, being sexually tortured—and torturing others—in a well-funded, soundproof hideaway, and badgering coeds with his intimate sex inquisition as he giddily recorded thousands of so-called sex "contacts." Laying the groundwork for his revolution, Kinsey ignored the World War and its tragic fallout. In 1938, Hitler occupied Austria and the Sudetenland in Czechoslovakia, and the world waited for his next boot to drop. Within a year, the Nazis took Czechoslovakia and Poland. Then, Britain, France, Australia, New Zealand, and Canada declared war on Germany. Although many countries were already at war, World War II is generally said to have begun when Germany invaded Poland, September 1, 1939, after which France and most British Empire and Commonwealth countries officially declared war on Germany. September 16, 1940, anticipating its entry into the battle, the United States began requiring all men between twenty-one and thirty years of age to register for service.

But Kinsey was unconstrained by war. He had important work to do and his own "revolution" was about to begin.

Who Did Kinsey Interview *During World War II*?

Thousands of film and radio announcements and public posters warned "DON'T TALK!" lest you say something that could harm our warriors. So in point of fact, the war made things easier for Kinsey. Since he was barred from questioning servicemen and women, he could only question people on the fringe, largely the deviants he preferred.

As noted, in 1940 The United States conscripted men into the service; 300,000 National Guard and 18,633 enlistees. Post 1941 Pearl Harbor, roughly two-thirds of our men were under arms and most of the rest, even conscientious objectors, were largely bound by the same military ethos. Since "moderate" felons (not violent rapists, etc,) were allowed to enlist,* most of the prisoners Kinsey interviewed during the war were indeed the dregs of the dregs.

From 1938 through 1940, his subjects were largely the homosexual demi monde ("450 homosexual"† and "110 inmates.")‡ From 1941-45 *at least 8,327*, or 68 percent of his total sample, would be draft dodgers, violent felons, homosexuals and other aberrants, available to answer Kinsey's 350 intimate questions.§

Post World War II, by 1946 Kinsey added "1,400 convicted sex offenders in penal institutions"¶ "two hundred sexual psychopath patients"** and well over 600 sexually abused boys.†† In sum, 86 percent of deviant "subjects" defined the Libido of The Greatest Generation!

During WWII, as men and women fought overseas to save the world, prostitutes, pedophiles, elitist homosexuals, and rapists were metamorphosed into graphs of masturbation, adultery, homosexuality, early sexual activity, bestiality, etc., that purported to represent the Greatest Generation. *Sabotage, not science.*

The chart at the top of the following page from *Sexual Behavior in the Human Male* (p. 10) provides dates and numbers of sex "histories" Kinsey says he gathered from 1938 to 1947. Instead, this chart is evidence that Kinsey used aberrant draft dodgers, like himself and his young staff, to libel, slander, and sabotage the Greatest Generation.

---

* Hans Mattick, "Parolees in the Army during World War II;" 24 Fed. Probation 49, 1960.

† Wardell Pomeroy, Dr. Kinsey and the Institute for Sex Research, Harper & Row, New York, 1972, p. 75.

‡ Pomeroy, ibid., pp. 70-72.

§ In the military vein, a Conscientious Objector had the right of appeal,. Website: http://home.earthlin.net.

¶ Pomeroy, ibid., pp. 208, 211

** Pomeroy, ibid, pp. 208, 211. In his 1949 testimony before the California legislature, Kinsey boasts, "Our survey of sex offenders began 10 years ago, early in the research . . . working rather closely with courts... [in] New York we have had constant contact over a long period of years."

†† Pomeroy, ibid., p. 83.

FIGURE 2
WORLD WAR II YEARS CIRCA 1941–1945
68% (~8,327) OF KINSEY SUBJECTS ARE WWII REJECTS
(POST WWII A MINIMUM OF 10,527 OR 86% DEVIANTS)

Year	Increment	Total
1938 (6 months)	62	62
1939	671	733
1940	959	1,692
1941	843	2,535
1942	816	3,351
1943	1,510	4,861
1944	2,490	7,351
1945	2,668	10,019
1946	1,467	11,486
1947 (part)	728	12,214

Source: *Sexual Behavior in the Human Male*, p 10.

The Team of Draft Dodgers

After the United States entered World War II on December 7, 1941, Kinsey tried but failed to get a deferment for Glenn Ramsey. To avoid being drafted into the army, Ramsey had joined the Army Air Force. Kinsey himself was draft-deferred due to age, childhood sickness, and fatherhood, but, thanks to pressure from the Rockefeller Foundation and Indiana University, Kinsey received draft deferments for all the rest of his strapping young male sex aides. Jim Jones writes:

> To secure deferments, Kinsey assured local draft boards that his project was crucial to the war effort. . . . He also stressed that the special qualifications and extensive training required of his co-workers made them difficult, if not impossible, to replace in the tight job market. To strengthen his position, *he persuaded officials from Indiana University, the NRC, and the Rockefeller Foundation to write letters to his staff members' draft boards.* Their support doubtless contributed to Kinsey's success[177] (emphasis added).

Kinsey's biographers say little about the war years, pretending the titanic struggle for global domination that killed tens of millions of people never happened. Pomeroy, Christenson, and gay activist Bill Condon (who produced the movie, *Kinsey)* all ignored the war. Jonathan Gathorne-Hardy mentioned that Kinsey's only concern had been to avoid the draft for his boys. Some facts finally leaked out in Jones's dissertation and his subsequent tome. "Kinsey employed no fewer than five draft-eligible men" during World War II, Jones said, implying there were even more men protected from service. Putting the best face possible on Kinsey's treachery, Jones says, "It was a testament to his single-mindedness that he considered his research more important" than the war.[178] Amazing. Even the atom bomb did not shake Kinsey's utter indifference to the years of slaughter and suffering.[179]

Instead, driving thousands of miles for sexual trysts, orgies, and "interviews," Kinsey and his band of Benedict Arnolds later "reported" on the sexual lives of contemporary civilian American men; but, while America's *best* men fought overseas to protect them, 68–86 percent of Kinsey's men dodged the draft.

During World War II, the Greatest Generation would have found these men treasonous. And for aiding and abetting draft dodgers, Kinsey and his team also would have been called criminals and traitors.

What protected Kinsey's lovers and aides? *The combined weight of the Rockefeller Foundation, Indiana University, the National Research Council, and Kinsey* kept his "boys" off the battlefield. Kinsey told the local draft boards that his handsome young Anglo-Saxon lads (the only kind he hired) served their country best by serving him. His men had "special qualifications," he argued, and could not be spared. Kinsey did not reveal that his co-workers' "special qualifications" included their facility as pimps, procurers, and pornography performers. Such men were, as Kinsey said, "difficult, if not impossible, to replace."[180] Actually, had Kinsey admitted his men were bisexual, homosexual, pornography stars, they would have been exempt from the draft anyway, as morally subversive, harmful to military morale and to security.[181]

So, while Axis Sally and Tokyo Rose exploited our GIs' contempt for the draft-dodging men back home, Kinsey and his colleagues did not have "a high old time" with soldiers' wives and sweethearts, but with each other, with each other's wives, with other bi/homosexual men and, arguably, with boys.

The War Effort

By 1941, while Germany's National Socialist machine was crushing almost all of Europe, Kinsey was commanding young girls to give him the sizes of their clitorises. While the Luftwaffe bombed London nightly and German soldiers slogged toward Moscow, Kinsey romped through Chicago's demimonde. And while Hitler's Gestapo and SS tortured, shot, hung, and gassed millions on their march toward world domination, the Kinsey lobby prepared a sexual revolution for Western society.

Jones said:

> Kinsey had to travel, and, like other Americans, he had to contend with rationing. Thanks to relentless petitioning, backed by strong letters from university officials, Kinsey managed to secure extra allotments of gasoline and tires. . . . Kinsey was able to work around wartime rationing, though it certainly did not make his life any easier.[182]

World War II rationing didn't make his life easier?

On August 31, 1944, General Patton reported that hundreds of GIs in the Third Army, having run out of gasoline and tires near the Moselle River just outside of Metz, France, were stranded, strafed, wounded, and killed like sitting ducks.[183] For lack of fuel and tires, *thousands* of warriors were wounded and died. These mothers' sons *gave their lives*, while Kinsey's team hoarded supplies so they could drive to theaters, colleges, hospitals, prisons, gay bars, and bathhouses to carouse with aberrant men who, like them, dodged the war. I am grateful to Jones for admitting that, after handling the "inconveniences" of draft dodging, Kinsey wangled military approval to pillage these supplies in order to conduct his personal "war effort."

Life was arduous, Kinsey whined to the Rockefeller Foundation with obvious emotion, complaining about sacrifices that he and his staff had endured[184] in carrying out his important sex study. What had Kinsey's sex-addicted gang "endured" during the war?

While war hospitals scrambled for every bit of apparatus they could find to save and care for wounded and dying soldiers, Kinsey also got "laboratory equipment despite multiple hardships imposed by the wartime emergency." Other researchers had "difficulties in obtaining certain materials and apparatus."[185] But with backing from the Rockefeller Foundation, the National Research Council, and Indiana University, Kinsey got what he wanted. His intimates in the National Research Council, for example, fulfilled Kinsey's orders during and after the war. That Kinsey and his lovers *lied to* get vital equipment, fuel, and tires is still, today, an outrage that demands public justice.

The Psychopathic Cult Leader

Most of the world's murderous leaders have been sexual deviants like Hitler and the allegedly prudish Stalin whose autographed collection of male nude drawings was on exhibit in Moscow in 2009.[186] A strait-laced cover appears to be advantageous for tyrants and bullies. So indeed was Kinsey. Jones says publicly Kinsey was "hailed" as an objective scientist but "privately, he had managed to function as a covert revolutionary who had used science to lay siege to middle-class morality."[187]

A *New Yorker* magazine excerpt from Jones's *Kinsey* book explained well the depth of the sexual saboteur's perversions. Jones wrote that Kinsey once circumcised himself without benefit of anesthesia.[188] In order to function sexually, often alone, Kinsey needed to perform *extremely* sadistic or masochistic acts.

The data all point to a lifetime of heterosexual impotence for Kinsey, who was also often impotent with *adult* men. But Kinsey *certainly* engaged in perverted sexual behavior with many men and probably also children during his "research." A lifelong sexual psychopath, Kinsey brought all of this experience to bear on his family, aides, followers, and "research."

Interestingly, Kinsey wasn't the only famous sexual psychopath to come of age at Indiana University. In the early 1950s, when Kinsey was the most famous "scientist" on campus—perhaps in the world—a young man named Jim Jones attended the university. Before the end of the decade, Jones founded a doomsday cult, the People's Temple. As the cult leader, Rev. Jim Jones engaged in sex with his followers to "subjugate and humiliate" them, an attorney later testified. But some members felt it was a "privilege" to have sex with him, said a follower and former Jones defense attorney, Larry Layton.[189] And at least one account claims he sexually abused a male congregation member in front of the followers.[190]

Kinsey—like Rev. Jones—was a charismatic leader, so sensitive to each subject's subtle movements that he could read his or her innermost thoughts. (More likely, followers come to believe that their innermost thoughts and desires are *whatever the leader tells them they are.*) Like Jones, Kinsey persuaded many people that it was a "privilege" to work in his harem, to remain loyal, to engage in sex with him. While Jones led 900 followers into mass suicide in Guyana in 1978, Kinsey went on to sabotage the moral landscape of the Western world.

Eminent criminology psychologists Robert Hare, PhD, and Paul Babiak, PhD, analyzed psychopathology in *Snakes in a Suit*. They note that psychopaths have three motivations: thrill-seeking, a pathological desire to win, and the inclination to hurt people. "The ability to get people to follow you is a leadership trait . . . but being charismatic to the point of manipulating people is a psychopathic trait."[191]

Kinsey's admiring biographer, Jones, acknowledged that Kinsey was "manipulative and aggressive," that he "abused his professional authority and betrayed his trust as a teacher."[192] If people did not say what Kinsey wanted, he denounced the resister "with considerable severity." Such sexual psychotics usually demand obedience—above all, *sexual* obedience—from their followers.

In one respect, Kinsey's work is invaluable as it documents the nature of the activities of predatory sexual psychopaths. Since this body of "work" turned a deviant young man into the father of the sexual revolution that changed Western culture, we may well view Kinsey as the most successful psychopathic sex cult leader in world history.

How did Kinsey force his students, staff, their wives, and myriad others to obey his will and to commit repeated obscene and deviant sexual acts? Why should we believe that Kinsey's staffers' *wives* were eager—in the 1940s—to perform sexually for Kinsey in soundproofed rooms at Indiana University or to be recorded making criminal sex films in his attic? How did he do it? A psychopathic cult leader, Kinsey chose pliable associates, and then tyrannized and emasculated them.

Like any cult leader, Kinsey handpicked his aides for their level of obedience: Handsome, Anglo-Saxon youth who were sexually available. He picked only those who were morally week, meek, and ambitious, and methodically surrounded himself with sycophants. Staff spouses, in turn, went to great lengths to preserve their social status as academic wives. They were obedient to their husbands' desires, and their husbands were obedient to Kinsey's desires. No one on the staff could dispute Kinsey. If they won such a dispute, they'd be gone. *But Kinsey would never have hired a challenger in the first place.*

Though starting as a frail, shy boy, Kinsey grew up to be an "alpha" adult bully who controlled his underlings physically, psychologically, and behaviorally. Pomeroy confessed, "*Kinsey dominated us.*" Kinsey used "sharp words, exaggerations and harsh language . . . determined to win arguments." He would even defend opinions "he had previously attacked."[193] Pomeroy mused, "Kinsey was in fact an aggressive individual . . . aggressive, too, when someone attempted to 'get something' on him." Pomeroy would be insulted and after "two or three weeks I would make an attempt at revenge by trying to trap him in some inconsistency,"[194] to no avail.

Both Pomeroy and Christenson admitted that Kinsey would alternate warm, fatherly approval with cold disapproval, using fear and shame to dominate his timorous underlings. Like any cult leader, Kinsey controlled all of them—and that control would last a lifetime. He used archetypal behavioral conditioning, such as erratic Pavlovian rewards and punishments, to subjugate his clique. Convinced that humans were no different from dogs, Kinsey, who studied Pavlov at Harvard, applied Pavlovian rat-and-dog training to create uniform obedience in the men who would serve him throughout his lifetime.[195]

But his control methodology could also be a case study of Stanley Milgram and Philip Zimbardo's findings on "Obedience to Authority."[196] These classic, chilling studies of blind obedience used a white-coated, authoritarian doctor who commanded college study participants to increase electric shocks to experimentation "subjects," who begged for mercy and writhed in pain. But these were actors, and the *real* subjects were the participants. Under orders at the controls, these participants delivered increasing shocks and increasing agony. While most participants resisted to some degree, nearly two-thirds ended up giving the "subject" what they thought was the maximum fatal electric shock.

Kinsey kept his team jumping for his favor—condemned one moment, sexually favored the next; insulted, and then lauded. Typical of pathological-conditioning victims, his staffers behaved like jealous siblings squabbling for parental approval, and Kinsey cruelly whipsawed his impotent subordinates to ensure their complete conformity at all times.

Pornographer William Dellenback described group sessions when they all sat around naked in Kinsey's bedroom and Kinsey told Dellenback to commit "solo" sex for him. "Looking back on that evening," biographer Jones reported, "Dellenback lamented, 'I didn't enjoy it,' adding that the entire experience was 'against my sense of propriety, I think.'"[197] (Dellenback, however, publicly voiced no qualms about filming *others* who were forced to perform for Kinsey's films.) Martin, for example, was also forced to commit solo sex for Kinsey's cameras and blushingly admitted, "I really wasn't interested, the idea kind of offended me."[198] In the end, rendered impotent by dear leader, Martin was humiliated. "I was such a failure nobody ever asked me again."

The rest of the staff, including Pomeroy and Gebhard, did as they were told. They had no "autonomy" but were "workhorses, harnessed" to Kinsey's will, said Pomeroy. No matter, he added. They "did not often resent" Kinsey, although "Gebhard felt some hostility toward Kinsey." Pomeroy added that "Paul perhaps more than I" was treated as a workhorse. Gebhard, who had a recent PhD in psychology from Harvard, "expected to be treated as a colleague, according to academic usage."[199] But he was on staff for a full two years before Kinsey allowed him to lecture. Worse, Kinsey sadistically excluded Gebhard as a coauthor on the *Male* volume.[200] Why? Well, try as he might, Gebhard was sexually impotent with Kinsey.

Once, when Gebhard had diarrhea, Kinsey instructed him to eat only citrus fruit. The submissive Gebhard ate fruit and, naturally, his diarrhea worsened. When Kinsey later caught Gebhard eating a hamburger, the biologist snarled, "Gebhard . . . sometimes I despair of you as a scientist."[201] "Kinsey would appear to soften and Paul would respond instantly," said Pomeroy. We could have "united . . . but . . . [t]he sense of hierarchy was always there," and Gebhard also found it difficult to adjust to "Prok's quick switches in attitude toward him."[202]

Pomeroy was not sexually aggressive enough to suit his boss, but at least he serviced Kinsey, so Kinsey preferred Pomeroy—despite his lack of credentials—to Gebhard. Pleased to have been favored, Pomeroy gushed, "Kinsey did treat me as a colleague, which I found extremely satisfying."[203]

Like any sex cult leader, Kinsey created "his own sexual utopia." But according to Jones, Kinsey's staff and their wives were not free, voluntary "participants in sexual liberation," but "pawns for Kinsey to manipulate and control," as "Kinsey decided what sex activity was staged, with whom and by whom."[204] Yet Jones calls Kinsey "the high priest of sexual liberation."

Tyrannical pansexuality was Kinsey's religion. The cardinal rule for the staff and their wives was that they must engage in sex, both on and off camera. The mandate was, "There should be no shame or guilt or repugnance attached to *any* sexual activity among senior staff members."[205] No guilt! The corollary to this supposedly detached scientific investigation was that anyone who felt embarrassed, coarsened, or dehumanized was guilty of repressed antisexuality, which would undermine "the work."

Jones said Kinsey would have been "saddened" to hear that so many of his team felt "coerced" into sex acts for and with him. This, said Jones, was not the "self-image" of the father of scientific sex, the man who was supposedly so "sensitive," so aware of truth, the scientist who recognized tall tales versus true confessions.

No, Kinsey was no scientist; he was a sex cult leader—utterly psychotic and vicious. His carefully engineered short hair and bow tie mask could not change that.

Kinsey's Orgy-Porgie Attic

An August, 1953 *Time* magazine story highlighted "the Kinsey's brick house (which he designed) behind a riotous growth of trees and shrubs (which he planted)."[206] But beyond those trees and inside that brick house, Kinsey was expanding upon his childhood trauma.

Biographer Jones documented that Kinsey's sexual self-abuse began in his parents' attic and continued with his youthful interest in "nature" photos and nudist magazines. Kinsey took his family on nudist vacations to the Smoky Mountains[207] and became an obsessive voyeur. And, just a short walk from the Indiana University campus, the adult Kinsey repaired to a hideaway, not unlike that of his youth. Jones reports that most of Kinsey's sex films were "done at Kinsey's home in one of the finished bedrooms in the attic."[208] No one could hear or see the group gropes in Kinsey's secret sex stage in his attic.

Pomeroy said Kinsey sought "original sources" to improve on the static naked pictures that so shaped his formative Scouting years. As his addiction and resources grew, Kinsey decided to film his own sex productions. "[A]t an early point" in the "research,"[209] Kinsey began to produce and direct his own pornographic nudist films, up in the Kinsey family home.

Clara provided Kinsey with the necessary social pretense. The subservient wife presented a maternal visage—the public face that attested to Kinsey's normalcy. But Clara Kinsey was a knowing accomplice to her husband's sabotage. James Jones documented her active role in Kinsey's pornography productions and homosexual trysts. Still, before her wedding, Clara could never have imagined she would end up being directed in filmed sex orgies and serving as a trading chip for Kinsey's access to young males, regarding vile child sex crimes.

As a sadomasochist, Kinsey naturally forced Clara and other subordinates into engaging in humiliating and illegal sex in his attic. After he launched his sex orgy programs in his home, his university colleagues would no longer hear Kinsey's cast screaming during the institute's sado-sexual torture "studies."[210]

While it appears that Kinsey acted out sexually with aides such as Pomeroy, Martin, Glenn Ramsey, and Earle Marsh,[211] we do not know how early this occurred. This information is carefully hidden by the Kinsey cult, which reveals only what Gathorne-Hardy calls, "always the official line."[212]

We do know that his was a criminally pornographic enterprise. Even in the 1950s, it was still illegal to film any sex act. (In later decades, this would change—thanks to Kinsey.) One of Kinsey's sadomasochistic sex partners, Earle Marsh, told BBC TV in 1996:

> Kinsey decided to film people having sex, using the attic of his own house as a location. I was in some, having some sexual contact, and many of us were. And, it was all done in secrecy of course. . . . At that time we would have lost our funding.[213]

And their jobs and freedom. Kinsey was "constantly apprehensive" that, if his sex films were exposed, "there is little reason to believe the Institute would have survived the publicity." *Yet, like any addict, he could not stop.*[214] He would have sacrificed his research, reputation, family, and job—even gone to jail—just to watch and film people, including himself, engaging in sex acts. This fits the definition of a voyeur and a psychopathic sexual addict, who is so aroused by his activities that he would sacrifice *everything* to continue.[215]

Pomeroy (who became a celebrated psychologist, sex therapist, and globally accredited sex-education swami) and his docile wife, Martha, made many Kinsey sex films.[216] Kinsey's bi/homosexual sex sadism star, Samuel Steward, also received a psychology degree and became known for work with young boys. With his wife Agnes, Gebhard, a neophyte psychologist and heir to the Kinsey throne, joined Kinsey's attic orgies by 1946 (or much, much earlier). Dellenback, Kinsey's unmarried photographer, also always obeyed Kinsey's humiliating sexual demands.

Clyde Martin (who eventually got his psychology degree) and his bride, Alice, performed for Kinsey's sex films but not *as a couple.*[217] Instead, they had sex with others or solo. Initially approved by Kinsey, Alice had a torrid affair with Gebhard, whom she then thought she loved. Perhaps this was why she refused sex with Martin as a "couple." According to Jones, Alice complained about "the sickening pressure" she was under to have sex on film with her spouse and other staff members. "I felt like my husband's career at the Institute depended on it."[218]

Well, it did. However, not all of Kinsey's "stars" were staff, wives, and students. University friends of a similar bent, their wives, and selected students were on Kinsey's sex casting couch call as required. But there was more. In the 2005 Yorkshire Television documentary, Gebhard calmly explained "that in conditions of the utmost secrecy, volunteers were taken up to the attic of Kinsey's home where a "workbench" was in place. . . . The best we could do was observe, and maybe stop-watch it, count the number of pelvic thrusts and so on."[219]

At least five homosexual headmasters at boys' schools in the Princeton area and one pedophile organization eagerly contributed sex assaults on boys to Kinsey's child pornography data.[220] Tripp and Dellenback also filmed the New York prostituted boys for Kinsey—at a few dollars per sex act.[221] Tripp became a credentialed psychologist and author, and eagerly displayed a nude sex photo of one of these boys to producer Tim Tate. Tripp said, "I got hold of a young German boy prostitute . . . who I photographed [in sex] with one of the younger ones." In "Secret History: Kinsey's Paedophiles," television interview, Tripp noted his sexual preference for canines. He also said:

> "Kinsey had a huge store of films done by myself, Bill [Dellenback] and other people. . . . Kinsey . . . would say 'Show me,' or 'Do you mind if I watch?' Or 'Let me come over.' . . . Whenever possible Kinsey did validate it."[222]

Indiana University had built a soundproofed room on campus for Kinsey, but he had the university tear it down and replace it with more heavily soundproofed walls and doors. Kinsey needed such soundproofing to muffle screams elicited by sexual torture. Kinsey's pornography, filmed in this room on campus as well as in his home attic, depicted not just criminal homosexual and heterosexual behaviors, but also violent sexual masochism and sadomasochism.

Although Kinsey longed to be a sex star, his friends said that the supposedly "open" sex guru had to "go into the bathroom to work himself up."[223] As an alternative, Kinsey needed a professional to sexually abuse him. One such was Earle Marsh, the active sadomasochist also known as Mr. Y.[224] Marsh often stayed in Kinsey's home for "consultation and sex." Jones quotes Marsh's raw details of sex acts with all of the senior staff and their wives, citing Clara, Martha Pomeroy, and their husbands. Marsh said, "Kinsey, of course, was an eager participant in these sessions."[225]

But for the most part, Kinsey's role in his films was reduced to demonstrating "solo" techniques.[226] Since he loved to show off his large sex organ, he found bizarre ways to perform on camera. Dellenback said, for example, he often filmed Kinsey, "engaged in masochistic" self-abuse. Indeed, Indiana University film recorded Kinsey inserting objects into his urethra, such as "a swizzle stick, the kind with a knob on the end." Or he would "tie a rope around his scrotum, and then simultaneously tug hard on the rope as he maneuvered the object deeper and deeper" or "wrap the other end around his hand and climb onto a chair and jump off."[227]

This taught the world about sex and started the sexual revolution, the field of sexology, school sex education, and its curriculum. (Fortunately for Clara's health, the Kinseys had long abandoned "the marital act.")[228] Clara mostly made persimmon pudding and dutifully covered up Kinsey's crimes until she died of natural causes at age eighty-two in Bloomington.

Her husband, however, paid a price for his disordered sexual life.

In 1956, at age sixty-two, Kinsey died, apparently of complications associated with "orchitis" which can be fatal. Jones discusses Kinsey's doctor as "pinpointing the testicles as the site of the infection."[229] Orchitis . . . marked by pain, swelling . . . usually due to gonorrhea, syphilis, filarial disease, or tuberculosis. . . . Traumatic orchitis [is] orchitis following trauma . . ."[230] He'd had hundreds of violent partners, hence, many sexually diseased partners, as well as significant trauma at minimum to his testicles and urethra. This death strongly suggests that Kinsey contracted venereal disease during his frantic frolics. This and the terrible trauma he inflicted for decades on his sexual organs no doubt led directly to his untimely death.

Kinsey's three surviving children were either teenagers or younger when pornography was being filmed upstairs.[231] In the 2005 PBS *American Experience* episode on Kinsey, his daughters admitted they knew their mother, father, and the Kinsey staff were making pornography, "the physiology involved in sex" in their family attic.

Kinsey's daughter, Anne Call, had refused for years to talk about her father but, when she was eighty, she wanted to correct the record. In her "open" home, she said, "Daddy was as pure a scientist as you will find." She added, "I'm just glad Mother wasn't alive to read" Jones's book, or Gathorne-Hardy's confirmations of the sex attic.[232] Call "absolutely" did not believe her father was bisexual or homosexual. No, never! He never had sex with Clyde Martin, "absolutely not." Her parents were typical academic conservatives. Did her mother have an affair with Martin? To that, the daughter of the man who proved that average Americans were wildly promiscuous gave a peculiar answer: "My mother would be the last person in the world to have an affair," Call said. "She was really pretty square. Their personal lives were pretty much by the rules of the day; you stayed true to the person you were married to."[233]

But the youngest son, Bruce Kinsey, contradicted his sister. Though he refused to answer questions about his father for years, he attended the 2005 premiere of *Kinsey* at Indiana University. There, he told university president Kenneth Gros Louis that the scenes of sexual "swinging" and filming of homosexual, heterosexual, and orgy-porgie sex in the Kinsey attic were all absolutely true. He begrudgingly, and apparently bitterly, admitted that this was part of his home life as a youth.[234]

[CHAPTER 4]

Toxic Consequences

> 39 per cent of 13 to 18-year-olds admitted sharing intimate pictures and videos with a boyfriend or girlfriend via sexting. . . More than one in four 13 year-olds have admitted they send and receive sexually explicit pictures of themselves via mobile phones.
>
> Telegraph.Co.UK, November 2009[235]

ALFRED KINSEY SOUGHT TO destroy the morality and religious legacy of Judeo-Christianity that had protected marriage, family, the authority of protective parents, and the sanctity of childhood. But packaging his lies as science, speaking directly to man's most base and powerful fears and urges, Kinsey deceived America. He affirmed and unleashed the collective sexual urges of a once largely self-controlled, decent people. And he did so at great cost, accomplishing on the home front what the Axis enemy's black propaganda failed to accomplish overseas: He sacrificed the reputations of America's women and men, demonizing and demoralizing our Greatest Generation.

To sabotage America's sexual morality and social fabric, Kinsey and his co-conspirators used a calculated pretense: science. But it was phony. Worse, Kinsey libeled our servicemen, our service women, and their grieving loved ones—while he indulged in orgies, lied to get draft deferments for his staff of sex partners, and even used scarce war supplies to engage in his treasonous pursuits. While the World War raged around him, Kinsey was indifferent to the lives lost and the sacrifices honorably given by the Greatest Generation.

FIGURE 3
MINIMUM ESTIMATES OF KINSEY'S CRIMINAL SAMPLE

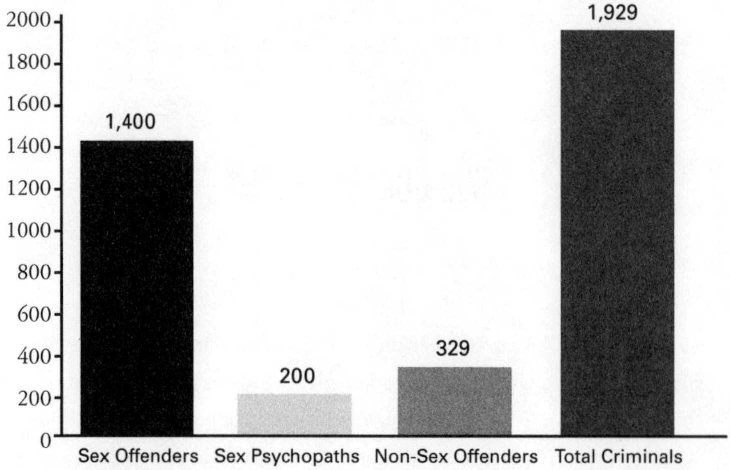

Kinsey's sample of "average" men, included large numbers of sex offenders, psychopaths and incarcerated crimals.

Libeling Our Legacy: A Media Blitz

When they published *Sexual Behavior of the Human Male* in 1948 and *Sexual Behavior of the Human Female* in 1953, Kinsey and his co-conspirators launched their campaign against our war heroes. They widely disseminated their "statistics" based on closet sex predators, psychopaths, and criminals (Figure 3). Michael Alvear chuckles in *Salon*, "50 percent of women were doing the hoochie-koochie before they got hitched."[236] *Life* magazine, said, "40% of women have been or will be unfaithful after marriage." (Figure 4)[237]

Kinsey appeared on the cover of the August 24, 1953 issue of *Time* that said, "*American culture was irrevocably changed. . . .* America wasn't ready for Kinsey's finding that 62% of women reported masturbating. . . . *These were, after all, America's mothers and mothers-to-be. . . .*"[238] An interview in the British Broadcasting Company's documentary, *Biography: Alfred C. Kinsey* sums up the reaction at the time. "Here [Kinsey] tells us in 1948 we've got this prudish society, and he tells us that more than 50% of women have had premarital intercourse," said Victor Cohn. "Well, wow, we didn't know that!"[239]

FIGURE 4

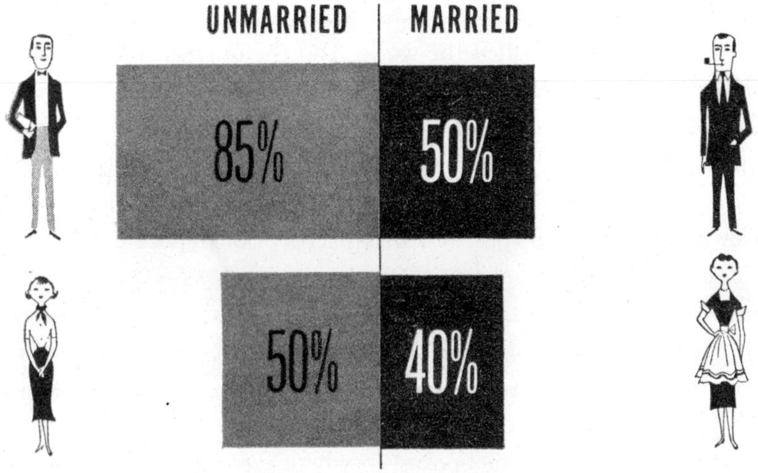

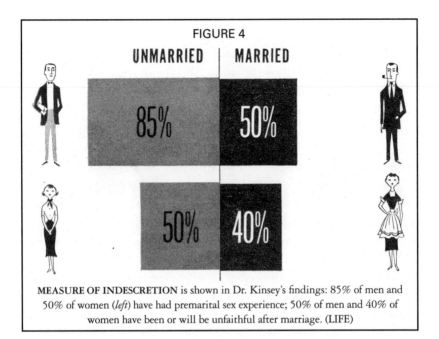

MEASURE OF INDESCRETION is shown in Dr. Kinsey's findings: 85% of men and 50% of women (*left*) have had premarital sex experience; 50% of men and 40% of women have been or will be unfaithful after marriage. (LIFE)

The shocking claims ultimately appeared in every major magazine, newspaper, and human sexuality textbook in the United States. The media unquestioningly bought Kinsey. Then they sold him to the nation.

Why?

"When K-Day finally arrived on August 20, 1953," the Kinsey Institute claims, people "rushed to their newsstands to find out what Dr. Kinsey and his colleagues had discovered about the sexual activities of American women." While some believed Kinsey, many "argued that the statistics couldn't be accurate because 'good' women would not have engaged in such activities, and if they had, they would not have revealed their experiences to Dr. Kinsey."[240] Was the American public *truly* eager to read Kinsey's findings?

The Kinsey Institute claims that its brilliant campaign was wholly unexpected. False. In fact, the Kinsey cadre had planned *for decades* to castrate our moral and spiritual legacy in an apparently "spontaneous" manner. By design, Kinsey's benefactors at the Rockefeller Foundation bankrolled aggressive publicity extravaganzas to boost sales of the volumes[241] and provided Kinsey—and his data—with seemingly impeccable credentials. Further, the Rockefeller Foundation was rich in allies that controlled the mass media. Like any war campaign, this support helped wage a mass media blitz.

Indiana University also provided financial support before, during, and after Kinsey published the work. And the university's patron, the Rockefeller Foundation, provided resources to prepare and carry out a substantial propaganda media blitzkrieg. As the first book's publication date approached, Indiana University wined and dined the most prominent reporters—supposedly objective journalists who then agreed to let Kinsey read and approve their articles prior to publication.

To control all media reports, Kinsey gave interviews *only* to those who agreed to sex interviews first. Then he controlled their sexual histories, likely using the information for blackmail purposes. At best, Kinsey follower, Scott McLemee, wrote in *Salon* that such sex files "gave a subtle, perhaps subconscious interest in confirming" Kinsey's "scientific rigor."[242]

"They were touting the book everywhere even though the statistics were appalling,"[243] said W. Allen Wallis, PhD, past president of the American Statistical Association. He recalled that an unprecedented quantity of mulberry-colored, hardcover copies of Kinsey's book flooded the health and medical profession. Though these were expensive volumes, he said, they went out gratis.

To indoctrinate a naïve populace with their destructive mindset, Kinsey's co-conspirators in the mass media blanketed the professions and academe with his black propaganda. By 1953, the lies were everywhere! Almost all magazines and newspapers—even the most popular and trusted—quoted Kinsey, blaming marital unhappiness on "the church, the school and the home."[244] According to the Kinsey Institute publicity, "Five national magazines hit the stands on K-Day—*Collier's*, *Time*, *Life*, *Woman's Home Companion*, and *Newsweek*. *Redbook* and *McCall's* appeared the following day.[245] Articles about the book and its media frenzy were published in newspapers around the country and the world, from the *Bloomington Herald-Times*, the Indiana *Daily Student*, and the *Indianapolis Star* to *The New York Times*, the *San Francisco Chronicle*, and the London *Sunday Dispatch*."[246]

Augmenting the media campaign, Kinsey lectured at colleges and hospitals worldwide, libeling the World War II generation to millions of overflow crowds of teachers and youths. Thousands of these worshipful Berkeley university Kinsey votaries would soon teach, train and spawn the hippie culture of the mid 1960s.

People repeated Kinsey's black propaganda so often and in so many venues that, finally, they began to believe them. Press, law journals, textbooks, television, novels, and films[247] hailed Kinsey's daring sexual honesty and labeled the Greatest Generation as "hypocrites," who only used church as a cover for their philandering[248] (as Kinsey actually did). Kinsey sycophant, Professor Vern Bullough, says, "The Kinsey message" was everywhere—in guides, articles, books, and novels like *The Fig Leaf, The Chapman Report, The Sex Probers, Miss Kinsey's Report*, and scores of others.[249]

As a result, millions of American elites parroted Kinsey's sabotage; that we could indulge in all manner of sexual depravity, *with no downside*. The original BBC television production on the sexual revolution, which A&E replayed in the United States, reinforced the Kinsey party line:

> America's idea of itself as a sexually conservative society was shattered forever. Things would never be the same again. Sociologically, it had a tremendous impact in this country. It was an event that just changed American social history, and I think world social history. It affected the way people looked, thought, talked and behaved about sex.[250]

Ignorant of the horrors of the 1860s sex traffic in New York City, and ridiculing Comstock as a foolish morals policeman, it was inconceivable that America would again be awash in gangs, drugs, sexual diseases, sexual crime, sex slavery, and trafficked children.

Such optimism would prove disastrous.

Toxic Fallout

Regurgitating Kinsey's fraud as scientific gospel, most scientists swallowed it whole. Some, though, did not. Abraham Maslow, MD, Lionel Trilling, PhD, and a score of others wrote about Kinsey's bad data. But even they could not have foreseen that Kinsey's cult would open the doors to sex as a field of science—or establish sexual anarchy as the norm.

Kinsey's fake statistics about parents were emotional poison that damaged subsequent generations, to the present day. Kinsey seduced the Greatest Generation's children—the Baby Boomers—who became the "Sex, drugs, rock 'n' roll" kids of the late 1960s and parented the Gen Xers of the 1980s, who parented today's "Porn Generation." It was exactly what Kinsey intended—but its virulence has likely surpassed even his expectations.

Armed with legitimate-looking statistics, Kinsey hypocritically alleged hypocrisy. He said our World War II heroes were adulterers and hypocrites, for whom moral integrity was a pretense. Constantly repeated, Kinsey's fraud eroded the trust that children had for their parents and spouses had in each other. As the delicate connection between Judeo-Christian morality and intimacy came unglued, insecurity crept into relationships, undermining marriage and eroding familial bonds.

From there, Kinsey argued that the Greatest Generation was *so* wildly immoral that we needed to reconsider our legal and social restrictions, even gut the laws that protected women and children from sexual assault. In the end, he and his co-conspirators sabotaged the way of life for which our honorable men and women had fought and, in great numbers, died.

In 1948, novelist Kathleen Norris warned in *Life* magazine about Kinsey's philosophy: "It can recede, I suppose, this civilization of ours, if in losing faith we lost all the rest. And the eternal animal in us, the flesh that looks only to flesh, will win the day."[251]

And so it has. We have paid dearly for Kinsey's sexual pathologies.

As Kinsey's conclusions spread from mass media outlets to college textbooks and then to high school, middle school, and even elementary children's lectures and texts, America's greatest strengths—our sexual reticence and commitment to God and family—would be branded as weakness: moral hypocrisy. In the end, Kinsey's black propaganda led to a drastic deterioration of American morals, changing Western society forever.

The British medical journal the *Lancet*, quoting Cole Porter's song about the sexual conduct of the World War II generation, ["According to the Kinsey Report,"] concluded that Kinsey, "an otherwise harmless student of the gall wasp, has left his former co-workers some explaining to do. The books launched the so-called sexual revolution, an era of sexual license" that brought a booming global trade in electronic pornography; annual international sex trafficking of up to eight hundred thousand women and children; domestic sex trafficking/

prostitution/stripping in the millions; unprecedented sexual violence against women and children; rampant eroticism in pop culture; high rates of unwed pregnancies; abortion on demand; skyrocketing rates of addiction to sex, pornography, and illicit drugs; failed marriages; widespread impotence; lost careers; financial ruin; sexually transmitted disease; and death.

Some revolution.

For years, people have charged that I track Kinsey and his followers the way a Nazi hunter tracks World War II war criminals—as if they were traitors, responsible for the deaths of untold millions of their countrymen. After all, they note, Kinsey and most of his original team are dead.

Yes, I still track the Kinsey cult, for their lobby were *and are* traitors to our Greatest Generation, our World War II warriors. Further, the Kinsey lobby's aggressive marketing of sexual license has unleashed rampant child sexual abuse, abortions, venereal diseases, AIDS, and serial killings; they *are* responsible for the deaths of untold millions of their countrymen—and their toxins have spread worldwide.

In his 1998 commentary in the *Encyclopedia Britannica*, Joseph Epstein notes that, "Kinsey's message—fornicate early, fornicate often, fornicate in every possible way—became the mantra of a sex-ridden age, *our* age, now desperate for a reformation of its own."[252]

In connecting the dots of this historical epoch, *the dark data speak for themselves*. The evidence shows that Alfred Kinsey and his psychopathic collaborators were the most effective fifth column in American history. The famed sociologist Pitirim Sorokin, PhD, said the evidence also shows that Kinsey and his followers' diabolical "sexualization of American culture . . . drastically and brutally affect[ed] the lives of millions. . . . What used to be considered morally reprehensible is now recommended as a positive value; what was once called demoralization is now styled moral progress and a new freedom."[253] The evidence shows that Kinsey succeeded, Sorokin also notes, by vilifying the entire World War II generation. It is time we united to restore honor to those whom Kinsey and his villianous co-conspirators defamed.

[CHAPTER 5]

Normalizing Sexual Pathology: Culture and Laws after Kinsey

> Kinsey's work, likened to the H-Bomb when it was published and the source of innumerable citations, references, comments and even jokes and songs, has formed the bedrock of all subsequent academic studies on human sexuality: it would be almost impossible to find an English-language book on human sexuality published since the 1950s which did not mention Kinsey. No other academic in the field of sexology (and precious few academics in any field) have been featured on the front cover of Time magazine or have sold so many copies of an academic textbook.[254]
>
> —Sarah Goode, *Paedophiles in Society* (2010)

IN HER NEW BRITISH text book, *Paedophiles in Society*, Professor Sarah Goode, PhD, documents Kinsey's work as "continued and developed by other researchers and writers." In her extensive research on the growth of pedophilia, Dr. Goode documented Kinsey's child sexuality views, "from birth have been taken up with gusto in certain quarters." Goode, a liberal researcher, notes that his studies have shaped "legislation, the gay rights movement and the field of sex education." In fact, says the psychologist, Kinsey's "has been the most important and influential work on human sexuality in the twentieth century" deeply influencing "science, the media, the law and public opinion."[255]

Another Britisher, John Bancroft, MD, was the fourth director of the Kinsey Institute. Handpicked, like all of the Institute's other directors, he continued to perpetuate the myth of Kinsey as an objective scientist for whom a serendipitous twist of fate led him to study sex. Yet in his introduction to the 1998 edition of the *Female* volume, Bancroft stated that Kinsey sought "a greater understanding of the varieties of sexual expression and a resulting greater tolerance of such variability."[256]

In more than a half-century since publication of the Kinsey Reports, the world's scientists, judges, educators, and parenting experts have transformed the man's psychosexual perversions into a scientific premise, a belief, which translated into behavior, ultimately sacrosanct in our laws and courts, classrooms, and doctors' offices. Now we are living with the fallout of Kinsey sadism and depravity.

Kinsey and his co-conspirators ambushed and vanquished three bedrock American values: the authority of Judeo-Christian sexual morals, the sanctity of marriage, and the protected innocence of children. Interrelated, these three values formed the basis of civilized society. Inverting them (through values-free education, sexual license, and child exploitation) leads inevitably to societal chaos and collapse. Kinsey and his zealots knew this. I propose that their lobby deliberately set out to cause America to implode. His disciples' devious call for participation in and toleration of sexual "variability" has given America six decades of sexual pathology, spreading daily in virulence and violence.

It is impossible to overstate the changes in American culture and society produced by Alfred Kinsey's attack on the morality of the Greatest Generation.

The doggedly libertarian *Salon's* Scott McLemee agreed with The National Research Council, that America can be divided into "pre-Kinsey" and "post-Kinsey" eras.[257] He said the "history of sex in America falls into two large, unequal, yet clearly defined periods. The first era belonged to the Puritans, the Victorians and related figures of restraint and misery. . . . This epoch of libidinal prohibition lasted until Jan. 4, 1948. . . . [w]hereupon, as the expression has it, the earth moved" with Kinsey's first book.[258]

Before publication of *Sexual Behavior in the Human Male*, we were largely a family-oriented, normal-minded, churchgoing, God-centered nation. We were *not* perfect. Racism, sexism, and bigotry are ever-present human failings. Yet our country was increasingly given to respectful tolerance and equal rights for women and for all races and religions, secular and even atheist. Due to our overall national mores, people worldwide flocked to our shores to partake of the nation's safety and opportunities. However, since Kinsey's publication, we became a country awash in divorce, pornography, sex addiction, venereal diseases, drug addiction, runaways, and sex crimes by and against adults and children. We have become a society that aborts tens of millions of babies, a society that repeatedly releases child rapists on parole, a society that inures us to increasing rates of sex crimes, of increasing savagery.

And so it turns out to be of significant public policy importance that, instead of being a normal family man, the father of the sexual revolution was a mad, sexual psychopath. While Kinsey claimed that the "sexual conflicts of youth" result from "prudish aversion" to youthful "participation" in "normal sexual activities,"[259] we know that a worldview that routinely involves young people in erotic experiments would serve the psychopathic Kinsey well. And, though he asserted that individuals and society suffer when we do not train our children in sexual techniques, *Kinsey's* sexual pathology devastated our public policies and national health, and the wellbeing and safety of our women and children.

Despite the fact that this saboteur said laws cannot "enforce morality," that is *exactly* what laws do, that is what laws *must* do. Kinsey claimed that "science" proved there is no moral or immoral, no right or wrong, no normal or abnormal. Therefore morality is whatever one chooses. Murderers could argue that murder should be legal, rapists could claim rape should be legal, and thieves can argue that theft should be legal. Following this ridiculous logic, the American Law Institute secretly fought the Founders' morality, working to establish their own value-free "morality" in laws *that served villains, pedophiles, and other deviants.*

A Legal Paradigm Shift: The American Law Institute's Model Penal Code

Kinsey's sexual propaganda dominated the now famous—or infamous—"sex offences" section of the American Law Institute's Model Penal Code (ALI-MPC) of 1955. The powerful Kinsey and ACLU lawyer, Morris Ernst, and the renowned historian/author, David Loth, enthused that the Kinsey Report did for sex what Columbus did for geography. However, unlike Columbus, the ALI-MPC authors, with Kinsey's aid, had mapped out well in advance how and where to use his scientific fraud in courts of law.

The first version of the ALI-MPC was distributed to legislators nationwide. It stressed "the authority of the 'social' sciences" to legalize all consensual fornication. The *Random House Dictionary* defines fornication as "voluntary sexual intercourse between two unmarried persons or two persons not married to one another." One of the many problems was that consensual fornication would be costly to society in many unseen ways, the obvious ways being the increased tax burden due to sexually transmitted diseases and illegitimate births, as well as the general destabilization of the family as fornication became common and consent became expected, subjecting women and children to additional, unanticipated physical and social pressures and consequences.

This loosening of moral absolutes certainly has caused and continues to cause many "subtle" changes in the human landscape. Before Kinsey, American laws protected women from what our hard-nosed Judeo-Christian patriarchy recognized as a predatory streak in their fellow men. However, if roughly half of women and men were fornicating *with no bad public health consequences* as Kinsey claimed, these carefully designed special privileges for women were obviously unnecessary. So, in 1955, Kinsey's sex frauds were carved into the American Law Institute's Model Penal Code. Sex science now participated fully in the protection of *predators*, to the injury of their victims. Perhaps more than anything else, the ALI-MPC exemplifies the fact that Kinsey's defamation of the Greatest Generation had profound fallout in all aspects of our moral and sexual life *and in the law*. Indeed, his propaganda affected the very essence of our society, spawning epidemics that threaten our children, our families, our marriages, our public safety, our quality of life, our very lives.

All of these changes have been and will continue to steamroll through our society. Starting with Alfred C. Kinsey, the Kinsey lobby *continues* to perpetuate the Kinsey Institute's agenda in *all* areas of human sexuality in our culture.

This is Kinsey's legacy.

> The "mainstream" Boston media didn't give "Slutcracker" negative reviews, although they did suggest it was "for adults only."[260] One review mentions that Clara "finds a sex toy" under the Christmas tree when, says the *Boston Phoenix*, we are treated to a "retelling of The Nutcracker . . . larger-than-life candy striped dildos and pole-dancing sugar plum fairies."
>
> —*SlutCracker*, Reviewed November 30, 2009[261]

Our laws are no longer based on Judeo-Christian morality, but on Kinsey's immoral "morality": an adulterous, fornicating, aborting, pornography-addicted, masturbating, impotent, sadistic, masochistic, bisexual, homosexual, exhibitionist, voyeuristic, and child-sexual-abusive world.

These truths are difficult to accept, yet crucial. America must come to understand what has gone wrong and how we changed from a family-oriented and flawed but honorable country to a sex-obsessed and violent one.

In *Ethical Issues in Sex Therapy*, pop sexologists Masters, Johnson, Kolodny, and Weems presented papers on the history of "Ethics of Sex Research Involving Children and the Mentally Retarded." Masters, Johnson, Kolodny, and their world-famous "sexperts" expressed no ethics problem when they reported the Kinsey team's criminal sexual abuse of 1,888 infants and children. No ethics violation. No problem. None, whatsoever.

Although ethics committees constantly testify on and make decisions about embryonic cloning, partial-birth abortion, compulsory sex-disease vaccinations for infants, assisted suicide—you name it—no national ethics organization has ever seen fit to investigate the Kinsey Institute's crimes, despite my efforts for thirty-five years. This is hardly reassuring.

Over the years, I have contacted many ethics groups about the criminal abuse of children evident in Kinsey's "data." I contacted the Hastings Center in New York. I contacted the ethics division of the U.S. Department of Health and Human Services. I reached out to scores of writers concerned with ethics. But no one wanted to know about these crimes, and none of America's ethics royalty has bothered to condemn the Kinsey abuse as of this writing. None.

I have often felt like John Adams in the Broadway play *1776*. "Is anyone there?" Adams cried out from his heart during the debate about declaring independence. "Does anyone care? Does anyone see what I see?" My earlier book, *Kinsey, Crimes and Consequences*, identifies the racist policies of the Kinsey Institute and of Kinsey's "studies." I document Kinsey's claim that these "experimental" babies and children were taken from the black community, the "ghetto." Still there is no outrage from academe or law.

Federal, state, and private grants generously continue to fund "research" in sex, "gender," and reproduction at the Kinsey Institute. Naturally, these funds pay for these sexperts' use of commercial pornography and production of their own. Why? Because today's sexologists are commonly addicted to pornography, imbibing it themselves, so they can use it for "therapy." This should not surprise us. Their founder, addicted as well, also made his own. As Masters and Johnson said, they all stand on "Kinsey's shoulders."

[CHAPTER 6]

Marriage, Family, and Parenting

> People will be involved in the attic with all kinds of sexual acts, and she'll come in with milk and cookies and towels for them to, you know, dry off and freshen up, and then milk and cookies and the next round of, you know, behavior will begin.
>
> —James Jones, "Social Science in America's Bedroom, Alfred Kinsey Measures Sexual Behavior"[262]

KINSEY BIOGRAPHER, JAMES JONES, paints a wholesome picture above of the famous man's dutiful wife and helpmate, Clara Kinsey. Despite Jones's sanitized depiction of the "you know, behavior," Clara Kinsey was accustomed to being degraded, right from her honeymoon, when she became the first permanent member of the sex guru's harem. From that day, Clara Kinsey no doubt bore the brunt of her husband's perverse wrath—and more—if she did not bow to his will. In standard Pavlovian conditioning mode, she jumped at the sound of the bell. And having sexually degraded herself, she degraded others, certainly allowing the abuse of Kinsey's experimental child "subjects."

Novelist T.C. Boyle was the only person on the *American Experience* television documentary who voiced any honest observation of the Kinseys' relationship, wondering about Clara's jealousy, loneliness, and any emotional harm. Pursuing the issue, Boyle coyly muses whether "love and romance . . . {can} be totally separated from the mechanical act of sex, the hormonal act of sex, as Kinsey would suggest." Of course,

Kinsey married Clara largely as a cover for his homosexuality and, when he promised to "love, honor and cherish" her, he lied.

So, what about love?

Clara's Wifely Duties

Despite the Kinsey daughter's claim that mom and dad were typical conservative parents, she couldn't have missed the atypical fact that their parents had separate bedrooms on separate *floors* of their home. Having given her the masculine nickname of "Mac," Kinsey replaced his bride with an endless parade of male lovers and "quickie" pick-ups. Kinsey did not just break his marriage vows, he trampled them into the mud, abandoning his wife's bed for seedy sodomy in bars, hotels, and bathhouses with multiple male "subjects."

Jones reported this account of the household arrangements by the sado-masochistic Earle Marsh, aka Mr. Y:

> During his visits to Bloomington, Mr. Y always stayed at the Kinseys'. . . . Kinsey's relationship with Clara was no longer passionate. . . . "They slept in different bedrooms. . . . I don't think he had sex with Mac to have sex, but if I was there we'd all have sex."[263]

Elaborating, Mr. Y. (Marsh) revealed to Jones:

> Kinsey and I'd be having sex upstairs and I'd go down[stairs] and have sex with Mac in the same house. She accepted what went on, you know. . . . Not that Clara had much choice, not if she wished to remain with her husband. Kinsey once said, "The reason she does [accept everything] is that she knows when I make up my mind to do something I do it," recalled Mr. Y.[264]

Marsh said Kinsey had a male harem and Clara had better be "open as hell." She often had sex with a man directly after Kinsey had used him. How mannerly. Divorce was unthinkable. She could only accept his table scraps. Clara would never have gone to court and divulged the real grounds for the divorce. Jones admitted that:

> No one felt the force of his unyielding demands more strongly than Clara, [who] went along with the filming . . . doing her best to throw herself into the role with the proper abandon as befitted the wife of the high priest of sexual liberation. Clara was filmed masturbating, and she was also filmed having sex with Pomeroy. . . . [She] was cooperative—anything he wanted.[265]

"I did see films of Kinsey masturbating," Jones acknowledged in his Yorkshire Television documentary. "I saw films of Mrs. Kinsey masturbating."[266] If Kinsey coerced his wife into doing that on camera, we can only imagine what the rest of her life was like.

Martin Dellenback told Jones that Clara did what Kinsey wanted "because she didn't have anything else." Clara was, in many ways, a victim of her times. Since Americans were truly traditional, and deeply committed to marital fidelity, how could she face the public shame of her life? All the excuses about her worship of Kinsey's vision ring false. Any knowledge of human love makes it clear that these activities were highly destructive to her, the other performers, to their marriages, and, therefore, to their children.

We know that Kinsey bullied women and that he bullied them into making his sex films. Clara was a party to this coercion. The novelist T.C. Boyle wondered whether the wives of Kinsey's team might have suffered emotionally. As the emotional traumas of living such lives escaped all the Kinsey biographers, so too did the fact that some of these wives might also have suffered *physical* harm, say from venereal diseases they might have contracted from bisexually experimenting husbands.

Hidden behind a falsified and idealized marriage model that the father of "sexology" held up to fool the world, the true Kinsey marriage was rife with sadistic masturbatory satisfactions and bi/homosexual adultery. Yes, the father of American sex "education," of "therapy," and of a sexual liberation cult, shaped millions of marriages in his deformed image. Specializing in primitive, painful, pathologic, and ultimately pathetic sex acts that humiliated and assaulted everyone involved, Kinsey himself *never* lived in a healthy marriage. Whatever it was, it was never love—by any stretch of the word.

Kinsey's Perverted Marriage Model

In Kinsey's research—as well as in his own marriage and sexual relationships, one thing was missing: the most important thing. Kinsey was incapable of researching or understanding or likely even contemplating or feeling *love*. Kinsey was psychologically and intellectually unable to support or even understand what keeps marriages intact; a good marriage is woven throughout with fidelity and love—both quite foreign to him. Kinsey utterly neglected the structure and physiology of the *emotional* and *spiritual* side of human sexual life.

Former Kinsey Institute librarian Cornelia Christenson, in *Kinsey: A Biography*, recalled a 1935 lecture that Kinsey gave on sexuality and "reproductive behavior." Though the talk allegedly predated Kinsey's academic interest in sex by three years, Christenson noted Kinsey's "interest in and concern for the problems arising from the social restrictions on man's biological nature." She quoted his conclusions:

> The ignorance of sexual structure and physiology, of the technique fundamental in the normal course of sexual activities and the prudish aversion to adequate participation in [sex, results in] broken marriages.[267]

Kinsey determined that this "ignorance of sexual structure and physiology"—the mechanical aspects of sex—caused marriages to fail. Since he had "practiced" a distorted form of sex on himself since he was a young boy, torturing his own sexual structure and physiology for more than three decades, he should have had a blissful marriage.

By his thinking, to keep marriages intact, society should lift restrictions that limit sexual behavior. Early in life, we should learn how to masturbate, copulate, and sodomize, he informed us, because ignorance would limit orgasms and lead to divorce. Comparing the post-Kinsey American divorce rate against the *enduring* marriages of the Greatest Generation, reveals these claims as ludicrous. Indeed, science confirms common sense, grandmothers, and biblical readings: that physical ignorance seldom causes marital failure. Although sometimes a major problem, ignorance has also unified many virginal newlyweds embarking on the great mystery and adventure of "the marital act."

But Kinsey took aim and fired directly into the heart of America's social vision—marriage—blaming *everything* from "high" rates of divorce and rape *to homosexuality* on sexual repression. He certainly knew that sexual *promiscuity* would inevitably lead to more divorce, the failed marriages, rape, and homosexuality (which it did). Thus the father of "the sexual revolution" was also the father of "no-fault-divorce," sexual addictions, *incontinence*, "early satisfaction of the sexual impulses," and so much more.

Marriage in the Greatest Generation

While Kinsey was busy sabotaging Americans with false claims of our sexual behavior, Hitler conquered Denmark, Holland, and Norway. France fell and England was destined to go next, while Italy followed the former teacher and dictator, Benito Mussolini. The United States rescued the Western world, and our World War II efforts turned wholly upon our soldiers' faith in God, their love of country, their love for their wives and families, and their selfless solidarity with their comrades in arms. Today, Europe is free *only* because the morals and values of our Greatest Generation strengthened *our* men and maintained *their* commitment to fight and die, if need be, to preserve freedom for America and for victims of tyranny abroad. Were it not for G.I. Joe's individual morality and honor, the Nazi jackboot would have squashed all of Europe. But after the war, Europeans quickly forgot this. In the years since, European and United Kingdom elitists often called Americans uptight, sexually repressed Puritans. This view widely missed the mark.

In fact, honest research confirms that, in pre-Kinsey America, "love" was in the air. Americans believed in sex, but held that "good sex" depended on love and marriage. In fact, most Americans planned to make a honeymoon gift to each other of their virginity.[268] It was the *American way.* Even by 1960, most college males still believed that "sex without love seemed utterly unethical." Interviewing two-hundred college men, Kinsey's libertarian psychologist friends, Phyllis and Eberhard Kronhausen, were surprised and appalled to discover that:

> The average modern college man is apt to say that he considers intercourse "too precious" to have with anyone except the girl he expects to marry and may actually abstain from all intercourse for that reason.[269]

The brilliant and touching letters between Abigail and John Adams—obviously virgins before their wedding—provides insight into the reality of pre-Kinsey American marriage "Alas!" Abigail wrote in December 1773. "How many snow banks divide thee and me . . . dearest Friend." The "one single expression," she said, "dwelt upon my mind and played about my Heart. . . ." Later, she begged, "Do not put such unlimited power into the hands of the husbands," and John wrote to her, "This is rather too coarse a compliment, but you are so saucy, I won't blot it out."[270]

To give children a *real* historical baseline for learning about marriage and Eros, sex education should focus on love letters between husbands and wives who, together, face challenges like hardship and war. Boys and girls would then understand that purity before the wedding day and fidelity afterward, rather than impediments to love, passion, and successful marriages—are commonly aids to it.

Unfortunately, the fallout from Kinsey's domestic black propaganda is apparent today, as American culture—and marriage—took a sharp turn.

Kinsey's Marriage Fraud

From stories such as King David and Bathsheba, Sir Lancelot and Queen Guinevere, and recorded histories such as Henry VIII and Anne Boleyn, we know that, throughout time, fornication and adultery have imperiled human peace and prosperity. Few men willingly rear other men's offspring. What's more, women who were known to be unchaste rarely could ascend to the throne or keep it, unchaste women of lower castes had difficulty marrying, and, by the time of the Greatest Generation, even men who themselves had "sowed their wild oats" sought to marry chaste women.

Was this "double-standard" unfair to women? *Of course it was!* On the other hand, the stress on chastity actually provided a *healthier and more civilized world for women and for their children*. Despite Kinsey's lies, American men *were* expected to be chaste, to save themselves for their beloved. But following Kinsey's *Male* book in 1948, the focus on chastity—and therefore fidelity and marriage—was reversed. Razing the "bourgeois notion" of heterosexual marriage and family, Kinsey fathered a sexual revolution that triggered a steady slide—a moral free-fall—from Indiana University to college professors to fraternity houses to bedrooms, and from "sex, drugs, and rock 'n' roll" to Woodstock, to music and the arts, and even to Big Pornography, inevitably profiting Big Pharmacology and big-business boardrooms.

Before Kinsey, "our boys" went off to war, leaving "for the duration"; unless they were killed or severely wounded, they would not be home until the war ended. Soldiers did not get stateside R & R or special leave for the holidays. Together with the emotional devastation of war, the long separations wrought changes in sons and husbands, who left as boys and returned as men. Having cheated death, they tried to get past the trauma of war. Our veterans cherished life. Creating families and children was a driving force, so they married immediately and started large families.[271] Births jumped to the highest in our nation's history:

1940	2,360,399
1946	3,470,000
1947	3,910,000[272]

The 2009 U.S. Centers for Disease Control and Prevention report, "Changing Patterns of Nonmarital Childbearing in the United States" revealed, with abortion and contraception freely available, in 2007 60% of births to women ages 20–24 were nonmarital, up from 52% in 2002; 32.2% of births to women 25–29 were nonmarital, up from one-quarter (25%) in 2002[273] with births to unmarried women totaling 1.7 million, 26% more than in 2002.[274]

Pre-Kinsey, notions of "illegitimacy" and "bastardy," tended to limit unmarried births despite restrictions on contraception and the criminalization of abortion. Although Aid to Dependent Children was created in 1936, in 1940 "virtually no illegitimate children and few nonwhites" were on its rolls. However, "illegitimacy in fact was at 7%

in 1940."[275] By 1950, youngsters under fifteen were the largest single population group in the country[276] with roughly 12 percent of these youngsters recorded as illegitimate.[277] Between 1940 and 1947, the Baby Boom increased the population by 12 million.[278]

Then, in 1948, Kinsey's bow-tied, crew-cut visage was in every magazine and newspaper. He spoke on the radio and appeared on the new television sets that showed up in even modest homes, all across the country. I remember hearing something about him proving that all adults were licentious sexual hypocrites. Thanks to the massive Rockefeller-funded publicity campaign for the Kinsey reports, I was not alone. Across America, the effects of Kinsey's propaganda on our World War II men and women and, subsequently, on their children, wildly skewed our perceptions of each other.

The "boringly faithful" Americans of the Greatest Generation naturally wondered who among their family, friends, neighbors, and fellow churchgoers were living this exciting, dissolute life that Kinsey described. Emily Mudd, a famous marriage counselor and Kinsey aficionado, reflected on the kinds of cartoons, jokes, remarks, and queries that spread like a flash flood across the country:

> Anyone who hears these [Kinsey] Reports, talks with their friends about them, and sees them in the different popular magazines, can't help but wonder where they as an individual fit into this or that pattern. We wonder about our friends and our associates.[279]

Some loyal spouses, who had never thought of straying, now doubted each other. And if adultery was so common and harmless, deception so easy, and jealousy so passé, maybe they, too, should taste the exciting, forbidden fruit before they grew too old? Further insecurity, demoralization, and pondering stirred among the Greatest Generation, prodded by bogus, misguided mental health experts. That is the nature and purpose of black propaganda.

Not only did men and women begin wondering which of Kinsey's statistics fit their own spouses, but their children, for the first time, began silently questioning their parents' morality. Hating to think about their parents sexual lives, and afraid of the possible answers, many young people simply didn't ask. But their moms' and dads' denials would not have mattered much anyway, since college professors and textbooks explained that their parents were so sexually repressed that they naturally lied to hide the shocking truth from their children. The Greatest Generation was branded a generation of hypocrites, living a lie of sexual licentiousness by night and hiding behind a veneer of upstanding citizenship by day.

Having assaulted the men of the generation in 1948, Kinsey and his co-saboteurs unleashed *Sexual Behavior in the Human Female* in 1953, assaulting the chastity of American women. That same year, the sex industry moved in as Hugh Hefner made his move in December 1953 with his first publication of *Playboy*, soon an icon on college campuses.

Branding America's women as morally loose, Kinsey's hostile scientism caused millions to wonder about their mothers, their sisters, and their girlfriends. Husbands wondered, too. Of course, no one could know that "wives and mothers" in Kinsey's "study" were mainly prostitutes whom Kinsey paid to be coded as typical American women.[280] This was no accident. Normal women wouldn't answer his sexual questions, and Kinsey eagerly sought abnormal people upon whom to "norm" his false data. He had sown the seeds of distrust. With his classic black propaganda, Kinsey undermined the trust and commitment of Americans to each other—and to the Founders' ideal of a virtuous, civilized people. It would wreak havoc.

Monumental Effect

America was the healthiest and wealthiest nation on Earth in the 1950s. With fewer educated elites and city folk, the Judeo-Christian ethic was the essence of our national persona—a great nation of laws, under God. The nation strove to uphold our pledge of allegiance and our National Anthem, believing in the morality that our parents taught us. We upheld the values of courage, faith, honesty, responsibility, self-control, virginity, honor, loyalty, and love of family and country.

Post-war, the Greatest Generation, as parents, taught their children that God always watched them, that all persons were equal in the image of God; that therefore homosexuality (pitiable but abnormal) was largely due to early neglect or sex abuse; that it was wrong to dress provocatively or view risqué pictures; that they should refrain from premarital sex; that they should stay faithful; and that absent brutal violence or alcoholism, they should try, try, try to stay married—if only for the security that it provided to their children. While such moral structures did have drawbacks, these values became meaningless if children believed that their parents commonly and hypocritically betrayed these values.

Returning from the war, our dazed fighters couldn't see what was about to punch them in the gut. Everywhere they turned, they heard they were sexual charlatans. It was wrong, insane. Yet, how many WWII survivors spent their last years pondering what *they* had done to create our immoral culture?

In her book *Daily Life in the United States, 1940–1959: Shifting Worlds,* historian Eugenia Kaledin writes, "No greater revolution took place during the 1950s than the shift in attitudes toward sex. By the end of the decade all institutional control over individual sexual behavior seemed to melt away. Beginning with the two gigantic Kinsey reports . . . the nation's mores were turned upside-down. . . ."[281]

On the heels of the *Male* volume in 1948, three major "companion" books would work to sabotage American law. The first out of the gate was *The Ethics of Sexual Acts* by Kinsey's friend, René Guyon, a closet French pedophile jurist. The second was *American Sexual Behavior and the Kinsey Report,* by author/historian David Loth and Kinsey's lawyer, Morris Ernst, the ACLU attorney. The third book was *Sex Habits of American Men,* a collection of essays, edited by journalist Albert Deutsch and written by world famous and stunningly foolish academicians. The drumbeat continued. Nationwide, thousands of articles and essays appeared by lawyers, judges, academics, anthropologists, psychiatrists, sociologists. Kinsey's cabal was on the move. Influential authors quoted Kinsey's bogus findings as fact, ridiculing all American sex laws and calling for reduction in and elimination of *all sex crime penalties*. By 1953, the unrelenting buzz instigated the Illinois General Assembly's Commission on Sex Offenders.

> The Kinsey Reports . . . permeate all present thinking on this subject. . . . [C]oncepts of [sexual] normality and abnormality . . . have little if any biological justification. . . . [Crime] prevention through . . . sex education for both adults and children may prove to be effective. . . . *A cultural tendency to overprotect women and children often . . . {is} more detrimental to the . . . victim than the offense itself*[282] (emphasis added).

Little did Americans know that the bell was tolling to end all such Judeo-Christian tendencies to "overprotect" women and children.

Until this turning point in our history, *half of our states outlawed a single act of unmarried, consensual, intercourse.* Of course, few Lover's Lane couples were dragged off to the lockup, but the law held out a clear "ideal" that had the direct effect of assuring most children an intact family, with a father and a mother and the very real opportunity for a stable and healthy life. Thus, constraining uncommitted passion had important social consequences, the same ones that had helped to produce the strong and moral nation from which the Greatest Generation emerged, the same morality that underpinned their ability to win World War II.

Today, as our society confronts the gamut of sexual dysfunction and atrocity, it is clear that to "overprotect" cultural tendencies have been diabolically destroyed. Meanwhile, back in 1953, the Illinois report *proves* that Kinsey intended his stealth design to deliver a death blow to our sex laws.

Harvard sociologist Pitirim Sorokin shook his head: "What used to be considered morally reprehensible is now . . . styled moral progress and a new freedom."[283]

Legal Protections for Women

In an angry screed in the *Washington Post* in 2004, law professor Jonathan Turley quoted Kinsey's adultery findings and concluded that such "science" proves that our laws still condemning adultery reflect "fundamentalist Islamic states."[284]

Like so many liberal "thinkers," Turley either needs to do some independent thinking or travel to the Middle East, for to compare American adultery laws to "Islamic" laws is shamefully uninformed. Pre-Kinsey, American adultery laws (which the Illinois Commission said "overprotected" women), in fact *shielded* women, *as well as their children and property*. Islamic fundamentalist laws, on the other hand, have always overprotected *men*. A Muslim man may legally have multiple wives—which we still call polygamous adultery—and he can *discard* any of his wives by merely saying three times that he is divorcing her. Once so divorced, such a Muslim wife is legally on her own, shamed without home, job, alimony, opportunities or children unless her husband grants his permission. Rare indeed is the Muslim woman who would dare to try to divorce her husband.[285]

The elevation of women, marriage, and premarital chastity—in both sexes—is a distinctively Western characteristic. It was the Western, Judeo-Christian belief that *each of us is made in God's image* that opened the door to equal legal rights for both sexes. Both the Old and New Testaments abhor divorce and, knowing men's sexual vulnerability to lust, warn men not to abandon the wife of their youth.

Prior to the Kinsey reports, American laws with regard to sex reflected the American ideal that it is critical for a civil society to honor women, wives, and mothers. To that end, the laws that governed the Greatest Generation favored women as the protectors of *marriage and family*. According to these laws, infidelity justified severe alimony payments. Courts found "fault" in divorce—and usually awarded child custody to betrayed moms. Such restrictions were the result of long political campaigns by ladies who convinced *voting gentlemen* that God would only bless husbands and an America that tried to live by the Ten Commandments.

Kinsey's Adultery

Kinsey's biographers pretended that his cruel betrayal of Clara and sexual prowling for handsome young bucks somehow did not poison their marriage! But infidelity crushes the heart and soul of the victimized spouse—usually, but not always, the wife. Traditionally, our laws clearly recognized the brutality of adultery, to the betrayed spouse, to the family, and to society. Yet Kinsey expected us simply to ignore the cost of infidelity: the wars fought down through the ages; the countless suicides and homicides; hundreds of years of literary, scientific, and scholarly treatises on love, jealousy, sex, and betrayal; and all the other reasons for laws that stood against adultery. Instead, Kinsey set out to banish normal and abnormal, moral and immoral, sin and redemption, good and bad, love and hate.

Primal human emotions are not so easily dismissed. I once knew an English woman who found her husband cheating on her. She grabbed a butcher knife and chased him all over the neighborhood, then stabbed him ten times. When he limped home from the hospital, she looked up coolly and cooed, "Tea, dear? One lump or two?" While I certainly do not advocate the release of such primitive emotions, as far as I know, he never cheated again.

Instead, what if, in marriage or in society, adulterers have a free pass?

At incalculable cost to our society, Kinsey has succeeded in largely granting them this.

Before Kinsey, adultery was both shameful and illegal. But when he claimed that a quarter of wives cheated on their husbands and most of the rest wanted to, he debunked the notion of female virtue. Such revelations increasingly devastated men's views of their wives and, in turn, their own fidelity.

Since then, America has largely decriminalized adultery. "No-fault" divorce, which all states legalized in full or in part by 1984, quadrupled divorce rates. Alimony essentially ended, impoverishing ex-wives (and their children). Wives lost homes, cars, other marital assets, and spousal support, which, until then, had been automatically awarded to betrayed spouses. Few protections remain for wives, except in community property states. Mothers of small children were forced to go to work. Subsequently, many women "chose" to maintain jobs after marriage "just in case," and this removed many mothers from their role as the primary caretakers of now, "latchkey" children.

Legalizing adultery was the job of Kinsey's black propaganda and, in time, the job of the educational arm of the American Bar Association, the American Law Institute Model Penal Code (ALI-MPC). The ALI-MPC wanted to decriminalize adultery, opening the door to "open marriage," "wife-swapping," "swinging," and "no-fault divorce." But according to the minutes of an ALI-MPC committee debate, an anonymous Nebraska lawyer was outraged by the proposal to decriminalize adultery. "I come from a section of the country," he told his elitist committee members, "where we still try to preserve the home and sanctity of the marriage."[286] Kinsey's morality, however, won the day and, eventually, the land.

According to historian David Allyn, another Kinsey aficionado:

> The committee voted . . . . to eliminate adultery from the model penal code. In fact, by the time the code was published in 1960, it closely matched Schwartz and Ploscowe's original intentions, which were based on the logic of the Kinsey reports. . . .[287]

Great. The ALI-MPC cited Kinsey's claim that "in an appreciable number of cases an experiment in adultery tends to confirm rather than disrupt the marriage."[288] The committee might have asked exactly *how many* adulterous marriages were "*confirmed*," what were the criteria for confirmation, how was the data collected, by whom, over what length of time, and was the alleged findings independently validated? Had they done so, they would have realized that Kinsey and the ALI-MPC had embarked on yet another Big Legal Lie. Considering Kinsey's torrid tumbles with a collection of desperate men and boys, Clara's perfunctory adultery "experiment" may have indeed "confirmed" their disordered marriage. Again, Kinsey justified his own deviant lifestyle and inflicted it on our nation and even on the world.

By statistically defaming wives (and, implicitly mothers, in the 1940s), Kinsey paved the way for no-fault divorce and an epidemic of single mothers. It did not matter to the ALI-MPC lawyers that Kinsey's World War II "sex survey" did not include servicewomen or women who otherwise worked for the government. No matter that most of Kinsey's "wives" were not actually married, but were prostitutes or women who lived with a man for "over a year"![289] Claiming adultery was widely practiced and trivial, Kinsey's ALI-MPC lied and liberated men from their moral responsibility to their wives and children.

As a result, the cult of sexual psychopaths and their abettors in media, law, clergy, government, and education, forever altered American social history. In time, the naïve cavalcade of sexual radicals of the 1960s began to question why they needed that "silly piece of paper anyway." In the wake, the breakdown of our society is powerful proof of the pernicious cost of divorce for adults and, especially, for children. For step by step, the laws we had always known to be *socially stabilizing* went by the wayside.

The Honorable Judge Morris Ploscowe was a major author of the ALI-MPC, which never questioned who comprised Kinsey's "average" World War II men or women or where Kinsey got infants and children to molest. Instead of really reading Kinsey's Swiss cheese of a study, Judge Ploscowe opined that, "It is obvious that our sex crime legislation is completely out of touch with the realities of individual living."[290]

Lawyer, Morris Ernst, excitedly explained:

> The whole of our laws and customs in sexual matters is based on the avowed desire to protect the family, and at the base of the family is the father. His behavior is revealed by the Kinsey Report to be quite different from anything the general public had supposed possible or reasonable.[291]

> It has been rather complacently assumed by a great many Americans that sexual activity for men outside the marriage bond is as rare as it is offensive to the publicly proclaimed standards of the people . . . strengthened by the bulk of popular literature and entertainment . . . [and] the almost savage penalties which many State laws attach to such activities [as adultery].[292]

Within a few years, our lawyers, judges, attorneys general, prosecutors, defense attorneys, and, indeed, our entire justice system, as Ronald Reagan observed in 1981, favored predators and ignored victims.[293] The Kinsey cult coached, disciplined, and drilled the justice system in jurisprudence, both politically and personally. Thus, only a handful of U.S. laws that once protected women and children (e.g., seduction; breach of promise to marry; alienation of affection; and criminal conversations) still live on some books. Some linger as remnants of the pre-Kinsey era. As of this writing, ten states, including Virginia, still have unused antifornication statutes that prohibit sex outside marriage.[294] Though prosecution for marital infidelity is rare, Virginia and twenty-three other states can still indict it. In fact, in September 2004, a former Virginia town attorney confessed to adultery and got twenty hours of community service as punishment.

Free Sex Is Not Free

Life magazine's cover photo on August 24, 1953, showed two little girls collecting seashells on the beach under the heading, "Kinsey Report on Women." A trusted magazine, *Life* gave Kinsey full exposure and full credibility, publishing Kinsey's "facts" about widespread "fornication" and "adultery" and saying that Kinsey's team knew more "about women than any men in the world." Of course, had the public known that these "scientists" were actually a handpicked gang of adulterous, bi-homosexual misogynists, the article never would have appeared.

Few Americans could avoid hearing and reading the adultery "data" from the Kinsey/Rockefeller cult although most average Americans rejected the bogus "findings." Academic elites were the first to accept the new "sex science" until, eventually, the oft-repeated "proof" of allegedly harmless and even healthy "free love" gained acceptance. Claiming to provide scientific justification for sex—early and often and with anyone or anything—the Kinsey fraud eventually rendered deviance as passé. In the process, vulnerable individuals followed the experts, wallowing in a wholly new configuration: not just premarital sex, but *loveless* sex. College anthropologists Nena and George O'Neill, PhDs, quoted Kinsey in their 1972 book, *Open Marriage*. The O'Neills sold Americans on adultery as a "restyled and updated type of monogamy"[295] through the same "swinging" and "wife-swapping" that sexually predatory fringe academicians had eagerly endorsed. According to the O'Neills:

> [After] reading the Kinsey reports (on *Sexual Behavior in the Human Male* in 1948 and *Sexual Behavior in the Human Female* in 1953) [we found] everybody else was apparently already doing it. What really went on in the sexual life of America had at last been made public through rigorous scientific research. Inhibitions began to look plain silly.[296]

Like Hugh Hefner, the O'Neills scorned the post-World War II ideal of togetherness in marriage, saying, "sexual fidelity is the false god of closed marriage," but, well, "the choice is entirely up to you." The cool, smart, smiling, educated O'Neills certainly wouldn't bow before that "false god"! After all, they said, our GIs sowed their wild oats with "frauleins and geishas, whether the husbands admitted it or not." Of course the authors had not served in the war.

Catch-22 author Joseph Heller did. He reported this about his bomb wing's bombardiers:

> Tom was only a few years older than I, no older than twenty-five, I'm sure, but he was already married and the father of an infant child he'd seen not more than a few times. He was resolutely intent on surviving to rejoin the family he missed so greatly, and he was increasingly and visibly perturbed that he might not succeed. It's a joy to me now to report that he did. . . . Hall A. Moody, my age or even younger, was married also, and

I relate with pride, not scorn, that neither he nor Tom Sloan ever exhibited even the slightest interest in sex with another woman.[297]

Certainly some men yielded to the trauma and terror of war. Returning, they would want to put their infidelities behind them, to rebuild their lives and families. Instead, the O'Neills said inhibitions were "plain silly" because everybody else was "swinging" and this made marriages solid. The O'Neills even advocated that wives should prepare for "multiple partners." Thou shalt commit multiple adultery—albeit responsibly.

On December 31, 2000, the *New York Times* included a review of the O'Neill legacy, pointing out that they had "underestimated jealousy in the book as a source of trouble": "When Nema interviewed the subjects years later, she found few of those with sexually open marriages had stayed married." Of the 100 or so couples Nena spoke with, the longest sexually open marriage was two years.[298]

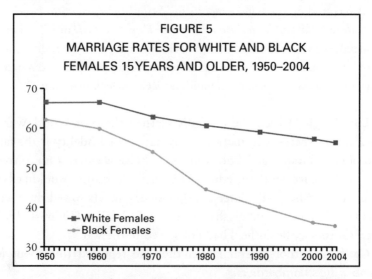

FIGURE 5
MARRIAGE RATES FOR WHITE AND BLACK FEMALES 15 YEARS AND OLDER, 1950–2004

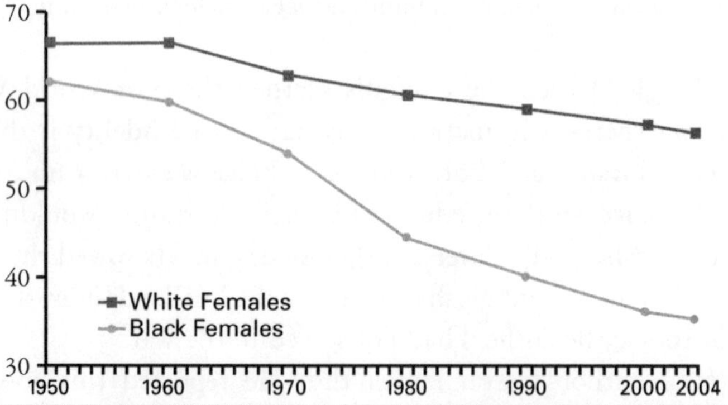

Note: 1950 and 1960 data is for 14 and older. **Source:** U.S. Census Bureau

Although the Pied Piper led the children of Hamelin into *mythical* destruction, Kinsey's black propaganda, popularized by "experts" like the O'Neills led women out of marriage (Figure 5), and married couples into adultery, divorce (figure 6), and *genuine* destruction. In 1968, these two PhDs lectured nationwide, singing their siren song that "marital freedom equals happiness." By 1974, the backlash over "wife swapping," "swinging," and failed "open marriages" caused the O'Neills to backpedal. In *Shifting Gears,* they denied that their advice had encouraged the divorce wreckage evident everywhere, ignoring the brazen facts before them of the increased harm to children who do not live with married parents. As if on cue, the couple reverted to blaming *their public* for the trauma they had inflicted with their "expert" psychobabble, charging they were misunderstood:

> [P]eople . . . consistently misinterpreted *Open Marriage.* The model is not a prescription for a swinging marriage, nor is it a prescription for lack of responsibility and caring. Open marriage is a . . . model for change and growth.[299]

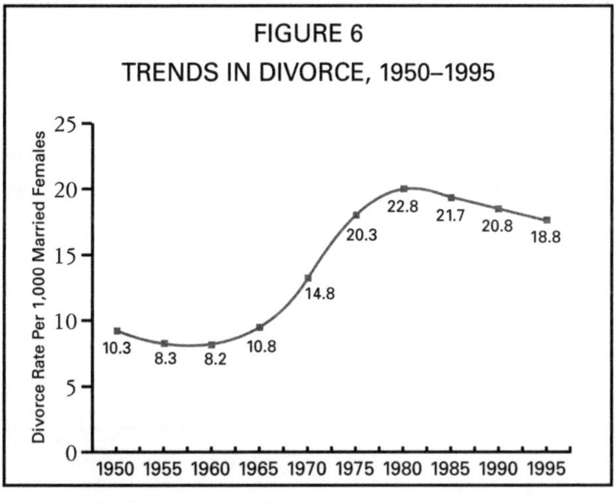

Source: Historical Statistics of the United States, Millennial Edition 2006, Vol. I, p. 688

Nine years after *Open Marriage,* Nena O'Neill belatedly tried to make amends in *The Marriage Premise* (1977). It was too late. In short order, the death knell struck for marriage. In the years since, adultery-driven divorces jumped off the charts, as did massive increases in adultery-driven battery, suicide, and even homicide. Testifying before Congress on May 3, 2006, Brookings Institution senior fellow Ron Haskins reported, "The three decades between the 1960s and 1990s, marriage rates fell dramatically . . . [whereas] during the 1970s and 1980s . . . divorce rates were rising . . . doubling between 1965 and 1975."[300]

Even the notably liberal Brookings Institution now admits that divorce has wreaked havoc with children and society—from schoolwork to delinquency and violence to suicidal conduct and more (Figure 7). (Gosh! Brookings ignored the high rates of violent and sexual child abuse in single-parent homes.)

Although the O'Neills dropped the swinging banner in 1977, others eagerly picked it up. In 1987, popular author and journalist Maggie Scarf, penned another typically Kinseyan marriage manual, *Intimate Partners: Patterns in Love and Marriage.* Like *Open Marriage* and *Shifting Gears*, Scarf's national best-seller regurgitated Kinsey's lies about the World War II generation:

> In the late 1940s and early 1950s, when Kinsey and his co-workers published their landmark findings . . . *the statistics on adultery took most people by surprise* . . . extramarital experiences were, apparently, *not at all uncommon*[301] (emphases added).

Like all subsequent Kinsey clones, Scarf dodged the most obvious questions. If adultery and random sexual behavior really was "not at all uncommon," why be "surprised by Kinsey's adultery data"? And as

FIGURE 7
WELL-BEING OF ADOLESCENTS
IF MORE LIVED WITH THEIR MARRIED PARENTS

Behavioral Problem	ACTUAL (2002)	PROJECTED
Repeated grade	6,948,530	–299,968
Suspended from school	8,570,096	–485,165
Delinquency	11,632,086	–216,498
Violence	11,490,072	–211,282
Therapy	3,412678	–247,799
Smoked in last month	5,083,513	–239,974
Thought of suicide	3,692,358	–83,469
Attempted suicide	636,164	–28,693

Note: Based on comparison of rates of behavioral problems in married-couple families and single-parent families from the National Longitudinal study of Adolescent Health, 2002. The "Projected" column extrapolates the incidence of each behavioral problem. If the same percentage of adolescents had lived in married-couple families as in 1980.
Source: Paul Amato, Future of Children, p. 89 (see footnote 6)

noted earlier, only 7 percent of single moms in 1940 had babies from "extramarital sex" when contraceptives were limited and abortion criminal? (Remember, in 1946, American marriages peaked at 16.4 per 1,000,[302] producing a million-plus *more* babies than in 1940.) So, if free sex was common, *where were all the babies?*

Scarf ignored the low divorce, illegitimacy, and venereal disease rates in pre-Kinsey America. He simply parroted Kinsey's fake data that 50 percent of husbands and 26 percent of wives committed adultery in the 1940s, and so on.[303] Hundreds or thousands of experts globally repeated Kinsey's false numbers, including Scarf and the O'Neills, praising his "methodology." Scarf did mention that, before Kinsey, adultery "was widely viewed as shameful and dishonorable." Yet, if one believes Kinsey's data, 26 percent of World War II wives were supposedly unfaithful with absolutely no bad results; by contrast, after the "free-sex" cult swept the country, marriages dropped by half—to 8.5 per 100,000 between 1959 and 1962.[304]

Unique among Kinsey's popularizers, Scarf *did admit* adultery causes powerful psychological effects although still ignoring the high price paid by children, especially as divorce and broken families commonly resulted. Her summary of how adultery affects a marriage is worthy of quoting almost in its entirety:

> *The discovery, by one partner, that the other is involved in an affair is usually experienced as a totally unexpected and catastrophic* event. It is a disaster, like a death—which, in an important sense, it actually is. It is the *death of that marriage's innocence*, the death of trust, the death of a naïve understanding of what the relationship itself is all about. The *vows of emotional and sexual exclusivity have been broken*, and the reactions, on the part of the betrayed mate, are *shock, anger, panic, and incredulity*. The marriage, as he or she knew and understood it, no longer exists, and suddenly, the "haven in a heartless world" feels frighteningly insecure and exposed. A fire storm of fierce emotionality—accusations and anger, on the part of the faithful partner[305] (emphases added).

And yet, we are to believe that this "disaster," this "catastrophic" event that brings "shock, anger, panic and incredulity," was occurring among 50 percent of husbands and 26 percent of wives, with *zero* public awareness or consequence until truth-telling Kinsey made it famous?

Naturally, promoting adultery as harmless and chic increased its frequency. Sociologist Arlene Skolnick, PhD, noted, "with the old norms and patterns no longer powerful and no new ones available, both young and older people improvised and experimented with . . . "swinging" or "mate-swapping" (at first called "wife-swapping"). She says these alternatives had little staying power and were "serious threats to the conventional family in the 1960s."[306]

Scarf observed that "in the decades following the publication of Kinsey's data," adultery increased among men and "*significantly*" increased among women. Sexual equality had allegedly arrived for women. She claimed half of wives were at the time unfaithful, which "represents a steep increase from the 26 percent infidelity rates among females that the Kinsey workers found in the early 1950s."[307]

FIGURE 8

NUMBER, RATE, AND PERCENT OF BIRTHS TO UNMARRIED WOMEN AND BIRTH RATE FOR MARRIED WOMEN, SELECTED YEARS 1950–2002

	BIRTHS TO UNMARRIED WOMEN			
Year	Number	Birth Rate (Per 1,000 Unwed Women Aged 15–44)	Percent (Of All Births)	Birth Rate for Married Women (Aged 15–44)
2002	1,358,768	43.6	33.8	NA
2001	1,349,249	43.8	33.5	88.7
2000	1,347,043	44.0	33.2	89.3
1999	1,308,560	44.4	33.0	86.5
1998	1,293,567	44.3	32.8	85.7
1997	1,257,444	44.0	32.4	84.3
1996	1,260,306	44.8	32.4	83.7
1995	1,253,976	45.1	32.2	83.7
1994	1,289,592	46.9	32.6	83.8
1993	1,240,172	45.3	31.0	86.8
1992	1,224,876	45.2	29.5	89.0
1991	1,213,769	45.2	29.5	89.9
1990	1,165,384	43.8	28.0	93.2
1985	828,174	32.8	22.0	93.3
1980	665,747	29.4	18.4	97.0
1970	398,700	26.4	10.7	121.1
1960	224,300	21.6	5.3	156.6
1950	141,600	14.1	3.9	141.0

NA—Not available

Source: National Vital Statistics Reports, v. 51, no. 2, December 18, 2002, p. 10; National Vital Statistics Reports, v. 51, no. 4, February 6, 2003, p. 14 (this report shows revised birth rate data for 2000 and 2001 based on populations consistent with the April 1, 2000 census); and National Vital Statistics Reports, v. 51, no. 11, June 25, 2003, p. 4.

The adultery increase is finally real, seen in the 750 percent increase in "illegitimacy" from 1950 to 2002 *despite legal contraception and abortion.* None of this is good for women, children or society. A flood of such sex "studies" and propaganda by seedy researchers have increased the acceptance of infidelity, divorce, and subsequently, "illegitimacy." Revolutionary sex researchers continue to toss out blue ribbon "studies" that "find" high rates of infidelity, while simultaneously ignoring its causes and tragic consequences.[309]

In the 1970s, every young couple I knew in Los Angeles (we were all liberal) engaged in adultery in order to "grow." They all, also, eventually divorced. *In every case, the break-up was due to an "open marriage,"* known to mankind for several millennia as toxic "adultery." One after another, husbands and wives abandoned their children and foolishly left their families to "find themselves" in communes, bars, beaches, and/or bathhouses. This, the experts explained, was because it was much better for the children if parents divorced rather than try to work out marital conflicts. As countless marriages fell apart, few questioned the wisdom of the Kinsey lobby—the O'Neills, Scarf, Masters and Johnson, and any of the myriad love groups and gurus from the 1950s to today. Caught up in the "progressive" excitement, marriages and love met disaster at every turn. Millions of couples bit into the forbidden fruit. And it was poison.

The Fallout from The New, "No-Fault" Divorce

Before the 1917 Russian revolution, religious law controlled family and marriage, restricting divorce and penalizing adultery. After their revolution, the Bolsheviks instituted "no-fault divorce." Our post-Kinsey culture was primed to adopt "no-fault" divorce and, unfortunately, the Kinsey cult didn't seem to mind a bit when "no-fault" divorce weakened marriage. But in time, it also harmed women's safety and financial equality. Bryce Christensen quoted radical feminist Betty Friedan admitting, "I think we made a mistake with no-fault divorce."[310]

Sex guru "Dr. Ruth" Westheimer didn't seem to mind when she voiced the implacable position of those who owe their livelihood and fame to Kinsey: "I don't care much about what is correct and what is not correct. Without him I wouldn't be Dr. Ruth!"[311]

Encouraging fornication and adultery, the ALI-MPC has demoralized marriage and families, telling the nation we did not "need to be good." Decades later, the ALI-MPC has harmed millions of women and children financially, morally, and physically. To their husbands, women gave their most significant "property" under common law—their virginity, innocence, modesty, youth, dreams, labor, and fidelity, as well as their children and, more subtly, their trust, dignity, and part of their humanity. In their middle years, millions of husbands shabbily dismissed these wives and mothers. And, as a final insult, our society and man-made laws have trivialized this betrayal.

Couples married young and naïve in America in the 1940s and 1950s. The proportion of American adults who are married declined from 95% in the 1950s to 72% in 1970 to 60% in 1998 and roughly 53% in 2009.[312] Although roughly 90% of adults marry at some time, American "men and women . . . marry for the first time an average of five years later than people did in the 1950s."[313]

It used to be that marriage was where one had a sexual relationship. Once love replaced marriage as justification for intercourse, it was not long before lust sufficed as adequate reason. Rolling down the slippery slope, such rationale has steadily degenerated. Today, forget marriage or love. Millions of young people live in an era of one-night stands, "booty calls," and "friends with benefits." It all started with Kinsey's phony statistic that half of "good" women were promiscuous. That moment in our history dramatically weakened women's hard-won power to withhold sex until men made a commitment to love and honor, and made it legal with a marriage certificate, that "little piece of paper."

But without the safety net of marriage, women lost virginity as their marital bargaining chip. "Free" sexual favors became increasingly expected as women traded on their sexual ability, availability, and agreeability in their search for some kind of lifelong stability. For many, the "nest" would not come. Instead, sex without love or commitment devastated millions of American women—and our society.

Prior to 1948, what types of men really were habitual fornicators and adulterers? Not even Hugh Hefner, the infamous pornographer-publisher of *Playboy* magazine, was "sexually active" before Kinsey. "The first time was in college," said Hefner in a January 11, 1976, interview with the Cleveland Ohio, *Sunday Plain Dealer*. "It was with the girl that I married." *Hefner was twenty-two when he lost his virginity*.[314]

Hefner believed Kinsey and credits him with transforming his Puritan values. Biographer Russell Miller writes in *Bunny* in 1984:

> It was the Kinsey Report that aroused his interest in sex . . . [due to] considerable frustration in his courtship of Millie. He began avidly reading . . . books on sex law, and any work with a vaguely erotic or pornographic content. That summer . . . Millie acquiesced to his urgent pleading to "go the whole way."[315]

He saw himself as Kinsey's populist. "Hefner recognized Kinsey as the incontrovertible word of the new God based on the new holy writ—demonstrable evidence," wrote Thomas Weyr. "Kinsey would add a dash of scientific truth to the *Playboy* mix."[316]

Much of Hefner's subsequent *Playboy* campaign for "no fault divorce" translated into legal change, which was bad news for women, children, and our civility. The Rockefeller-funded cabal—ALI-MPC, Kinsey, *Playboy,* and others—would emerge as something akin to a reality-twisted, *1984*-type Ministry of Truth.

Citing Kinsey's "data" and aping the *Playboy* and Bolshevik tradition, the ALI-MPC sent the 1955 Model Penal Code to all American state legislatures. California, where seduction had been a felony in 1948, passed "no-fault divorce" in 1969. This completely destigmatized adultery. Soon, every state in the union adopted the ALI-MPC recommendations for "no-fault" divorce, all or in part. Adultery no longer carried the old cultural onus of shame. Millions of marriages collapsed under the weight of sexual experiments.

The social expectation of faithfulness and the cost of alimony payments that had restrained many potentially errant husbands and fathers, and that had fed, clothed, and protected their children, were ridiculed as old-fashioned sexual repression and Puritanism. With that ridicule was a perceived "right" to other violations. "Rainbow Retreat," apparently the first "battered women's" shelter, opened in 1973 in Phoenix, Arizona. Desertion, as well as wife and child battery, began to surface as a nationwide calamity.[317]

Even battered, betrayed, and abandoned wives of thirty years' duration were frequently convinced that they should reject alimony as these behaviors were "normal" and because they were suddenly "equal" under the law. It took years for these discarded homemakers to realize that this new law afforded no equality. Their job opportunities were, at best, entry-level, meager, and low-paid. Moreover, alimony and other deterrents against battery and betrayal by husbands *turned out to have been a major support of the civil society*. Without these safeguards, millions of abused and fatherless children became dependent on welfare. Mothers, seeking father figures for their children, too often exposed their little ones to transient male figures, followed by unparalleled violence, neglect, and worse.

The "no-fault" fallout would go on to cause catastrophes of epic proportions.

Family Chaos in the Wake of Easy Divorce

Kinsey's black propaganda assault on women in his *Female* book asserted that illicit sex and adultery did not increase illegitimacy, venereal disease, divorce, abortion, homicide, or sex crimes. The reason, of course, was that all of these measures of social chaos were modestly low until the 1960s. Because there had not yet been an epidemic of sex crimes, sexually transmitted diseases, divorce, or illegitimacy, Kinsey's cult used his black propaganda about frequent fornication to justify abandoning social restraints. The data, after all, supposedly implied that, since we were already "doing it" without any negative fallout, there was nothing to worry about—we should just be more honest about what we were doing.

But the harmful "ripple effect" of depicting fornication and adultery as normal is seen in the titanic swells of crime and of increasing depravity ever since (Figure 9). In secret or in public, adultery is neither a "private" vice nor "a victimless" crime. Besides injuring the betrayed spouse, adultery demoralizes friends, family, and society. The children suffering through an adulterous marriage are ordinarily deeply wounded and vulnerable to myriad difficulties in their own lives. After fifty years of Kinsey-era disordered and broken families, some states are reassessing their position on adultery. A few, for instance, have initiated legislation to repeal "no-fault" divorce statutes, and to reestablish adultery as grounds for "fault" divorce.[318] Certainly some marriages are tragic. However, in no way does adultery "confirm" marriage. It destroys marriage.

And, while divorce devastates adults, it has an exponentially more serious effect on children, whose private world is A-bombed. They are left reeling from shock, which radiates out from the private to the public world. Bob Just wrote of his parents' divorce when he was five. "The great wisdom of building a family," Just mused, "is that you stay together for the sake of the children if for no other reason. . . ."[319] The product of a family that did not do that, Just speaks of a lifetime of "fear and anger":

> And there are millions of other Americans coming up behind me with the same demons. We are not just a social problem, but also a growing political force. In fact, America's ability to maintain her freedoms may ultimately depend on there being some kind of massive national healing. . . .[320]

The sexual "freedom" of adultery spawned separations and divorces that, in turn, bred parental hostility, child abandonment, lonely latchkey children, and child runaways. *Two million runaway and homeless children live on America's streets.* This is not little Johnny packing cookies, an apple, and his toy harmonica in a handkerchief to "run away" to the backyard. One out of every seven children *really* runs away before age eighteen.[321] The outcome is disastrous: 75 percent of runaways who are missing "for two or more weeks will become involved in theft, alcohol, drugs, or pornography." One of every three runaway boys and girls is prostituted "[w]ithin 48 hours of leaving home."[322]

According to the U.S. Department of Justice (DoJ) 2002 *National Incidence Studies of Missing, Abducted, Runaway or Thrownaway Children* (NISMART) report, 1,315,600 children go missing each year. Of those, 203,900 are family abductions and 58,200 non-family abductions, leaving 1,053,500 runaway or thrownaway children! Many of these youngsters return home or are returned in a day or two. But all of these children, adrift from home, directly reflect the trauma inflicted on children today from divorce, single-parent homes, battery, and incestuous abuse. That there are no press headlines, no in-depth television coverage, no *Oprah* interviews, about a million missing children is very revealing. The Kinseyan "sexual revolution" has hardly improved the lives of children.

When authorities ask runaways why they fled home, most report

SELECTED FINDINGS

CHILD DEPICTIONS

BASIC FACTS:

49% (2,971) photographs
34% (2,016) cartoons
17% (1,011) illustrations

PRINCIPAL CHILD	AND	OTHER CHARACTER *Where Depicted*
47% female 32% male 21% both/other	*SEX*	49% male 35% female 16% both/other
39% 3–11 years 26% 12–17 years 16% fetus–2 years 14% pseudo children(*) 5% unspecified	*AGE*	79% adults 7% 3–11 years 7% 12–17 years 6% unspecified 2% fetus–2 years
85% Caucasian 3% Black 12% Other minority	*RACE*	85% Caucasian 3% Black 12% Other minority

SAMPLE CHILD DEPICTIONS (NONADDITIVE)

29% nude/genital display (visual only)
21% visually exposed/sexualized
20% genital activity
16% sexual encounter with adult
10% force
10% killing/murder/maiming
6% internal genital ("pink") exposure (visuals only coded)
4% sex with animals/objects

SHARE OF CHILD DEPICTIONS BY MAGAZINE**

Playboy: 8 avg/issue (5% of *Playboy* cartoons/visuals)
Penthouse: 6 avg/issue (4% of *Penthouse* cartoons/visuals)
Hustler: 14 avg/issue (12% of *Hustler* cartoons/visuals)
Playboy highest year: 1972 (N=187, 16 per issue)
Penthouse highest year: 1972 (N=31.or 11 per issue)
Hustler highest year: 1978 (N=228, or 19 per issue)

Over 9,000 scenarios in *Playboy*, *Penthouse* and *Hustler* were identified as depicting characters under 18 years of age. From this population pool, a mere 6,004 scenarios met the project's unusually narrow criteria for the analysts of child depictions.11

ADULT CRIME AND VIOLENCE DEPICTIONS

BASIC FACTS:***

42% (6,273) photographs
36% (5,338) cartoons
22% (3,243) illustrations

VICTIM	AND	OFFENDER *Where Depicted*
46% male 43% female 11% both/other	*SEX*	54% male 22% female 24% both/other
66% 18-39 years 15% 40-60 years 3% 61+ years 16% unspec/mixed	*AGE*	57% 19-39years 17% 40-60 years 3% 61+ years 23% unspec/mixed
85% Caucasian 2% Black 13% Other minority	*RACE*	82% Caucasian 2% Black 16% Other minority

SAMPLE CRIME AND VIOLENCE DEPICTIONS (NONADDITIVE)

56% violent prop, (Visual only)
32% nude and/or sexualized victims
14% killing/murder
14% assault/battery
12% sex dealing/prostitution
12% violent sex act
12% other violent activity
11% white collar crime

SHARE OF CRIME AND VIOLENCE DEPICTIONS BY MAGAZINE

Playboy: 21 avg/issue (12% of cartoons/visuals)
Penthouse: 16 avg/issue (10% of cartoons/visuals)
Hustler: 32 avg/issue (26% of cartoons/visuals)
Playboy highest year: 1976 (N=490, or 41 per issue)
Penthouse highest year: 1980 (N=271, or 23 per issue)
Hustler highest year: 1984 (N=568, or 47 per issue)

AGGREGATE SHARE OF CHILDREN, CRIME AND VIOLENCE BY MAGAZINE

Playboy: 29 average per issue
Penthouse: 22 average per issue
Hustler: 46 average per issue

---

*The description of "pseudo-child" provided in the Attorney General's Commission on Poritogrtphy (1986, Vol. I, p. 618) rest "Pseudo-child pornography or 'teasers' involve women allegedly over the age eighteen who are 'presented in such away as to make them appear to be children or youths.' Models used in such publications are chosen for their youthful appearance (e.g., in females, slim build and small breast); and are presented with various accoutrements designed to enhance the illusion of immaturity (e.g., hair in ponytails or ringlets, toys, teddy bears, etc.). 'Pseudo-child pornography is of concern since it may appeal to the same tastes and may evoke responses similar or identical to those elicited by true child pornography."

**For rationale of estimates, see *Overview of Project* (Volume I), Table I, "Average Total Number of Features Per Magazine,", and Table II, "Average Number of Cartoons and Visuals Per Issue Containing Child Imagery" (pp. 95-96).

***For rationale of final 14,854 estimate, (originally 14,692) see *Overview Project* (Volume I), Table I, "Average Total Number of Features Per Magazine" (p 95), and Tables "Crime and Violence Data" (p. 133), "Crime and Violence Cartoon Data" (p. 134), and "Crime and Violence Visual Data" (p. 137).v

The Institute for Media Education
Box 7404
Arlington, VA 22207

Non-Profit Org.
U.S. Postage
Paid
Birmingham, AL
Permit No. 60

abuse. Yet our pornography-tolerant justice system does little to protect these children when they return to their parents, who are often alcoholic, adulterous, and/or pornographically sexually and physically abusive. Such children are destined, for the most part, to become the next generation of teen parents acting out their damage on their own children. Our broken homes have fed:

- Increased poverty and welfare, especially among single mothers;
- Increased pornography consumption, including in the home;
- Increased parental abuse and neglect, triggering sexually active, traumatized children;[323]
- Increased mothers' boyfriends sexually "acting out," etc.;[324]
- Increased childhood abuse by drug-using, disordered, incarcerated, and/or abandoning parents;[325]
- Increased State aid, prisons, half-way houses, medicalized youths, mentally ill adults;
- Increased child runaways, child prostitution, child pornography, child substance abuse;
- Increased "retrained" judges who trivialize violence, pornography addiction, drug use and incest in favor of the more affluent parent;[326]
- Increased battery, homicides, suicides, and multiple drug and alcohol addictions;
- Increasingly high taxes to control, treat, and remedy these problems.

With divorce come child custody battles. Before Kinsey, rare was the adulterer who gained child custody; a guilty dad paid alimony and child support, and lost his home and other major possessions. Certainly, scheming wives harmed some innocent parties, but, today, protective parents sometimes give up on the legal system, snatch their children and flee, rather than let the court place their children with an abusive ex-husband or ex-wife. The DoJ crime data show that, in one year, 203,900 children were kidnapped by "a parent or family member"[327] (Figure 10).

Typical of the reality of 58,200 children kidnapped by nonfamily members in 1999 is the September 5, 1982 abduction of "Johnny" Gosch, a twelve-year-old Iowa paperboy. His mother Noreen's efforts to find her son created needed public awareness of the authenticity of child

FIGURE 10

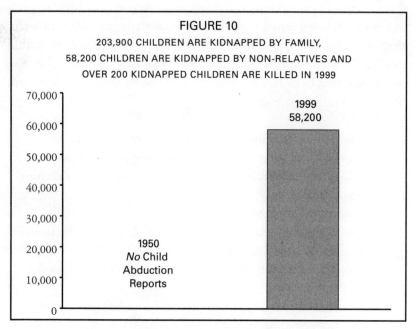

203,900 CHILDREN ARE KIDNAPPED BY FAMILY,
58,200 CHILDREN ARE KIDNAPPED BY NON-RELATIVES AND
OVER 200 KIDNAPPED CHILDREN ARE KILLED IN 1999

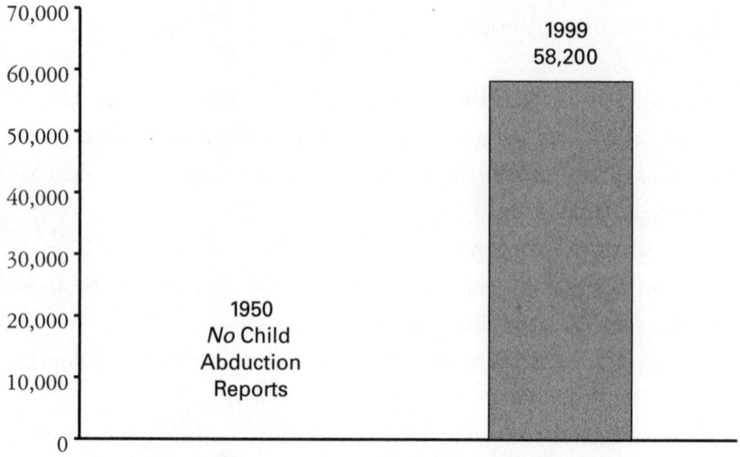

In 1950 there are zero child non-kin kidnapping reports.
Source: missingkids.com/en_US/timeline/flash.html

abductions and sexually trafficked with over two hundred children murdered each year. Authorities have not found Johnny while scores of other children are similarly snatched and trafficked (see the Franklin Cover up) confirmed even in our law courts.[328] A society without two parents caring for their children endangers its children and its civility.

In 1950, the U.S. Census Bureau reported that 43 percent of American children were at home, with their mothers caring for them, while their fathers worked full-time to provide for their families. By 1990, a scant 18 percent of American children had such stable homes. Black families had disintegrated even more rapidly than white families. Liberal black journalist William Raspberry observed in the *Washington Post* that black families were "failing":

> When [Senator Daniel] Moynihan issued his controversial study [40 years ago], roughly a quarter of black babies were born out of wedlock; moreover, it was largely a low-income phenomenon. The proportion now tops two-thirds, with little prospect of significant decline, and has moved up the socioeconomic scale.[329]

In *The Family in America*, Bryce Christensen, PhD, addressed some of the appalling societal consequences of divorce. He said so-called no-fault divorce statutes—spinning off from 1971[330]—drove up state divorce rates "by some 20 to 25%" by 1989.[331] In most of the thirty-two states that implemented no-fault divorce during the divorce boom (1965–1974), statistically, the change "resulted in a substantial number of divorces that would not have occurred otherwise."[332]

"No-fault" divorce swelled the ranks of "displaced homemakers" as divorced men moved on to sexual frolics with younger women. The new Kinsey era of socially and legally permitted fornication shifted men's focus from seeking "the woman meant for him," his "soul mate," his wife—who would be the devoted and caring mother of his children—to having sex with a growing pantheon of sexy "playmates." Seduced by their new role, these boys playing at being men increasingly neglected or refused to pay alimony and child support. Every form of abuse increased.

The troubled and troubling children of divorce made their mark in the juvenile crime statistics. These children later crowded unemployment offices, prisons, and therapists' couches, often adjudicated and counseled by those sharing similar but more controlled emotional disorders. Those who survived parental abuse, neglect, or divorce had experienced betrayal at the most intimate level of the heart. Many if not most would be, at a minimum, suspicious of love in the future.

Most Americans had understood and agreed that fathers should care financially and emotionally for their children. Christensen said that, historically in America, if you "bore the title 'father,' you 'bore also the title of provider.'" Pre-Kinsey, if a girl became pregnant outside of marriage, her family and the general community often pressured the young man into fulfilling his manly responsibilities in what was commonly known as "a shotgun wedding." Before Kinsey, American character did not largely center on the right to be "happy," have sex, and to consume products; rather, American character upheld the "duty to provide for the unborn child and its mother," and the child's right to be recognized as legitimate—and always as *wanted*. Abortion, viewed as murder of one's unborn child, strongly focused American females' character on the merits of chastity. Post-Kinsey, gone was the clarity about the economic and social stigmas that had kept many frisky young men and women virginal until marriage—and faithful within it.

Turning to that massive increase in the number of single mothers raising children without child support, and battling the inevitable child poverty, neglect, illness, and criminality, Christensen wrote:

> America's policymakers have given little or no regard to the social ideal of wedlock. Though zealous to reduce the child poverty which parental divorce has caused, they have shrunk from the task of preventing divorce in the first place. Indeed, the policymakers pushing for tougher measures to collect child support have generally acquiesced in the liberal no-fault divorce statutes, which helped to drive up the divorce rate in the first place. . . . It is now easier to dispose of an unwanted spouse of twenty years than to fire an unwanted employee of one year.[333]

Great consequence has turned on the difference between "fault-based" and "no-fault" divorce. Before Kinsey, an adulterous spouse forfeited custody of the children. Before Kinsey, win or lose, most fathers thought it their manly obligation to shoulder the burden of proper child support. Once lawmakers eliminated "fault" from child custody proceedings, adulterous fathers or mothers could retain custody. Neither party was "innocent," neither was "betrayed." There were only betrayed children.

Increasingly strict laws to collect child support from "deadbeat dads" brought about fierce custody battles, which treated children as commodities. The parent who "won" custody of the child also "won" child support from the other parent, regardless of that parent's sex or ability to pay. In the post-Kinsey family, a parent might have to pay child support to an "ex" who casually brought lovers—male or female, or both—into the child's home to frolic in the living room and bedroom.

As divorced mothers sought new partners, neglect and sexual abuse of children increased in frequency. It is common knowledge that physical and sexual abuse of children, including child murder, is especially linked to the boyfriend/stepfather scenario.[334] On the other hand, even in cases where there was ample proof that adulterous fathers battered and deserted their wives and children, convicted felons and incest offenders have actually *gained* custody of their children, often because these men had higher incomes than their ex-wives.[335]

Those who pushed for "no-fault" divorce said they aimed to "strengthen wedlock . . . by helping men and women trapped in bad marriages to move into good marriages." Indeed, this finally enabled many people to leave alcoholic, violent, or adulterous spouses, without having to prove adultery or violence. In this way, no-fault divorce helped those who could not prove fault, lacked resources, or preferred not to air dirty laundry.

Nevertheless, divorce skyrocketed—and left children in a no-win situation. Whether their mother stayed with or left a violent husband, he still beat the children. Often, too, such children suffered sexual assault. Daughters of batterers are 6.5 times more likely to become victims of father-daughter incest than are other girls.[336]

The problem is that, when the "scientists" wreaked havoc on our laws concerning sex and family, they also jettisoned sin and guilt. When a society no longer condemns the man who dumps his middle-aged wife for a "trophy bride," and coworkers no longer ostracize sexually exploitive male or female colleagues, more and more men will mistreat women and children. This is no surprise. And this is why Kinsey's effect on children—including as victims of sexual abuse—has been profound and far-reaching.

More recently, it even turns out that girls who grow up without fathers at home may actually reach puberty at unnaturally young ages.[337] In her 1997-breakthrough scientific journal article, Marcia E. Herman-Giddens, MD, found that little girls were entering puberty abnormally "earlier than their mothers did." If her father is absent, or if a girl grows up in a home with a nonbiological male figure, puberty tends to occur earlier. Among the variables that may explain this change in development, Herman-Giddens adds that the increasingly overt sexuality of popular media may not only cause copycat imitation among girls, but may also play a role in precocious pubertal development.

Parenting, Permissiveness, and the Predatory Era

Adulterous couples reaped their own rewards. When children were involved, the disastrous penalties of broken vows were visited upon the children, unto future generations.

Up to and including the men and women of World War II, Americans had always surmounted great adversity, due largely to their serious, religiously grounded ethical beliefs. But then, elitist "experts" weakened parents' moral confidence. While the Greatest Generation struggled to get their lives on track, they fell into Kinsey's trap, when

PhDs everywhere sabotaged their child-raising skills. *As families were uprooted and toppled, their children became vulnerable prey.*

The renowned 1950s psychologist Erich Fromm said that even the mature adult longs for "rootedness, for . . . mother, blood and soil."[338] But rootedness, as well as mother love, patriotism, and even the God of their parents, were stolen from the children born in that era. Their moral inheritance was purloined by those who bore false witness against their parents, libeling those who saved the world in World War II and whom Tom Brokaw rightly called the Greatest Generation.

The illustrious sociologist Christopher Lasch, PhD, wondered why a generation unsusceptible to extreme hedonism "raised a generation that was."[339] Normalizing hedonism in ways Freud never would—or could—Kinsey's attack on parents' customs and self-confidence left them dependent upon experts who urged permissiveness "to fill their children's needs. . .repudiating the serviceable practices of the past."[340] Lasch wrote extensively about the "permissiveness" of the child-raising experts of the late 1940s. He reported one mother saying, "If anything had been drummed into her in her years of motherhood, it was that you mustn't squelch the young. It might stunt their precious development."[341] Said Lasch, the "routinized half-truths of the experts" became "the laws of living"[342] as "modern parents repudiated the serviceable practices of the past."

Tired, confused, and hopeful, postwar parents heeded the "experts," and the "experts" heeded Kinsey's "sexperts." According to Lasch, the prescription for parents was that "the child should have every wish and need met, should not have the experience of being refused."[343] No surprise, then, that many thousands of these children later fled their folks' hearth and home for "sex, drugs and rock and roll." Still, in the late 1950s, Lasch recalls a colleague's weary comment, that fathers and mothers need to be able to "say 'No' without going through an elaborate song and dance."[344] Lasch observed:

> The severe criticism of the average mother's way with her children coming from social workers, psychiatrists, and educators has helped to destroy a great complacency which was formerly the young mother's protection. . . . *The dictum that mother knows best and the dogma of the natural instincts of motherhood* have so fallen in disfavor as to be available refuges only for the ignorant or the stubborn[345] (emphasis added).

Why had parents failed? Why had they been conned by supercilious "experts" whose parenting prescriptions were diametrically opposed to the teaching of Scripture and of their own parents? Their parents—the non-college-educated Depression Generation—admired education and passed on this deference to their children. As a result, the struggling Greatest Generation was vulnerable as the experts purged "the cult of virginity" with candid school "sex education."[346]

Even before *Sexual Behavior in the Human Male*, a few voices cried out in the wilderness against these modern child-raising trends. Often blamed for the excesses of the permissiveness camp, pediatrician Benjamin Spock, MD, was actually one of its critics, seeking to restore the wisdom of the *parent* in the face of an exaggerated concern for the child's "self-expression."

With a few of his peers in the 1940s and 1950s, Spock had realized, somewhat belatedly it is true, that experts' advice actually *harmed* children's welfare. Even before millions of Baby Boomers were fleeing home to go find "sex, drugs and rock and roll," Spock recognized that "expert" advice undermined parents' confidence. In his post-World War II (1946) book, *Baby and Child Care*, he warns parents *not* to heed the experts:

> [Many parents] felt somehow that they had failed to do for their children what their parents had done for them, and yet, they did not know why, or wherein they had failed, or what they could do about it.[347]

The consequences were dire: *Increasingly, parents were becoming what Kinsey had falsely painted them to be.* By the late 1960s, we were becoming what Kinsey said we were in 1948: promiscuous hypocrites. Losing themselves to the hedonism that "sexperts" prescribed for them, many parents turned a blind eye to their children's need for comforting structure, discipline, nurturing, and even obedience. With proponents in media, education, and law, Kinsey stripped parents of the ethical authority to direct their children's moral lives. "The children born . . . to World War II heroes became the rebels and dropouts of the sixties and seventies," said Lasch. "Demanding and reproachful, they simultaneously *condemned their parents' values and criticized their failure to live up to them.*"[348]

Their failure to live up to their values?

Their parents fought and died in World War II to preserve those very values for their children!

But how else could Baby Boomers respond, believing that their lives and their parents' lives were built on lies, hypocrisy, and secret sexual perversions? How bitter, how desperate were thousands of youths who *silently* suspected their parents' lives were a sham? Never really knowing what drove them to distrust, thousands of children left home at the first opportunity, both defying and emulating their parents' alleged sexual hypocrisy (as in the 1967 film, *The Graduate*), celebrating "free love," and drugs.

In the end, the Greatest Generation won at the battlefront but lost the home front, and Kinsey's black propaganda was a self-fulfilling prophesy: With a vengeance, Baby Boomers believed Kinsey and his champions—and raised *their* children accordingly. Kinsey's disastrous effect on American life has become evident in our daily diet of pornography, lust, sex, rape, torture, and murder. In our common language and media, this barrage obscured the images of godliness, purity, honor, modesty, and self-control.

The seeds were sown. Millions of young adults believed Kinsey. They did not know—no one knew—that Kinsey was a saboteur. And their parents could not know that drugs, booze, and free love would lay waste their World War II sacrifices, that their children would reject the integrity of their parents—the generation that saved the world in their lifetime. Sadly, the seeds spread into the wind, into the fertile soil of the American psyche, weakening our faith in our traditions, in each other, and in our parents.

Biographer Barry Miles, who wrote about Allen Ginsberg, William Burroughs, Jack Kerouac, and the Beat Movement, revels in the era:

> The years 1965 and 1971 . . . revolutionized western—and eventually global—culture. . . . Long hair, grass and LSD, free love, rock music and the great festivals from Monterey to Woodstock, antiwar protests and political activism, communes . . . personal transformation in therapies and practices from EST to gestalt. . . . the hippies were defined by virtually everything so-called straight society was not.[349]

Too many children had found themselves neglected, frightened, abandoned, angry, and, increasingly, sexually molested by their parents' passing lovers.

An even darker picture then emerged from Kinsey's false data, and led directly to the general demise of childhood security. Kinsey's euphemism for sexual abuse—mere sexual "contact"—was being *normalized* and *mainstreamed* as a beneficial technique of child-raising, though it was advocated by a man who himself lived a life of grotesque and latent or active pederast perversions. The implications for society of normalizing child sexual abuse have become almost inconceivably catastrophic.

Our Greatest Generation didn't know it then, but the so-called experts' advice on *all* moral issues reared a largely confused, rebellious, and enraged generation that, in turn, gave birth to today's growing population of lethargy, as well as sexual criminals and predators. The children would soon strike back.

First, Kinsey's black propaganda replaced the age-old wisdom of our Greatest Generation. Then, experts' parenting prescriptions superseded the maternal instincts of Baby Boomers, as parents. Of course, permissive parenting easily unraveled our cultural norms.

Renowned child psychiatrist Lawrence Kubie, a strong supporter of Kinsey and his fraudulent data on child sexuality, was a typical child-rearing "expert." He declared:

> [O]ur responsibility, as experts . . . is to re-examine critically everything which used to be left to mother's or father's uninformed impulses, under such euphemistic clichés as "instinct" and "love," lest mother-love mask self-love and father-love mask unconscious impulses to destroy.[350]

Ideologues carefully replaced the old-fashioned value of love with new scientific black propaganda, infusing the new message into families in a modern way. Just after the war ended, for the first time in human history, images, ideas, and relationships of all kinds entered the home via the mesmerizing light of television, which educated, entertained, influenced, deceived, tempted, and too often corrupted, and distanced family members.

But why was the Greatest Generation so easily swayed by "experts," who preached child-rearing practices that were not only in conflict with but diametrically opposed to the practices of their own Depression-era parents?

Depression-era parents survived World War I and then the Great Depression before raising large families. With meager resources, few Americans in the 1920s were fortunate enough to attend high school. Remember, his official biographer Cornelia Christenson quotes Kinsey saying that "less than 1%" of men during his term of research, attended college.[351] The parents of the Greatest Generation had *great respect* for higher education as the way up in the world. Those with college degrees held the public's trust, respect, confidence, and better and more secure jobs. The Depression Generation passed this trust in educated professionals on to their children, the Greatest Generation, who created their own large families in the 1940s and 1950s. They, too, tended to believe that educated child experts knew more about raising good, healthy, and noble children than did their own parents.

Yet, the more the Greatest Generation followed the directions of university-trained experts, the more Grandpa and Grandma shook their heads, as they watched their children devalue and replace their common law, Judeo-Christian values with those of the sexual elites. For centuries, worldwide elitist sexual revolutionaries advocated free sex, but not until Kinsey's books was their narcissism able to overtake and overwhelm the American psyche.[352]

Kinsey's Lies Fuel the Sixties Generation

During the 1960s and 1970s, the mass media, Hollywood, college professors, and child-raising "experts" proclaimed the rebels and dropouts of the 60s and 70s to be more moral than their parents. Many students of human behavior have struggled to understand what happened in the 1960s. Judge Robert Bork quoted an Israeli visitor's attempt to grasp why many American children of that decade rebelled so violently against their parents.

"Their fathers gave them prosperity and freedom," The Israeli said, "and so they hate their fathers." At first blush, Bork thought this was just "a biting comment on the ingratitude of that generation."[353] But Bork decided, the visitor had "a deeper insight." What was it?

For the answer, Bork referred his readers to sociologist Helmut Schoeck's work on "envy." Schoeck argued that the children of the Greatest Generation "strike out in senseless acts of vandalism as a result of their vague envy of a world of affluence they did not create but enjoyed with a sense of guilt."[354]

Schoeck might rightly be accused of psychobabble. In most industrial nations—especially the United States—the children of immigrants usually became more affluent than their parents had been;

usually, these children were aware of the sacrifices that had earned their subsequent affluence and they were, then, deeply grateful to their parents. On the other hand, if the children of the Greatest Generation believed that their parents' lives—and their own—were built on lies and deception, on hypocrisy and secret sexual perversions, their vandalism becomes far more understandable, even predictable.

Lasch, like Bork, also puzzled over what "blew up" American sexuality and morality among the children of World War II. As noted, Lasch blames their "parents' . . . failure to live up to . . . their values."[355] But that makes no sense. *Their parents fought and died in World War II to preserve those values*. Repeated often enough, the self-styled authorities succeeded in sabotaging World War II parents, destroying families, devastating children, turning Americans against a system that had produced so much for so many—and opening our doors wide to the brave new world of sexual anarchy.

Today, we live with the fallout from Kinsey's black propaganda campaign to destroy marriage and the family. For example, the data are quite clear that the absence of a biological father in the household leaves children significantly more vulnerable to early sexual activity, alcohol and drug abuse, and even criminal activity.

Indeed, the lies about the Greatest Generation launched a tidal wave of cynicism and violent crime, said Neil Postman, PhD, largely "generated by our children, children post-1960s."[356] By 1979, "serious child crime" reached a staggering 11,000 brutal felonies that year. Postman, then chairman of the Department of Culture and Communications at New York University, described a dramatic increase in serious crimes (i.e., murder, forcible rape, robbery, and aggravated assault) committed by American children. Postman reported that:

- In 1950, adults committed 215 serious crimes for each crime committed by a child;
- By 1960, adults committed 8 serious crimes for each crime committed by a child;
- By 1979, adults committed 5.5 serious crimes for each crime committed by a child.[357]

And adult crime *exploded* during these years! In 1979, more than "400,000 adults were arrested for serious crimes, representing .2430% of the adult population; indeed, adult crime tripled from 1950 to

FIGURE 11

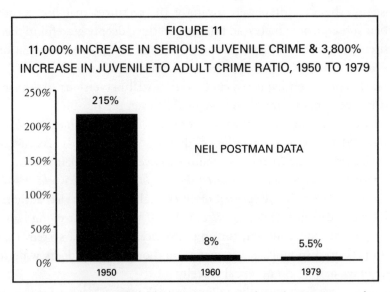

11,000% INCREASE IN SERIOUS JUVENILE CRIME & 3,800% INCREASE IN JUVENILE TO ADULT CRIME RATIO, 1950 TO 1979

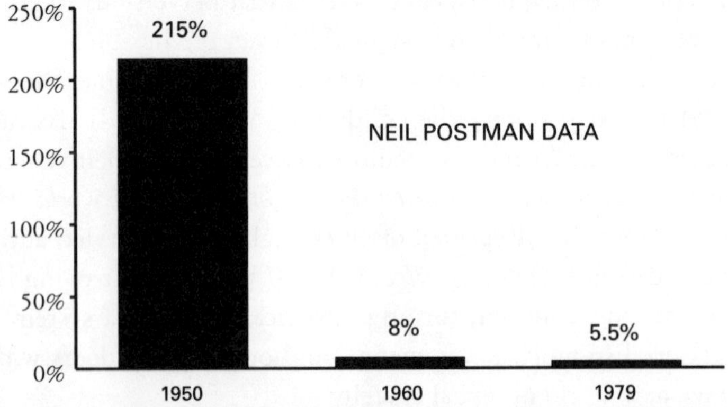

Postman, *The Disappearance of Childhood*: in 1950 nationwide, "only 170 persons under age of fifteen were arrested" for murder, forcible rape, robbery or aggravated assault (.0004 of juveniles), p. 134.

1979."[358] At the same time, Postman reported, "serious child crime" *soared a staggering 11,000%.* Postman observes the obvious about the children of the Greatest Generation: "If America can be said to be drowning in a tidal wave of crime, then the wave has mostly been generated by our children."

By the 1980s, Baby Boomer parents became what Ben Shapiro calls "The Porn Generation." Our innocence had come to an end. Dancing cheek to cheek was out. "Hooking up," "Sexting" by teenagers to friends and "Choo-Choo" orgies were in.[359] According to Shapiro:

> This is the tried-and-true hypocrisy charge: If you've sinned, you can't advocate morality. Falsely implicating millions of Americans in immoral sexual behavior was certainly an effective way of neutralizing societal morality. The only way to alleviate guilt became abdication of moral sexual standards. And when the chief goal is erasing guilt, even for immoral actions, all that remains is narcissism.[360]

Sabotage indeed.

[CHAPTER 7]

Pandering, Promiscuity, and Pornography

> Some women don't seem to recognize that anything that's too easy to get is not desirable. If a girl holds herself at so little value that she will sleep with one man after another, then other people will also hold her at very little value."[361]
>
> —Katharine Hepburn, *Ladies Home Journal*, January 1984

The Repressed Church, School, and Home

With the most up-to-date science telling both husbands and wives that their spouses secretly craved outside liaisons, marriages began to implode. Concerned about the trend, naïve and trusting average Americans searched for answers. Kinsey's cult just happened to have them. In 1953, the popular *Colliers Magazine* reviewed Kinsey's sex "data" and explained that bedrock American institutions inhibited sexual expression. One of the Rockefellers' many mass-media shills, *Colliers* quoted Kinsey to its readers:

> "It is the church, the school, the home . . . which are the chief sources of the sexual inhibitions, the distaste for all aspects of sex, and the feelings of guilt which many females carry with them into marriage. The solution, [Kinsey] infers from the statistics (and most Americans are likely to disagree violently), is to permit greater freedom before marriage."[362]

But those societies that have accepted sexual license have always reaped social chaos. Once the sexual genie escapes the bottle, everyone suffers. Historian, British scholar J.D. Unwin once set out to prove that *no* relationship existed between sexual behavior and culture, but years of study persuaded him that *there is a direct correlation between sexual morals and the rise or fall of a nation*. In 1934, Unwin reported in *Sex and Culture* that human liberty depends wholly on monogamy, and that social energy, justice, and success "in conquest, in art and science" depended completely on marriage and monogamy. In 1936, Raymond Firth described Unwin's conclusion:

> The cultural achievement of a people can be correlated with the degree of sexual continence they observe, and indeed is directly based upon it. Societies such as the Masai, the Andamanese or the Haida, which place no restrictions on sexual play or upon the early satisfaction of the sexual impulses, are at a "dead level of conception"; they possess the power of reason but they do not apply it to the world of their experience; a sense of responsibility has no place in their social vision.[363]

When Kinsey was fifteen, the famed deaf and blind author and lecturer Helen Keller repeated the same warning that most of the medical profession did. In 1909, she said women and children always paid the price of "free love." Candidly addressing issues of health, sex, marriage and family, Helen Keller wrote her article, "I Must Speak," in a time when adult and child prostitution were fraying the edges of society. "The most common cause of blindness is ophthalmia of the newborn," Keller wrote. "One pupil in every three at the institution for the blind in New York City was blinded by this disease. What is the cause[?] . . . [Her husband] . . . has contracted the infection in licentious relations before or since marriage."[364]

Keller said the truth about syphilis and gonorrhea—the only two prevalent venereal diseases of the era—was sorely needed. "Surgeons attributed three-fourths of the surgical operations on women to this disease; one-fourth is a very conservative reckoning."[365] Blind herself, Keller recorded the "bitter harvest" of such blindness, with syphilitic children reared in poorhouses and scores of young, once-healthy women dying in great pain and misery as a direct result of sexual license.

Still, Kinsey promoted his bogus "proof" that promiscuity bore no bad fruit to a public and an educational system increasingly ignorant of history. Indeed, this would become his lifelong mantra.

Before Kinsey, young women were divided into two groups—the fortunate "good girls" and the unfortunate "bad girls." Men would toy with "bad" girls and marry "good" ones. Understanding this reality, religious groups often tried to rescue the "bad girls" and help them rejoin society. But Kinsey, with the help of his pamphleteer, Hugh Hefner, essentially redefined *all* females as the "bad girls next door."

The experience of the last fifty years proves the historical accuracy of the maxim that women use sex to get love and men use love to get sex. As it turns out, a realistic appreciation of this human weakness had been the basis of our protective sex laws. So, once we destigmatized adultery and legalized fornication and cohabitation, the violent fallout in the West was inevitable.

Just a Piece of Paper?

Most of the pre-Kinsey generation found transcendence and sexual security through the church- and synagogue-taught beliefs of chastity, love, marriage, fidelity, and bearing and raising children. These values were transformed, then, into hard work, self-governance, and service to God and country. But Kinsey sacrificed those values on the altar of his pagan dogma, that a civilized society can healthfully separate sex from love, commitment, respect, and procreation.

Repeated often enough, Kinsey's spurious "data" on fornication created widespread distrust, not just between husbands and wives but also between unmarried women and men. A marriage license would soon be pooh-poohed as that mere "piece of paper." Love—not marriage—would be the reason for having intercourse. And inevitably, physical lust was adequate qualification for a "roll in the hay."

A witnessed marriage contract publicly assured women of a reliable life partner, safety from venereal disease, rape, and myriad other catastrophes. While marriage gave men great power over their wives, it also provided a sense of duty beyond the self; care and protection for their children. The couple would strike a bargain based on the assumption of a gentlemanly, even loving husband, who would not abuse his economic and physical advantages. Once women lost their most powerful bargaining chip for marriage—their virginity—they had to resort to a backup bargaining tool—sexual availability and agreeability. However, marital sex was commonly a joyful pleasure for both, assuming the couple had continued to honor one another. But contractual, monogamous, marital commitment has been the foundation of civil society, and the backup plan wasn't likely to lead to lifelong stability for women.

Based on the common law, America's legal system *did* reject Kinsey's bogus "findings" that justified early sex with as many "partners" of as many ages, sexes, and even species as possible.[366] Most Americans also rejected it—at first. Soon, however, more and more people yielded to the relentless mantra of supposedly harmless and healthy "free love." Acceptance of Kinsey's dogma percolated downward from university professors, until it became the new "sex science" religion. Kinsey's fake "data" would slowly normalize sexual anarchy.

Embraced and repeated by the intellectual elite, Kinsey's black propaganda inevitably spilled over into all forms of education and entertainment, where it took on a life—and false truth—of its own. By 1964 a *Time* cover story marveled that "Sexuality and open nudity became prevalent on the avant-garde stage. . . . The rebels of the 60s are adrift in a sea of permissiveness."[367]

Bitch, Cow, or Female Goat

In unprecedented numbers, children went off to college, where their professors taught them that their parents' love was a cover for envy and fear, and that virginity and sexual fidelity were abnormal, even deviant. Children of the Baby Boom slowly began rejecting everything their parents had fought to preserve in World War II. President of Barnard College at Columbia University in 1948, Millicent C. McIntosh, PhD, warned that Kinsey lined "up statistics which seem to show that [woman] is not really different from the bitch or the cow or the female goat."[368]

In 1953, said McIntosh, college girls felt trapped by Kinsey's statistics and wondered whether they were "normal" if they were not having relations. At the same time, many college boys "felt that they were not actually virile if they could not keep up with the statistics Dr. Kinsey presents."[369] But McIntosh observed, if they heard Kinsey's big lie often enough, people begin to believe it, "no matter how much they may realize in their more lucid moments that they should not swallow it whole."[370]

Even fornication-friendly Margaret Mead, PhD, warned that Kinsey, who referred to reproductive sex as "outlet," was training the public to "confuse sex with excretion—excremental rather than sacramental." Mead agreed that Kinsey "suggests no way of choosing between a woman and a sheep."[371]

Kinsey's black propaganda worked. Americans believed scientists, and put their stock in the declarations of the experts. How bitter, how desperate children must have been, thinking that their parents—and, therefore, their own lives—were a sham and a farce? How disillusioning and depressing for young, hopeful, idealistic boys and girls! So it was that, once they accepted Kinsey's deviant data as true, the children of our Greatest Generation shifted their "moral sanctions."

Ever since December 1953, *Playboy* magazine has touted the sexual revolution and especially Kinsey, and also regularly promoted illicit sex and drugs. The vulnerable *feeling* of betrayal had become a quivering state of rage by the 1960s.[372] The horrors of Vietnam further fueled the depression and despair of many young Americans, such that radical students rioted, started fires, screamed obscenities, hurled rocks at police, and set off bombs. Some waved the banners of the Communist enemy and chanted "Ho, Ho, Ho Chi Minh!" Many staged violent, drunken, drugged sit-ins. They raged at stunned, cowering, cowardly, foolish, and clueless university administrators and radical teachers who, at heart, and even publically, often both led and encouraged with the youthful revolutionary leftists.

The 1955 ALI-MPC quoted Kinsey, claiming, "Pre-marital intercourse is also very common and widely tolerated, so that prosecution for this offense is rare."[373] In fact, we have shown premarital intercourse was hardly common *or* widespread. Regarding Kinsey's data on "working class" males, the pre-Kinsey national "hard data" statistics on venereal disease, illegitimacy, and abortion fully disprove the claims that ours was a nation of promiscuous women and men.[374] But despite solid evidence to the contrary, the ALI-MPC swallowed and regurgitated Kinsey's absurd statement with no attempt to validate his "research." *Despite Kinsey's claims, no reliable data suggests sexual ethics were less conservative in working class communities*. The hard data on "illegitimacy" and venereal diseases confirm the facts. Promiscuity was known to be a dead end for women: *Few men and significantly fewer women of any class were promiscuous*. Yet the ALI-MPC cited Kinsey's snide ridicule of America's moral creed:

> [I]n a heterogeneous community such as ours, different individuals and groups have widely divergent views of the seriousness of various moral derelictions. . . . The immorality of the extra-marital fondle or kiss may have to receive legislative concern once we embark on the task of enforcing morals.[375]

This loosening on moral imperatives, moral absolutes, is certainly causing many such "subtle" changes in the human landscape. Over the years, American moral laws *had* grown to protect women from what our hard-nosed Judeo-Christian patriarchy recognized as a predatory streak in their fellow men. However, if most women and men were fornicating *with no bad public health consequences*, these carefully designed special privileges for women would have to go. So, in 1955, Kinsey's sex frauds were carved into the American Law Institute's Model Penal Code. Sex science would now participate fully in the protection of the predators, to the injury of their victims. Kinsey's sabotage of the Greatest Generation had profound fallout in the law with regard to protections for unmarried women.

The American Law Institute-Model Penal Code

The ALI-MPC was enacted all or in part by every state legislature, weakening or eliminating laws that, while restrictive, turned out to have protected the interests of women and children: fornication, cohabitation, seduction, breach of promise, prostitution and yes, even laws restricting public access to contraception outside of marriage.

In promoting premarital and extramarital sex, Kinsey's reports had wide-reaching effects on sexual relationships outside of marriage, as rampant promiscuity led to increases in venereal diseases, illegitimacy, and, yes, prostitution. Contraception was broadly legalized in 1965.

With widespread reliance on contraception instead of abstinance, promiscuity multiplied exponentially as did "illegitimacy." Following legal access to abortion, genital herpes and AIDS had devastated our country and many parts of the world. What's more, we associate various debilitating and fatal illnesses with many forms of contraception, even the "Pill," which—for forty years—experts insisted was completely harmless and even beneficial to health. Far from it.

Before Kinsey, prostitution was illegal. Since Kinsey, it became viewed as such a "victimless crime," that sex therapy surrogates (prostitutes) can practice in some states to "treat" impotence. Acceptance of prostitution and sex-for-profit further legitimized pornography, spawning increases in sexual abuse, incest and domestic and international human sex trafficking.

1960 Joe and Jane College Are Virgins

By the early 1960s, Phyllis and Eberhard Kronhausen, PhDs, Scandinavian free-sex radicals, advocated pornography for all. The Kronhausens later built an "erotic" museum in Sweden, where liberated parents might even bring the little kiddies. In 1960, even the Kronhausens grudgingly lamented that our college youth were still the *antithesis* of Kinsey's aberrant population.[376] Despite the agendas of such sexual elitists, American colleges had no "co-ed dorms" in 1960. Just as we called men in the service "our boys," we offered added protection to college students by giving them a grace period in which to mature. They were still "girls" and "boys." Many colleges could expel those girls and boys if they were not in their dorms before the doors closed at midnight. Further, sleeping around got a girl a very bad reputation, and it was similarly bad form for a boy to brag about any such conquest. The *Washington Post* recently noted that during the sexual revolution it was "collegiate etiquette" to hang "a tie or sock from a doorknob signifying privacy required." Now "Tufts might be the first college in the nation to make explicit what other schools have only hinted at: It is not cool to have sex in front of your roommate."[377]

Certainly before Kinsey the "patriarchy" believed females could easily be seduced into sexual behavior contrary to their own interests and that of society. Such men viewed females as the "weaker" sex, and as a higher moral and empathetic sex, deserving of protection from exploitive, wily, physically stronger men on the prowl, but they couldn't have foreseen the college "hook up culture." For hard data, from early in the last century, confirms pre-Kinsey *male* chastity, as well.

Heeding the claims about the spread of gonorrhea and syphilis, New York City mandated premarital VD testing in 1935. According to those records, "the positive rate for syphilis during the first year of compulsory testing was only 1.34%." Even "liberated" men had to admit that "it's possible the prevalence of the disease was exaggerated. . . [and] that the respectable types who got marriage licenses were at low risk for sexually transmitted disease."[378]

To their dismay, the Kronhausens, describing the sex lives of two hundred male college students in the early 1960s, concluded in a huff that, even in 1960, "Joe College" was still a virgin. Those suave Kronhausens were offended. They chose to hide the percentages, stating only:

> No Sex Without Love: Many of the students were as blushingly romantic about sex morals as any girl of their age would be. To these young men, sex without love seemed utterly unethical. Some of them did not even think it right to kiss a girl unless they were "in love."[379]
>
> Premarital Intercourse: In the college group as a whole one still finds considerable resistance toward premarital intercourse. What has changed in terms of sex mores between the attitudes of the older generation . . . [has been,] as Kinsey puts it, the "rationalizations" which serve to justify this resistance against premarital intercourse.[380]

Shame! Good gracious! But thanks to such bona fide "sexologists," see how advanced and "liberated" we are now! In 1960, the two researchers groaned to think that that many college men found premarital intercourse unacceptable due to "morals" and "religious tenets." Even more depressing to the sexperts was the fact that *most* college men objected to premarital sex *for emotional and ethical reasons*. Our free love advocates fretted that Joe College found intercourse *"too precious"* to share with anyone but his fiancée or even his wife. The Kronhausens were shocked, aghast, and selflessly determined to help Kinsey rid the nation of such obvious sexual self-discipline.[381]

Everyone Likes Children

Reluctantly, contemptuously, and even scornfully, the Kronhausens admitted that Joe College *did* abstain—because he and "lower educational groups . . . overvalued virginity" in themselves but especially in women.

Of course, the truth was—and is—that appropriately valuing virginity in women and in men had no fatal downsides versus enormous personal, societal, and economic benefits. But of course, the Kronhausens were not interested in such practicalities.

Nor was Hugh Hefner.

With his pushing and prodding, the drug culture of the 1960s and 1970s exploded as pushers found new young buyers who sought to numb their pain pharmacologically. Too well do I remember such a tragedy. My neighbors, Joe and Catherine Reilly (fictitious names to protect their privacy), were long-suffering stoics from the Greatest Generation. Their daughter, "Cindy" and her hubby would lie around stoned while their small daughter roamed, half-dressed, through the neighborhood. "Aren't you worried she'll be hurt or molested?" I asked. "No," laughed the modernized beguiled parents. "Everyone likes her." Like thousands of other children, their sweet little girl was fecklessly exposed and was indeed harmed.

At the first opportunity, millions of Baby Boomers fled their parents' comfortable homes to defy their (falsely labeled "hypocritical") Mom and Dad by joining hippie "free love" communes. The "free love" movement of the 1960s advocated unattached, uncommitted sex. With the arrival of the contraceptive birth control pill early in the decade and some states' legalization of aborting babies, women increasingly offered their sexual favors, Kinsey style.

"Shotgun weddings" became outmoded. Instead, men increasingly abandoned women of all ages, races, and religions to single-mother poverty. Women were commonly injured by sex without love or commitment. The devastation of such fornication (as well as "no-fault" adultery) was enormous, not to mention the unparalleled impact on children. By the mid-1960s, women who survived the toll of multiple partners, venereal disease, and traumatic abortions were often left permanently scarred—physically and emotionally barren.

Neither the bloody three-year Korean War that began in 1950, nor the civil rights struggle that began in the mid-1950s, nor the horror of the Vietnam War that began silently in the early 1960s, nor the assassinations of Robert Kennedy and Martin Luther King in 1968, explain the *sexual* self-destructiveness of so many American young people.

The quote "Make Love, Not War" was the spirit of the 1960s. However, Joseph Heller saw the late 1950s and early 1960s as disasters: when drugs destroyed so many of his old Coney Island friends: "Sex was often fused with drug use, and many claimed to enjoy their sexual experiences more when high on marijuana, mescaline, or LSD. Group sex and orgies became commonplace in some circles."[382]

By the end of the '60s, typical Americans could no longer avoid the media's "expert" focus on the joys of "free" sex without love or marriage. By 1972, Nena and George O'Neill's best-selling book *Open Marriage*, popularized "swinging" and "wife-swapping," selling Americans on adultery as a "restyled and updated type of monogamy."[383]

Attempting to get men to "pop the question," educated, attractive, young single women took to engaging in sexual antics that were once even too degrading for most prostitutes. Telling themselves that they were indifferent to wedding bells, highly educated, financially secure, and "sexually free" academic or businesswomen breathlessly awaited a man's marital proposal. Of course, it was unlikely to come. Such women commonly were devastated by sex without love or commitment.

"The Booty Call" on His Cell Phone Speed Dial

Politically correct, sexology-trained professional Ian Kerner wanted to legitimize homosexuality, sodomy, and much of the Kinsey model. But even this so-called "Sex-Doctor to Generations X & Y" began to wonder:

> In the very first episode of [the television show] *Sex and the City*, Carrie Bradshaw posed a question: "In an age when a woman has access to the same money and opportunities as a man, can she also have sex like a man? Can women pursue sex for the sole sake of pleasure, without any emotion or deeper sense of attachment? Can she hook up casually without feeling post-orgasm regret?"[384]

Kerner said "post-orgasm regret" was often accompanied by "sadness or anger." "[T]he female orgasm releases a burst of oxytocin, also known as the cuddle hormone," that causes a connection often even to the one-night-fellow. Contrary to established propaganda, this quizzical therapist found that women's "orgasm" without love could be more depressing than masturbation. Like most sexologists of the Kinsey cult, Kerner doubtless *never really read* Kinsey's so-called "scientific" research. He, like the others, just accepted all of Kinsey's claims, thinking they were science. After Kerner saw the Fox film, *Kinsey*, he had other misgivings:

> Kinsey was more interested in sex as a pure physiological act than as an emotional expression of love. . . . Watching the film, I was struck by a scene in which Kinsey's assistant and protégé—distraught at the toll that casual sex has taken on his life and the subsequent indifference of his mentor—shouts at him, "You think sex—f**king—is just something, but you're wrong. It's the whole thing. And if you don't watch out, it will cut you wide open!"[385]

For Kerner, that cinematic scene in *Kinsey* was like "a lightning bolt." He noticed that "millions" of women seek love "in the age of the booty call," that sex "matters"—even if you pretend it doesn't. So enlightened was Kerner that he seemed to think he had discovered the wheel, even though our grandparents and the Bible and our heritage had preached the same thing, all along.

Kerner noticed that sex could be "magical, but it also has the potential to debase and destroy." Still, even as a pornographically modified sexologist, he wondered why so many women he counseled were being destroyed by sex? The answer is clear to those who consider the question carefully, those who value history and literature, or those who still have common sense: Sex without marital commitment retards love.

True to his sexual indoctrination, Kerner values erotic liberation. Yet he is troubled. What do women get today instead of love, marriage, children, and grandchildren? Kerner's answer is that women get "orgasms" that represent "some guy's ability to add your phone number to his cell phone's speed dial."[386]

The cost of sexual sabotage to society is high. Kinsey saw sex as separate from our mind-body-heart-soul—separate from love and commitment—allegedly what we do with our body has no lamentable physical or emotional effects. Really?

Sex without Soul

For sixty years, Kinsey's own baleful vision has separated sex and body from brain and love. He succeeded in this because "scientists" bowed to *his* delusions. Naturally, the working public always pays economically, emotionally, physically, and civilly for the errors of elitist, magical, psychotic visionaries.

Predictably, devaluing virginity and chastity came at a great price. Along with skyrocketing rates of illegitimacy and abortion, countless college students and other Baby Boomers fell victim to a growing infestation of sexually-transmitted diseases—genital herpes, human papilloma virus (HPV), chlamydia, and other venereal epidemics—not to mention depression, heartbreak, alcohol, drug, and sex addictions. Topping off the list, in 1981, the era ushered in the deadly AIDS virus. The statistics on all of these post-Kinsey diseases are sobering. *Reclaiming America* noted this venereal disease fallout in "The Truth About Alfred Kinsey."[387] America's sexual revolution, predicated on Kinsey and his "scientific research," has had a profound and devastating impact on our children and our society. The current claim that pre-Kinsey Americans were as promiscuous as subsequent generations is either based on *illiteracy* or premeditated lies. In fact:

- Births to *unmarried* teenagers ages 15–19 years jumped *254%* from 1950 to 1992.[388] After 1973, with contraception and abortion available, we can conservatively estimate a *tripled* increase in teen sexual intercourse to at least 600%, since "Planned Parenthood"—not parents—managed the sexual lives of American youth.
- The *Medical Encyclopedia* identifies almost 12 million new cases of VD every year, almost 65% under the age of 25 and one-fourth are teenagers.[389]
- In 1994 alone, the total known cost for VD in the United States was more than $16 billion.[390]

- U.S. carriers of AIDS in 2006 are estimated at 36,828, and deaths at 14,016, largely unchanged since 2002, despite massive educational efforts to stem the epidemic.[391]

This epidemic of venereal diseases follows almost *five decades of classroom sex sabotage by* Planned Parenthood, SIECUS, et al. Further, *Reclaiming America* reported that Planned Parenthood ended the lives of 244,628 unborn American babies in 2003.[392] This group received $350 million dollars in federal taxpayer money in 2008, and is supposed to increase their grants in 2010—roughly a million dollars a day—to encourage promiscuity and kill the results.[393]

Pediatrician Meg Meeker, MD, writes in *Epidemic: How Teen Sex Is Killing Our Kids* that sexually transmitted diseases (STDs) are crippling and killing children. Meeker reports that nearly 50 percent of children have had sex by grade twelve and about 25 percent of these are infected with an STD; chlamydia and genital herpes have skyrocketed 500 percent among white teenagers in the last twenty years, resulting in infertility, divorce, depression, suicidal attempts, and on and on.

According to the government-funded National Longitudinal Survey of Adolescent Health, the Heritage Foundation reported in 2005:

> This year, nearly 3 million teens will become infected. Overall, roughly one-quarter of the nation's sexually active teens have been infected by a sexually transmitted disease (STD).[394]

No Moral or Immoral, Right or Wrong

The American taxpayer has been "forced to finance a substantial portion of this group's grotesque agenda."[395] Despite its ongoing record of sabotage, injuring minors, Planned Parenthood annually dips into the federal pork barrel for millions of dollars in government grants and contracts.[396] Whose special interests do our elected officials serve by funding this wealthy and influential sex organization?

Society must weigh other consequences of the growth in our society's tolerance for and acceptance of even extremely overt sexual deviance. "Kinsey's explicit goal," wrote liberal author Scott Stossel, was to strip sex from religion and morality and give sex over to a new "sex science." That goal is now fully achieved. Stossel quotes Kinsey:

> Whatever the moral interpretation . . . there is no scientific reason for considering particular types of sexual activity as intrinsically, in their biological origins, normal or abnormal. . . . Present-day legal determination of sexual acts which are acceptable, or "natural," and those which are "contrary to nature" are not based on data obtained from biologists, nor from nature herself.[397]

"[W]hatever the surveys found was 'natural' and whatever was 'natural' was 'normal' and whatever was 'normal' was morally okay," Stossel wrote. "In other words, [Kinsey] sought to demolish 'normal' as a meaningful category of sexual behavior." He concluded that under cover of pseudo-science, Kinsey successfully divorced sex "from questions of moral value and social custom."[398]

Do we wonder why?

Clearly, Kinsey sought to use his "work" to legitimize and normalize his own deviancy. Indeed, the notorious sex guru may well have been the father of sexual perversion—including bestiality—that most Americans regard as revolting and unthinkable, with good reason.

But Kinsey championed these bizarre and barbaric practices, and even blamed the Old Testament and the Talmud for the ban on what he called "matings between individuals of different species." Blasphemously, Kinsey likened laws against sex with animals to:

> [Biblical] taboos which made certain foods clean and other foods unclean. The student of human folkways is inclined to see a considerable body of superstition in the origins of all such taboos [for] human contacts with animals of other species have been known since the dawn of history.[399]

Kinsey's "Inerspecific" (Bestiality) Contacts

Of course, rape, torture, murder, and cannibalism have also "been known since the dawn of history," but they are still barbaric deeds that

Judeo-Christianity—and any civilized culture—considers more than "taboo," but criminal. Such judgments protect the civil society.

Paul Robinson, a Kinsey friend, wrote that Kinsey "evaluated every form of sexual activity in terms of its role in the sexual lives of the lower species . . . [as] natural because they conformed to 'basic mammalian patterns.'" He added that Kinsey's "naturalism received its most forcible expression in those Chapters of the Reports treating sexual contacts between human beings and animals of other species, or interspecific contacts, as he preferred to call them."[400]

Kinsey said that sex with animals offers a "psychological intensity comparable to that in exclusively human sexual relations." We might wonder how Kinsey would know such a thing. But Kinsey provided other clues, claiming that human "enjoyment" of bestiality required satisfying the animal with an orgasm. Kinsey also dubbed most animal sex as "homosexual." Why? Because, said Kinsey, female animals show no erotic arousal and fail to reach orgasm. Finally, Kinsey felt losing "an affectional relation with the particular animal," could traumatize the human lover. Taken together, it is rational to consider Kinsey's descriptions of bestiality as autobiographical, as Robinson suspected. In fact, Kinsey felt "erotic responses to human[s]" and to animals are the same. And, interestingly, Robinson points out that, in all of Kinsey's writings, only when the zoologist described bestiality did he mention love. Robinson wrote:

> Thus he found it entirely credible that a man might fall passionately in love with his dog, and that the affection could be returned in kind: "The elements that are involved in sexual contacts between the human and animals of other species are at no point basically different from those that are involved in erotic responses to human situations." In effect, Kinsey refused to grant the human realm a unique place in the larger order of things. Indeed, it was precisely the pretension to such specialness, he believed, that accounted for most of our sexual miseries.[401]

Diagnostic and Statistical Manual of Mental Disorders (DSM)

Today, bestiality/zoophile Web sites abound. Indeed, the American Psychiatric Association's (APA's) *Diagnostic and Statistical Manual of*

Mental Disorders (*DSM*) no longer classifies sex with animals as a pathology, "unless accompanied by distress or interference with normal functioning." Though these erudite psychiatrists might at least be concerned about disease transmission or even the animal's distress, the *DSM* committee increasingly concerns itself solely with achieving orgasms—any and all orgasms—having relied on Kinsey's data as the "science" that normalized even the most barbaric and inhumane behaviors.

How could the APA normalize and destigmatize such extreme pathological, sexual perversions as bestiality? "Only a zoophile writes this way about sex with animals," murmured a renowned psychiatrist, when I presented Kinsey's statements. "Kinsey sees no difference between Romeo and Juliet and Romeo and Rover!" But he said, "Don't give my name."

In the beginning, Kinsey libeled the Judeo-Christian Greatest Generation. In the end, nearly sixty years after the Kinsey reports, his cultic lobby has resurrected the Ancient Theology: Baal Peor, Priapus worship, wrapped in scientific robes. Kinsey's cult sabotaged the reality of "morality" by claiming to prove scientifically that there is *no* right or wrong, *no* good or bad, *no* moral or immoral, and *no* normalcy or deviance. In Kinsey's world, we can do no wrong except, perhaps, to uphold our traditional, Judeo-Christian values. In Kinsey's world, the only perverts are virgin men and women who marry, stay faithful, bear children, and raise them in a wholesome, intact home.

[CHAPTER 8]

Big Pornography as Sexual Sabotage

> Kinsey opened the floodgate of the AIDS epidemic, rampant abortion, pornography, increased divorce, and the sexual anarchy America faces today.
>
> —Michael Savage, PhD, 2005

Hepburn as Witness: Off the Pedestal and into Pornography

The famous actress, Kate Hepburn, is certainly another liberal witness to Kinsey's sexual sabotage warning that women have gone from "the pedestal . . . into pornography . . . now merely sex objects."[402]—decades before the violence and degradation now known as "gonzo porn!" With regard to pornography, the world has indeed changed in the years since Kinsey published his black propaganda. Hefner's launch of *Playboy* in December 1953 genuflected to Kinsey, saying his was the most important book "of the year. . . . I did a research paper comparing the statistics in the Kinsey report and U.S. laws."[403]

Thus, one man's vision changes another man's life and, then, the world—as Hugh Hefner and his magazine, *Playboy,* did eventually conquer the world. "We have our own flag and a Bunny army," Hefner exulted in 1970.

Hefner recognized Kinsey as the incontrovertible word of the new God.[404] Indeed, Hefner saw himself as Kinsey's publicist.

Hugh Hefner launched *Playboy* in December 1953, eight years after the war's end and a scant five years after the publication of *Sexual*

Behavior in the Human Male. The magazine was Hefner's Kinseyan outreach to college males. He declared that *Playboy* would be Kinsey's mouthpiece and Hefner would be "Kinsey's pamphleteer," branding the college population with Kinsey's black propaganda. Hefner openly parroted Kinsey, falsely describing "the hypocrisy . . . the gap between what we said and what we actually did."[405] Of course, Hefner was actually the poster boy for male virginity.

It would bring more bad news for women, children, and our civility, as Kinsey moved sex from the "marital embrace" into a standalone, recreational industry—with millions of sexual-disease and impotence victims ultimately filling the coffers of the elated pharmaceutical companies.

But conventional wisdom argues that "porn" simply increases libido. Are we giving pornography a bum rap when we hold it accountable for disease, impotence, and abuse? After all, what's wrong with porn? Is it really such a bad thing?

Yes, pornography is a *very* bad thing.

Hefner Trains Joe College: How to Seduce a Virgin

Until the Kinsey and Hefner media frenzy claimed to prove widespread female sexual promiscuity, *it was a crime to seduce a female in thirty-six out of forty-eight states*, plus Washington, D.C.[406] "Seduction" was defined as "intercourse with a girl of previous chaste character by means of various deceptions, artifices or promises."[407]

Brian Donovan, a sociology professor at the University of Kansas, noted that women in the "Progressive era (1900–1920)" brought "felony charges against men who reneged on their promises of marriage. New York's seduction law not only criminalized betrayal but it also functioned as a tool in the prosecution of sexual assault."[408]

Such a view of women's rights came under attack when *Playboy's* first issue, with Marilyn Monroe on the cover, told its naïve consumers to renounce marriage, arguing that women are all just "Miss GOLD DIGGER," after men's money. With the inaugural issue, Hefner editorialized about his hedonist "*Playboy* philosophy." He would hire no married men. Quoting his guru, Alfred Kinsey, Hefner sought to eliminate the "togetherness" marital ideal that had characterized our nation:

> If you are a man between 18 and 80, *Playboy* is for you. . . . If you're somebody's sister, wife, or mother-in-law and picked us up by mistake, please pass us along to the man in your life and get back to your *Ladies' Home Companion*. . . . We believe . . . we are filling a publishing need only slightly *less* important than the one just taken care of by the Kinsey Report.[409]

Based on Kinsey's phony statistics, Hefner launched this effort to resist marriage, defend adultery, and call for changes in U.S. laws, namely to end alimony for jettisoned wives. Much of Hefner's ongoing *Playboy* campaign for "no-fault divorce" translated into legal change, as the Rockefeller-funded Kinsey-*Playboy* cabal emerged touting mechanistic sex for our brave new world.

First, seduction became legalized—as state legislators believed the ALI-MPC calling for modernizing our "restrictive" sex laws. Thus, promising marriage and tricking girls into sex lost its unambiguous moral and criminal stain. Soon, uneasy seducers could be "cool," and follow *Playboy*'s lead, without fearing a jail sentence.

Nine months after Hefner's first *Playboy* issue, he published his Joe College seduction manual, "X Virginity: An Important Treatise on a Very Important Subject." Here, *Playboy* urged bachelors to seduce virgins by dangling love, marriage, and family before their eyes. In fact, although in some states seduction would still have been a criminal offense, Hefner's September 1954, issue declared open season on virgins:

> You must now face up to the problem of virginity in your female friends and acquaintances. . . . You will, of course, meet a certain amount of intellectual resistance from young ladies who have been previously misguided by narrow minded mothers, teachers, maiden aunts, etc. *The purpose of this article is to show you how such resistance to learning (a form of social lag) can be most easily overcome* (emphasis added).[410]

Clearly, in Hefner's view, most coeds *were* virgins. "Spreading the good news . . . is what this article is about," claimed *Playboy*. After achieving success in "deflowering" (the common term at the time for a girl's first sex experience) a reticent co-ed, go on to others.

Though the founding patriarchs sought to protect female vulnerability by controlling male predation, Hefner made it clear: Those days were gone. *Playboy* advises its naïve reader to give her just enough alcohol to release her inhibitions. Promise her anything, certainly marriage. If need be "emphasize the intellectual rather than physical." In this regard, the *Playboy* author says Freud and Kinsey "have done more for sex than any other men who ever lived."

Playboy advises selecting "a suitable subject and, these days, that can sometimes be more of a problem than you might assume." But the magazine provides several strategies—*The Alcoholic Approach, The Intellectual Approach, The Freudian Approach, The Atomic Age Approach, The Snob Approach, The Persistent Approach,* and, of course, *The Kinsey Approach*:

> You will meet, too, from time to time, the . . . girl who wants to conform . . . to do whatever everyone else is doing. For Miss Common Denominator, we suggest Kinsey' last volume, *Sexual Behavior in the Human Female.* You can prove almost anything with this book . . . like 81% of all American women pet, 60% have premarital intercourse, 75% of the women who experience sex have no regrets afterward [and] . . . make better adjustments after marriage. . . . The idea is to bowl her over with the sheer mass of your statistics—all proving that simply everybody is enjoying sex this season. Losing her virginity will seem very unimportant compared to the fear of being different.[411]

"Everyman" Is a Playboy

With its first issue, *Playboy* displayed the air-brushed "girls next door" to every man or boy who could pay the price of the magazine. Married or single, Everyman and Everyboy could be a play-boy forever. Later seeing himself as *Playboy's* January 1954 bow-tied rabbit, sandwiched between two women in swimsuits and heels, indeed, in 1955, Hefner explained his "Playmates":

> It's natural to think of the pulchritudinous Playmates as existing in a world apart. Actually, potential Playmates are all around you: the new secretary at your office, the doe-eyed beauty who sat opposite you at lunch yesterday, the girl who sells your shirts and ties in your favorite store.[412]

By the 1950s, although psychologist Abraham Maslow, PhD, was still advocating women's "self-actualization primarily as wives and mothers," dozens of writers had already cited the same "evidence from the Kinsey report that persuaded Betty Friedan of a link between women's emancipation and their greater capacity for sexual fulfillment."[413] Finally, after ten years of their husbands' lusting for Miss June, July, and August, the closet Communist Betty Friedan[414] put down *Das Kapital*, her broom and mop—and the feminist movement was born. In *The Feminine Mystique* (1963), Friedan expressed the betrayal of college-educated "super wives" and "super moms" who married for "love" and "togetherness" only to find *their college-educated husbands dragging Playboy paper-doll fantasies into the conjugal bed.*[415]

In 1963, hubby claimed that he "read" *Playboy* for the "articles." Wives who objected were told they were "jealous" or had "no sense of humor." The Vietnam War might become a political issue in the late 1960s, but, armed with Kinsey's lies, Hefner and his paper dolls had created another issue, rocking and revolutionizing the marriage bed. The national view of sex and love would never be the same.

In *Love and Will* (1969), psychotherapist Rollo May, PhD, noted the "sexual fascism," the "detached, mechanical, uninviting, vacuous—typical schizoid faces" of the women sold by *Playboy.* He said, famously, that Hefner "shifted the fig leaf from the genitals to the face."[416] In fact, Hefner hijacked Judeo-Christian virtue, seducing men and boys to trade in their beloved "sweetheart" for interchangeable, monthly paper-doll "playmates."[417]

As men suddenly questioned the integrity of their wives and girlfriends (as well as parents and friends), May predicted that Kinsey's attack on intimacy in sex would *increase* male hostility and *impotence:*

> In an amazingly short period following World War I, we shifted from acting as though sex did not exist at all to being obsessed with it. . . . [418] From bishops to biologists, everyone is in on the act. . . . [Note the] whole turgid flood of post-Kinsey utilitarianism. . . .[419] Couples place great emphasis on bookkeeping and timetables in their love-making—a practice confirmed and standardized by Kinsey. . . .[420] Where the Victorian didn't want anyone to know that

> he or she had sexual feelings, we are ashamed if we do not. . . . The Victorian nice man or woman was guilty if he or she did experience sex; now we are guilty if we *don't.*[421] [We] feel less in order to perform better! My impression is that impotence is increasing . . . it is becoming harder for the young man as well as the old to take "yes" for an answer.[422]

In fact, just as he was recognized as "the father of the sexual revolution," the impotent Kinsey should be known as "the father of the impotence evolution"—the one being the natural outgrowth of the other. Sad as it is, this state of affairs is also glaringly apt—even predictable—since Kinsey himself suffered from Traumatic Masturbatory Syndrome (TMS). Though people considered masturbation taboo in Kinsey's day, not so today. Now it is, instead, taboo to admit that masturbation can be addictive—and that chronic masturbation can cause impotence. Indeed, mass retailing of pornography in recent decades has led to "Clinical Traumatic Masturbatory Syndrome" (TMS).[423] Lawrence Sank, PhD, of the Center for Cognitive Therapy in Bethesda, Maryland, discussed TMS in a 1998 article in *the Journal of Sex and Marital Therapy*. According to Sank, TMS results from "masturbating prone. It causes severe sexual dysfunction in most males who practice it . . . leading to 'a long history of sexual failure.'"[424]

But the cost of pornography is much more devastating than the masturbation based impotence men inflict upon themselves. The vast world of Internet pornography has obviously made female, male, and child sexual abuse ever more common. A 2002 article in the *Duke Law Review* notes:

> Parents arrested for the online sharing of explicit photos of their own children are just one example of how child pornography, though extremely socially unacceptable, is an already created and unfortunately booming market.[425]

We trace this victimization back to the Kinseys, who used their colleagues, subjects, and, not unlikely, their own children in their attic porn.

Pornography's Power over the Brain: Mirror Neurons

Science magazine has reported for decades on the "mirror mechanism," whereby the human brain links visual to motor neurons. When we watch an event, our bodies physically mirror the excitement we feel were we actually involved in the event. Significantly, *watching a film triggers the same neurochemical sites as watching an actual event*. Neuroscientist Gregg Miller reported:

> This [mirroring] process is why the tarantula scene in Dr. No gives people the heebie-jeebies, and why we flinch when we see someone cut her finger with a kitchen knife.[426]

Although the intensity is normally less, our "reproductive" organs are similarly stirred if we witness sexual actions, even animal coital actions. As in "monkey see, monkey do," our brains translate the highly intense or intimate actions we observe into our body's neural and motor activity. Therefore, exposing children to animal or human mating is perilous premature "learning by imitation." In his research on mirror neurons, Miller reports:

> Actual touch and the observed touch elicited similar activity in the subjects' secondary somato-sensory cortex, an area involved in processing touch. . . . It's as if the brain translates vision into sensation.[427]

Miller added, "If you see someone behaving badly, a sadist, you hopefully don't share their joy." Unfortunately, "hope" clashes here with reality, as Kinsey's facial expression clearly demonstrated when he forced small children to watch a film of porcupines violently mating. This revealing photograph is a classic example of how "people with impaired emotional experience are also impaired at recognizing, judging, or caring about emotions in others."[428]

Researchers at the University of Picardie Jules Verne in France studied young male volunteers who viewed neutral films as well as videos "of men stroking naked women. . . . fellatio and engaging in intercourse." The fMRI scans and the men's "penile plethysmograph" (a tube that measures erection) were in concert. The men got erections, and the brain lit up. It turned out that the *erections followed the mirror neurons—that is called a "cause-effect" relationship*. "The activation comes before the erection." The study finds the viewers' mirror neurons automatically imitate the pornography to produce erections.[429]

Jonah Lehrer, author of *Proust Was a Neuroscientist*, writes that pornography "works by convincing us that we are not watching porn. We think we are inside the screen, doing the deed." A study in *Neuroimage* also found that "looking at still pictures of naked people triggered our mirror neurons into action, as the brain began pretending that it was actually having sex, and not just looking at smutty pictures in a science lab."[430] Thus, viewing still or moving pornography automatically triggers (solo) masturbation, or coitus, or sodomy with a willing or unwilling adult or child, lest one become frustrated, anxious, angry, and depressed indeed! Hence: cause=effect=and widespread pornography addictions set crimes.

The Erototoxic Virus

*S*ociopolitical essayist Jason Miller, a typical, liberal college graduate and former pornography consumer, casts no stones at porn users. Instead, Miller would have them admit its "virus-like" harm—both to them and to all society. He describes his "relationship," typical of millions of similar men, with one "liberated" woman:

> She was so damaged by pornography that despite her attractive physical appearance, she saw herself as ugly and overweight. Her ex-husband had been addicted to pornography. He was physically abusive, insisted on watching porn movies while they had sex, and forced her to act out the parts of the women in the movies. Based on those experiences, she lived in a nightmare world of virtually endless and hopeless psychological competition with fantasy women. She was comparing herself to air-brushed, surgically-enhanced women whom pornographers portrayed as compliant sex partners with endless cravings for hot . . . delights such as these do not occur in nature.[431]

An August 1974 pornographic *Playboy* cartoon shows a young couple in bed, naked. The male is grinning at a large *Playboy* centerfold nude photo that he has placed across the body of the beautiful young woman upon whom he is mating. As in similar other *Playboy* cartoons and illustrations, the female is not a "mate" but reduced to serving as a *Playboy* receptacle. She looks up and asks, plaintively, "Are you sure you still love me, Henry?" This has become the reality in millions of homes and university dorm rooms. "Henry's" daily parade of pornographic "paper dolls" (and often his own hand) is more key than his once-beloved mate, triggering what one psychiatrist calls his "squirt reflex." What a tradeoff! Impotent without pornographic images in his mind, Henry is like millions of men, boys, and increasingly women and girls worldwide.

Playboy publishers are on record as being *fully* aware that they are creating *impotent male users and addiction to their products*. They feed this fear with images of all wives as fat, old, ugly, having sex with the family dog or as sexy adulterous swingers. *Playboy* published thousands of cartoons, jokes and articles with these ideals, while threatening their consumers' potency. *Playboy* "jokes" that doctors, lawyers, pilots, professors, preachers, writers, artists, and men are "too small" or impotent, endangered by women. Typically, November 1983, Interlandi "jokes" that Shakespeare is impotent, "Well, Mr. 'To Be or Not to Be,' is it to be or not to be?"

Emasculation by pornographers is happening on a global scale. Worse, such *Playboy* pornography (circa 1970s) included the thrill of rape, as in a *Playboy,* September 1971 image of a chained woman about to be raped by two train engineers. Such constant propaganda helped fuel scientists, like evolutionary psychologists, Randy Thornhill and Craig Palmer who argue that rape is normal, for "natural selection has furnished men with behaviours that makes it easier for them to commit rape."[432]

The FBI admitted that "forcible" rape in the United States increased a staggering 418 percent in thirty-nine years (this statistic only includes reported female victims *over age* twelve),[433] while the population increased a mere 52 percent.[434] In fact, when society sufficiently abhors and punishes rape and anything that supports it, rape decreases. When society pardons rape, it increases.

Pornography is the bible and the bile of the "human sexuality" movement.

And it is toxic, an erototoxin.

Many pornography victims have testified to *Playboy*'s role in their victimization (see the Attorney General's Commission on Pornography, July, 1986). Consider the testimony of addiction therapist Mary Anne Layden, PhD, of the Department of Psychiatry at the University of Pennsylvania. An expert witness on pornography effects before the U.S. Senate in 1999, Lyden said:

1. I treat sexual violence victims, perpetrators, and sex addicts.
2. Every case of sexual violence that I have treated has involved pornography.
3. Sexual violence and pathology involves distortions called permission-giving beliefs.
4. Many psychological problems and social problems show traces of these distortions.
5. The media spreads the distortion called Pornography Distortion.
6. Research finds that pornography spreads these distorted beliefs including the belief that children are not harmed by pornography.
7. Visual images are mentally stored facts, events.
8. Visual images are stored permanently.
9. Children are especially vulnerable to images.
10. The Internet contains the three factors that produce antisocial behavior in children.
11. Sexual violence and pathology are frequent.
12. We cannot accept a society where the factors that hurt children are spread in schools and libraries.[435]

Playboy Led Consumers to Incest

Hugh Hefner long called himself "Kinsey's pamphleteer." By 2003, David Shaw, writing in the *Los Angeles Times*, quoted the king of porn as boasting that "After 50 years of *Playboy*, we all live in Hef's world":

> We all now live, to some extent, in a *Playboy* world. I can see the effects of the magazine and its campaign for sexual openness everywhere. . . . When George Will was here the other day, interviewing me, he said, "You won, and he's right. It's nice to have gone through

the battles with all those Puritans, all those forces of repression and hypocrisy, and to live long enough to see the victory parade."[436]

But *who* are "we"? *Who* really "won"?

Clearly, *Playboy* won. Big Pornography won.

Playboy has always had a corner on the market, but it was not long the only magazine on the market. It took fifteen years before *Playboy* was followed by a more degrading magazine, *Penthouse*. Ten years after *Penthouse* was on the newsstands, *Hustler* emerged, adding brutal depictions of bestiality, scatology, and racism that had been finessed in *Playboy* and *Penthouse*. From there, dozens of pornographic picture books came out of the woodwork.

Wardell Pomeroy's pornographic addictions, begun in the Kinsey attic, made him a natural fit for employment by Big Pornography. Pomeroy was a paid advisor, consultant, and expert witness for *Penthouse Forum Variations*, the pornographic publication that taught bestiality, sadism, homosexuality, bisexuality, and incest, which the magazine euphemistically dubbed "Home Sex."

One of many *Penthouse* titillating incest articles by Pomeroy came sandwiched between two planted editorial "letters," allegedly from young women who were thrilled at their incestuous lives. The texts of both letters are deliberately pornographic. One of them recalled the "memory" of a "five or six" year-old having sex each morning with papa. That editorial plant, disguised as a young woman, was very graphic and explained, "It felt marvelous."[437] The other *Penthouse* letter alleged that a young girl's lust seduced her handsome, intelligent dad. Mom found out, joined them in a trio and, yes, you guessed it, all three lived "happily ever after."

Penthouse perpetuated the rape and incest theme with "Wicked Wanda," a comic strip starting in 1973 that copied *Playboy's* "Little Annie Fanny" comic strip, that began in October 1962. The Playboy strip's underlying pedophile core is based on its inspiration—Harold Gray's *Little Orphan Annie*. *Playboy's* Annie Fanny is a massive-breasted blonde innocent, stripped naked and often gang raped from 1962 to 1988, and again briefly in 1998. "Wicked Wanda," the *Penthouse* copy, is raven-haired, huge-breasted, naked, wicked, and depraved. Her blonde childlike sidekick, "Candyfloss," wearing white and pink communion-like dresses prior to various rapes, is the *Penthouse* pedophile hook.

The December 1977 issue of *Penthouse* initiated the magazine's big incest campaign with "Incest: The Last Taboo" by their flaccid writer Philip Nobile. Although Nobile used *Penthouse Forum* to push incest, he reported that same year that Willard Gaylin, MD, a psychiatrist at Columbia Medical School, was "appalled" by the promotion of "positive incest." Gaylin viewed incest as a problem not unlike that of homosexuality; it "implies that some wrong has already occurred," that incest revealed a disordered, diseased family life. He added, "A child will have plenty of intercourse in life, but he or she is going to have only one crack at a caring parent." Said Nobile, "Despite Kinsey's statistics, Gaylin remains unconvinced of non-traumatic incest." Gaylin said he had more trust in "the wisdom of the Old and New Testaments and every other religious group" and wouldn't believe in positive incest if "it lay down on his couch."[438] Nobile also quotes Abraham Kardiner, MD, a psychiatrist specializing in incest, who thought that such articles "will throw a monkey wrench into society by introducing the idea that incest is beautiful. . . . The family is in enough trouble already from homosexuality."[439]

But Nobile panders incest. In page upon page of *Penthouse*, millions of users lusted after unattainable, inaccessible *young* women whose illustrated pictures and photographic montages provoked consumers for sex. Psychologist and "men's rights" advocate Warren Farrell, PhD, answered the dilemmas for millions of frustrated, aroused men and boys, and even women and girls:

> When I get my most glowing positive cases. . . . incest is part of the family's open, sensual style of life, wherein sex is an outgrowth of warmth and affection. It is more likely that the father has good sex with his wife, and his wife is likely to know and approve—and in one or two cases to join in.[440]

Statistically, some percentage of those reading Farrell will have acted out his story on hapless children. Nobile and Farrell, Gebhard, Pomeroy, and others used the media to urge son, brother, uncle, father, aunt, or mother to rape and/or sodomize their children in the comfort of their own homes. Many sexually aroused and frustrated readers would put down these magazines and feel "naturally" neuronally driven to sexually assault the young child asleep—or hiding—in the next room. In the evening, child incest victims often hide in closets, under beds, or on window ledges, hoping to escape the "open, sensual style" of their "warm and affectionate" family predators.

December 1977, the same month and year that *Penthouse* promoted incest, the next magazine in the bookstore rack, *Playboy,* did the same thing in a special piece about three sisters seducing daddy.[441] *Playboy,* however, had pushed incest since its first issues, via Hefner's carefully selected cartoons. We *must* wonder how many children have endured the years of incest that the Kinsey/Hefner, et al cult advocated.

On the other hand, psychologists, psychiatrists, social workers, and others who created, shaped, and "accredited" their profession as "sex experts" are also incest pushers. These self-certified "sexperts" testified in all major obscenity, pornography, sodomy, and homosexuality cases and even child custody cases, that pornography and incest are harmless and can even be "enriching" for children. The sexperts' diseased view of children and sex has infected all our lives, without exception![442]

Children in Playboy

In 1989, as the Principal Investigator for the U.S. Department of Justice (DoJ), Office of Juvenile Justice and Delinquency Prevention (OJJDP), I completed a study, *Images of Children, Crime & Violence in Playboy, Penthouse and Hustler.* For this study, our coders identified *Playboy* with 1,196 cartoons of children, most of them sexualized, and with 1,849 visuals of children under eighteen, also usually sexualized by implication or association with the "centerfold" photo and other techniques. Measuring the "softest" *Playboy* pornography for its toxic treatment of eros, implicates its followers as producing measurably stronger erototoxins.

For example, in August 1975, *Playboy* ran a full-page, full-color pornographic advertisement for its harder "erototoxic"—as I call it—satellite publication, *OUI*. In this large photo, a teenager, "Jane," lay naked on a bare mattress handcuffed to the tarnished metal bed frame, wearing only sheer black stockings, which suggest her harlotry to blur adult sexuality with youth. The text traffics "Jane" directly into the brains, mirrored memories, and bodies of millions of *Playboy* consumers:

> *How One Family Solved Its Discipline Problem*
>
> This is Jane. When she is nice, she is very, very nice. But when she is naughty, she has to be punished. Lately, Jane has been very, very naughty. That is why, in the current issue of *OUI* magazine, Jane is pictured in a variety of poses that restrict her movement . . . it's for her own good. And not incidentally, your pleasure. And it's only in *OUI*.[443]

Elsewhere, *Playboy* used the ploy of "discussing a foreign film" to undermine its consumers' awareness of being brainwashed. In one clip, a father holds his young "retarded nymphet" upside down, exposing her reproductive organs as he is about to rape her.[444] Another *Playboy* "film clip" displays the back of a man's head as his "tween" daughter apparently presses papa toward her crotch.[445] *Playboy* also highlights photographer David Hamilton's "artsy" simulated lesbian scenes between nude teenagers.[446]

In our DoJ study, from December 1953 to December 1984, our coders identified 266 *Playboy* visuals of children systemically depicted in some degree of nudity, like "Jane," the "retarded nymphet," Hamilton's naked little girls, "innocent" nude teenage "lovers," and so on. Of these, 129 visuals were in a "home/doorway/yard" and another sixty-six in a "bed/bedroom/hotel room." In the 1,849 *Playboy* child visuals that our coders identified, we found 688 "other characters"; of these, almost 400 were "incest" visuals: 54.1% were sexually linked to a parent, 9.3% to an "other relative," 8.6% to an "older sibling," 4.9% to an unspecified relative, and 1.2% to a grandparent.[447]

Playboy Photographer as "Father Knows Best"

In February, 1979, *Playboy* ran a photo story, "Father Knows Best," which reported that "photographer Ron Vogel has been snapping pictures of his daughter ever since she was a baby. At 21, she's still his favorite model." Indeed, Vogel pimps his naked daughter directly into the neurochemistry of millions of *Playboy*-using fathers. The article says in their "nudist family," Lexi always competed with the naked models for her father's attention. Right.

A multiple-page spread of photos of Lexi show Dad tying up his daughter in naught but leather trappings to leave her anatomically, graphically exposed. Perusing Vogel's exploited daughter, *Playboy's* aroused dads are naïvely excited by an innate sense of fear and shame beyond their normal aroused state, while *Playboy* and Vogel share the images as though they are oh, so casual and, well, asexual.

But these pictures are imbedded forever in viewers' brains. And some dads, identifying with the handsome young photographer (in several intimate photos with his daughter,) will decide they, too, can take naked photos of their daughters—perhaps to send some to *Playboy*. Few *Playboy* users suspect that they have been tricked and manipulated into viewing their own daughters—and others—as welcoming, incestuous sexual targets. But many dads, thinking it was their own idea, will act out on their daughters, and never know *why* they had these overwhelming, frightening, and devastating urges. They were conned by *Playboy* and Ron Vogel. Some father.

"She Digs Forceful Figures, So Come on Strong, Big Daddy"

Playboy also published a series of sadistic child molestation photos by J. Frederick Smith. One naked girl, allegedly an adolescent, is eroticized and sadistically posed like Christ on the cross—but laid out horizontally. *Playboy* tells its consumers the "hung up miss" will accept abuse, "albeit with clenched teeth."[448] Adjacent to this, *Playboy* displays another of Smith's photographs: a sleeping girl, supposedly about eight years old, lies naked with her hair in pigtails, on full-color Disney character sheets as she holds a Raggedy Anne Doll. *Playboy*'s accompanying text is unashamed as it obviously panders incestuous violent rape:

> *Baby Doll. It's easy to feel paternalistic toward the cuddly type above. Naturally, she digs forceful father figures, so come on strong, Big Daddy* (November 1971).

The *Playboy Advisor* column, formerly penned by James R. Petersen, is one of the magazine's regular features. Petersen, who lectures nationwide in colleges, was identified some years ago as the country's most popular sex education resource. Posing as a savvy sex "advisor," Petersen wrote responses to letters allegedly from juvenile and adult readers who sought advice about wines, orgasms, sound systems, and so on. In the magazine's May 1987 issue, a clearly planted letter asks how to be safe from AIDS. In response, Petersen directs millions of American men to find "virgins or very young lovers" in order to "cut down your chances of being exposed to the virus."[449]

Intermingled with such incest and child-abuse sabotage, the monthly "centerfolds" include photographs of the Playboy Playmates throughout their childhoods. Typical captions for these child photos include:

"8 Weeks: My first centerfold!"[450]
"Age 1: Already Playmate Material"[451]
"Age 5: My 1st topless picture."[452]

Cartoons as Propaganda

A 2006 California health department advertising campaign featured cartoon characters shaped like male genitalia; the campaign advocated STD testing for San Francisco's bisexual and homosexual men. A study of the casual effect of the ads found that, in neighborhoods where the ads appeared on billboards and bus shelters, "Between 40 and 60% of survey respondents who were aware" of the risqué ads said they had recently tested. Thus, the officials said, the cartoons changed attitudes and conduct.[453]

So, too, *Playboy*, *Penthouse*, and *Hustler* cartoons change attitudes and conduct. Cartoons urging sex with children appeared in *Playboy* in a systematic manner from *1954 to 1984!* In 1954, several cartoons had little boys seeking sex with adult women. One cartoon was drawn by Hefner. The cartoon depicts three boys closely examining semi-nude pictures of women on a burlesque theater display, while a fourth lad, looking fully satisfied, is watching a dog. One of the boys explains why "Joey" is not looking at pictures of the naked women: "Joey ain't interested—he's got a sister."[454]

In 1968, *Playboy's* "Straw Man" from the *Wizard of Oz* hints that he wants to have sex with flat-chested Dorothy. However, many consumers would think it was their own "dirty minds" that thought "sex" when the Straw Man leered at a confused Dorothy and asked, "*Would you like to know what I really want?*"[455] By 1978, the Straw Man, Cowardly Lion, and the Tin Man gang rape Dorothy—full assault and in full color in *Playboy*. Dorothy is sprawled out on the Yellow Brick Road, complaining to a police officer who does nothing, though her shirt is torn open so we can see the exaggerated breasts drawn by one of *Playboy's* main child sex-abuse artists, Michael Ffokers (aka: Brian Davis).

So, no, it wasn't the consumers' pedophile minds—*not yet*. It was *Playboy*'s closet pedophile seeding pedophile fantasies among their naïve "readers." Soon enough, millions of consumers *would* get the Dorothy rape and find it "funny." Playboy used fairy tales and other forms of illusion and fantasy as a standard conditioning device to circumvent the consumer's suspicions that the magazine was grooming him to be a pedophile. But by 1971, incest appeared often in *Playboy* cartoons, and routine viewing would change these consumers. Of all *Playboy* child cartoons, 390 took place in a "home/doorway/yard," and forty-seven included the child in a direct "sexual encounter with family member."

On the graphic evidence, Hefner personally culled about 400 cartoons from roughly 200,000 submissions each year for thirty years from December 1953 to the 1990s, documented in my book, *Soft Porn Plays Hardball.*[456] Thus, Hefner *himself* mindfully selected and published the monthly child cartoons that included "gang rapes of children" and sexual abuse by benevolent father figures. Despite our devastating child pornography research findings in our DoJ study, *Playboy* lied in response:

> If other magazines are publishing cartoons of "gang rapes of children, fathers sexually abusing daughters, benevolent or father figures raping or murdering young girls," *PLAYBOY* never has, never will. Our readers know that. And lying with statistics is still lying.[457]

The distribution of my United States DoJ Office of Juvenile Justice and Delinquency Prevention Executive Summary twenty-four-page précis, with its graphic anthology of child pornography examples in *Playboy*, *Penthouse*, and *Hustler*, troubled many of the magazine consumers who saw it. In February 1986, *Playboy* finally reprinted one of its letters to the editor, requesting *Playboy's* comment about the study.[458] *Playboy* did not directly answer the letter, but excused it as a case of lumping *Playboy* together with other magazines.[459]

Two years later, Burton Joseph, the *Playboy* lawyer and former chairman of the Media Coalition, said that pornographic child pictures in *Playboy* are "extremely rare and occurred mostly in older issues." He admitted that *Playboy* does run cartoons with children being sexually molested, but (as *Hustler's* Larry Flynt claimed about "Chester the Molester") these child pornographic jokes were just "commentaries on society's defects."[460]

Joseph also faulted my OJJDP study, saying we overcounted incidents of child-abuse cartoons in *Playboy.* For example, Joseph falsely claimed that we counted each panel of *Playboy*'s "Little Annie Fanny" comic strip as a separate cartoon, thus inflating the numbers.[461] However, having read my OJJDP report, Joseph knew that our research *analyzed no comic strip* characters. *Playboy's* Annie, however, was a pseudo child raped by hundreds of bug-eyed males in each comic strip. Ho, ho. Coincidentally, the year Joseph made this statement, "Little Annie Fanny" was removed from *Playboy* magazine. Such a coincidence.

Playboy Cartoonists Blame Child Victims

In his 2009 book, *Empire of Illusion*, Pulitzer Prize winner Chris Hedges notes the sexual sabotage of pornography. He says television's "*The Girls Next Door*, which stars the octogenarian Hugh Hefner and girlfriends young enough to be his granddaughters, *is spiced up with undertones of incest and pedophilia*."[462]

Brainwashing viewers with incest and pedophilia has always been a Playboy subtext. When readers of the February 1971 *Playboy* turned the pages from the sexually arousing naked women, they came upon a black and white cartoon of a middle-class living room. There, *Playboy*'s artist "Cole" drew an old man leeringly imagining his granddaughter naked as his wife innocently comments to a friend that the old fellow loves his grandchild.[463]

Alongside incest, seventy-two *Playboy* cartoons had a child involved in "prostitution, sex buying or barter, massage parlor activity and dealing." That is, "incest" for pay.

Considering that cartoons are especially appealing to youngsters, who stop to study and look at them, "child sex" cartoons are particularly insidious.

Claiming to have selected all the *Playboy* cartoons until the '90s, Hugh Hefner would have chosen this incest cartoon, drawn by "Ffolkes," a *Playboy* cartoonist who published at least thirty-five child abuse funnies. In this one, the girl is depicted as about six years old, with the naked exaggerated breasts that *Playboy* commonly draws on its child sex victims, to blur the child's age and confuse and arouse consumers. This girl is voluntarily, happily prostituting herself to a male relative, dad or uncle. Ffolkes (and Hefner) have the child archly say to the man: "But first of all we have to ask Teddy's permission, and that costs $40."[464]

In May 1974, the Hefner-Ffolkes' team again aroused, confused, and desensitized *Playboy* reader-participants with their "happy incest" theme. In this scene, a naked little girl of roughly eight years is with an old man in his bed. Looking like Shirley Temple, the curly-top child (with naked exaggerated breasts) talks to mom on the bedside telephone. Grinning, she says, "Uncle William and I are playing a game of consequences."

In another example of children as willing victims, Bill Lee depicts a four-year-old tyke confounding her would-be molester. "No thank you nice man," she says. "I don't want to go for a ride in your car. Why don't we just go up to my place and ball?"[465]

Typical of *Playboy's* "child entrapment" theme, these cartoonists blame their victims and render the naïve children unhurt by whatever transpires (as is always the case with "Little Annie Fanny"). Often, such cartoons show a "clever" adult male who tricks a child into sex by saying it will cure her hiccups, fix a headache, or serve as her "consequence" for losing her game, and so on. Some argue that these cartoons are "nonviolent," but it is *ludicrous* to excuse something as "nonviolent" when it instructs in trickery to violate a child or woman. All such images are violent and predatory by definition.

Brooke Shields, "Sugar and Spice" Child Pornography Published by *Playboy Press*

In 1983, the case of *Shields v. Gross* dealt with parents selling their children for sexual purposes. At age eighteen, the teenage actress, Brooke Shields (b. 1965), sought to halt the distribution of naked photographs taken of her by Garry Gross when she was ten years old. Shields's *mother* allowed her to be marketed as an oiled nude with coiffed hair and heavy "adult" makeup for photographic use to *Playboy Press*. The lawsuit stated:

> [Plaintiff] had been a child model and in 1975, when she was 10 years of age . . . a series of photographs to be financed by *Playboy* Press, required plaintiff to pose nude in a bathtub . . . used not only in "Sugar and Spice" but also, to the knowledge of plaintiff and her mother, in other publications and in a display of larger-than-life photo enlargements in the windows of a store on Fifth Avenue in New York City.[466]

Today, we recognize these oiled and naked images as child pornography and, therefore, as *illegal*! But for his own private reasons, the New York judge ruled *against* the rights of Brooke Shields to retrieve her naked photos. The New York Court of Appeals, soon to be Chief Judge, Sol Wachtler, concurred in the 1983 decision. Less than ten years later, Wachtler was arrested and convicted of sexual crimes involving an underage child.[467] Apparently, his earlier judicial decisions are not being revisited based on his inherent conflict of interest.

The court allowed Gross to distribute and sell his photos of the naked Brooke Shields wherever he wished. Like most children controlled by errant parents, Shields had nowhere to hide! Charles Jourdan's Fifth Avenue shoe salon displayed photos of ten-year-old Brooke, "promising even greater reaction," says a well-satisfied *Playboy Press*. *Penthouse* and similar outlets reproduced these photos and sold them to consumers. In its introduction to a series of naked images of the young Shields, *Playboy Press* stated, "We knew we were onto someone altogether different when we saw these photos by Garry Gross." *Playboy Press* says these are photos of "a little girl" who "projects an identifiable sensuality . . . inside that little girl there's a sexual woman hiding."[468]

Hiding?!

As often as possible in 1978, *Playboy* exploited the twelve-year-old in the film, *Pretty Baby*, which was set in 1917. In March, *Playboy* printed an outcut showing Shields in bed with her naked mom (played by liberal Susan Sarandon), as a potential customer looks on. The idea here was that of a mother-daughter sex act—common to prostituted women and children at the time.

Playboy, Erototoxins Belittle Incest Trauma

Kinsey's efforts to downplay the medical and emotional consequences of incestuous abuse showed up in psychiatrist Judith Herman, MD's *Father-Daughter Incest:*

> Kinsey himself, though he never denied the reality of child sexual abuse, did as much as he could to minimize its importance. Some 80% of the women who had experienced a childhood sexual approach by an adult reported to Kinsey's investigative team that they had been frightened and upset by the incident. Kinsey cavalierly belittled these reports. He hastened to assure the public that children should not be upset by these experiences. If they were, this was the fault not of the sexual aggressor, but of prudish parents and teachers who caused the child to become "hysterical."[469]

It is amazing that a feminist scholar like Herman missed Kinsey's brazen data that proved that he was *at best* an academic pimp and procurer of mass child rape, if not a child rapist himself. Herman also missed Kinsey's claim that, of 4,441 women he interviewed, *none* were *ever* harmed by a sexual encounter. Historically, it is difficult for one scholar to see the pathology of another.

Belittlement of incest trauma dominated Kinsey's studies—and those of his collaborators—creating the field of human sexuality and mass sex education. Prevalent in *Playboy* and other pornographic publications, such belittlement then wormed its way into mass media and the modern American culture, especially law and school sex education. For example, the "incest" citation in the free encyclopedia, *Wikipedia* (founded by a Jimmy Wales, cited as a pioneering pornographer[470]) quotes Kinsey zealot and pedophile advocate Floyd Martinson, who parroted Kinsey's incest frauds:

> Incest is also an important part of sexual exploration by children, especially in families with children of the same age. A study by Floyd Martinson found that 10–15% of college students had had a childhood sexual experience with a brother or sister (see child sexuality).[471]

The Academic Pedophile Lobby

Floyd Martinson, PhD, edited *Children and Sex* in 1981 with another pedophile advocate, Larry Constantine, PhD. Both men are celebrated for their claims on "Infant and Child Sexuality: Capacity and Experience."[472] In his presentation in Wales at the British Psychological Association Conference, Martinson encouraged "infant and child sexual activity."[473] Not surprisingly, Martinson is cited favorably in *Paidika, The Journal of Paedophilia,* a child molester magazine designed to promote the acceptance of pedophilia and pornography. *Paidika* said "paedophilia has been, and remains, a legitimate and productive part of the totality of human experience . . ."[474]

This advocacy would cause many—perhaps most—people to conclude that Martinson is a closet pedophile—or pederast. He was also a *child sexuality expert* for *Playboy*. To sway hesitant parents and arouse *Playboy's* readers, Martinson reiterated Kinsey's claims of infant sexuality. The *Playboy* editor sighs, consider "your wasted youth," when you know that erotic excitement starts "in the womb," and that little boys can have orgasms by "their first birthday."[475]

Martinson's assertion was "gaining currency within the sex establishment [that] very young children should be allowed, and perhaps encouraged, to conduct a full sex life without interference from parents and the law."[476] Says sports and sexuality expert, psychiatrist Linnea Smith, MD:

> While society is looking at ways to draw the line and say clearly that adolescent girls are not "fair game" we see on *Playboy's* March 1996 cover, a knock-kneed adolescent in a parochial school uniform depicted as the "stripper next door" ever ready to symbolically

> sexually service all male viewers. *Playboy* continues its practice of sexualizing extreme youth, innocence, vulnerability, and submission. *Playboy* is flagrantly glamorizing the adolescent student as a sexual target and perpetuating the propaganda of pedophiles that children solicit sex from adults. Catholic schoolgirls as a genre of criminal child pornography and pseudochild adult bookstore porn is standard fare. Recycling these images in a more legitimized commercial sex format only multiplies the harm.
>
> A New York judge commented that, ". . .A society that loses its sense of outrage is doomed to extinction." Where is the outrage of child advocates, parents, all citizens? A society cannot continue to abandon its responsibility to its children for humanitarian reasons as well as its own future. [477]

But Floyd Martinson claimed people foolishly feared incest. Though he did not admit to personal experience, Martinson wrote of "father's drunken condition" and daughter's delight in "the sensual experience." Father, he says, didn't know what he was doing. Daughter, he says, did. Father made "love" to the child. Martinson assured us the child "liked the sensation" so she "let it continue for awhile." The sexpert's Old Pedophile Tale hasn't a shred of credence. Still, did any sexpert researchers follow the so-called delighted daughter for the next few decades, to see what long-term consequences resulted from the "sensual experience" of being raped by a drunken father?

Beyond gagging and choking, real incest symptoms include bulimia (to shrink from sight), obesity, wearing baggy clothing or many layers of clothing (in an attempt to cover up from peering eyes and to provide protection by appearing larger), eating disorders, substance abuse, perfectionism (an attempt to overcompensate for feelings of worthlessness), depression, suicidal ideation, promiscuity, prostitution, self-harm, phobias, homosexuality, and more. Martinson ignores and hides the common results of incest.[478]

Child Pornography Sabotage Feeding Pedophiles[479]

Across the nation, educated and economically secure friends, neighbors, educators, judges, teachers, lawyers, doctors, college presidents, and even a Nobel prize-winner have been arrested for possession of child pornography as well as for child sexual abuse.

We've had safe public libraries for over one hundred years! One might say we have "turned a corner" in society. What is on the other side?

According to PedoWatch, a pedophile monitoring group, "online pedophiles are telling each other to use public libraries to download child pornography," but PedoWatch is "working with law enforcement worldwide to remove child pornography and child luring activity, and currently works with . . . law enforcement . . . to monitor the activities of online pedophiles."[480] According to Donna Rice Hughes in her March 2000 Senate Hearing testimony, public libraries are a "breeding ground" for sexual attacks on children.

Consider the following data, excerpted from *Enough Is Enough, Safety 101*:[481]

- 40% of arrested child pornography possessors were "dual offenders" who both sexually victimized children and possessed child pornography.
- 83% had images involving children between ages 6 and 12; 39% were children ages 3 to 5; 19% had images of infants and toddlers under age 3.[482]
- Internet child pornography images increased 1500% since 1997.
- Approximately 20% of all Internet pornography involves children.[483]
- Child pornography was a $3 billion annual industry in 2005—it has grown since.[484]
- Child pornography reports increased 39% in 2004. Over 20,000 children are sexualized on the Internet weekly.
- More babies and toddlers are appearing and abuse is more torturous and sadistic.
- Children are between six and twelve, and getting younger.[485]
- Most illegal sites are hosted in the United States.[486]
- The U.S. Customs Service notes over 100,000 Web sites with child pornography.
- Amazon.com "subscribers" use credit cards for a monthly fee of between $30 and $50 to download photos and videos, or a one-time fee of a few dollars for single images.[487]

CHILD SEXUAL ABUSE IS OBVIOUS BUT HERE ARE "STUDIES":[488]

- A New Zealand Internal Affairs study connected viewing child pornography with committing child sexual abuse (New Zealand's Department of Internal Affairs, 2006).[489]
- *The American Journal of Preventive Medicine* reports one in six men as sexual abuse child victims.
- Almost 40% of perpetrators were female (*The American Journal of Preventive Medicine*, June 2005).
- One in four women report childhood sex abuse, largely by males (study as above).
- $19 billion is generated annually on the street from human trafficking (Christine Dolan, The Global Coalition to End Human Trafficking NOW).[490]
- "The Global Coalition to End Human Trafficking NOW" cites 10 million children prostituted worldwide.

ONLINE SEXUAL PREDATORS[491]

- 40% charged with child pornography admit to sexually abusing children (Reuters, 2003).
- The Butner study found 85% of offenders for child pornography also molested children.[492]
- One in five children who use computer chat rooms has been approached over the Internet by pedophiles (Det. Chief Super. Keith Akerman, Telegraph.co.uk, January 2002).
- 1 in 33 received AGGRESSIVE sexual solicitation (asked to meet, called them via phone, sent mail, money or gifts) (Online Victimization, NCMEC, June 2000).
- 25% told a parent (Online Victimization, NCMEC, June 2000).

YOUTH

- Children go missing at 750,000 per year, 62,500 per month, 14,423, per week, 2,054 per day, and 85 per hour, 3 children every 2 minutes. (NCMEC Online Victimization: A report on the nation's Youth April 3, 2000).
- 90% of teens go online, 74% at home, 31% from their bedroom (The Kaiser Family Foundation in consultation with International Communications Research, 2001).

- 44% of children polled visited sexual sites.
- 43% say they have no Internet use rules in their homes (Time/CNN Poll, 2000).
- 75% of parents say they know where children spend time online, but,
- 58% of teens say they accessed objectionable Web sites: 39% offensive music, 25% sexual content, 20% violence. (Source: WebSense, *USA Today*, October 10–12, 1999).
- Pornographers disguise their sites (i.e., "stealth" sites) including Disney, Barbie, ESPN, etc., to entrap children (Cyveillance Study, March 1999).
- 62% of parents of teenagers are unaware that their children have accessed objectionable Web sites (Yankelovich Partners Study, September 1999).
- 95% of all 15- to 17-year-olds go online, with 70% accidentally seeing pornography, 23% "very" or "somewhat" often; 55% of those exposed say they were "not too" or "not at all" upset, 45% were "very" or "somewhat" upset.[493]
- 26 popular child characters, like My Little Pony, Action Man, link to porn sites, 30% hard-core (Envisional 2000).

Pornography and the Law

In 1967, the *Colorado Law Review* published "The Legal Enforcement of Morality," that relied on Kinsey's "data" to sabotage the American "common law" standards of virtue, honor, and chastity. "Kinsey reports that in some groups among lower social levels," the article explained to its audience of lawyers, "it is virtually impossible to find a single male who has not had sexual intercourse by the time he reaches his mid-teens."[494] The author of that article was none other than *Playboy* magazine publisher, Hugh Hefner—Kinsey's "pamphleteer."

(Since Kinsey claimed to interview 1,400 sex offenders, any *real scientist* would report on what percentage of the sex offenders had sex by "his mid-teens." Not the Kinsey team.)

The Kinsey Institute and Hefner were on a roll. Sexual purity, chastity, and modesty—the ideal of American culture—were being ripped away. Mass media penetrated almost all American homes, delivering a steady diet of sex, at best, and predatory perversion at worst. Discussions about sexuality were beginning to spill from research circles and academe to higher education and, eventually, "sex education" infiltrated nearly every school in the country. Sex-related disorders would soon exact a painful cost, individually and collectively. Nationwide, states were mugging our common law base of history and bible for "scientific laws" based on Kinsey. They were liberalizing their sex laws, usually for the first time since statehood.[495] The legalization of *seduction,* breach of promise, fornication, adultery, and pornography jump-started our national sexual-dysfunction epidemic.

Before Kinsey, exhibitionism, voyeurism, and pornography were illegal. Now, for the most part, they are legal. Obscenity, however, was illegal—and still is. The issue today is how we define "obscene." Again, the turning point in our history was 1955, with the ALI-MPC:

OBSCENITY: PRE-KINSEY ILLEGAL. POST- KINSEY ILLEGAL.

The slippage is so dramatic that, although obscenity is *still illegal*, most sexual materials mass distributed now would have been defined as illegal obscenity pre-Kinsey.

Exhibitionism and Voyeurism: Pre-Kinsey *illegal*; Post-Kinsey largely legal.

Exhibitionism is legal in the media and tolerated elsewhere. We see prostitution, stripping, pseudo-child pornography, sado-masochism, and bestiality in "entertainment" and in school sex education, bookstores, and libraries; this creates voyeurs of all onlookers, hence de facto legalization of voyeurism, et al.

Pornography/Erototoxins: Pre-Kinsey *illegal*; Post-Kinsey legal.

Pornography is more profitable than legitimate film and increasingly part of legitimate films, plays, and even dance. Kinsey, a pornography-masturbatory addict and masochistic orchitis sufferer, claimed pornography was neither addictive nor harmful, and of course, *more intelligent* men use it. In 1953, "Kinsey's pamphleteer," Hugh Hefner, launched *Playboy*. After 1957, pornography spread as the U.S. Supreme Court used the Kinseyan ALI-MPC definition of obscenity to legalize "soft" pornography. This triggered mass production of deviant pornography and, eventually, sadistic adult and child pornography, prostitution, child sexual abuse, rape, and general social disorder.

Recently, liberal radio host Michael Goldfarb professed puzzlement about The Motion Picture Production *Code* of 1930, the *Hays Code*, which had prevented the filming of "immoral" words, plots, and scenes. Since today's system permits almost anything to be filmed and then "rates" the results, Goldfarb mused, "The irony is that the arrival of censorship initiated Hollywood's Golden Age."[496]

Actually, this really is not ironic. We are most creative when forced to think and to limit what we do—else the bad always drives out the good. So, thanks to the promorality Hays Code—which was based on what the religious public agreed to view—my friends and I grew up watching great classic films, serious films that were complex and grimly realistic and entertaining comics, musicals, and dramas with clean humor. There was seldom anything inching toward sexual exploitation—and the cinematic words didn't need ellipses. We spent our Saturday afternoons with commonly witty fictional heroines and independent-minded heroes who were strong, clever, and, yes, moral.

In these productions, the characters overcame obstacles, fell in love and married, forever. None of these films were erotic or pornographic. Excluding fallen angels like Mae West and Jean Harlow, almost all of the sensual film heroines *and heroes* of the 1940s were played as honorable virgins—adults who postponed sex until marriage. Why didn't the public mock such performances? Because these chaste portrayals were close enough to the audience's *reality*. The entertainment was believable because *art imitated life*. Remember, Kinsey himself claimed he was a virgin before marriage. Clara was certainly a virgin before marriage. Clyde Martin was a virgin before Kinsey seduced him. Vincent Nowlis and his wife were virgins before marriage. Even *Playboy*'s Hugh Hefner is on record as having been a (heterosexual) virgin until reading Kinsey's claims about everyone else's libidinous lives.

Today, people generally believe that we have no laws against obscenity. This is not so. Even the Federal Communications Commission declares on its Web site: (2010) "It's Against the Law": "*Obscene material is not protected by the First Amendment to the Constitution and cannot be broadcast at any time*" (italics added).[497] Most professionally made "sex" materials today are, however, legally obscene in that "The Supreme Court has established that, to be obscene, material must meet a three-pronged test:"

1. "An average person, applying contemporary community standards, must find that the material, as a whole, appeals to the prurient interest;
2. The material must depict or describe, in a patently offensive way, sexual conduct specifically defined by applicable law; and
3. The material, taken as a whole, must lack serious literary, artistic, political, or scientific value."[498]

Since *all public sex acts are still illegal*, (so prurient and absent literary, artistic, political or scientific value) *all pornography seen in public is actually illegal*. One cannot walk naked in public, copulate or commit sodomy, or sexual torture in the public square, even in the midst of political, artistic, or scientific discourse. So, doing so in public films, stage, or magazines is definitively, scientifically "obscene." Obscene material is still obscene *and illegal*, even if our government elite does not prosecute naked public sex acts in the media as criminal.

The decadence, disease, and despoiling of 1860 New York City has returned with a vengeance. With the end of World War II and Kinsey's onslaught, books and movies too soon included vulgar swear words, violence, and graphic sex scenes. Content that was virtually pornographic was *everywhere*. U.S. Supreme Court Justice Antonin Scalia, in a dissent on an obscenity ruling said:

> The First Amendment explicitly protects "the freedom of speech [and] of the press"—oral and written speech—not "expressive conduct." [V]irtually every law restricts conduct. . . . The purpose of Indiana's nudity law would be violated, I think, if 60,000 fully consenting adults crowded into the Hoosierdome to display their genitals to one another, even if there were not an offended innocent in the crowd.[499]

The Sabotaged Porn Generation

Post-Kinsey, thanks to the ALI-MPC and Hugh Hefner and his ilk, pornography has become a part of the American landscape. The billion-dollar Big Pornography enterprise has merged with most major media outlets from Time-Warner to Fox, Disney, hotel chains from Marriot to Sheraton, (though *Omni* deliberately divested from in-room pornography),[500] and other media control agents. So it was not surprising when the 1981 *New York v. Ferber* decision to legalize pornographic child sexual abuse *was completely censored by the national "free press" media*, though one *New York Times* item briefly appeared (an editorial supporting *the five judge decision* to legalize child pornography as "freedom of speech"). Similarly, the controlled media ignores pornography, which is commonly implicit in rapes and sex murders.

According to Family Safe Media, the pornography industry generates $12 billion dollars in annual revenue, which is more money than every NBA, NFL, and MLB team combined, and more money than ABC, NBC, and CBS combined. That money is *power*—buying votes, grants, and appointments in political, social, and academic systems.[501]

Internet Pornography

The following data are excerpted from *Enough is Enough, Safety 101*:[502]

- In 2006, 87% of university students polled have virtual sex largely via Instant Messenger, webcam, and telephone.[503]
- In 2004, there were 420 million pages of pornography . . . the majority. . . . {apparently} owned by less than 50 companies.[504]
- The largest group of viewers of Internet porn are children between ages 12 and 17.[505]
- Sex is the #1 searched for topic on the Internet.[506]
- 58% of the public surveyed wanted government restriction of Internet pornography even if the materials were legal in books and magazines."[507]
- Commercial pornography sites:
  - 74% display free teaser porn images on the homepage and porn banner ads.
  - 66% did not warn of adult content.
  - 11% warned, but did not say "sexually explicit content" on the homepage.
  - 25% prevented users from exiting the site (mousetrapping).
  - Only 3% even "required" adult verification.
- 32 million women visited at least one pornography Web site in one month of 2004.[508]

- 41% of women said they viewed or downloaded pornographic pictures, movies.[509]
- 25 million Americans allegedly visit cyber-sex sites between 1 and 10 hours per week; 4.7 million over 11 hours per week.[510]
- At least 200,000 Internet users are hooked on porn sites, X-rated chat rooms or other sexual materials online.[511]

Pornography Breeds Its Own, Sabotaged Employees of the Industry[512]

1. The Pornographic Industry Breeds/Lures a Damaged Population as Its Employees:
   - 90% are child sexual abuse survivors.[513]
   - Degrading, dehumanizing acts that are required of employees exacerbate disorders.
   - USA/UK welfare, police agencies must "offer/mandate counseling" for staff who "*view objectionable material*" based on resulting trauma.[514]
2. Secondary Negative Effects of Pornographic Workplace on Performers:
   - Sexually Transmitted Diseases
   - 66% to 99% of pornography performers admit to herpes, *a non-curable disease.*[515]
   - Chlamydia/gonorrhea is 10× greater than the rate among LA County 20–24 year olds.[516]
   - 25 HIV cases were reported by Adult Industry Medical Healthcare since 2004.[517]
   - 70% of STDs in the porn industry occur in females.[518]
   - Mental Health/Disabilities of Pornographic Workplace Employees
   - Suicide and suicidal ideation[519]
   - Post-traumatic stress disorder[520]
   - Sexual trauma[521]
   - Prostitution activities[522]
   - Sexual addiction[523]
   - Substance abuse[524]

3. Public Costs: Sex performers, traumatized by a brutal workplace, typically last "*three months to three years*"[525] putting most on the dole:
    - *Mental Health*—Drug/alcohol/abortion/abuse—require rehabilitation.
    - *Hospitalization*—Drug overdoses/suicides/auto accidents, etc.—need medical aid.
    - *Government Services*—Pregnancies/abortions/PTSD—require social services.
    - *Child Protection Services*—Child abuse/neglect/battery/foster care, etc.
    - *Women, Infant Children (WIC)*—Penury: food/nutrition for women, children.
    - *Unemployable*—Job gap, common lack of high school diploma and dysfunctions.
    - *Law Enforcement*—Prostitution/domestic violence require police, judicial time.
    - *Jails and Prisons*—Drugs/prostitution/DUI/domestic violence, parole, jail.
4. Pornographers Dodge Taxes, Federal and State Workplace Safety Laws:[526]
    - In *Robert Deupree, Petitioner, v. Workers' Compensation Appeals Board*, etc.,[527] (08-815) Mar. 2, 2009, a pornographic performer contracted HIV allegedly due to employer-violation of standard workplace safety practices.

      The U.S. Supreme Court ruled the plaintiff (who like most pornographic performers suffers from multiple pre-existing pathologies) was an *employee*, thus entitled to workplace safety. The blood-borne pathogens standard for "employee" protection is violated by most pornographers, who commonly demand release of semen, fecal matter, blood and "other potentially infectious material ("OPIM").[528] Mrs. Shelley Lubben, former "porn star"[529]concludes, "the majority of pornographic films currently produced involve direct contac*t betwee*n skin or mucous membranes and blood, semen, vaginal fluid, saliva and other OPIM. Since these exchanges of potentially hazardous fluids clearly violate even minimal health safety measures, the majority of pornographic films being produced would be in violation of extant safety laws."

> "In addition, recognizing pornographic performers as employees—directed and controlled by the employer[530]—will finally provide these commonly already disabled pornographic employees with the health insurance, tax supports and disability benefits commonly provided by employers to other workers in the United States of America."

The character of the progeny of The Greatest Generation is being sabotaged; degraded by an anti–Judeo-Christian, mass sexual abuse industry. Naturally, regular users of pornography are more likely to have sexually callous attitudes and accept the rape myth (that when a woman says "no," she means "yes").[531] The Internet has changed how Americans send and receive mail, how they work and socialize, and also how and with whom they view—and make—pornography. The most stunning shift in our vision of ourselves appears to be the fact that children are now challenging the Big Porn Mandarins by making and distributing pornographic videos and images of themselves, for free, on the Internet. The impact of pornography upon incest and family safety, solvency is and will be staggering.

With the arrival of Internet pornography, the newspapers daily report arrests of predators and the recovery of victims—of abduction, rape, and murder. A "civil war" is being waged sabotaging the most vulnerable Americans at home, at work, on our streets, in our libraries, on our campuses, everywhere.

[CHAPTER 9]

Sex Educators as Sexual Saboteurs

> *Hands down*, if you'll pardon the expression, the real big daddy of pedophilia chic could only be Alfred Kinsey, could only be the long-dead Alfred C. Kinsey . . . . How did Kinsey and his team get away with it? "As we can see now," wrote Tom Bethell in his excellent review of the Kinsey facts for the May 1996 *American Spectator*, "science had vast prestige at the time and Kinsey exploited it. Any perversion could be concealed beneath the scientist's smock and the posture of detached observation."[532]
>
> —Mary Eberstadt, the *Weekly Standard*, June 17, 1996

> Any sort of sexual education that anybody has had in the past 50 years came right from the [Kinsey] Institute . . . . So his impact is enormous and in ways that it's probably impossible for us to completely grasp. . . . When Kinsey published that information, he changed our culture completely.[533]
>
> —Laura Linney, who starred as Mrs. Kinsey in the 2004 film, *Kinsey*

IN 1948, I WAS blissfully unaware when Kinsey published his much-ballyhooed *Male* report. But it did not take long for me to feel its direct effects. A scant two years later, my coed junior high school "health" class watched a highly inappropriate animated cartoon of animals mating. While the boys leered and hooted, the girls giggled and blushed. Our avant-garde "health" teacher appeared oblivious to the student discomfort. I am reminded now of the photo of Kinsey and Co., gleefully screening a porcupine mating film to a group of clearly traumatized children. I, for one, stalked out, out of my "sex ed" class sensing that something mean-spirited and ugly was being forced upon us. At the time, I did not know what it was. I was unaware of the phony "health" connection that today dominates the Western world's increasingly malevolent forms of "sex education."

Kinsey's "Pioneering" Research Was Not the First

Publicity campaigns designed to sustain Kinsey's false findings have told Americans for decades that Kinsey was the *first* to investigate sex and call for sexual "toleration." That is untrue; European sex "science" radicals preceded Kinsey. For example, by 1895, the German homosexual movement had grown so rapidly that that they were a major power lobby. In 1897, Magnus Hirschfeld, MD, Founder of the Institute for Sexual Sciences and a bizarre bisexual, had already launched international conferences on "sex science" and homosexual "rights."[534]

In his book *The Sexual Modernists*, University of California at San Diego sociologist, Jack Douglas, described the European sexuality movement at the turn of the twentieth century:

> The standard picture presented by sexual modernists today depicts a few lonely culture heroes, especially Havelock Ellis and Sigmund Freud, suddenly launching a revolution against massive Victorian sexual repression. This picture is completely false. Havelock Ellis' work was built on a mass of earlier scholarly and scientific work, all carefully footnoted, and Freud drew almost all of his major ideas from Ellis and other sex researchers and from literature and philosophy.[535]

Douglas described sex research journals that included extensive case studies of all forms of sexual activity. But the dialogue was vigorous. Scholars energetically challenged both "repression" and licentiousness. Douglas wrote:

> What is striking, by contrast with our own day, in which there is a reigning dogmatism of sexual modernism, is how lively and undogmatic the massive controversies over sexuality were.[536]

In 1948, learning of Sigmund Freud's "penis envy" theory (that girls envied the male sex organ), I recall thinking that whoever believed that was an idiot, since millions of teenage girls, like me, had never even *seen* the organ in question, much less envied it. In 1948, we might envy a pretty sweater, driving a convertible, or traveling to Paris, but *not* a penis—or the "power" for which it supposedly stood. I concluded that penis envy was Freud's problem.

Turns out, Freud's other problem was covering up crimes of several of his aristocratic, "free-spirited" colleagues, who were sexually abusing their daughters. Thanks to a daring exposé by Freudian psychiatrist Jeffrey Masson, PhD, we know that having been condemned by his medical colleagues for exposing the trauma of incest, Freud invented a literary "scientific" theory to ingratiate himself back into medical society. Should patients complain of incest, Freud said they lied to cover up their own erotic desires.[537] Freud gave his rejection of incest classical Greek archetypes, Oedipus and Electra, and, *abracadabra!* a great theory was born. Freud contended that boys lust for Mom and girls lust for Dad. His medical colleagues (especially the guilty offenders) liked that idea and welcomed Freud back into his place in the medical pantheon.

Freud's fraud then had the ruinous effect of blaming the victims and trivializing incest and child abuse. (At least he warned parents to resist their toddlers' supposed carnal desires, whereas Kinsey argued that sex with adults could *aid* the tots.)

After Freud, and as early as 1940, libertarian marriage and health educator Ray Abrams praised his colleagues for attacking "patriarchal" marriage and family courses, sexual morality and "the cult of virginity."[538] In just another decade, academe regarded the 1940s as "the Dark Age of 'traditional' parenthood—a period in which 'sex education' didn't amount to much more than a brief embarrassed conversation."[539] But in this climate, in 1941, the Rockefeller Foundation started funding Kinsey's sex studies and the next year began funding the Planned Parenthood Federation of America, which soon became the country's leading provider of both promiscuous classroom sex miseducation and the end result, pandemic juvenile STDs, failed contraception, and teenage abortions.

Through the 1940s, being a virgin bride or bridegroom meant one *chose* to wait for one's *soul mate*. Sexuality information focused on staying chaste, preserving virginity until marriage, and rearing children as a coupled family, hardly glamorous, but workable. Parents were in charge of disseminating this information. By law and by custom, parents protected children from sexual talk and images; they *never* would have imagined exposing children to *normal* sex, much less sodomy or other "perversions."

Having been slapped down by the Hays campaign, television and films, cartoons, advertisements, comics and books drastically curtailed sexual exploitation. Pre-Kinsey in Missouri, for example, sex talk was a crime if it took place in the hearing of anyone under twenty-one. However, by 1973, important Missouri lawyers argued that rape and child abuse "carry extremely severe punishment. . . . Those few who are punished are dealt with cruelly, to the satisfaction of no one except a shrinking frenetic fringe of maniacal moralists." In 1973's *Missouri*, Judge Orville Richardson wrote that heavy "penalties for rape, sodomy, and sexual abuse in the first degree should apply [ONLY] to victims under age 12."

> The label "rapist" is a damaging one and should not be used in the statutory non-consent cases . . . The Code reserves that term for the most heinous sexual offender. . . . For, one may have sex with a "fully consenting . . . social companion . . . of 12 years of age."[540]

Even by 1944, writes education researcher Randy Engel, efforts were afoot to professionalize sex as a field, to train lawmakers, judges and teachers in the "realities of human sexuality." They just required a conservative-appearing, credentialed American spokesman.[541]

Although GI Joe saved the world from Nazism, urbane European elites in 1945 still mocked American adherence to biblical laws, especially the ideals of chastity and fidelity.[542] Filled with a burgeoning homosexual and academic sexual-freedom movement, Europe had produced a growing cadre of "sexperts," including Havelock Ellis, Albert Moll, Theodor van de Velde, Magnus Hirschfeld, Bronislaw Malinowski, Sigmund Freud, Wilhelm Reich, Max Marcuse, and René Guyon. A few Americans joined their ranks: Margaret Mead, Margaret Sanger, Harry Benjamin, and Robert Dickinson among them.

Not surprisingly, like Kinsey, the biographies of such sexual radicals often exposed secret sexual preferences that augured the author's allegedly objective "data." At the turn of the century, the civilized world was sufficiently liberalized to let affluent intellectuals even take up the crusade of perverse, brutal sadosexual aristocrats, such as the Marquis de Sade. Self-styled freethinkers, who saw themselves as "sexperts" and, as such, the legitimate progenitors of the super race, created the sexual and eugenic "reform" movements to end sex laws and create a godless super race.

Education historian Mary Shivanandan, PhD, summarized the key child "developmental theories of the 20th century," psychoanalytical theorists Sigmund Freud; Eric Erikson; maturational theorists Arnold Gesell and Robert Havighurst; cognitive theorists Jean Piaget, Lawrence Kohlberg, and Albert Bandura; humanists Carl Rogers and Abraham Maslow; and the child-cage-building B.F. Skinner. *Not one* of these, theorists ever advocated sex for children—let alone adult sex acts *with* children.[543]

Even Freud began his career by noting that sexually violated children suffered grave consequences in adulthood, as it crippled mature development. So Freud argued *against* incest, at least until his livelihood was threatened by his Viennese colleagues. So, in the entire field of social "science," *only* Alfred Kinsey asserted that sexual satisfaction was developmentally beneficial in childhood.[544] *This fact alone establishes Kinsey as the sole foundation of modern "sex education."*

With deliberate and almost military precision, and cloaked in his carefully maintained conservative disguise, Kinsey dethroned and buried the elitist Sigmund Freud as the West's reigning sex guru, with his message that, sexually *anything goes*. Once the elites bought it, the common law, Judeo-Christian morality began to crumble.

Charlotte Iserbyt was President Ronald Reagan's senior policy advisor for educational research and improvement. In her chronology of the assault on American education, Iserbyt quotes from William Z. Foster, who was national chairman of the Communist Party USA. Foster called for education to be "cleansed of religious, patriotic and other features of the bourgeois ideology . . . present obsolete methods of teaching will be superseded by a scientific pedagogy. . . . God will be banished from the laboratories as well as from the schools."[545]

Iserbyt points out that Foster's methods for "communizing" traditional American schooling in the 1930s are in place today; consider the "scientific pedagogy" we see in Outcome-Based Education (OBE), Mastery Learning, Direct Instruction (Pavlov/Skinner), and Kinseyan Sex Education.[546]

In 1932, the National Education Association (NEA) created a "Policies Commission" to revolutionize American education. In 1944 their "Planners" would eliminate local school control "without seeming to do so." Like Kinsey at Indiana University, the NEA got sex education into schools by training children to ask for it. A "girl" will ask to study "sex and love, and marriage. . . . There's nothing more important to boys and girls of our age, and for most of us there isn't any place else we can go for help."[547]

Iserbyt writes that "Radical, un-Americans . . . and their paid staffs," supported by nonprofit foundations, catapulted their social engineering missiles at "the *Constitution of the United States of America* and its *Bill of Rights*." According to Iserbyt:

> In 1948 . . . . Professors B.F. Skinner and Alfred C. Kinsey published their books, *Walden Two* and *Sexual Behavior in the Human Male,* respectively. Skinner's novel, *Walden Two*, recommended—amongst other radical things—that "children be reared by the state, to be trained from birth to demonstrate only desirable characteristics and behavior." Kinsey, as a taxonomic scientist, wrested human sexuality from the constraints of love and marriage . . . a shift which would affect the legal and medical professions.[548]

Their little secret group of "Planners," would, said Iserbyt, "separate man from his God-given, freedom-providing identity." Now, children would be trained "for the benefit of *society as a whole.*" "Kinsey, Skinner, and other secret 'Planners' provided the ingredients for future moral chaos with which we are struggling today."[549]

Sexologist Harry Benjamin, MD, was a close friend and correspondent of Kinsey's, as well as of French pedophile jurist, René Guyon. In his introduction to Guyon's 1948 book, Benjamin wrote, "It probably comes as a jolt to many, even open-minded people, when they realize that chastity cannot be a virtue because it is not a natural state."[550]

In *The Closing of the American Mind* (1987), Professor Allan Bloom charged that the student uprisings of the 1960s and 1970s ended real American education. He compared the New Left university takeover to "Nazi Youth, the Woodstock concert to the Nuremberg Rally" and charged that cowardly and narcissistic professors were reviving their ignorant support of pre-World War II fascists. Journalist Richard

Bernstein said academic multiculturalists were the "Red Guards of China's Great Proletarian Cultural Revolution," who engaged in acts of "terror," "atrocity," "assault," and "dictatorship." Liberal educator Lawrence Levine wrote that the late Page Smith called the university "a classic Frankenstein monster" and compared the process of achieving university tenure "to ancient rites of human sacrifice." In his best-selling *Illiberal Education*, Dinesh D'Souza asserted that by the time students graduate, universities have taught them that "all rules are unjust. . . . "[551]

But that *was* just the beginning! Today, thanks to a group of psychopaths, including pedophiles and pederasts, funneled into schools via the NEA, Planned Parenthood, the Sex Information and Education Council of the United States (SIECUS) and the like, millions of children believe "all rules are unjust," especially sexual rules; and that therefore chastity is neither natural nor a virtue. Not coincidentally, modernity is a state of sexual immorality, pandemic child sexual abuse, disease, and cultural suicide.

How Sexology Wormed Itself Into an "Academic" Field

Kinsey was our first and loudest sex educator. The Rockefeller Foundation funded his massive publicity machine, operating on the assumption that if you tell a big enough lie often enough people will believe it. Indeed, the *Male* volume allegedly sold over 250,000 copies (a large number were actually given away by the publisher) Kinsey became a media darling, wrapping European aristocratic sexual decadence in red, white, and blue—and using purportedly objective, homegrown "statistics" to peddle sexual "modernism" to Middle America.[552] Thus, one man's psychopathic mission—and the eagerness of opinion-molders who could propagate it—repudiated the Greatest Generation and normalized decadence in the United States. What's more, Kinsey's work was translated into a dozen languages,"[553] seeding a new, western international academic field: sexology.

Until Kinsey, colleges did not teach "human sexuality" or "sexology." However, after Kinsey published *Sexual Behavior in the Human Male* in 1948 and *Sexual Behavior in the Human Female* in 1953, eager Ivy League professors began teaching Kinsey's books to millions of students—never mind that the books actually contained fabricated data that Kinsey used to legitimize his own manic sexual perversions! Trained to believe Kinsey, students worldwide were inspired to support his risk-free promiscuity "findings" in their own behavior and sex studies.

Shocked by the inexplicable sexual changes that swept across the country in the 1950s, the Greatest Generation had no idea that these changes stemmed from false "data" and a carefully orchestrated publicity campaign that sexually defamed them. Then, their lives got more confusing as "expert" warnings bombarded our World War II parents and threatened dire consequences if they did not indulge their children in every way. Says Lasch, our parents "felt somehow that they had failed to do for their children what their parents had done for them, and yet, they did not know why, or wherein they had failed, or what they could do about it."[554] For example, in 1958, groundbreaking sociologists saw freedom on the horizon: "the American family is in a stage of transition from the older patriarchal family to a system of a democratic, equalitarian arrangement."[555]

Of course, Kinsey and his co-conspirators had a much more nefarious plan for subverting Western civilization.[556] And, in time, they would win.

In 1954, literary critic Lionel Trilling worried that, in the past, only those "committed to morality . . . religion, social philosophy, and literature" addressed sex. Now, with Kinsey, science, had "the authority to speak decisively on the matter."[557] Just around the corner, in 1955, the National Association of Secondary School Principals provided education and training standards for "separate degrees for those qualified as sex educators."[558] By 1957, Kinseyan adherents were organizing to credential one another as "sexologists." Wardell Pomeroy (one of Kinsey's many lovers) founded the Society for the Scientific Study of Sex (SSSS), which claimed to be the first organization dedicated to the systematic study of sexuality.

One after another, year after year, "experts" emerged, debunking moral and marital traditions and justifying, with their "science," greater and more dangerous perversions. By 1962, psychiatric criminologist Ralph Slovenko, PhD, used Kinsey to argue that, "even at the age of four or five, [a child's] seductiveness may be so powerful as to overwhelm the adult into committing the offense. . . . Often the young female is the initiator and seducer."

In 1960, the Conference on Children and Youth, staffed with

Kinseyans, advocated bringing such "education" into all our educational institutions. For its scientific "authority," the field (surprise!) would rely on Kinsey's data. In 1964, homosexual activist Deryck Calderwood, PhD, (an SSSS member), got approval via the New York University health/education department to give sex education certificates to students. By 1968, another homosexual activist, Kenneth George, PhD, was similarly approved by the University of Pennsylvania health department. Kinseyan sexual advocacy would now become accredited and internationally recognized. We were, "on our way" so to speak.

That same year, *Playboy's* Hugh Hefner used some of his sex profits to help Kinsey co-author, Wardell Pomeroy, and his colleagues create the Sexuality Information and Education Council of the United States (SIECUS). This group, dedicated to "sex and sexuality education, sexual health, and sexual rights," became one of the most important forces in American sex education.

In 1967, the American Society for Sex Educators, Counselors, and Therapists (ASSECT) were formed to promote and train practitioners in what they called "Kinseyan sexuality." Absent any objective, proven standards, ASSECT, Deryck Calderwood, PhD, and Kenneth George, PhD, were certifying students as qualified sexual health analysts based on Kinsey's frauds and similar perverse writings.

Also in 1968, The Institute for the Advanced Study of Human Sexuality (IASHS) (formally the National Sex and Drug Forum) opened their store-front doors in San Francisco. Soon, with Kinsey co-author Wardell Pomeroy as their academic dean, the IASHS was passing out sex certificates and "degrees." The IASHS gave degrees to pupils who took months, even years of pornography viewing for class credit. IASHS students also learned erotic massage, self-massage, masturbation, sex education design and curriculum development for children, the nation, and the world.

Kinseyan training and certification soon spread to Japan, India, South America, England, Israel, and elsewhere. Shortly after 1968, IASHS graduates could be found endorsing child sex abuse and incest in the pages of *Playboy*, *Penthouse*, and *Hustler*.

Yes, the "sexperts" took over. They answered questions children never asked, creating *their* liberated sexual paradise. Little did the Greatest Generation know that Kinsey and these "experts" were sexual saboteurs, hijacking their children and grandchildren, steering them away from traditional healthy parenthood and values and advocating Kinsey's preposterous idée fixe: that children are sexual from birth.

Pornographers Invest in Sexuality "Research" Sabotage

In 1968, Hugh Hefner awarded the first of many grants to William Masters and Virginia E. Johnson to train sex professionals in *his* Kinseyan sexuality. In 1969, Hefner quietly funded a study by the Kinsey Institute and the University of Chicago; not coincidentally, the study recommended to the President's Commission on Obscenity and Pornography that all pornography be legalized.[559]

In 1970, Playboy Enterprises funded a University of Minnesota program to "change the attitudes of men and women medical students" toward sexuality; using pornography to "desensitize" future doctors to their patients' sexual peculiarities. This program was spread to medical schools worldwide, to further normalize pornography.

In 1971, sexuality students began to receive college credit during the IASHS's infamous *F**karama* [asterisks inserted], the institute's Sexual Attitude Restructuring (SAR) program. This pornographic film series—often shown to students on fourteen or more screens at the same time—included child, bestial, bisexual, group, and homosexual pornography. Recruiting applicants "off the streets," the IASHS required only that the recruit reject traditional sexual values. Using this conditioning, the IASHS trained students via pornography, the Kinsey Reports, erotic massage, sex surrogate therapy (prostitution), self-massage (masturbation), the forensic defense of pornography, and so on. Students also created sex-education curricula for all age groups, and sold these programs to public, private, and parochial schools.

Citing Kinsey's "findings," in 1973 a group of violent bi/homosexual bullies stormed the American Psychiatric Association (APA) conference and demanded that "homosexuality" be removed from the list of psychological disorders in its Diagnostic and Statistical Manual. Unaccustomed to violence, the frightened psychiatrists quickly agreed.[560] That same year, pedophile advocate, John De Cecco, PhD, a San Francisco State University psychologist, became the first editor of the *Journal of Homosexuality.* Also in 1973, Kinseyan educators John Gagnon, PhD, and William Simon, PhD, published *Sexual Conduct:*

The Social Sources of Human Sexuality. On the heels of those milestones, the World Health Organization (WHO) recommended in 1974 that sexology be recognized as an autonomous discipline in the education and training of health professionals. In 1976, the most influential of the various sexologists formed the World Association for Sexology (WAS), which, in turn, founded the World Congress of Sexology.

In 1977, the IASHS training center sold its own photographs of naked children, posed pornographically, to *Hustler* magazine. The IASHS's "minister of photography" included the photos to illustrate an IASHS article that argued for legalizing incest and child abuse. The photographs were released in 1977 as a coffee-table picture book, *Meditations on the Gift of Sexuality*,[561] which also included photos of naked IASHS faculty, staff, students, and friends engaging in masturbation, sodomy, and group orgies. These pathologically disordered deviants are the sex educators and designers of national and global school sex education curricula.

For its part, Playboy Enterprises funded the *National Education Association* (NEA) in 1978. A year later, Pomeroy is on record as seeking funds from the "Adult Film Association annual convention in February of 1979" to film child pornography.562 Though Pomeroy died in 2001, the IASHS lives on. As of this writing, the IASHS awards a doctorate of education, four graduate degrees, and seven credentials, including credentials for safe sex and erotic massage. Students can earn a state-approved "Sexological Bodywork Certificate," which critics of the measure called a prostitution degree masquerading as a health strategy.[563] The IASHS course description promises "ecstatic and erotic states," and points out that the "erotic education is communal. Each person touches and coaches every other person. . . . Diversity in sexual preference and gender" is taught, as are "masturbation skills."[564]

Originally, the course description correctly states that it "would not have been possible even a decade ago." Much of the original text is now missing online, and students are told, "For more information, please contact us." Thanks to Kinsey's growing army of disciples who continue to promote Kinseyan pathologies, "what is appropriate in erotic education have shifted." Indeed! Now, home study for this certification includes "baby massage" instruction along with "erotic massage, sex coaching, anal pleasure" and more. Chilling.

The Sex Education Bandwagon

After the 1981 genital herpes scare, another sexually transmitted disease burst onto the scene: Gay-Related Infectious Disease (GRID). Soon, the politically hot disease was renamed AIDS, which was later correlated with a preceding condition, HIV. Though both diseases—and roughly twenty-five others—result from the canon of Kinseyan promiscuity, sexologists fail to reveal this irony. Instead, they respond with advocacy for condoms, abortions, childhood STD vaccines, and similar cover-ups.

We must blame SIECUS and its handmaiden, Planned Parenthood, for the eroticized classroom. The former executive director of SIECUS, Ann Welbourne-Moglia, PhD, stated that AIDS was a time of "rare opportunity." Why? To "educate about AIDS," we must teach "about sexuality in general."[565] SIECUS and Planned Parenthood never sought to teach chaste health to schoolchildren. No. Welbourne-Moglia and her cult used AIDS to *institutionalize* "outercourse": mutual masturbation, oral and anal sodomy, and, of course, pornography. The idea that children *should* have sex before marriage, in order to be healthy, was long Kinsey's mission, and Planned Parenthood's mission, as well.

In 1981, *Playboy* Enterprises had funded Planned Parenthood, the ACLU, and the Media Coalition, which was defending child pornography in the New York case, *People v. Ferber*. Though the New York judges had approved Ferber's child pornography on the basis of "free speech," the U.S. Supreme Court unanimously reversed the decision in 1982, citing the nation's "compelling interest" in prohibiting child sexual abuse (gosh!). *Playboy* continued to fight on many fronts. In 1983, for example, to boost the scientific paradigm of Kinseyan sexuality, *Playboy* funded scores of sex-training universities, including Vanderbilt, UCLA, and NYU.[566]

In 1979, after the Adult Film Association refused to fund Wardell Pomeroy's IASHS production of child pornography films, a disappointed Pomeroy crafted "standards" to train sexologists. In 1986, he and his sexologist clan created the American Board of Sexology (ABS) to "diplomate to sexologists who meet its rigorous standards." Pomeroy's Kinsey clones also formed a bogus SSSS Commission on

Accreditation, for "Human Sexuality Programs" and "Sex Education Curricula" that would accredit only Kinseyan school sex education programs and curricula.[567]

Meanwhile, the ALI-MPC succeeded in influencing the legalization of abortion and pornography, and reducing punishments for sex-crime violations, so that Planned Parenthood, SIECUS, and ASSECT were free to exploit children's open minds with sex "education" curricula in private, public, and parochial schools. Attempting to normalize promiscuity, sodomy, "outercourse," therapeutic pornography, sadomasochism, and masturbatory addictions, they introduced curricula to schools from kindergarten through postgraduate degree programs. By 1990, the American Academy of Clinical Sexologist (AACS) added its bogus accreditation program to the mix, claiming that it would give professional recognition for qualified physicians, sex therapists, and sex counselors.[568]

In 1996, SIECUS published its "Position Statement on Sexually Explicit Materials," telling children, parents, and teachers that "sexually explicit visual, printed, or on-line materials can be valuable educational or personal aids."[569] The original statement, in the author's archive, adds that its information for children helps in "reduc[ing] ignorance and confusion . . . [and] contributing to a wholesome concept of sexuality."[570] Recent online iterations of this coda continue, "supporting the sexual rights of all," that would include children. However this new version claims to deplore, "violence, exploitation, or degradation, or the portrayal of children in sexually explicit materials."[571] Meanwhile, hundreds of thousands of IASHS graduates asserted their "Basic Sexual Rights," according to the Institute, including the right to all things consensual, including incest, child prostitution, child pornography, bestiality, and all other sex acts if allegedly *consensual*.[572]

After nearly sixty years of indoctrinating the young and not-so-young, "sexology" has arrived. Now, it has blossomed into an educational field and research industry that permeates all areas of human sexuality. *The Sex Industrial Complex* is complete, as sexologists recommend all manner of sexual promiscuity while pharmaceutical companies line up to sign the sexologists' dance cards and, subsequently, profit from the resulting psychosexual disorders.[573]

Legitimizing "Sex Education" and *The Sex Industrial Complex*

Author Beverly Newman, then of Ivy Tech College in Indianapolis, argues that American sex education was particularly founded upon the Kinsey dogma so that the world would also have to believe Kinsey's claims about the Greatest Generation. Kinsey, she muses, "never should have been walking the streets freely, let alone administering a major university institution. . . . The shameful Kinsey's legacy continues to menace the lives of America's children."[574] Indeed.

From the courts and professors to teachers and children, Kinsey's dogma percolated downward. Using a "Graffiti Board" to desensitize students via "dirty words," sex educators taught children about "nudity, adolescent pregnancy, masturbation, abortion, homosexuality, contraception, divorce, group sex and extramarital sex relation."[575] By 1973, "Thanks to Kinsey, every form of deviance is promulgated throughout our schools," reported psychiatrist Charles Socarides, MD."[576] "Kinsey stated it very clearly . . . that . . . any kind of sex was normal."[577]

As attorney Ben Shapiro, the iconoclastic young author of *Porn Generation*, has noted, infiltrators such as SIECUS, Planned Parenthood, and their satellites have commandeered our schools, launching their amoral, immoral plan for sexually fixating our children:

> They have used sex education as a means of indoctrinating children into a cult of moral relativism and hedonism. Following in the footsteps of Alfred Kinsey and his trumped-up research, the sex-education movement has viewed its goal as the promotion of an acceptant and inevitable attitude about teen promiscuity.
>
> "[Our goal] is to be ready as educators and parents to help young people obtain sex satisfaction before marriage," wrote Planned Parenthood staffer Lena Levine in 1953. "By sanctioning sex before marriage, we will prevent fear and guilt."
>
> Fifty-two years later, Levine's dream has come true—we live in a society where condoms are dispensed to seventh-graders, where twelve-year-olds are told about the glories of oral sex and where children are given the "opportunity to develop their values and increase self-

FIGURE 12
SCIENTIFIC AUTHORITY FOR THE SEX INDUSTRY COMPLEX (SIC) IN THE 20TH–21ST CENTURY

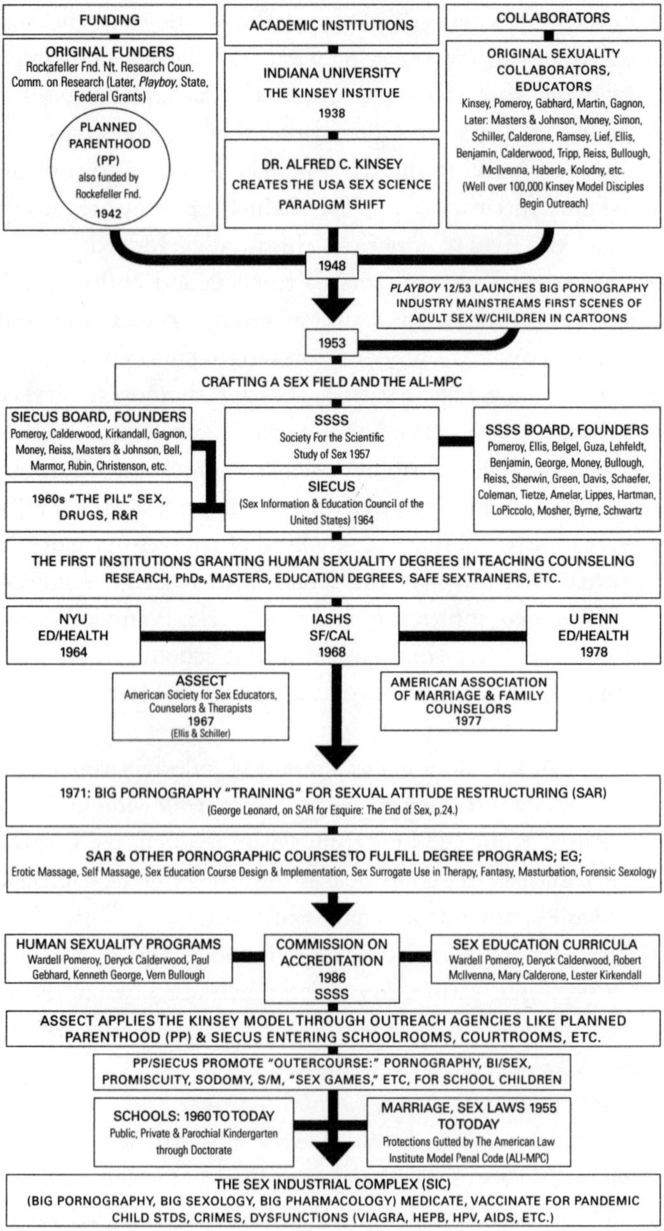

FUNDING
ACADEMIC INSTITUTIONS
COLLABORATORS
ORIGINAL FUNDERS
Rockafeller Fnd. Nt. Research Coun. Comm. on Research (Later, *Playboy*, State, Federal Grants)
PLANNED PARENTHOOD (PP) also funded by Rockefeller Fnd. 1942
INDIANA UNIVERSITY THE KINSEY INSTITUE 1938
DR. ALFRED C. KINSEY CREATES THE USA SEX SCIENCE PARADIGM SHIFT
ORIGINAL SEXUALITY COLLABORATORS, EDUCATORS
Kinsey, Pomeroy, Gabhard, Martin, Gagnon, Later: Masters & Johnson, Money, Simon, Schiller, Calderone, Ramsey, Lief, Ellis, Benjamin, Calderwood, Tripp, Reiss, Bullough, McIlvenna, Haberle, Kolodny, etc.
(Well over 100,000 Kinsey Model Disciples Begin Outreach)
1948
PLAYBOY 12/53 LAUNCHES BIG PORNOGRAPHY INDUSTRY MAINSTREAMS FIRST SCENES OF ADULT SEX W/CHILDREN IN CARTOONS
1953
CRAFTING A SEX FIELD AND THE ALI-MPC
SIECUS BOARD, FOUNDERS
Pomeroy, Calderwood, Kirkandall, Gagnon, Money, Reiss, Masters & Johnson, Bell, Marmor, Rubin, Christenson, etc.
1960s "THE PILL" SEX, DRUGS, R&R
SSSS
Society For the Scientific Study of Sex 1957
SIECUS
(Sex Information & Education Council of the United States) 1964
SSSS BOARD, FOUNDERS
Pomeroy, Ellis, Belgel, Guza, Lehfeldt, Benjamin, George, Money, Bullough, Reiss, Sherwin, Green, Davis, Schaefer, Coleman, Tietze, Amelar, Lippes, Hartman, LoPiccolo, Mosher, Byrne, Schwartz
THE FIRST INSTITUTIONS GRANTING HUMAN SEXUALITY DEGREES IN TEACHING COUNSELING RESEARCH, PhDs, MASTERS, EDUCATION DEGREES, SAFE SEX TRAINERS, ETC.
NYU ED/HEALTH 1964
IASHS SF/CAL 1968
U PENN ED/HEALTH 1978
ASSECT
American Society for Sex Educators, Counselors & Therapists 1967
(Ellis & Schiller)
AMERICAN ASSOCIATION OF MARRIAGE & FAMILY COUNSELORS 1977
1971: BIG PORNOGRAPHY "TRAINING" FOR SEXUAL ATTITUDE RESTRUCTURING (SAR)
(George Leonard, on SAR for Esquire: The End of Sex, p.24.)
SAR & OTHER PORNOGRAPHIC COURSES TO FULFILL DEGREE PROGRAMS; EG;
Erotic Massage, Self Massage, Sex Education Course Design & Implementation, Sex Surrogate Use in Therapy, Fantasy, Masturbation, Forensic Sexology
HUMAN SEXUALITY PROGRAMS
Wardell Pomeroy, Deryck Calderwood, Paul Gebhard, Kenneth George, Vern Bullough
COMMISSION ON ACCREDITATION 1986 SSSS
SEX EDUCATION CURRICULA
Wardell Pomeroy, Deryck Calderwood, Robert McIlvenna, Mary Calderone, Lester Kirkendall
ASSECT APPLIES THE KINSEY MODEL THROUGH OUTREACH AGENCIES LIKE PLANNED PARENTHOOD (PP) & SIECUS ENTERING SCHOOLROOMS, COURTROOMS, ETC.
PP/SIECUS PROMOTE "OUTERCOURSE:" PORNOGRAPHY, BI/SEX, PROMISCUITY, SODOMY, S/M, "SEX GAMES," ETC, FOR SCHOOL CHILDREN
SCHOOLS: 1960 TO TODAY
Public, Private & Parochial Kindergarten through Doctorate
MARRIAGE, SEX LAWS 1955 TO TODAY
Protections Gutted by The American Law Institute Model Penal Code (ALI-MPC)
THE SEX INDUSTRIAL COMPLEX (SIC)
(BIG PORNOGRAPHY, BIG SEXOLOGY, BIG PHARMACOLOGY) MEDICATE, VACCINATE FOR PANDEMIC CHILD STDS, CRIMES, DYSFUNCTIONS (VIAGRA, HEPB, HPV, AIDS, ETC.)

esteem," to quote Debra W. Hafner, former president of the Sexuality Information and Education Council of the United States [SIECUS].[578]

However, one can never prevent fear and guilt. Rather, we merely shift what we fear and feel guilty about.

Standing on Kinsey's "revelations" about the Greatest Generation's alleged promiscuity and children's alleged carnality, Kinsey's lobbyists morphed into child sex "educators." Thus, Kinsey's "sex education" monopoly became entrenched in "higher education," where research efforts work in tandem with education to continue Kinsey's "work," more than fifty years after his death. Indeed, Kinsey's atrocities endure in "sex education" and "human sexuality" textbooks worldwide—in secular, private, and parochial schools, as Kinsey remains the unquestioned authority for the absurd assertion that children *need* sex and, therefore, promiscuity-pushing sexual "information."

But there had to be more to this story. How could these lies legally enter the education system? It is no accident that Kinsey's message to "fornicate early, fornicate often, fornicate in every possible way" is now legally and socially in place,[579] with adult authority figures teaching R-rated and even X-rated classes to primary school boys and girls. Yet if Kinsey is now suffering a public disrobing, his intellectual heirs display their researches still. For a final model of pedophilia chic—this one tricked out with all the requisite charts, tables, models, and talk of methodology—consider a volume published in 1993 by Prometheus Books.

Much of the answer lies in Kinsey's *global* reach. We see his fallout in dozens of international "sexuality" organizations and congresses, all of which stand on the frauds of Kinsey's cadre. It starts with SIECUS and Planned Parenthood. To these forces, add the following and *many, many new* satellite academic pornographers as well as blatant pedophile/pederast organizations such as NAMBLA (North American Man-Boy Love Association) that salutes Kinsey on their Web site, The Childhood Sensuality Circle, the René Guyon Society, and the like.[580]

- The World Association of Sexology
- The International Society for Sexual Medicine (ISSM)

- The International Society for The Study Of Women's Sexual Health
- The Finnish Association for Sexology (typical of all national "westernized" sexuality organizations) with international outreach via UNESCO
- The Society for the Scientific Study of Sexuality
- The Woodhull Freedom Foundation (Carole Queen, PhD, says she is a "Daughter" of Kinsey)
- The Center for Sex and Culture[581]

As Kinsey's *domestic* "disinformation" lobby has worked to catastrophic effect, the results *inside* the United States are bad enough, but these groups provide exclusively pro-Kinsey data[582] with untold *international* consequences as well. Consider the "work" of Vern Bullough, PhD, a (deceased) distinguished professor emeritus of Natural and Social Sciences, State University of New York, later California State Northridge, and one editor for *The Journal of Paedophilia*.[583] Although Kinsey researched Americans, Bullough declared that Kinsey's study "came to be a worldwide source . . . and set standards for sex . . . everywhere."[584] Everywhere, indeed. By defaming our Greatest Generation, Kinsey moved sex out of the "bailiwick of the religious," creating its own scientific "field" of pleasure, including prostitution/pornography and possibilities, said the distinguished professor emeritus.

"Many years ago," after scrapping religious and medical concerns,[585] Bullough and a coalition trained a new lobby of believers in Kinseyan cultic sexuality, conducting "workshops for educators, therapists, and various professionals on such topics as . . . homosexuality, transvestism, *adult child sexual interactions*, sex and the single parent" (emphasis added).[586]

Bullough's trainees included "large numbers of religious professionals as registrants,"[587] who took copious notes on "almost any topic dealing with human sexuality."[588] But if not from our medical, moral, or literary past, where did his coalition of "sexperts" find the "science" to teach these topics? Our new sex "information," modern "sex education," and all its fallout are the legacies of Kinsey—a sexual psychopath—and his cult of followers! After Kinsey died, sex "trainers," coalitions, and "institutes" popped up in storefronts and at colleges everywhere.

Sex Education into Colleges

Soon, Kinsey's sex-education monopoly became well-entrenched in what is known as "higher education." For example, in 1994, Tennessee legislators,[589] reacting to the massive increases in teen STDS, rapes, and abortions, voted to fund only sex courses that taught abstinence before marriage. The next year, however, the Tennessee Department of Education *itself* secretly published a *Lifetime Wellness Curriculum* that instructed captive schoolchildren in oral and anal sodomy and dismissed marriage as a mere "parenting" and financial option. Never mind that this violated the law.[590]

In 2006, Robert Crooks, PhD, and Karla Baur, PhD, assessed the effect of the 1948 and 1953 Kinsey reports on our culture today, writing, "The surprising statistics on same-sex behavior, masturbation and novel acts in the bedroom contributed to the growing acceptance of a variety of sexual behaviors."[591] They would know. Crooks and Baur had a lot to do with acceptance of those "surprising statistics."

In 1983, they first published their college text, *Our Sexuality*. It has been reissued regularly since then. One of hundreds of similar college texts, *Our Sexuality* continues to teach that normal men and women of the 1920s through the 1940s were promiscuous, that children want and deserve to have sex, that we should normalize and encourage masturbation and homosexuality. Heralded as the "most authoritative college textbook available on human sexuality" (2005 version), *Our Sexuality* cites Kinsey as the world's sexual expert, and advances the entire range of Kinseyan cant and ideology.

Relying *wholly* on Kinseyan "scientists," Crooks and Baur reject our common laws, Judeo-Christian sexuality within the framework of marriage and family, but promote Kinseyan "sex-positive" attitudes. They ask *no* questions about Kinsey's "data" on women's sexuality, (including his preposterous assertion that, out of 4,441 women, not one suffered rape or childhood harm from sexual assault). They ignore the growing body of ethical medical and psychological research that demonstrates the disastrous, lifelong effects of pornography and child sex abuse. Kinsey's claims served Crooks and Baur's sociopolitical agenda, their academic careers, and that of the new "sexuality field" and its lobby.

The authors eagerly celebrate and support Kinsey's pederast notion of infant "orgasms." Too eagerly, they hide the truth that Kinsey got his "child sexuality data" from adult rapists of children shamefully regurgitating Kinsey's frauds of multiple sex crimes against children as research. Unabashed, Crooks and Baur reiterate Kinsey's cruel fantasies—and teach millions of college students to emulate them. What of these readers, these students, who go on to become the next crop of professional "experts," conducting "tests" and lecturing and testifying in courts worldwide, *believing* that Kinsey proved that child and even infant sexuality is an active volcano requiring release?

Our Sexuality is *not* unique in teaching collegians that it is harmful to thwart children's "sexuality"—a lie that has brought graphic, even pornographic *mis*education into most of America's schoolrooms. College students, now imbibing such "science," are our next generation of parents, professors, psychologists, marriage counselors, social workers, daycare workers, adoption workers, camp counselors, physicians, nurses, clergy, lawyers, lawmakers, law enforcement officers, *judges,* journalists, writers, artists, presidents—and *teachers*.

Sexualizing America's Classrooms

Before Kinsey, home economics, health, or physical education teachers taught about menstruation, reproduction, and, sometimes, marital behavior. From biology class to instruction on finances, these lessons taught that sex was good, but only in marriage, for reasons of health, happiness, and societal well-being. Simple. On to history and math. But once Kinsey sexualized America's children from birth onward, school activists argued that their districts needed trained instructors—"experts"—to teach students about sex. Soon, classes that were euphemistically called "sex education," "family life," "health," "hygiene," "abstinence," or "diversity," "hate crimes" and, later, "AIDS awareness," infected most American schools.

Since the U.S. Supreme Court ruled the Ten Commandments could not be displayed on school house walls, huge school AIDS posters went up in their place, allegedly to warn students about AIDS. Some of these advertisements are graphically provocative. Some include a homoerotic sub text, others use the AIDS threat as a vehicle to market pornography—heterosexual, bisexual, whatever.

Published for our children by all the "right" health departments, one poster, prominently displayed in some California schools, included graphic drawings of splayed female genitalia and a very large, erect phallus. This poster graphically demonstrated how to put a condom on the phallus, how to use "dental dams" to prevent AIDS during both sodomies, and how to clean your needles if the child is shooting up with drugs. How informative.

Eventually, public health data confirmed the obvious: The more children who received Kinsey-type "sex education," the more children suffered from sexual disease infections and socio-sexual pathologies. Still, thanks to the Kinsey cult, the responsibility for sex "education" was wrested from parents to Kinseyan-trained schoolteachers. Then, the gloves came off. Children learned about sex *only* from Kinsey-baptized missionaries. Within decades, Kinsey's disciples even assaulted the youngest child's psyche with deviant sexual stimulation, relabeled as "education."

Planned Parenthood and SIECUS took the lessons of Kinsey's pedophile "experiments" into almost every North American classroom—and many in Europe, too.

I propose that a valuable sex-education exercise would be to have students watch old *Popeye* cartoons, as when Popeye defends Olive Oyl and Sweet Pea, or *Sense and Sensibility* or the *Thin Man* films about Nick and Nora Charles. Or, better yet, read love letters between husbands and wives, married for fifty years while they endured war, poverty, and hardship: presidential couples like Julia and Ulysses S. Grant and Abigail and John Adams.

Of course, over the protests of parents and priests, America's schools, even Catholic schools, have used coarsening sex "education" programs for decades—even though official Catholic Church teaching from Rome condemns graphic sex lessons and insists that parents are the "primary educators" of their children. The Texans for Life Coalition complained about south-Texas Catholic schools on its 2008 Web site:

> Specifically, kindergartners are taught about the sexual intercourse of their parents, third graders (ages 7 and 8) are given the particulars of pedophilia and individual and mutual masturbation ("often accompanied or caused by reading or watching sexually graphic materials"). Oral sex is described in detail at the fourth grade level.

By the seventh grade, the topics are anal sex, impotency, sex toys, "S&M" (Sadism & Masochism), and bestiality. At every level . . . there is a subtle attempt to make all types of sexual activity appear normal and acceptable.[592]

The governing idea is that sex education should be left to parents but, at the same time, they do not have the "relevant knowledge" to be qualified to talk to their kids about sex. It would follow that, since Kinsey's supposedly healthy ideas have spread across the world, "sex education" should have created healthier, happier children and solid marriages and families. Unfortunately—and obviously—this is not so.

Changing the Game

Remember, *Planned Parenthood News* asserted in 1953 that helping everyone enjoy guilt-free sexual satisfaction before marriage was a goal to which it should aspire. In that same publication, Lena Levine added, "[W]e must be ready to provide young boys and girls with the best contraceptive measures available . . . to achieve sexual satisfaction without having to risk possible pregnancy."[593] Forty years later, they were still at it. In 1996, the Planned Parenthood Federation of America Bulletin wrote, "The solution is to teach young people how to experience sexual pleasure, instead of teaching them to not have sex."[594]

Emphasizing "sexual satisfaction" in its constant tirade, Planned Parenthood and SIECUS teach libido techniques. Opposing Judeo-Christian morals, both groups have told children that sex—with themselves, other children, even adults—is their birthright, and any morality that would repress them from full sexual expression (such as their parents' moral tradition) was foolish.

Adults often "overprotect" kids, wrote the Planned Parenthood Federation of America in the 1987 booklet, *Human Sexuality: What Children Should Know and When They Should Know It*. "Nowhere is this 'overprotection' more evident than in the area of sexuality. For children to make healthy and helpful choices regarding sexuality throughout their lives, they must be encouraged to make their own choices from the youngest ages."[595]

Undermining parents at every turn, Planned Parenthood long maintained this know-it-all-attitude despite its failure to aid children in *any* healthy manner. "If your parents are stupid enough to deny you access to birth control, and you are under 18, you can get it on your own," encouraged a 1986 Planned Parenthood advertisement in the *Dallas Observer.*[596] Lecturing students at Ramona High School in Riverside, California, in 1986, a Planned Parenthood employee said, "At Planned Parenthood you can also get birth control without the consent or knowledge of your parents. So, if you are 14, 15 or 16 and you come to Planned Parenthood, we won't tell your parents you've been there. We swear we won't tell your parents."[597] A 2003 teenwire.com posting read: "[T]ake the useful, smart stuff you've learned from your folks and kick the crap to the curb."[598]

Presumably eager to help students discern the smart stuff from the "crap," SIECUS and Planned Parenthood armed educators with pornographic films, magazines, books, and sex "games" for children. Eventually, Planned Parenthood's Kinseyan "sex ed" curricula provided graphic masturbation lessons as well as live demonstrations with cucumbers and bananas. Instructors provided children with "contraceptive information" and even directions on how to do "it." Both organizations trained would-be professionals and children about the virtues of oral and anal sodomy and sex "toys." After AIDS hit, SIECUS and Planned Parenthood were too late with too little. Now they added condoms and "dental dams" to their menu. Stressing sexual "diversity," instructors taught children to experiment with pseudo-erotic acts in groups, alone as well as homosexually and heterosexually. "Don't rob yourself of joy," instructed the Rocky Mountain Planned Parenthood in 1981, "by focusing on old-fashioned ideas about what's 'normal' or 'nice.'"[599]

Once SIECUS and Planned Parenthood had sexually indoctrinated children, they then directed them to local "health clinics." Before Planned Parenthood's official opening in 1943, its "birth control" clinics were somewhat operational, largely to prevent pregnancy; with little discussion of venereal disease; they distributed condoms, not to promote "safe-sex" but to limit births. Only after the genital herpes and AIDS epidemics of the 1980s did Planned Parenthood begin advocating condoms use for "safe sex."

Unfortunately, condoms and "dental dams" did little to prevent VD and pregnancies from childish fornication, so Planned Parenthood abandoned "safe" sex and began advocating "*safer*" sex—while treating pandemic rates of venereal disease and aborting roughly 1.5 million babies a year in "reproductive health" clinics.[600] In the 1960s, Planned Parenthood enjoyed its coming-out decade. When birth control was removed from obscenity statutes, the doors swung open. In 1968, Planned Parenthood got its first federal grant, from the Office of Economic Opportunity. It was a rare opportunity indeed.

In the 1970s, Congress enacted Title X, funneling billions of dollars into Planned Parenthood's programs. But the biggest opportunity came with the 1973 Supreme Court decision in *Roe v. Wade*, which legalized abortion on demand.[601] Planned Parenthood bombarded America's schoolchildren with "sex ed"—instructions for heterosexual intercourse and all manner of deviant sex, showcased in what it called sexually "positive" film pornography, again neglecting "negative" issues, like venereal disease or pregnancy. When the time came, of course, they were more than willing to *treat* STDs and *perform* abortions. Indeed, the very group whose aggressive sexual propaganda had helped breed these personal disasters rakes in billions of dollars cleaning them up.[602]

Pushing Teen Sex

Consider Planned Parenthood's illustrated brochure, *You've Changed the Combination* distributed to tenth grade children nationwide beginning in 1974. Using frank language, the brochure dismisses the emotional and the disease complications of casual sex that it encourages. The brochure tells millions of teenagers to have relations with their friends and, really, anyone else—except "victims." According to the teenage training manual:

- "There are only two basic kinds of sex: sex with victims and sex without. Sex with victims is always wrong. Sex without is always right" (p. 10).
- "Sex is best between friends. Not quickest, just best" (p. 9).
- A girl might be "too high" to remember that she stopped taking "the pill" (p. 11).

- Boys should "ask" before having (illegal) intercourse with a minor (p. 12).
- An adult, who was "married and ha[s] two children" is okay for sex (p. 11).
- Sex with blushing young girls is okay if boys "ask" first (p. 11).
- "If this is a one nighter, and you don't intend to be around, say so . . . " (p. 12).
- If this is a girl you've just met and she agrees, you're in the clear, provided that she's old enough to have some sense" (p. 12).
- Women "freely chose" prostitution so you can pay for it (p.18).
- "Do you want a virgin to marry? Buy one. There are girls in that business too. Marriage is the price you'll pay, and you'll get the virgin. Very temporarily" (p. 18).

Of course, these pathological directions are also *criminal,* riddled with lies and future pain, disease, fear, shame, tragedy, even fatalities, for the children trained to believe its callous Kinseyan message.

Planned Parenthood criminally tells millions of teen readers to ask a girl who is "high" on drugs for consent before having sex (p. 11). *Ridiculous!* Boys should *never* have sex with someone who is "high" or who "may not be thinking clearly" (or at all!) This is "uninformed" consent, a crime. The sexperts tell the youngsters, "If she's young, always ask" (p. 12). How young might a "blushing young girl" be? And how old is "old enough"?

Beyond such egregious, illegal messages suborning crimes (and many more), the school sexperts claim that, if girls refuse sex before marriage, it is a form of *prostitution*, since men end up "paying" for sex by marrying. (This echoes the position of pornographers, prostitution lobbyists, and international "Human Sexuality" training institutions.) Planned Parenthood here works to psychologically sabotage, brainwash American schoolchildren with emotional shock and desensitization, to strip away their moral training so they will experiment with sexual pathologies that will have destroyed many thousands of lives.

This booklet is sexual sabotage. It endangers the health and welfare of children and contributes to the delinquency of minors, violating both state and federal laws. Still, Planned Parenthood continues to defraud city, county, state, and federal governments, obtaining millions of grant monies to miseducate teachers and students about the realities of sex acts in the lives of adolescents. Predictably, this booklet is not an isolated example.

Who *are* these malevolent "sexperts?" Consider Planned Parenthood's "Teenwire.com" Web site, which includes a "question and answer" section for children, without requiring parental consent (often in violation of laws). In one typical posting, an alleged teenager asks: "How do i know if my girlfriend is having a real *orgasm* when i give her *oral sex?*"[603]

For starters Planned Parenthood's educator does not answer, "Son, how old are you? How old is this girl? You are too young for sex. Have you been tested for any STDs? Do your parents know you are sexually active?" No, Planned Parenthood's answer is pure Kinseyan propaganda, referring to girls as women and presuming that these teens have multiple partners:

> The only way to know for sure is to ask! So you know, many women—about one out of three—have trouble reaching orgasm when having *sex* with a partner. And most women experience orgasm through clitoral stimulation rather than through *vaginal* penetration. Some women will *fake orgasm* to make their partners feel good. . . . But it may take time to earn the trust for a fully honest conversation.[604]

This "expert" indicates that the teens (*who are not* yet "women"), should build a fully honest relationship—yet urges sexual involvement—then pornographically describes methods the boy might try to stimulate the girl although such sex technique is well beyond the scope of the *alleged* boy's question. Finally, the Planned Parenthood expert adds, "communication with a partner is very important," and that they should talk about what "feels good" or bad. The "expert" subsequently acknowledged, "unprotected oral sex" *can* result in several STDs, although "risks are relatively lower than those of unprotected vaginal or anal sex." Unaware of the child's age, the Planned Parenthood expert never raises issues of promiscuity or, God forbid, abstinence. Instead, the expert suggests ways to lower the oral VD risks: "[U]se a Glyde® dam to cover the v— or a—." So the boy might sodomize his friend to protect himself from VD![605]

Though the Planned Parenthood "experts" advise that sexually active teens should have each other's consent, without pressuring to get it, they do not address the issues of alcohol or drug use, pornography, or promises, in obtaining that consent. They tell kids to be "honest," then dishonestly ignore that, while their emotions may be genuine, kids are still immature. So when they tell the teens to protect each other against physical or emotional harm, they *know the reality* that teen relationships are fleeting, that hearts break, and, worse, *promiscuity itself* results in physical harm—even incurable venereal diseases, for example. While Planned Parenthood warns them to guard against pregnancy and STDs, they give no real discouragement, no condom failure rates and so on. For decades the organization steers young people into sexual encounters, hiding the dire consequences of such interactions.

Consider the following teenwire.com exchange, dated December 20, 2006. I have edited it to avoid obvious pornographic terms:

> Im having a big problem—sex just doesnt feel good for me anymore. When i have sex and even if i go really fast and try to reach orgasm i cant even feel a good sensation. Im 15 years old. Is something wrong? Its like my penis is numb, when i [***] i cant even feel it and i get so tired of doing it, i dont even get to [ejaculate]. I think something is really wrong, please help![606]

Obsessive masturbation and pornography use are the common causes of such problems, but Planned Parenthood's Teenwire "expert" ignores this fact, since Planned Parenthood panders both pornography and masturbation as normal. Instead, the expert suggests the boy see "a clinician," as his problem may be due to medication the boy might take.

In 2007 Teenwire entries included a girl who just had an abortion, someone with hepatitis wondering about infecting her boyfriend, and similar stories. Planned Parenthood's "experts" never changed their tune, just prescribed lots of sex, condom use, and Big Pharma when the time comes.

Planned Parenthood operates several similar Web sites that children worldwide can visit. One such is *Scarleteen.com.*

> It's back to school for you and back to the basics here at Scarleteen. How about adding some sexuality primers from our articles, blog and advice answers to your DIY sex ed course load this year?
>
> Do you have your prereqs on sexual orientation? We've got The Bees and . . . the Bees: A Homosexuality and Bisexuality Primer for you. Thinking about coming out this year? Here's a guide on How to Come Out of the Closet Without Tripping Over Your Laundry.[607]

Scarleteen.com, Planned Parenthood brags under the heading, "The Information and education you need to help find the you in sexuality":

> Many of the textbooks that are used in public school sex education classes in 1999 would've been considered "pornographic" or "obscene" 20 or 30 years ago. Most people use "kinky" to refer to sexual behavior considered "abnormal" in our society (a value judgment, not a definition). That does not mean they are abnormal. However, not too long ago oral sex was considered abnormal or deviant, as was masturbation, mutual masturbation, anal sex, and more. Many people use the term "kinky" to describe themselves proudly.[608]

In another entry, a teen allegedly writes:

> Dear Experts, I look at porno sites but I got all A for my subjects. People say looking at those sites affect your school work, but since i think i'm not affected, should i stop it? If i should, how?

Answering, Planned Parenthood deliberately dodges the pesky problem that obscenity is illegal for everyone and pornography is *illegal for minors*. They reply:

> Pornography (also known as porn or porno) is sexually arousing imagery. Some people prefer to call it erotica because the word pornography is sometimes used to describe material that may be considered offensive and obscene. In any case, many people enjoy using pornography or erotica as a part of their sex play—alone or with a partner . . . [extensive pornographic details omitted here]. There is no indication that using pornography causes problems as long as it does not interfere with other aspects of a person's life. Hope this information helps![609]

Ongoing and Systemic Promotion of Teen Sex

In 2004, Planned Parenthood published a pornographic comic book, *It's Perfectly Normal*, for fifth to ninth graders. That year, they sold more than one million copies of the sexual sabotage: assorted sex acts and full frontal nudity largely of pubescent children fully illustrated. It would not be out of place on the walls of a ruined Roman brothel in Pompeii.[610]

Famed advice columnist, Ann Landers, hailed *It's Perfectly Normal* as a great book, saying that *children would enjoy the pictures*. To this statement, the Christian, conservative author Lee Duigon replied, "Ann has apparently been hanging around the Kinsey Institute crowd, which thinks child molestation is just part of a good scientific inquiry into sex."[611] Elsewhere, Duigon writes:

> [D]id you know that the anus is a "sex organ" (p. 23, 26)? Did you know that the one and only reason people object to homosexuality is because "their views are often based on misinformation, not on facts" (p. 17–18)? [Or that] although "some religions call masturbation a sin," the "fact" is that "masturbation cannot hurt you" (p. 48) [And that abortion is always right if the baby is unwanted?] [612]

As it turns out, extreme abuse of one's sex organs can induce massive trauma, and, as we saw with Kinsey, much worse.[613] As children followed Planned Parenthood's sex prescription, the organization opened neighborhood "clinics" to handle a booming business. The organization aborted millions of babies in these "clinics." Still, Planned Parenthood offered no aid to women whose breast cancer might be traced to those abortions, or to women dying from AIDS or cervical cancers or other promiscuity-based diseases, all direct results of Planned Parenthood's rigorously advocated sexual freedom.

Indeed, a pattern of lying to schoolchildren dominates Planned Parenthood's advice in government-sanctioned, tax-subsidized obscenity and pornography. In *Brave New World,* Aldous Huxley said the State could control the people if it could train schoolchildren to have sex. In *1984,* George Orwell writes that the State could control the people by giving them pornography. Both were on target. Thomas Sowell said:

CAUSAL EFFECT OF KINSEY'S FRAUDULENT "DATA"

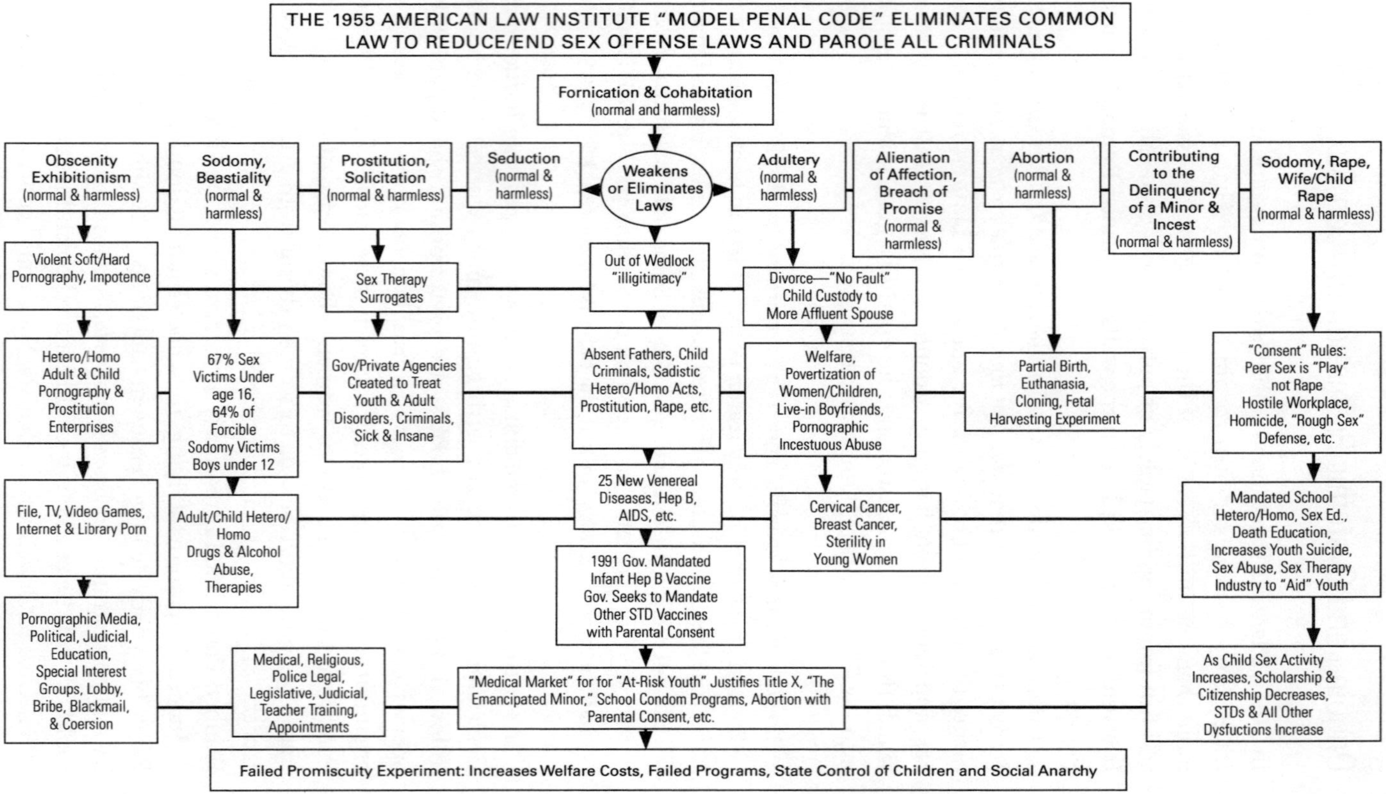

> The techniques of brainwashing. . . .are routinely used in psychological conditioning programs imposed on American school children. These include emotional shock and desensitization. . . stripping away defenses. . . and *inducing acceptance of alternative values*. . . . [614]

This description well defines the Rockefeller-funded Kinsey attack on Greatest Generation's morals. This is vividly displayed in the 1974 Rocky Mountain Planned Parenthood booklet, *You've Changed the Combination!*, which "shocked and desensitized" ninth grade students with pornographic drawings of nude, *Playboy*-style, large-breasted women towering over wimpy nude males, drawn without genitalia: that is, visually castrated.

You've Changed the Combination! warned naïve boys and girls that parents—who fear homosexuality—"force" boys to become *heterosexual*. "Your parents do not want you to be a homosexual," the manual states, "so they begin to focus you on girls sexually about the time you hit puberty" (p. 5). Brutally desensitizing impressionable boys, the authors instruct them to reject girls, who expect boys to open doors for them, pay the costs of an invited date, or to proffer other gentlemanly courtesies. Such girls, the pamphlet said, are not advanced (p. 8–9).

However the "good news" is in a new study Drs. John and Loretta Jemmott of the University of Pennsylvania that joins a long list of evaluations demonstrating the effectiveness of abstinence education. Robert Rector, Senior Research Fellow at The Heritage Foundation, confirmed the new study supports eleven of fifteen studies finding abstinence programs effective in reducing sexual activity. The Jemmott study finds that not only is real abstinence education highly effective in reducing youthful sexual activity, but that the "safe sex" and "comprehensive" sex ed programs addressed above are counterproductive.[615]

[CHAPTER 10]

Abortion Educator Saboteurs

> I fear the power of choice over life or death at human hands. I see no human being whom I could ever trust with such power—not myself, not any other. Human wisdom, human integrity are not great enough. Since the fetus is a creature already alive and in the process of development, to kill it is to choose death over life. At what point shall we allow this choice? . . . At no point, I repeat, either as life begins or as life ends, for we who are human beings cannot, for our own safety, be allowed to choose death, life being all we know.
>
> —Novelist Pearl S. Buck[616]

Kinsey's Amazing Data on Abortion

Three years after Kinsey's death, his disciples acknowledged that there was a dearth of "factual data" on the reproductive consequences of human sexuality—on births or abortions among married or unmarried females. So they said they would provide this "much-needed, factual information." The result was Kinsey's posthumous third volume, *Pregnancy, Birth and Abortion*, published by Kinsey Institute director Paul Gebhard and colleagues in 1958.

Gebhard's report detailed Kinsey's magical "findings," which he had allegedly recorded about abortion and contraception that his bogus female subjects used.[617] While this amazing information exists nowhere in Kinsey's first two volumes, the elite academic and legal professions accepted *Pregnancy, Birth and Abortion* at face value.

The true agenda of the eugenic Kinseyans was to encourage abortions among lower-income, minority, and "feeble-minded" women. To do so, they ignored the realities of Kinsey's study population and argued in *Pregnancy, Birth and Abortion* that their study population approximated the "socio-economic upper 20 percent of the urban population," though they acknowledged that this group might "include an overrepresentation of women who have been separated, divorced, or widowed." In fact, it included an overrepresentation of prostitutes, whom he disguised in his "data" as normal married women: Susie Homemaker and Rosie the Riveter.

The documentation of these interviews is off-limits to anyone but Kinsey Institute insiders; *to this day, no one has verified Kinsey's numbers.* But among these "elite" white women, they claimed, "between one quarter and one fifth had an induced abortion,"[618] and, of "pre-marital pregnancies that ended before marriage, 6 percent were live births, 5 percent spontaneous abortions, and 89 percent induced abortions."[619] So, only after Kinsey's death did his successors suddenly produce the statistic that 89 percent of single pregnant women and 25 percent of married pregnant women had aborted their babies—so popular, allegedly, was *illegal* abortion in America during World War II (even though, in wartime, women usually cling desperately to the children of fathers who may never return).

In fact, this was *zero* "science" here.

Abortion as Big Business

As millions of women have created and terminated babies, emotions run high for and against legalized abortion. How can they not? Pro-life activists view the killing of a child in the womb as the murder of an innocent life. On the other side of the debate, pro-abortion activists call unborn babies fetuses, lumps of "tissue," and "parasites." They are adamant that women have the legal right to kill them. After all, the unborn, they claim, feel no pain. So women are trained to distance themselves from the growing human being in their bellies as they fall prey to barbaric schemes *unimaginable* to women of The Greatest Generation.

Once abortion was legalized, Planned Parenthood clinics were a gold mine. To abort babies, they built an entire industry—with facilities, pharmaceuticals, pills, potions, therapeutic services, and medical professionals. In the economics of abortion, the earlier girls had sex, especially unmarried girls, the more babies, and the more would need to be aborted.

By 1971, Big Pharma and Big Sexology got their hands on millions of children in the healthcare system. But by 1976, heeding the outraged roar of a residually moralistic American public, Congress cut federal Medicaid funds for abortion, except in cases of life endangerment, rape, and/or incest. No free abortions for casual promiscuity. Nonetheless, thanks to the sexual revolution, sexual promiscuity increased, and the profits of Big Pharma and Big Sexology increased exponentially anyway. Sex, after all, was like cigarettes:[620] The sooner children started having sex or smoking, the greater the probability they would be *permanent* pawns of the sex and/or cigarette/alcohol/drug industries. And that was good for business.

At first, the abortions themselves were the moneymaker for Planned Parenthood and other abortion mills. But in time, as medical technology advanced, a great deal of money could be made by actually selling the "lump of tissue" in whole or in parts.

In partial birth abortion, the so-called *physician* pulls a live baby feet-first from his or her mother's womb, and then he stabs the infant through the back of the skull, to kill him or her.[621] For many of us, it is difficult to believe that this is legal in the United States of America, but this grizzly operation is performed all over the country by doctors who swore to uphold the Hippocratic Oath.

Partial-birth abortion, however, is preferable to the alternative, Dilatation and Evacuation (D&E). In D&E, the physician inserts an instrument into the womb to kill the baby. According to Life Dynamics, this method "delivers pieces of macerated organs that are usually unsuitable for fetal research, transplantation, etc. This may be the main reason for [pro-abortionists] vehement defense of the practice of partial-birth abortion."[622] Partial birth abortion, in which most of the baby is aborted intact, is *most* profitable.[623] And this is why the Sex Industry Complex (SIC) lobbies *so hard* to maintain their legal right to do it.

How could Americans have come to the brutal mass murder of

infants, sacrificing children for profit? The pathological Kinsey sect deserves some credit. The Kinsey lobby and the SIC worked for decades to solidify the sexual revolution, promoting promiscuity and fighting legal limits on everything from obscenity to abortion. They pushed us down the slippery slope, such that the Greatest Generation, looking down from the peak, would scarcely recognize their own descendents or the culture in which they live. Because women have become responsible for both conceiving and destroying their babies, and because women are now trained to distance themselves from the children in their wombs, too many *can* and *do* fall prey to violence unimaginable to women of the Greatest Generation.

Although human cloning is still on the drawing board, Big Pharma finds it especially valuable to harvest baby body parts from late-term abortions. The growing human trafficking in children now also includes embryonic body parts. It is unconscionable to pretend that entrepreneurs are not already using embryonic researchers as customers, a marketing opportunity for a profitable global trade in body parts, including embryonic stem cells.

According to the National Right to Life Web site:

> Embryonic stem cells are taken from aborted fetuses or clinically produced embryos. Adult stem cells are obtained from born children or adults. To date, research using embryonic stem cells has not had favorable results, while that using adult stem cells have in been very positive. . . Research cloning involves cloning human embryos for purposes such as pulling stem cells, after which the embryos die. Reproductive cloning involves allowing the cloned embryo to grow and be born.[624]

From embryonic stem-cell research to cloning and other fetal experiments, where does our scientific establishment draw the line? In H.G. Wells's 1896 novel, *The Island of Dr. Moreau*, a medical researcher creates an island of human-animal hybrids, "Leopard-Man" and "Swine-Folk." Frighteningly, one hundred years later, life imitates art. Modern researchers use *in vitro* manipulation, inserting embryonic cells from one species into the blastocyst of another. The resulting creature has the features of both species.[625] It is, indeed, a brave new world.

Science aside, the killing of children *inside* the womb naturally metastasized into violating—and even killing—children *outside* the womb. The next step, then, is that in addition to permitting mothers and doctors to kill unborn babies, we approve of violating and killing other people as the Incas and other prior civilizations did through child sacrifice. The evidence shows that maintaining a civilization depends on the severest of restraints, which *must* be found in our laws, for the *law* is our teacher, codifying our ideals if not always our actions.

So what, then, if authorities decide it is legitimate to kill brain-damaged people, whom the elitists first dehumanized as "vegetables"? That same society will eventually find it acceptable *and even prudent* to kill the sick, the old, and other burdensome people.

Once it gets a degree of societal freedom, evil knows no bounds.

That the legalization of abortion revolutionized America's social and moral order is agreed. We might also legitimately see the selling of infant body parts as exchanging the Judeo-Christian moral view for a neo-pagan moral view. We would do well to remember that this exchange has consequences.

Taxpayers Fund Planned Parenthood's Sexual Sabotage

American taxpayers gave Planned Parenthood more than $1.49 billion in the seven years after June 30, 1997. What for? Planned Parenthood admits "that it performed over a million (1,398,574) abortions from 1997 to 2003. . . . [With] profits of $350 million . . . government grants and contracts continue to be a large and growing portion of Planned Parenthood's revenue, growing from $165 million in 1997–98 to more than $265 million in 2003–04"[626] and $272 million for 2007.[627]

The STOPP chart reflects Planned Parenthood Federation of America's (PPFA) yearly abortion profits for 1977 to 2002. "[B]ased upon an estimated average cost of an abortion in each year," PPFA would have earned roughly $985,000,000 from aborting babies during 1977–2002.[628]

Planned Parenthood's sabotage of the unborn started even earlier. "[B]abies are not sweet little things," said the PPFA's Five-Year Plan

FIGURE 13
ESTIMATED PLANNED PARENTHOOD ABORTION INCOME 1977–2002

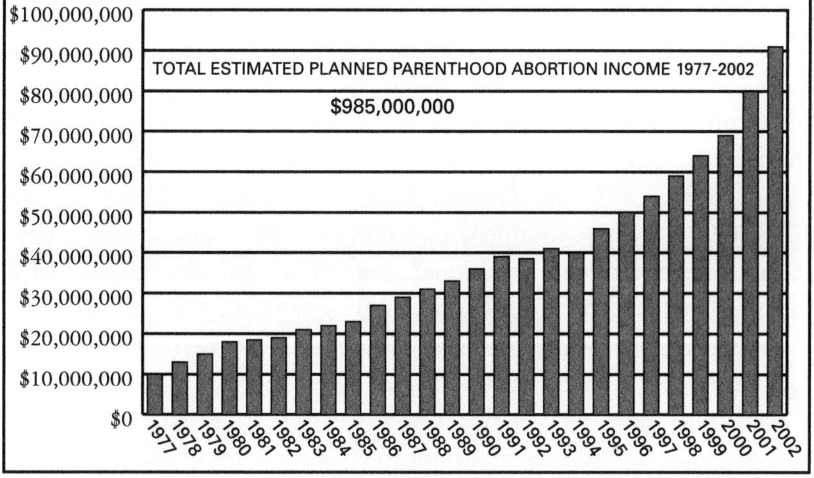

Source: Abortion numbers from Planned Parenthood Federation of America Service Report 1987, 1994, and Annual Reports 1994/95–2002/03. Abortion income estimated by STOPP International.

for 1975–1980. "They wet and dirty themselves, they get sick and they're very expensive to take care of. . . . Emphasis shall be put on services to . . . teenagers and young adults."

"Unwanted pregnancy should be considered a sexually transmitted condition of epidemic proportion," wrote David A. Grimes and Willard Cates, Jr., Association of Planned Parenthood Physicians (APPF) in a 1976 article. They added, "Legal abortion is an effective, safe, and curative treatment for that condition." ("Abortion as a Treatment for Unwanted Pregnancy: The Number Two Sexually Transmitted 'Disease.'")[629] (Figure 13)

More than twenty years later, according to Gloria Feldt, then-president of the PPFA, Planned Parenthood has "taken unequivocal and courageous stands . . . working for minors' access to abortion and contraception . . . and leading the way for abortion."[630]

Sad, but true.

In fact, Planned Parenthood and Big Pharma are leading the way in *profiting* from abortion, venereal disease treatment, and vaccines for sexual diseases. This profit depends upon *increasing* juvenile sexual promiscuity. Without massive teen fornication, Planned Parenthood would shrink drastically. Hence, since the late 1960s, Planned Parenthood has disguised titillating, Kinsey-based sex training as "sex education" for the "benefit" of millions of schoolchildren.

Not surprisingly, with billions in government grants and contracts over the last decades, Planned Parenthood invested millions in classroom promiscuity training, using *our* money to lie to our youth—and to do them fatal harm.

In *Making a Bloody Fortune*, Kelly Hollowell, MD, asked why Planned Parenthood's raunchy teen outreach Web site, teenwire.com, taught teenagers "the nutritional value of semen" also provided by another teen advisor "Go Ask Alice" along with the calorie content of "serving" of "a man's ejaculation." Expert "Alice" doesn't suggest *any* negatives in the girl's consumption of sperm, nor her age or the word "man" not "boy" to describe her partner(s). Alice is encouraging. Sperm is low in calories (important to youngsters these days). She adds that "gulping gallons" a day isn't a "substitute for real nutritious cuisine."[631] A review of both advice sites finds training for anal sex, oral sex and orientation experimentation. (Figure 14)

FIGURE 14

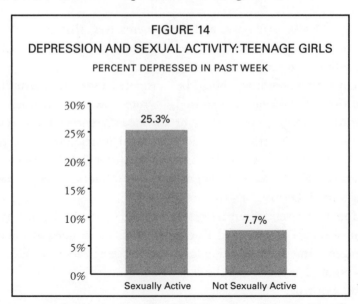

DEPRESSION AND SEXUAL ACTIVITY: TEENAGE GIRLS

PERCENT DEPRESSED IN PAST WEEK

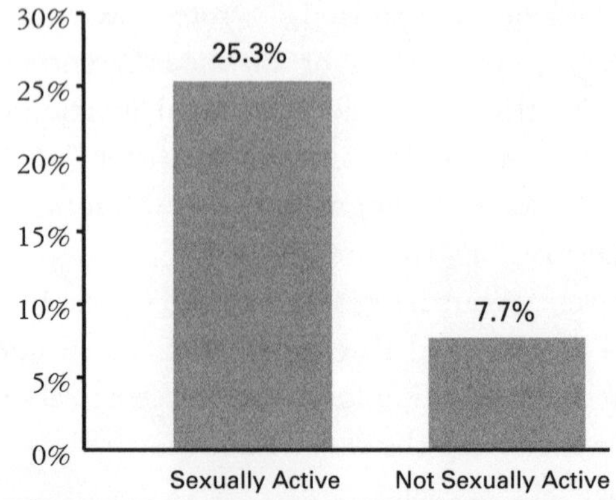

Source: National Logitudinal Survey of Adolescent Health, Wave II. 1996

Note: Teenage girls aged 14 to 17. Depressed means the girl responded that she felt depressed "a lot of the time" or "most or all of the time."

Sex "Ed" Shocked and Disturbed Teens

By the 1980s, Planned Parenthood's sex "education" lectures were often crudely pornographic. George Grant's *Grand Illusions: The Legacy of Planned Parenthood* details important testimony by girls who sat through a Planned Parenthood presentation on sex, contraception, pregnancy, and abortion. Grant writes, "Catherine told me later. . . 'I've never seen pornography before.'" After, the speaker passed a condom package to each girl and told the boys to "hold up a finger so that the girls could practice contraceptive application." The "shell-shocked" students followed orders.[632] As the class ended, some of the girls quietly cried. One ran out and vomited and another fainted. One girl reported that a "peer training project" had "filled her mind with all sorts of obscene ideas," "pushed her into sex," and "forced her into an abortion." In the end, she "hated what she'd become." Children's emotions are delicate and complex; indeed Catherine said one girl committed suicide.[633]

According to Grant, Planned Parenthood's Louis Harris 1986 national opinion survey found that:

- More than 87% of surveyed teens opposed in-school "comprehensive sexuality services";
- 67% said they didn't want "such services near their schools";
- 28% said they had had sexual intercourse;
- Almost all who had intercourse blamed "peer pressure;"
- Nearly 80% said they were too young to have intercourse.[634]

Planned Parenthood, though, did not listen to its own study. On an endless mission to force promiscuity on American youth, the organization does not care about venereal infections and abortions or depression and suicide. "The teens in the poll admitted that their comprehensive sex education courses had affected their behavior," Grant wrote.

"There was a fifty percent higher rate of sexual activity for them after the classes." Sadly, their understanding of the consequences of such activity was not correspondingly enhanced.[635] I'm reminded of the same reaction by teenagers to the subtly pro-grass film strip,

"Marijuana Update." After it was screened by the health teacher at Shaker Heights High School in the 1970s, one youth reported to me, "My friends left saying they were going to go get high!"

FIGURE 15
TEEN SUICIDE RATE

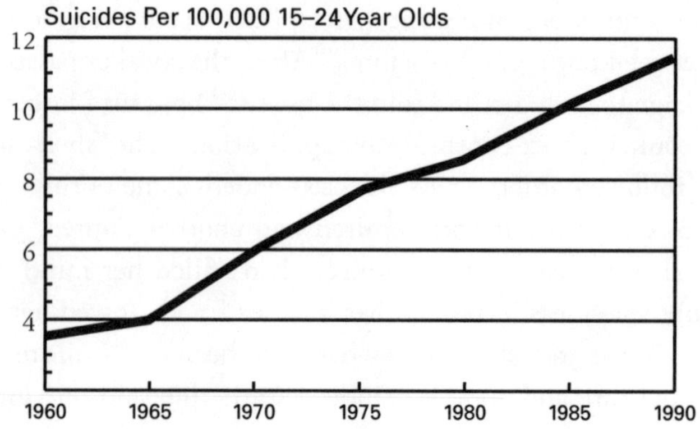

Source: National Center for Health Statistics

Preying upon schoolchildren, Planned Parenthood and SIECUS are but two of several evil, fraudulent, occult-like "sex-education" programs that perpetuate the Kinseyan sexual-revolution model. Their barbaric "sexperts" have been "educating" our children for more than half a century. Sadly, if they measure their success in pandemic childhood venereal disease, abortion, suicide, homicide, rape, child sexual abuse, depression, and despair, they have succeeded (Figure 15). Despite the horror stories, it is a miracle that *some* American youths retain their chastity, decency, and sensitivity. We should thank them and their parents.

Sexual Abuse of Students Explodes

Those who think that "educators," especially *female* teachers, cannot be pedophiles and pederasts have not been paying attention. Such naïveté has cost millions of children their innocence. Today, we have an epidemic of direct violation of children by educators—men *and* women.

Post-Kinsey, with pornography addiction running rampant, many teachers and other academic "professionals" have been convicted of Internet child pornography and other child abuse crimes. And schools and public libraries have increasingly housed predators—authorities who are dangerous to girls and boys.[636]

According to a 2004 *Education Week* report, Hofstra University professor Charol Shakeshaft reviewed published research, examining previous studies on "Educator Sexual Misconduct: A Synthesis of Existing Literature." Shakeshaft concluded that "the physical sexual abuse of students in schools is likely more than 100 times the abuse by priests."[637]

And no wonder! Our schools are filled with teachers who were sexually "trained" (as were many Catholic seminarians) by Kinseyan sex "educators." *Millions* of children might be victims of sexual misconduct by such eroticized teachers and other public school and library employees. Shakeshaft reports that school employees targeted roughly 10% of students with unwanted sexual attention—from libidinous remarks to rape.

A 2003 report by Grettje Timmerman supports Shakeshaft's findings. Timmerman found that a stunning 20% of girls and 8% of boys had been sexually harassed by an adult in school. Additionally, in a survey of high school graduates 17.7% of males and 82.2% of females reported sexual harassment by faculty or staff during their school careers. 13.5% of those surveyed said they had engaged in sexual intercourse with a teacher.[638] Several other studies confirm that sexual harassment in secondary schools is widespread, a "frequent public occurrence in the school culture."[639]

Survivors of Educator Sexual Abuse and Misconduct Emerge (SESAME)

While judges, prosecutors, and doctors have been convicted of child sexual abuse, the great majority of child predators seek out paid or volunteer positions that give them legitimate, easy access to children in schools, libraries, and churches and as music teachers, coaches, youth leaders, etc.

Survivors of Educator Sexual Abuse and Misconduct Emerge (SESAME), is an organization of educator abuse victims and their families. Organized to inform Americans about the toxic fallout from giving unquestioned authority to those in positions of educational guidance over children, SESAME provides a "Voice for the Prevention of Sexual Exploitation, Abuse, and Harassment of Students by Teachers and Other School Staff."

Pointing to a predatory subset of the teaching population, SESAME documented that sexual assault of children is not uncommon among educators, including those in schools and public libraries.[640] SESAME reported, "The best estimate is that 15% of students will be sexually abused by a member of the school staff during their school career."[641] "Many abusers are in positions of power or trust in relation to their victims which makes it easier to overcome a child's resistance."[642]

We now know that Kinsey, for example, "was deeply influenced in his "work" by five pedophile "headmasters who were quite clear they had very warm relationships with young adolescent boys of twelve or thirteen [in one New England area]."[643] Today, with many opportunities to eroticize schools and libraries, we must be concerned that adults who are "helping" children to understand their sexuality, are actually pedophiles or, at least, naïve supporters. Particularly as pornography seduces and habituates educated men and women, children are increasingly at risk from this growing molester constituency.[644]

Consider the case of the president of Washington, D.C.'s American University. Richard Berendzen, PhD, was convicted of terrorizing women with obscene phone calls, requesting sex with their children. Using pornography at his desk, Berendzen called one woman, claiming to have a four-year-old sex slave caged in his basement. Forewarned by university authorities that the police were about to drag him off, Berendzen employed a standard legal dodge—fleeing to the Johns Hopkins sex clinic for "treatment." In three weeks, "therapists" (who shared the pedophile bias of the Johns Hopkins sex clinic founder, John Money, PhD, pronounced Berendzen recovered. Soon he returned to teach AU students and, now, as an approved victim, he lectures at child protection conferences on his own early incest abuse. The heroic woman who turned him in—an incest victim herself—had to move from her home, without recourse or recovery from her presidential violation.

Like most sexual psychopaths, Berendzen tried to protect himself by collecting men around him who hid similar secrets—or who were unquestioningly obedient to authority. Not coincidentally then, in 1986, five years before Berendzen's capture, a nine-year-old girl reported that the AU psychology department head, Elliot McGinnies, PhD, molested her in his trailer at The Pine Tree Nudist Colony in Crownsville, Maryland.[645] McGinnies also ran the legal dodge—sprinting off to a mental health clinic before facing the courtroom. Eventually he received a confusing sort of clearance from the local judge with no explanation as to why the liberated nudist needed a quick therapy dose prior to his amnesty.[646] Apparently degrees in higher education *do not* necessarily restrain predatory child molesters.

A major problem, educator sexual abuse has increased with the mainstreaming of pornographic stimuli. Clearly, *we are in an era of serious sexual addiction and dysfunction*—estimated by some as perhaps half of our male population and a smaller but significant number of our female population.[647] Therefore, allowing *any* adult to provide *any* graphic sexual information to children places those children at risk. The educator who does so is suspect; there is no longer *any justification* for special rights for librarians to expose children to "harmful matter."[648] An informed and sophisticated distrust of *anyone* who presents such material to children is vital to the health and welfare of America's youth.

News Flash: Epidemic *Female* Teacher Pedophiles

In 2005–2010 news about female teachers molesting students bombarded us. Although the number of male teacher-molesters has rabidly increased in the "Internet" years, the female pedophile epidemic is especially telling; this toxic flood lays at the feet of the sexual revolution and *certainly* at mainstream pornography.

On October 20, 2005, Andy Decker raised useful questions about female teacher-abusers in an Internet essay on *Free Republic*, citing the *Peoria Journal Star*. Decker provided a list of such women, "a coast to coast sample of those who work in public schools as bus drivers, substitutes, and full-time teachers." Many if not most of these teachers are NEA members, he notes. These names only capture *some* of those charged from 2003 to 2009 of heterosexual and some homosexual abuse of vulnerable students. See TeacherCrime.com. The Web site itself indicates that it is not responsible for its content nor does it validate the claims against the individuals listed on the site. So check press reports on the Internet for local, national, and international updates on these charges to verify if the accused has been found *innocent or guilty* of the charges in a court of law. *This is not a complete list*:

Robin Gialanella
Stephanie Burleson
Shelley Allen
Sandra "Beth" Geisel
Maria Saco
Amber Marshall
Elisa Kawasaki
Nicola Prentice
Elizabeth Miklosovic
Rhianna Ellis
Samantha Solomon
Gwen Ann Cardozo
Elizabeth Stow
Lynn Samuels
Nicole Andrea Barnhart
Laura Lynn Findlay
Kelly Lynn Dalecki
Lakina Stutts
Rachelle Vantucci
Donna Carr Galloway
Carol Flannigan
Toni Lynn Woods
Amber S. Jennings
Debra Lafave
Kim Alexander
Kathy Denise White
Susanne Eble
Rebecca Boicelli
Angela M. Stellwag
Bethany Sherrill
Harriet Laquette Gordon
Katherine Tew
Adrianne Hockett
Margaret de Barraicua
Mary Kay Letourneau
Melissa Michelle Deel
Nicole Pomerleau
Sarah Saslorio
Laura L. Findlay
Pamela Charles
Christina Gallagher
Lisa Suitter
Tiffany Copley
Tammy Lee Huggins
Pamela Rogers Turner
LaDona Rangel
Melissa Daw Green
Kimberly Merson
Georgianne Harrell[649]

Andy Decker notes the gross "sexualization of our nation" and the "double standards" of very light punishments for female pedophiles. Decker asks: What is the NEA's role in this flood of teacher abusers? What are the states doing about these public employees? What attention are we giving to this problem?[650]

Apparently, not enough. On December 22, 2006, WorldNetDaily published a record of female pedophile teachers, starting with Stephanie

Giambelluca. Police say the sexual abuse of a twelve-year-old male student was recorded on videotape by the boy's babysitter.[651] Here are a few more examples:

Amber Marshall, 23: Indiana teacher, confessed to sex with several high school students.[652]

Amy Gail Lilley, 36: Florida softball coach, two years of house arrest and eight years of probation for sex with a fifteen-year-old girl.[653]

Angela Comer, 26: Kentucky, fled with her fourteen-year-old male student, pled guilty.[654]

Angela Stellwag, 24: a New Jersey mayor's daughter and substitute teacher pled guilty to having sex in her apartment with a fourteen-year-old boy.

Beth Raymond, 31: Connecticut private-school employee was sentenced to eighteen months in prison for sexual assault of a juvenile male.[655]

Brandy Lynn Gonzales, 27: Texas teacher pled guilty to sexually assaulting five elementary school students with her husband, who pled guilty to sex acts with one teen.[656]

Cameo Patch, 29: Utah substitute teacher, guilty of having sex with a seventeen-year-old high school male. She received no jail time.[657]

Laura J. Obzera: Bolingbrook Illinois elementary school nurse confessed to sex with a boy.[658]

Jessica Bailey Wishnask: North Carolina, middle school teacher caught in "Intimate contact" with a boy.[659]

Tawni Wimberley, 29: Arizona technology teacher, pled guilty to sex with two male minors.[660]

Gay Turley, 42: Arizona PE teacher, softball coach, pled guilty to sex with a former girl student.[661]

Heather Chesser, 27: Tennessee, substitute teacher at alternate school pled guilty to statutory rape of a boy student.[662]

Jennifer Mally, 27: Arizona, married English teacher, cheerleader, guilty of sex with boy student.[663]

Carol Flannigan, 50: Florida, music teacher convicted of sex with eleven-year-old student and his father.[664]

Carrie McCandless, 29: Colorado social-studies teacher (married to the principal), pled guilty to sex with a boy.[665]

Cathy Heminghaus, 46: Missouri special-ed teacher, convicted of statutory sodomy on two middle-school boy students.[666]

Christine Scarlett, 36: Ohio high school English teacher, pled guilty to sex with a seventeen-year-old student, gave birth to his son, was fired, and served a short sentence.[667]

Darcie Esson, 32: Colorado English teacher, pled guilty to sex with a seventeen-year-old student on the floor of her hotel room (while her two small children and their seventeen-year-old babysitter, slept in the same room).[668]

Deborah Reeder, 45: Florida teacher, pled guilty to sex with her son's seventeen-year-old boy friend.[669]

Diane DeMartini-Scully, 45: New York school psychologist at a Long Island middle school, jailed for sex with a sixteen-year-old, supplying him with drugs and condoms for sex with a thirteen-year-old girl.[670]

Erica Rutters, 29: Pennsylvania teacher at a Christian academy, pled guilty to corruption of a minor, got three years probation.[671]

Franca and Antonia Munoz-Juvera, 26: California math and chemistry teachers and twin sisters, convicted of molestation of an underage female student. A female roommate who "facilitated the crime" was also convicted.[672]

Jacquelyn Faith Garrison, 19: North Carolina substitute teacher at a high school, pled guilty to an improper relationship with a fifteen-year-old student.[673]

Janelle Marie Bird, 24: Florida Christian school teacher, acted out sexually with a fifteen-year-old student and got two years in state prison.[674]

Kristen Margrif, 27: Michigan teacher, received a one-year delayed sentence for sex with a sixteen-year-old student.[675]

Kristi Dance Oakes, 32: Tennessee biology teacher resigned from her high school post. She pled guilty, receiving up to six months in jail.[676]

Laura Lynn Findlay, 30: Michigan band teacher at a middle school, charged with sex with at least five young students. Sentenced to seven to twenty-five years in prison.[677]

Michelle Kush, 29: Kentucky substitute teacher at a high school, committed two counts of rape and sodomy with a fifteen-year-old boy. She got sixty days in jail, thirty days house arrest, and five years probation.[678]

Pamela Balogh, 39: New Jersey gym teacher and coach at a Catholic high school, pled guilty to sex with a fifteen-year-old female student over ten months.[679]

Pamela Rogers Turner, 27: Tennessee model-turned-elementary teacher, guilty of sex with a thirteen-year-old boy. After sentencing, she sent the boy nude photos and sex videos of herself and got seven years in prison for parole violations.[680]

Robin Winkis, 29: Pennsylvania high school English teacher, pled guilty to sex with a seventeen-year-old boy and was sentenced to two to twenty-three months in jail.[681]

Traci Tapp, 28: New Jersey gym teacher at a New Jersey high school, pled guilty to sex with three sixteen-year-old students and got no jail time.[682]

For extensive January 2010 updates see "WOMEN WITH TROUBLES,"[683] identifying women arrested for child sexual abuse, including female teacher-abusers.[684] The use of pornography by educators and administrators had been rampant for years. The pervasive acceptance of pornography is the elephant in the room, the toxins in the sexual waters, the "tipping point" for most, if not all these predators. Consider these school reports of male and female predators:

- A school superintendent had an affair with the president of the parent-teacher organization, exchanging emails with sexual pictures of children.[685]
- The president of the Broward Teachers Union mailed Internet pornography to a police officer posing as a fourteen-year-old girl.[686]
- An Iowa middle school principal was arrested for child pornography and "sexual exploitation of a minor."[687]
- A New Jersey school superintendent was arrested for sexually-explicit Internet conversations with what he thought was a thirteen-year-old girl.[688]
- An Illinois school superintendent used the school district computer to view Internet pornography.[689]
- A college professor was arrested for distributing thousands of child-pornography images on the Internet, pandering obscenity involving a minor, promoting prostitution, unauthorized use of property, wiretapping, and tampering with evidence.[690]
- A Wisconsin teacher was arrested for child enticement and solicitation for "using the Internet to arrange a sexual encounter with a police officer posing as a fourteen-year-old girl."[691]

- A Massachusetts high school teacher engaged in online sex acts after recruiting teenage girls to watch him.[692]
- A Maryland drama teacher was indicted for child pornography.[693]
- An Orange County, California school bus driver was convicted December 2009 of molesting and taking pornographic photos of three girls.[694]
- Scores of school bus drivers have been arrested for child pornography. One in Maryland was charged with sodomy, aggravated sexual abuse, sexual abuse, and endangering the welfare of a child.[695]
- An Oklahoma Sunday-school teacher got over twenty-four years in prison for Internet-associated sex crimes against minors.[696]
- Sex abuse at the premier American Boychoir School in Trenton, New Jersey, was so pervasive that administrators who sodomized male students thought molestation produced a world-class choir, according to a lawyer for a former victim.[697]
- A former Warwick high school coach allegedly seduced and had sex with a fifteen-year-old girl at his home when his wife and children were out.[698]
- An elementary school educator in Virginia was charged with having images of nude youths and using his computer to solicit children.[699]
- Child pornography was found on a California math teacher's home computer.[700]

[CHAPTER 11]

Sabotaging Schools and Libraries

> Banned Books Week is not a celebration of free speech. It's a way for leftwing bureaucrats to bully ordinary citizens by stigmatizing those who complain with nasty names such as "bigots," "screamers," and "book burners." The purpose is to intimidate parents from ever complaining about books that are given to their own children.
>
> —Phyllis Schlafly, *Eagle Forum*, December 4, 2009

Sabotaging Your Public Library: A Tax-Paid Peep Show

Schools are not the only place where child sex abuse is prevalent, and teachers are not the only predators. Conservative leaders like attorney and former public school teacher, Phyllis Schlafly, have long argued that our libraries were under the control of sexual saboteurs, men and women who sought to overturn parental rights in favor of those of elitist revolutionaries.

All of our lives, most of us have gone to public libraries, finding them wholly safe and friendly environments. However, due to the forceful defense of pedophile rights by members of the American Library Association (ALA), child molesters now feel free to carry on their activities *in our public libraries*.

One paroled pedophile crawled under a library table and molested a six-year-old girl at a Spokane, Washington public library.[701] Her father had walked away to get her first library card. Typically, the predator's lawyer argued that the convicted child molester needed more "treatment." He will serve "at least 15 years."

The ALA has battled all attempts by sane, independent-minded Americans to reinstate laws that will protect our rights to a safe and civilized public library that excludes known psychopaths.

We might ponder how the righteous librarian with the horn-rimmed glasses degenerated into a peep show proprietor. The NEA and the ALA refused to self-police, so, in 2000, Congress passed the Children's Internet Protection Act, which required schools and libraries to use filtering software to block Internet material considered obscene or harmful to minors. The U.S. Supreme Court reaffirmed the law against a challenge in 2003. Those who refuse to comply—as some librarians do—have lost significant federal funding for their communities.[702] Based on "free speech," they defend their actions despite direct harm to children and the general community. Defending pornography rights is standard Kinseyan education, which the librarians received in their college educations.

But of course, Big Pornography has rewarded ALA leaders (who protect *their* sexual secrets) for its support for years.[703] The pornography industry (the "Sex Industrial Complex") has publicly funded the ALA, which is also a member of "The Media Coalition" (also funded by Big Pornography). On the evidence, these entities have conflicts of interest between their duty to society and their fiduciary duty to Big Pornography. Given the incestuous relationship between these organizations, it is no surprise that the ALA often acts as a friend of pornographers in court cases. In *New York v. Ferber,*[704] for example, the ALA fought for Ferber, a child pornography distributor, arguing that filming for-profit child sexual abuse qualified as *freedom of expression*! This was not an isolated effort. In 1994, the ALA again pleaded for Big Pornography's right to sexually exploit children; the United States District of Columbia Court of Appeals repudiated this case.[705]

The ALA-Playboy-NAMBLA Connection

In 1993, San Francisco's ALA allowed the North American Man Boy Love Association (NAMBLA) to use a library room as a meeting place for their regular monthly meetings. The local television station,

KRON, broadcast a report by Gregg Lyon, who noted the NAMBLA mission to help their members safely meet and molest children. "We're talking about children as young as three years old."[706] According to KRON's report:

> The . . . . San Francisco Public Library on a Saturday afternoon: downstairs, children—some with parents, some by themselves. And upstairs, this scene captured by our Target 4 hidden camera. This is the regular monthly meeting of NAMBLA, the North American Man-Boy Love Association. This is not a counseling session, not an attempt to help NAMBLA members control their lust for children. Quite the opposite. On this day the group discussed putting together a calendar of nude boys as a fundraiser.[707]

Lending our tax-funded facilities and the ALA's considerable prestige to aid pederasts and child pornographers reveals the ALA leaders' commitment to normalize a historically "anti-American" cultural standard: adult sexual assault of children. Preserving "free speech" for predators or a safe environment for their victims?

Freedom to Read . . . Or Freedom to Rape?

The ALA refused to filter criminal and violent obscenity, even from children, and even despite a mandate from legislators; for years the ALA's pornographer elite has controlled our libraries and librarians. For example, and no doubt influencing ALA's support of pornographers in scores of judicial cases, *Playboy* has given substantial donations to The American Library Association's "Freedom To Read Foundation." For substantiation, see "A Look at the Playboy Foundation's record." [708]

When the ALA works to bring "harmful matter" *produced by one of its financial patrons* into our libraries, a significant conflict of interest is obvious. For example, the ALA defended using children of all ages in the most vile obscenity, as in the *Ferber* case. The ALA defended *Playboy* via its "Freedom to Read Foundation" in the 1996 case, *Playboy v. United States*.[709] In service to their pornographic patrons, the ALA rode roughshod over the public interest with the "Freedom to Read Foundation," while the American people were trying to eliminate "signal bleed, the partial reception" of pornographic cable television shows "in the homes of nonsubscribers to that programming." That the ALA is in direct conflict with the majority of the tax-paying public is visible by the hostile reactions of the polity to the ALA effort to turn *our public libraries* into local dirty bookstore monopolies.

"Are Children Safe in Public Libraries?" NO, not at all safe. What *normal* person would use a library computer to view pornography? And where do they take their arousal? On January 11, 2010, even the *San Francisco Chronicle* reported, "The bathrooms often have proved downright scary, with people doing drugs, bathing in the sinks and having sex in the stalls. . . . But the library has, well, begun to turn the page on the problem by hiring what is believed to be the country's first full-time psychiatric social worker stationed in a public library," to watch the bathrooms. How civilized.

On point, Safe Libraries also reported suggestions by a reporter from January 9, 2010 that "patrons have been caught performing sex acts in the library bathrooms and between library stacks. Always bring hand sanitizer when visiting the computer lab. . . .people are viewing pornography on these computers and well . . .masturbating. Library staff rarely ever cleans the keyboards and mice are in the computer labs so they are NASTY! So if using library computers, please bring hand sanitizer. . ."[710]

Ah, education. Realistically, computers are so inexpensive now that only the most out-of-control predators would risk using pornography in a public library. The fact remains that non-filtered libraries *do* attract predators. For example:

- A paroled pedophile used the Grand Rapids, Michigan Library to email "nude photos of himself to a fourteen-year-old girl."[711]
- A Pell City Board of Education Alabama chamber of commerce chairman used the Homewood public library to access child pornography.[712]
- A Chicago paroled pedophile "downloaded child pornography from computers at the Vernon Hills Public Library," and returned to download more child pornography.[713]
- A fifty-five-year-old Chicago librarian was found with a suitcase of computer-generated images of children as young as six years, performing various sexual acts.[714]

- A paroled predator was caught downloading pornography at a Perris, California library.
- A twice-convicted incest/child molester left his resume and child pornography in a bathroom at the Cleveland Public Library.[715]
- In 2006, CBS Broadcasting reported, "Thirty-three sex crimes were committed at Chicago's Harold Washington Library alone in the last three years."
- "[A]t Chicago libraries . . . we could actually see a patron looking at porn simply by standing on a city street and looking through the window."[716]

Obviously, pedophiles—including known sex offenders—access pornography and look for child victims in our public libraries.

In 2003, the ALA encouraged librarians to reject the Children's Internet Protection Act that would protect children from library pornography and get their funds elsewhere. The U.S. Supreme Court upheld the CIPA on June 23, 2003, allowing budgets to be withheld absent blocking software. "The 6–3 Supreme Court ruling held that CIPA does not violate the First Amendment because public libraries do not offer Internet access "to create a public forum for Web publishers [but] to facilitate research, learning, and recreational pursuits by furnishing materials of requisite and appropriate quality." As to filters' tendency to block constitutionally protected speech, the then Chief Justice William H. Rehnquist wrote that, because CIPA allows librarians to disable a filter "without significant delay on an adult user's request," the goal of "protecting young library users from material inappropriate for minors" outweighs any temporary inconvenience to adults."[717]

Sabotaging Religious and Secular Educators on Human Sexuality

Remember, for the last forty years—until the recent growth of serious "intimacy" training for Christian sex addicts—religious *and* secular educators also received "human sexuality" training from Kinsey disciples. Shakeshaft reported that 10,667 youths reported sexual abuse by priests in more than five decades, from 1950 to 2002, while roughly 290,000 youths endured some sort of sexual abuse by a *public school employee* in just *one* decade, 1991 to 2000. The Catholic League for Religious and Civil Rights asked why the mass media ignored the Shakeshaft report: "Isn't it news that the number of public school students who have been abused by a school employee is more than 100 times greater than the number of minors who have been abused by priests?"[718]

Still, media coverage of the Catholic priest abuse scandal was relentless. The *National Catholic Register* pointed out the bias, reporting, "a search on the media database LexisNexis for 'Carol Shakeshaft' turned up no articles eight days after' the *Education Week* report."[719]

Unfortunately, Catholic libraries and institutions had long (naïvely) relied on the same sexuality "professionals" that teach students in other schools and colleges. These are "sex-ed" teachers in the Planned Parenthood vein, as all such "credible" educators used Kinseyan pansexual books to sweep aside the traditional view of American—and certainly Catholic—morality. Many of the Church's key sexuality advisors became entrenched protagonists of Kinsey Institute bi/homosexual pathologies.

Michael Rose's *Good bye! Good Men* and similar reports on the downside of homosexuality document some consequences of Catholic institutions, particularly seminaries, that relied on Kinseyan dogma. Such pathological training materials were often used in seminary admissions criteria, psychological testing, teaching, textbooks, and "counseling." Screening psychologists purged many priesthood candidates as "immature" because they rebuffed the "diversity" that the psychologist or diocesan hierarchy pandered. Thus, a few key homosexual Catholic bishops and other leaders destroyed the vocational aims of legitimate Catholics, from the early 1970s, accepting instead potential and active homosexual pederasts and licentious heterosexuals, who would keep their crimes secret. Sexually harassed or dismissed, seminarians represent a class of potential plaintiffs for suffering under the auspices of these bogus sexperts. Having written extensively on this issue, I have urged the Catholic public to sue those who held themselves out as "sexperts," for such sexperts were responsible for purging orthodox seminarians, especially those who rejected homosexual experimentation as legitimate Catholic theology.

Two glaring examples stand out, illustrating how the Church's response to sexuality fell into the hands of saboteurs. First, on the evidence, many seminarians were trained in sexuality via the program George Leonard described in *Esquire*, "Sexual Attitude Restructuring" (SAR, later called "Reassessment").[720] Pomeroy's IASHS created the so-called "f**karama" program, a "sensory overload" of brainwashing via up to fourteen screens of all manner of simultaneous pornography.

Second, according to the *Boston Globe* and the homosexual periodical, *The Advocate*, Fred Berlin, MD, is a major Catholic commission advisor on issues of child sex abuse.[721] In 1994, Berlin was course director for a training program sold to judges, "health professionals," lawyers, legislators, police officers, and child advocacy workers. Among other things, Berlin taught that "pedophilia . . . can be effectively controlled with appropriate psychiatric intervention." To that end, Berlin co-founded a celebrated sexual training and treatment center, the Johns Hopkins Sexual Disorders Clinic, with his mentor, John Money, PhD.[722] In an interview with the pedophile periodical, the *Journal of Paedophilia,* John Money said that their clinic was designed to offer "leeway to judges" to free convicted child molesters.[723] Money further offered that adult sex with children is normal and often beneficial and stated, "regarding paedophilia [*sic*] that I would never report anybody."[724] A dedicated Kinsey disciple, Money was a mentor for June Reinisch (the third Kinsey Institute director), and served on the advisory boards of the Kinsey Institute and Big Pornography's incest-pushing periodical, *Penthouse Forum*.[725]

Thus, Money—and Berlin—present the Catholic Church with a problem. The founder of St. Luke's Institute, Rev. Michael R. Peterson, MD (who died of AIDS), *urged* the church to rely on Berlin and Money in a 1985 paper, after warning the clergy that they should avoid potential abuse suits by following the well-qualified Money and Berlin:

> [T]he two mental health professionals are considered by me and most people in the field as the two U.S. experts and ones who have had good success in treatment of the paraphilic disorders in the past fifteen years (circa 1970) at their Clinic.[726]

But Berlin and Money promised child molesters a free ride. "We will not, however, report to your Probation Officer information you tell us as a part of the normal doctor-patient privileged relationship," said their official welcoming paperwork.[727] Several articles from Maryland papers also document Berlin's efforts to "exempt specialists from reporting pedophiles even when their crimes continue during treatment."[728]

By 1988, "at least eight men [were] convicted of sexually abusing Maryland children while under treatment" at the Johns Hopkins clinic.[729] The Maryland attorney general rejected Berlin's demand that he be allowed to cover up ongoing child rape by his patients, though we have no evidence that Berlin has complied. Now, Paul McHugh, MD, former Johns Hopkins director of psychiatry and a member of the Baltimore Archdiocese's Independent Review Board on Child Sexual Matters, oversaw Berlin's efforts to protect active pedophiles in treatment at Johns Hopkins.[730] And the sickness spreads. St. Luke's is a primary treatment center for pedophile priests.[731] The current director, Rev. Stephen J. Rossetti, naturally praises Money and Berlin, since he shares their cover-up policies.

> [St. Luke's] officials maintained that they were not legally required to make such [ABUSE] reports, and they argued that doing so would violate doctor-patient confidentiality.[732]

Thus, Kinseyan psychopaths provided guidance to Catholic leaders and other religious denominations, just as they assisted those in other "helping" professions. With such training, it is not surprising that sexual abuse of children by "educators" and other experts worsens each year.

Church advisers—like Peterson, Money, and Berlin—and their institutional sponsors, such as Johns Hopkins University, the Kinsey Institute, and the Institute for the Advanced Study of Human Sexuality, etc., are highly *vulnerable for medical malpractice, fraud, negligence, and other claims*. Berlin's claims of pedophile priest cures would have meant that many "treated" pederasts and pedophiles have returned to their duties. Of course, even the Government Accounting Office's 1996 report on sex offenders—spanning fifty years and five hundred therapeutic programs—found no form of psychotherapy that actually stopped such predators.[733]

As an educational endeavor, the work of Kinsey in the 1940s united deviant sexuality with operant conditioning to initiate an earnest attack on the American educational system. In its breadth and depth, it worked. Since 1955, Planned Parenthood and SIECUS taught Kinsey's bi/homosexual pornographic lunacy to public, private, and parochial youth, from kindergarten school and public libraries through postgraduate programs. And since Kinsey, the madness of American "sex education" has fueled the profits and power of the Sex Industrial Complex, while every sexual trauma has skyrocketed.

Conservative attorney, and former school teacher, Phyllis Schlafly, recently asked, "Who defines American culture?" She wrote that the "Policies Commission" to revolutionize education stalled until the 1960s. Many children were taught not only the "basics, but also values such as honesty and patriotism."[734] By the late 1960s, though, millions of children danced to the Kinsey/Guyon tune: "chastity cannot be a virtue because it is not a natural state." This immorality came courtesy of a gang of sexual psychopaths—Kinsey Institute clones who trained SIECUS and Planned Parenthood to be our nation's "sex educators." Kinsey's pathologies thus sabotaged education and public and school libraries, seeping into the cracks of our shaky "learning" system, causing sexual suicide.

Now librarians eagerly stock the Kinsey clan, Planned Parenthood, SIECUS materials. Yet, on October 23, 2009, Parents and Friends of Ex-Gays & Gays (PFOX) reported that *Ex-Gay books are banned*, that books like *My Genes Made Me Do It!: A Scientific Look at Sexual Orientation* that finds sexuality determined by nurture not just biology, "can't get a spot on the school library shelf." Nor can *You Don't Have to Be Gay*," author Jeff Konrad's struggle to overcome his unwanted same-sex attractions. PFOX argues that libraries only shelve books that push bi/homosexuality. They say, as of October 2009, "Baby Be-Bop," is on the shelves for children. It has sex scenes in bathroom stalls with men the "gay" teen "never talks to." *Love & Sex: Ten Stories of Truth*, describes a boy's sex with his tutor, "Matt." His "d— was smashed between his stomach and my thigh. And as his hand jerked up and down on me his hips humped with the same rhythm." These are not "banned" books.[735]

Thus have Kinsey's pathologies percolated down through the educational system; AIDS gave the sex-ed lobby a blank check. Purporting to save children's lives, the disordered "experts" promoted every form of deviant sex. In tandem, the American Library Association, with ties to the pornography industry, turned the local library into a local peep show as pornographers and pedophiles reaped financial rewards and child victims.

In education's eroticized culture, sexual abuse of students exploded. Arrests of teachers, administrators, and librarians have become commonplace, while Kinsey's pathological training also encouraged priest abuse.

Since 2000, America's college-educated movers and shakers have exponentially *increased* their reliance on Kinsey, arguably more than doubling the references to his "data." While computerized records only began in the early 1980s, Kinsey's initial impact on our laws and social conduct occurred between 1948 and 1960. Likely, Kinsey and his disciples control 95 percent of all college texts, reports, essays, and opinion on sexuality from 1948 until today.

With authority figures teaching students to masturbate and put condoms on one another's fingers in enlightened classrooms across America, it is no accident that Kinsey's message to "fornicate early, fornicate often, fornicate in every possible way" is now entrenched, legally and socially.[736] As noted earlier, if a dirty old man (or woman) in the park put a condom on a cucumber in front of kids, he'd go to an institution for the criminally insane. But if a teacher does the same in the classroom—and requires students to participate—we pay him (or her) $60,000 a year and call him a "family life educator."

[CHAPTER 12]

Pandemic, Predatory Criminals

The simple and rather frightening truth is that under circumstances of legal and social permissiveness, people will engage in the most outrageous criminal behavior.[737]

—Hannah Arendt, Philosopher, *Eichmann in Jerusalem*

IN *ATKINS V. VIRGINIA* (2002), Daryl Atkins abducted and killed an innocent airman. Because a psychologist found Atkins "mildly mentally retarded" the Court majority ruled Atkins should not get the death penalty. Justice Scalia protested that the founders did not excuse the mentally retarded from capital punishment, and protested that since the majority objected to capital punishment at all, it was not the Constitution but "the feelings and intuition of a majority of the Justices that count . . . the perceptions of decency, or of penology, or of mercy, entertained . . . by the majority of the small and unrepresentative segment of our society that sits on this Court."[738]

The ideas of judges have consequences.

Once the academic elite began its black propaganda campaign in 1948, the increase in all forms of sexual abuse was preordained. Since the Greatest Generation stood in the way of this brave new world, Kinsey needed to marginalize fathers in order to capture their children. That is what happened. Many men—even fathers, and even judges and future judges—believed Kinsey, who effectively eliminated fathers as the moral and legal protectors and providers for their families. Women and children are on their own.

Kinsey's sex science frauds claimed widespread sexual promiscuity, spawning the sexual "freedom" of adultery and an epidemic of divorce that, in turn, increased child abandonment, child crime, and child victimization.

Though I was a child in the big "sin city" of Los Angeles in 1948, my world was safe and innocent. But the Kinsey lobby soon bred sexual predators by the thousands—eventually by the tens of thousands. Justifying and then legalizing their perverted crimes, and instilling distrust and fear between men and women, the Kinsey cult ate away at our civility. Our American progenitors had battled black slavery, sex slavery, wage slavery, economic depressions, foreign and domestic wars, and massive waves of immigration. Thanks to the common law's Judeo-Christian political and social moral vision—the "Protestant work ethic"—a twentieth-century middle class emerged. This culture prized hard work as salvation and stressed the importance of sobriety (both sexual and intoxicant). With this ethic and commitment to God as the bedrock of our national prosperity, America became affluent.

In 1932, well before Kinsey burst onto the front pages of national and international acclaim, his close friend, French pedophile judge, René Guyon, had worked out the legislative strategy in 1932 for abolishing child protections. In fact, Guyon helped craft the legal language that Kinsey asserted as his own words in both his *Male* and *Female* volumes, brazenly portraying adult sexual abuse of children as natural—as basic as eating or breathing. Guyon argued that chastity was abnormal but any sex act—anything—was normal. The flyleaf of Guyon's book *Sex Life and Sex Ethics* (1933) said:

> He proceeds to the discussion of onanism, incest, homosexuality, fetishism, and even such "extraordinary" variations as necrophilia and coprophilia, all of which he considers to fall within the limits of the normal.[739]

This Guyon book was issued in English coterminous with Kinsey's *Male* volume, wrapped in the mantle of Kinsey's authority as he quoted from Kinsey's just-published 1948 "findings." Once Kinsey "proved" that it was both commonplace and natural to commit all manner of deviant sexual offenses, the law soon followed suit, insulating offenders from legal recrimination, rather than protecting women and children from their predation. Kinsey's legal followers saw to it that such attitudes were adopted into American law.

Before Kinsey, our laws had come to reflect the delicacy of human emotions, the harm of domestic betrayal, the critical importance of sexual dignity for all people. Enter Kinsey, who, himself, served on the Illinois Commission on Sex Offenders' workgroup to devise the "Framework for Sex Offender Law." Blaming the lack of sex education for high levels of sex crimes in the early 1950s, Kinseyan reformers testified tirelessly before state legislatures and asserted in professional, academic, and legal literature that "sex education" would reduce the number of sex crimes and high recidivism rates.[740]

Law reformers promoted Kinsey's fundamental assertion that human beings are sexual from birth.[741] In the world of law, this came to mean that *small children could be "provocateurs."* For example, Kinsey's colleague, the oft-quoted psychiatrist and law professor, Ralph Slovenko, *accuses very young victims of seducing their molesters*. Recall that he says, "*Even at the age of four or five, this seductiveness may be so powerful* as to *overwhelm the adult* into committing the offense" (emphasis added).[742]

Kinsey supported other "researchers" we now know to be pedophiles and pederasts. Indeed, Lloyd DeMause, PhD, editor of the *Journal of Psychohistory*, reports that most sex "researchers" shared—and still share—Kinsey's legally certifiable sexual pathologies.[743] Like Kinsey, they used "science" to legitimize and legalize their own pathologies, to increase acceptance among mental health professionals, and to promote the idea that sexual abuse was harmless for child and adult.

Redefining children as sexual (implicitly capable of consent) soon dramatically *increased* plea bargains reduced down to non-sex crimes, non-felonies. This had the unanticipated result of lowering sex crime rates *by reclassification*, reducing penalties for child molestation and rape, to allow paroles and pardons, even for repeat sexual predators.

As the legislatures and courts applied these changes to the law, they ignored thousands of years of history, literature, and painfully gained knowledge of human sexual behavior. Instead, our society's elite deferred to Kinsey and suddenly reclassified immoral sexual conduct *as having no public health consequences*.[744]

Judges and Lawyers Worship at the Kinsey Temple

As soon as the "K-bomb" hit the streets, penologists, legislators, and lawyers traveled regularly to Bloomington to worship at the feet of the Great Man. From him, lawyers, legislators, and judges learned how to gut our laws, using what some knew—and some did not know—were his Big Lies. According to the Rockefeller Foundation's Alan Gregg in 1950, Kinsey collaborated with law and justice professionals, reportedly meeting with "about one well-qualified visitor a day; penologists, sociologists, legislative experts, psychologists, doctors of medicine, lawyers and directors of welfare and social work, ministers and teachers."[745] In turn, Kinsey often received kudos for the lawyerly language in his two books. In fact, as noted, he parroted (plagiarized) the legal verbiage of Judge Guyon and American Civil Liberties Union (ACLU) lawyer Morris Ernst. Thus, within a few years, Kinsey's pathological influence was visible throughout our legal culture and among all the professions that Gregg listed in 1950.

In December 2006, Ed Hynes, Vice President of Morality in Media, wrote in obscenitycrimes.org, that the "'Sexual revolution' began with child abuse." Hynes levels the charge that "Kinsey and his staff separated morality from intimacy. It was the start of the so-called sexual revolution, an era of sexual license . . ."

The "sexual revolution" was based on Kinsey's claim that we are sexual from birth—a claim that emerged directly from sexual abuse on children and babies producing innumerable negative developments in predatory crime, including a booming global trade in adult and child Internet pornography, sexual violence against women and children, and international trafficking of 600,000 to 800,000 women (and more children) annually for prostitution, plus millions more trafficked, abused, raped, and murdered.

"Some revolution," concluded Mr. Haynes.[746]

Backed by the Rockefeller Foundation and "others," Kinsey, a mad sexual psychopath, and his cult followers sabotaged every state legislature in the Union, gutted our laws, and revolutionized American sexual life to mirror their own perversions.

So, in the end, Kinsey's real crime was *crime*. Though it was illegal before and after the Kinsey reports, the seriousness of rape diminished drastically in the post-Kinsey years, as people began to believe that women might have contrived rape charges for devious reasons. Judges began ruling rape as "overenthusiastic sex" and a "victimless crime"—giving legal standing later to "rough sex" *as a murder defense.*

The issue of statutory rape became pivotal. Since the Kinsey reports promoted children as "sexual from birth," American law softened with regard to the sexuality of minors and eased laws protecting children, lowering the age of consent, fostering the view that adult sex with juveniles is victimless. And that was only the beginning.

Kinsey changed the laws protecting women and children using the American Law Institute Model Penal Code.

The American Law Institute's Model Penal Code (ALI-MPC)

In 1948, attorney Louis B. Schwartz reviewed Kinsey's *Male* Volume in the *University of Pennsylvania Law Review* for bench and bar, providing new language that would legalize formerly proscribed sexual conduct. Schwartz wrote:

> To reveal that certain behavior patterns are widespread, that they are a product of environment, opportunity, age and other factors over which the individual has little control, that they are not objectively harmful except as a result of society's efforts at repression . . . to suggest that the law ought not to punish and that psychiatrists might better devote themselves to reassuring the sexual deviate rather than attention to "redirect behavior" . . . all these add up to a denial that sexual "perversion" is an evil.[747]

The American Law Institute (ALI), founded in 1923, joined the American Bar Association (ABA) in 1947, beginning a "national program of continuing education of the bar."[748] In 1948, the Carnegie Foundation funded the ALI to "educate" and, in 1950, the Rockefeller Foundation stepped in to finance the ALI's new "Model Penal Code" (MPC).[749] By 1955, the ALI—Schwartz as well as judges, lawyers, and a support cadre from psychiatry—created the new American Law Institute Model Penal Code (ALI-MPC), which relied heavily on Kinsey's sexuality "data." Immediately, the ABA adopted it and the ALI used the code

FIGURE 16—THE ALI MODEL PENAL CODE (MPC) REMOVES PROTECTIONS FOR WOMEN & CHILDREN U.S. JUSTICE SYSTEM 1948 –TODAY: EXPERTS USURP JURY OF ONE'S PEERS

ALI-MPC ADVISORS/LAW

JUDGES:

Curtis Bok, Judge, Court of Common Pleas, Philadelphia, PA
Charles D. Breitel, Justice, New York Supreme Court, New York, NY
Gerald F Flood, Judge, Court of Common Pleas, Philadelphia, PA
Stanley H Fuld, Judge (Ret.) United States Court of Appeals, Second Circuit, New York, NY
John J. Parker, Cheif Judge, United States Court of Appeals, Fourth Circut, Charlotte, NC
Orie L. Phillips, Chief Judge, United States Court of Appeals, Tenth Circuit, Denver, CO
Joseph Sloane, Judge, Court of Common Pleas, Philadelphia, PA

LAW SCHOOLS:

Dale E. Bennett, Louisiana State University Law School, Baton Rouge, LA
George H. Dession, Professor of Law, Yale Law School, New Haven, CT
Sheldon Glueck, Professor of Law, Law School of Harvard University, Cambridge, MA
Jerome Hall, Professor of Law, Indiana University School of Law, Bloomington, IN
Albert J. Harno, Deen, University of Illinois, College of Law, Urbane, IL
Henry M. Hart, Professor of Law, Law School of Harvard University, Cambridge, MA
Jerome Michael, Professor of Law, Columbia University School of Law, New York, NY (Deceased 1953).
Frank J. Remington, Associate Professor of Law, University of Wisconsin Law School, Madison, WI
John Barker-Waite, Professor of Law, University of California, Hastings College of Law, San Francisco, CA

CORRECTIONS/JUSTICE:

Sanford Bates, Commissioner, Department of Institutions and Agencies, State of New Jersey, Trenton, NJ
Winfre Overholser, M.D., Superintendent, St. Elizabeth's Hospital, Federal Security Agency, Washington, D.C.
James V. Bennett, Director, Bureau of Prisons, Department of Justice, Washington, D.C.
Samuel Dash, Acting District Attorney, Philadelphia, PA
Florence M. Kelly, Attorney-in-Charge, Legal Aid Society, Criminal Courts Branch, New York, NY
Joseph Saralite, Chief Assistant District Attorney, New York County, New York, NY

PRE-1948

COMMON LAW

Only lawful sexual congress is marital heterosexual coitus

POST-1948

KINSEY REPORTS (KR): *The Advent of "Consent"*

KR falsely claim that 95% of white men would be sex offenders, were the common law enforced:

- 69% frequent prostitutes (prostitution is illegal)
- 85% have pre-marital sex (fornication is illegal)
- 50% commit adultery (adultery is illegal)
- 10%–37% are somewhat homosexual (sodomy is illegal)

While of white women KR falsely claim that:

- 0% are harmed by rape
- 50% have pre-marital sex (fornication is illegal)
- 26% commit and 50% desire adultery (adultery is illegal)
- 87% of pregnant single women abort (abortion is illegal)
- 25% of wives abort (illegal)

Of children, KR falsely claim that 100% are orgasmic from birth, hence:

- Children can benefit from sex with adults and even incest (illegal)
- Children need early, explicit school sex education (illegal)
- Children need masturbation, hetero/homosexual acts taught (illegal)

Of parole, KR falsely claim that sex offenders rarely repeat sex crimes

1950

Rockefeller Funds ALI Model Penal Code

1952

Herbert Wechsler, Harvard Law Review, Call for ALI-MPC

1955

AUTHORS/ REPORTERS OF ALI-MPC

Herbert Wechsler, Chief (*Lawyer*)
Louis B. Schwartz, Assoc (*Lawyer*)
Morris Ploscowe, Accoc. (*Judge*)
Paul Tappan, Assoc. (*Lawyer/Sociologist*)

ALI-MPC #4 "SEX OFFENSES" DRAFT SENT TO STATES

1948

FOUR BOOKS CALL FOR "SCIENCE-BASED" SEX LAW REFORMS

- *Sex Habits of American Men, A Symposium on the Kinsey Report*
  Edited by Albert Deutsch
- *American Sexual Behaviour and the Kinsey Report*
  Morris Ernst & David Loth
- *The Ethics of Sexual Acts*
  René Guyon (French Pedophile Jurist)
- *About the Kinsey Report*
  Edited by Donald Porter Geddes & Enid Currie

ALI MPC ADVISORS/THERAPEUTIC SCIENCES

SOCIOLOGY/ENGLISH:

Ernest W. Burgess, Professor of Sociology, University of Chicago, Chicago, IL
Kenneth D. Johnson, Dean, New York School of Social Work, New York, NY
Thorster Selfin, Professor of Sociology, University of Pennsylvania, Philadelphia, PA
Lionel Trilling, Professor of English, Columbia University, New York, NY

PSYCHIATRY/MENTAL HYGIENE

Lawrence Z. Freedman, M.D., School of Medicine, Department of Psychiatry and Mental Hygiene, Yale University, New Haven, CT
Manfred S. Guttmacher, M.D., Chief Medical Officer, Supreme Bench of Baltimore, Baltimore, MD

OTHERS:

Leonard S. Cottrell, Russell Sage Foundation, New York, NY
Thomas D. McBride, Philadelphia, PA
Timothy N. Pfeiffer, New York, NY
Floyd E. Thompson, Chicago, IL
Harrison Tween, President, The American Law Institute, New York, NY
Herbert F. Goodrich, Director The American Law Institute, Philadelphia PA

1956	1962	1963	1963	1967	1969	1970	1971	1956	1970	1972	1971	1972	1972	1974	1978	1978	1979	
WI	IL	MN	NM	NY	GA	KA	NJ	OR	MD	MA	CN	CO	ID	KY	MS	MO	MI	ALL OTHER STATES

ALI MPC #4 "SEX OFFENSES" DRAFT ADOPTED/ADOPTED BY ALL STATES

STATE LEGISLATURES

MEDICINE/ PSYCHIATRY | COURTS | LAW ENFORCEMENT | CORRECTIONS | LEGAL PROFESSION & LAW SCHOOLS | PUBLIC/PRIVATE EDUCATION to train future lawyers, judges, and law school professors. State by state, the "ALI-MPC" altered our nation's sex-crime statutes.

According to Kinsey's authorized biographer, Jonathan Gathorne-Hardy, the ALI-MPC was Kinsey's work, "virtually a Kinsey document."[750] True, 100 percent of the 1955 ALI-MPC's footnote justifications for reducing or abolishing penalties for sex crimes quoted Kinsey as proof.[751]

The Kinsey Institute had to have loved it. The ALI-MPC proffered "evidence" to justify legalizing—or, in the interim, liberalizing—*all* of the Kinsey cabals' sexual perversions.

The ALI-MPC's deliberate, systematic assault on the safety of women and children should be required reading for everyone who studies the law. This code was the Kinseyan change agent that caused a paradigm shift from the common law—which arguably protected crime victims—to Kinsey's bogus pseudoscientific law, that clearly protected predators and blamed victims. Thus, the privileging of predators was a Kinsey Institute achievement, with the support of our legal institutions. Kinsey's prominence in the ALI Model Penal Code was no "coincidence." It was a done deal, because Kinsey's "data" justified elitist laws to end old-fashioned "common laws." And they did.

In 1955, the ALI-MPC soon reached all American legislators (Figure 16). Then it lightened or ended penalties for obscenity, adultery, prostitution, abortion, rape, sodomy, child molestation, and so on. In the most predatory crimes, changes would include:

- *Contributing to the delinquency of a minor:* Pre-Kinsey, illegal; post-Kinsey, what was illegal in every state in the union (adults describing sexual conduct and showing sexually explicit pictures to children) based on "sex education" became legal in schools and libraries, leading to lightening penalties for similar conduct in the wider society as well.
- As Kinsey and sexology's academe increasingly claimed sex with children is victimless, crimes against children increased. In 1999, the FBI cited 58,200 children kidnapped by non-family members and over a million throwaway and kidnapped by family members. Children became roughly 80% of reported rape victims.
- *Prostitution:* Pre-Kinsey, illegal. Post-Kinsey, sometimes legalized or trivialized as a "victimless crime."

- Kinsey claims that use of prostitutes was widespread and harmless (he offered no reports of sexually transmitted diseases, illegitimacy, alcoholism, battery or other negative consequences). This eased restraint of and punishment for prostitution. For example, sex therapy "surrogates" (prostitutes) are still legal in some states as a form of impotence treatment, further legitimizing sex-for-profit, a precursor to today's human sex traffic. In fact, in 2010, the widespread practice of child prostitution in Georgia has resulted in Senate Bill 304 to legalize child prostitution, umm, to protect children, in a manner of speaking.[752]
- Hence, prostituting ones children under age sixteen could be legal in Georgia! Imagine the increase in Georgia's housing market! Clever!
- *Rape/Statutory Rape:* Pre-Kinsey, illegal; Post-Kinsey, penalties reduced.
- Pre-Kinsey, premarital sex seriously decreased a woman's marriage opportunities and her legal credibility, so woman's legal standing largely rested on her virginity. Therefore, rape was a serious crime; eighteen states allowed the death penalty for rape—most of the rest, life or long sentences. But the 1955 ALI-MPC said women and children are seldom raped—that they made up most charges. Judges began to rule rape as "overenthusiastic sex," a "victimless crime"—giving legal standing later to "rough sex" as a murder defense. By 1958, for no recorded reason, the FBI excluded *statutory rape* and children under twelve, from its Uniform Crime Reports on rape crimes.

Kinsey's Data "Permeate All Present Thinking On This Subject."[753]

Kinsey worked to revise sex laws with the Illinois, New Jersey, New York, Delaware, Wyoming, and Oregon sex commissions.[754] In 1949, he testified before the California Subcommittee on Sex Crimes, claiming that his sex studies found "that 95% of the [male] population has actuality engaged in sexual activities, which are contrary to the law."[755] A year later, a New Jersey report on sex deviation praised Kinsey. By

1951, explaining its own findings, the Illinois sex offender commission acknowledged that *"the Kinsey findings . . .permeate all present thinking on this subject."*[756]

An unconscionable consequence of the ALI-MPC has been the transfer of decision-making authority from judges and juries to sexperts because, as professor Herbert Wechsler wrote in the 1952 *Harvard Law Review*, "Judges have no special expertise or insight. . .that warrants giving them a decisive voice" in the "determination of the treatment of offenders." He urged that judges "should be superseded by a dispositions board that would draw personnel of equal weight from social work, psychiatry, penology and education."[757] Moreover, *juries were no longer permitted to hear all the evidence about the accused lest it "prejudice" their view of his/her guilt*. Thus, Kinsey's influence on the ALI-MPC significantly curbed the uniquely American system—a jury "of one's peers."

And so it was that the train had left the station, metaphorically stopping at every state in the union to deliver Kinsey's sexual news to America's lawmakers. Predictably, a toxic bias favoring predators came to dominate our laws.

In 1948, penologists were already citing Kinsey to eliminate life imprisonment and the death penalty for rape. For example, in his 1948 essay on sex and the law, Judge Morris Ploscowe wrote that "Illicit sex activity is so widespread" that "95 per cent of the total population could be convicted as sex offenders."[758] Thus, he said, sexual misconduct was a nonproblem, as prohibitions are "inherently unenforceable" since "the law attempts to forbid an activity which responds to a wide human need."[759]

Kinsey's black propaganda spread. Columbia University law professor Beryl H. Levy declared that Kinsey's "data" reflected "contemporary values." Like Kinsey, in his *Sexology* article Mr. Levy described rape as naturally, and therefore easily forgotten by young victims.[760] The new ALI-MPC would soon abolish "unrealistic" rape and statutory rape in all fifty states.

So Kinsey, a certifiably mad sexual psychopath, advised state legislative committees on how to rewrite our laws based on his personal sexuality model.[761] "Follow me," he said. "It'll be great!" They did. And it was great—for grooming sexual psychopaths.

It has not been great for women and children.

Wechsler said *the purpose* of the ALI-MPC was *to reduce crime from its "high" rate in 1952. On the evidence, then, the ALI-MPC is a total, absolute failure.* Women and children are raped and battered over 100 percent more today. Since the ALI-MPC, we have seen massive increases in violent crime with rape jumping off the charts.

FIGURE 17
VIOLENT CRIME 1951–1997
NUMBER OF OFFENSES

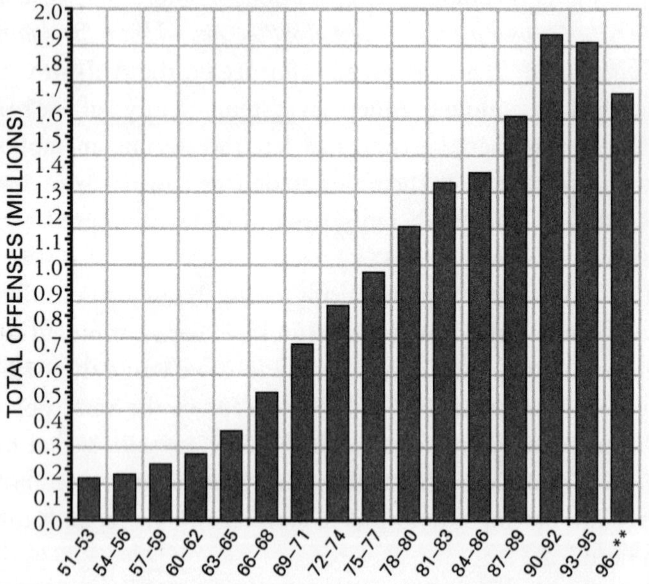

Basic data from *Statistical Abstracts of the United States* and the Department of Commerce, Census Bureau

All of this is thanks to the Kinsey cult, who mainstreamed their "she-says-no-but-she-means-yes" theory of human sexuality into our laws. That was the first time anyone (except for admitted rapists in courtrooms) had ever asserted that children who screamed, wept, fainted, and fought to get away from their rapists actually derived "pleasure from the situation."[762] Subsequently, Kinseyan sexperts repeated the claim that women cry rape so they can "enjoy" sex without feeling guilty.

Propaganda Sabotage Legitimizes Rape

> The difference between a rape and a good time depends on whether the girl's parents were awake when she finally came home.[763]
>
> —Alfred C. Kinsey

While men under the patriarchy gave male seducers criminal penalties, Hugh Hefner, by contrast, provided a seduction manual to Joe College in his 1954 *Playboy* issue on virginity, in which *Playboy* advised readers to attack the mind, not the body, after selecting "a suitable subject." Hefner trained his college users in seduction over rape:

> Boys are bigger than girls. And some guys figure that's all the advantage they need to make any seduction a success. *Trouble is, that ain't seduction.* . . . you've got to win over the lady's mind first. The muscle method is too often confused with a dirty four letter word spelled r-a-p-e. . . . Such goings on can lead to . . . long jail sentences.[764]

How good of Hef to advise his readers on how to avoid jail. Instead, he outlines various alternative approaches for seducing a young virgin: release her inhibitions with alcohol, promise her anything, or use Kinsey to "emphasize the intellectual rather than physical."

Beyond the obvious encouragement to trick and seduce young virgins, such publishers are on record as *fully aware* that their "readers" come to view the pornographic fantasy world *as their own possible reality*. Starting with Hugh Hefner, Kinsey's cult picked up the baton as *Playboy* sought to conquer virginity—and women—with thousands of seduction, rape, and gang rape jokes, stories, and cartoons for American men, our future national leaders.[765]

After more than half a century of mainstreamed pornography, users are inured to normal, marital sexual relations—often rendered impotent. To be momentarily virile, they require increasingly energizing stimuli—images of sex linked to hate, anger, shame, or violence, in an endless cycle that encourages copycat crimes.

In a more recent justification for sexual violence, anthropologist Craig Palmer and biologist Randy Thornhill, claimed in 2000 that rape is "a natural biological phenomenon," a desire to reproduce, and a "product of the human evolutionary heritage."[766] With slipshod scholarship and execrable ethics, Palmer and Thornhill's logic ignored the massive increase in rapes of infertile infants, children, young boys, and elder women—not to mention the overwhelming negative sociological effects of rape on all its recipients.

Liberals also neglect to explain why rape, like homosexuality, if it is a natural, biological phenomenon, increases and decreases with the era and culture. Were such conduct "natural," like breathing, it should remain at the same level cross-culturally and over time. But rape rates, like "sexual orientation," fluctuate depending on the belief system and the stimuli in the culture.[767] When society, especially male leaders, sufficiently abhor and punish rape and anything that supports it, rape decreases. When alpha males pardon rape, it increases.

"Utmost Resistance" and Other Prosecutorial Impediments

Unaware that Kinsey's WWII criminals were their legal model, the ALI-MPC imposed new rules about rape and gang-rape. If defendants' lawyers accused a victim of a "racy" past, they could label her a "prostitute." And if lawyers said a foolish young girl engaged in casual sex, or drinking, *she* would be blamed for her own rape, reported David Bryden in the *Buffalo Criminal Law Review*.[768]

In 1961, Berl Levy snidely asked, "What is Rape?" He remarked in 1961 that courts must recognize the "utmost resistance" theory:

> It must be shown that the woman fought back like a tiger . . . resisted with all her might and main and with every means at her disposal: punching, scratching, biting, kicking, screaming, etc. . . . *Some experts have expressed the opinion that it is well-nigh impossible for a man to rape a woman of ordinary good health and strength*[769] (emphasis added).

Feminist lawyer, Susan Estrich, added that forcible rapes are graded. "If serious bodily injury is inflicted, forcible rape is a first degree felony," she said.[770] But what is "serious" bodily harm? Is not rape itself "serious bodily harm"? Estrich observed that homosexual rape—sodomy—is even seen "as a lesser felony."[771]

In her famous 1986 *Yale Law Review* article "Rape," Estrich expressed her confusion with the ALI-MPC's rape "innovations," which perplexed her.[772] She was not alone. Juries were so confused that they often acted more leniently than they intended. Estrich was irate. The more liberated society got, the more men raped women and then children, and the lighter their punishments. Why did her liberal male colleagues, judges, lawyers, her friends, treat rape more casually than did traditional, "unliberated" patriarchal American men?

Kinsey's black propaganda was so successful that, under the *1980* ALI-MPC, *unlike other crimes*, "rape and sexual assault require corroboration or a 'fresh complaint' of the victim's testimony."[773] Even if the victim met this requirement, the new ALI-MPC ordered juries to hear "cautionary instructions" about the victim's possible tainted history and testimony.[774] Then, liberal courts demanded extensive "corroboration" of the victim's testimony and proof of her "chastity." So under the new MPC, judges gave wide leeway to rapists' lawyers to portray victims as promiscuous and, presumably, willing participants.

The Kinseyans also shortened the statutes of limitations. Pre-Kinsey, 33 percent of states had no statute of limitations on rape reports. The sex lobby promptly reversed this. In 2000, Iowa law set a three-year statute of limitations for most rape cases, five years if the victim was a minor. New York's statute became five years, extending five more if the victim did not know the predator. In 2005, Florida, Nevada, and New Jersey were on record at five years, with longer time frames due largely to the development of efficient DNA evidence, which could convict the predator(s).[775]

Kinsey Cultists "Liberate" Rape Penalties

Pre-Kinsey American men often shared President Theodore Roosevelt's view of rape, as he expressed it in his Sixth Annual Message to Congress in 1906. Rape, he believed, was the most horrific of all crimes because even murder was usually a male-on-male battle, commonly acted out on a somewhat even playing field. But rape preys on women, unable to protect themselves.

Current university "liberal" male and institutional feminist dogma insists that there were more rapes pre-Kinsey, under the "patriarchy."

They argue that women made fewer reports because of the draconian culture. But this argument is illogical, given the tough rape laws that enabled rape victims to come forward. In 1780, rape—right up there with murder, sodomy, burglary, robbery, arson, and treason against the commonwealth—was aggressively prosecuted.[776]

According to Massachusetts court records (1698–1797), the rate rape peaked in 1725–1734 at *3.5 rapes per 100,000 population*;[777] Moreover, during those ninety-nine years, the all-male jury tended to believe rape charges and punish predators accordingly. By 2008, Massachusetts rape is recorded at *25.6 per 100,000 population*.[778] This is a 550 percent rape increase and the latter data exclude the rapes of children under age twelve.

We've come a long way, but is this where we want to be?

The millions of adult and child rape victims are *a legacy of the Kinsey Institute's sexual revolution.* With the first Kinsey report, Judge Morris Ploscowe argued for "Lightening Sex Crime Penalties." He reported the 1948 penalties for rape (Figure 18):

- 19 states: death, life, or a long term (three of these mandated death)
- 27 states: twenty years or more, up to life
- Pennsylvania: fifteen years[779]

FIGURE 18
PRE-KINSEY ALI-MPC USA
1948 RAPE PENALTIES

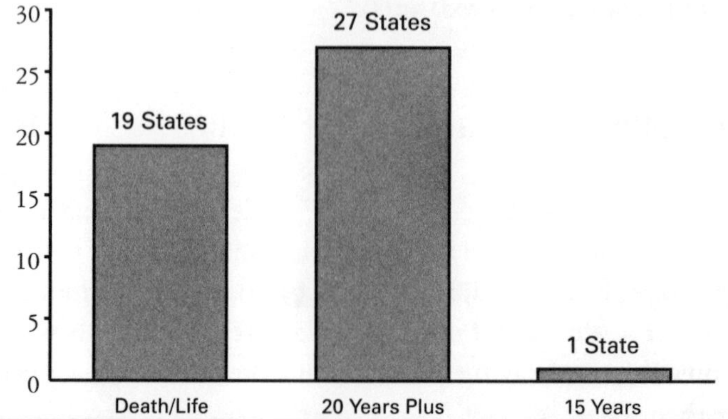

Source: Ploscowe in Deutch, *Sex Habits of American Men*, p. 135

In practice, convicted rapists often got jail and a public horsewhipping. Unlike the post-Kinsey restrictions on victims, women could report rape *whenever they felt ready*, and cases could be prosecuted regardless of any statute of limitations. Even by the early 1950s, a third of our states *had no statute of limitations* for rape reports.[780]

As a result, most rape-minded men tempered their lust because of draconian laws and the wrath of legal penalties imposed by other men. Rape laws upheld colonial restraints such that, when a man had sex with an unmarried girl or woman, he was viewed as the villain. In Alabama, for example, men who committed rape were stricken from the voting records, when or if they emerged from prison. Such severe pre-Kinsey penalties protected women and children.

No more.

Whittling away at protections against rape, the *new* 1980 MPC changed America's rape laws dramatically. Citing a few of the several thousand University Law Review Journals that affirmatively cite the Kinsey reports, Professor Linda Jeffrey, PhD, and Col. Ronald Ray (Ret.) summarized the sabotage of sex-crime laws[781] that:

- Legalized all sex by "consenting adults";[782]
- Condemned judicial bias against "sex offenders";[783]
- Reduced sex crime penalties;[784]
- Viewed boy prostitution as trivial;[785]
- Rejected "common law" Judeo-Christian standards of virtue honor and chastity;[786]
- Legalized homosexuality;[787]
- Provided "beneficent concern for pedophiles";[788]
- Reduced sex law penalties;[789]
- Claimed that young children are seducers;[790]
- Argued that we must legalize all prostitution.[791]

Rehabilitating Sexual Predators—And Letting Them Go

The original ALI-MPC wrote that "a majority of authorities find that the sex offender in general is not a recidivist." Defying all common sense and knowledge, this preposterous "scientific" decree emerged from the Kinsey-based *California Sex Crimes Report 1950–1953*. Since Kinsey claimed "that 95% of the [male] population has actuality engaged in sexual activities which are contrary to the law," he urged parole for all rapists, even murderers. Kinsey urged, "lessening the penalty." Why? Well, others grant "parole immediately in 80% of . . . sex cases."[792]

Kinsey disciple John Gagnon bragged that educated people nationwide were echoing Kinsey's theories:

> A more modest and less violent image of the sex offender began to appear in the public press. Rather than focusing on rare violent events, attention began to be paid to the majority of people whose offenses were occasional, who had no criminal pasts, and who were responsive to treatment.[793]

But Gagnon never—nor anyone else—possessed or discovered a "treatment" that worked on sexual predators, *ever*. Still, he claimed, with "an increase in public sexual knowledge . . . new ways of thinking about the relationship between sex and law began to emerge . . . Pivotal to these conceptions was the distinction between victim and victimless [sex] in the 1950s."[794] Crediting Kinsey for research into "unconventional sex," Gagnon said Kinsey's work led to current views that "[m]ost sex offenders were not "sex fiends" and few were violent or dangerous, or likely to repeat their crimes.[795]

Adding bad logic to Kinsey's bad data, sex reformers argued that we cannot prosecute 1 percent of men for sex acts that are common to 95 percent of all men; we must either arrest *all* men or pardon the 1 percent, end punishment, and provide therapy. Of course, this makes no distinction with regard to the severity of those "sex acts." For example, before Kinsey, America's penal codes, based on common law, defined sex crimes as both "Offenses Against Persons" and "Crimes Against Morals." In their argument that 95 percent of men broke sex laws, the sexologists make no distinction between crimes against morals (say public cursing) and predatory crime (rape/murder). No matter. In books and publicity brochures, Kinseyan sexperts regularly perpetuated the low-recidivism myth discussed in more detail shortly. This fraud created revolving doors for sex predators who go into short-term prison sentences and "treatment" and out to commit new rapes and even murders.

Authorities soon wanted "therapy" for predators so they could learn to "control" their urges. Bear in mind that therapy for sex offenders is costly. A 2009 National Institute of Justice conference noted probation as preferable to jail, "It's about 78 dollars a day per prisoner and about 3 dollars and 42 cents per day for somebody on probation."[796]

In 1993, the U.S. Senate passed the "National Crime Victims' Right Week,"[797] so I suppose we can account as moral progress that, once a year, we "recognize" new victims of violent sex crimes with ceremonies and suchlike. Similarly, in 1996, President Bill Clinton and Senator Howell Heflin (D-AL), proposed the U.S. Constitution add a "Victims' Rights" Amendment to give rights to victims.[798] Hmmm. So instead of imposing severe penalties—capital punishment or life without parole for violent criminals—or even requiring a legal moratorium on media glorification of rape and murder, we *resolved* to honor victims' "rights."

As of this writing, however, few states inform rape victims whether their rapist has AIDS or other communicable diseases. In Florida, a rape victim, who was denied her rapist's medical records "due to privacy considerations," asked, "Why does he have any privacy rights? He certainly disregarded mine."

One of the victims' rights measures was to include:

> The right to be notified of a parole hearing, the right to speak or present written testimony, the right to be notified of the release of the criminal and the right to restitution from the defendant.[799]

But why do courts parole these violent criminals in the first place?

Following Kinsey's WWII "data" that rape was the natural and normal reaction to any available female, victims often had fewer rights than their attackers. So our legal institutions allowed—and continue to allow—Kinseyan focus on rehabilitation and parole for rapists and murderers, so these violent predators could continue to victimize.

As unpleasant as it is, life imprisonment or the death penalty are the only guarantees of the "rights" of victims.

The Result: A Rape Victim Every 45 Seconds

What if women really enjoy rape? What if the public accepted the idea that women *wanted* "hot" sex but were too restrained by society to admit it? She says "NO" but she really means "YES!" If this is true, wouldn't the public consider rape harmless, natural, biological? And shouldn't we change our laws to accommodate this view? If we did change our laws to give this implicit permission on behalf of women, what would happen?

Of course, the rape rate would increase.

And of course, this is *exactly* what has happened, year after year, decade after decade, since the 1955 ALI-MPC. Heralding the toxic fallout of Kinsey's "liberated" sexuality, the nation adopted the behavior of a sexual psychopath (Kinsey) and nationalized sexual psychopathology.

In 1940, *LOOK* magazine reported that there were about 100 murders per year in Harlem, "but rape is very rare."[800] Then, on the heels of Kinsey's 1948 and 1953 books, New York saw a major change in the view of women and children, sex and crime. In 1965, some 2,320 forcible rapes were reported in New York.[801] By 1985, there were 5,706.[802] Then, rapes of women and children eclipsed men's murders of men—*a major shift in aggressive focus.*

The authors of *Transforming a Rape Culture* asked, do "rape and sexual assault truly permeate this society, or are we hearing about the sensationalized, isolated cases? Has the rate of sexual violence really increased?" In 1996, sociologist Peggy Sanday, in *A Woman Scorned,* reported on national twenty-year rape increases per capita. "Between 1935 and 1956 arrest rates for rape nearly doubled, as did the rates for other sexual offenses."[803] Sanday noted that a tragic loss of believability for women came with sexual license, a legal version of the "she *meant* yes" phenomenon.

Given the judicial indifference toward rape victims, Washington, D.C. saw the first "Rape Crisis Center," as a small group of women organized to offset the increasingly tolerant "justice system."[804] Now, hundreds of centers offer a broad spectrum of services to sexual assault victims. Because the centers do not require the victims to make police reports, these centers *reduce* the number of rapes included in the FBI Uniform Crime Report.

By 1998, an analysis, *Rape in America*, by the U.S. Department of Justice (DoJ) with the Centers for Disease Control and Prevention reported on interviews with 8,000 women and 8,000 men. They found that "1 in 6 women experienced an attempted rape or a completed rape"; more than half (54 percent) were minors at the time and 22 percent were under age twelve. In the same study, one in thirty-three men reported that they had experienced a sexual assault.[805] Other research finds one in six men reported sexual assault.[806] Boys aged twelve through seventeen were found to be two to three times more likely to be sexually assaulted than adults.[807] Other DoJ data identify *64 percent of forcible sodomy victims as boys under age twelve.*[808]

Crime steadily escalated from the 1960s onward, and *rape far outstripped all other violent crime.* According to Violent Crime data from the FBI "Index of Crime, United States 1960–1999," the population grew 52 percent in thirty-nine years, 1960–1999. At the same time, violent crime grew 396 percent. Rape raised the average, increasing 418 percent.

FIGURE 19

FBI INDEX OF CRIME 1960–1999 GROWTH IN SEVEN TOP CRIMINAL OFFENSES

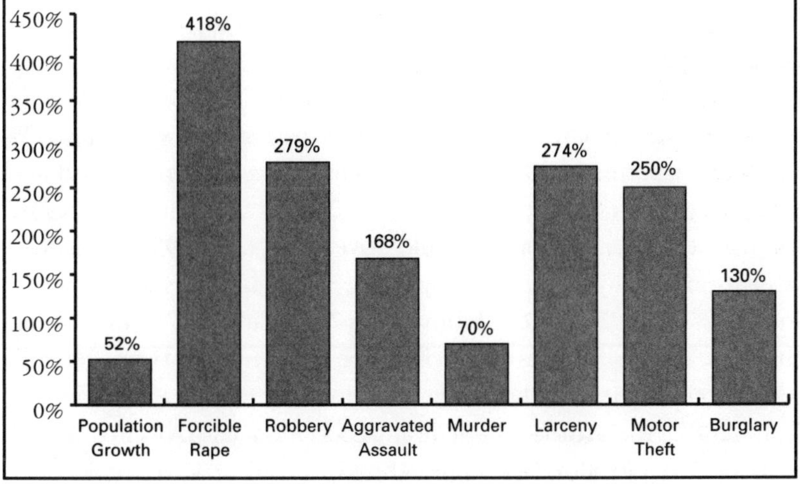

Source: Data for seven major crimes, FBI CJIS, faxed page number unreadable, January 16, 2001

FIGURE 20

Year	Population	Growth Since Last Decade	Annual Growth Rate
2000	8,008,278	9.36440%	0.899%
1990	7,322,564	3.54833%	0.349%
1980	7,071,639	-10.42733%	-1.095%
1970	7,0894,862	1.45050%	0.144%
1960	7,781,984	-1.39348	-0.140%
1950	7,891,957	5.86133%	0.571%
1940	7,454,995	7.56876%	0.732%
1930	6,930,446	23.31549%	2.118%

15.5% NYC Population Growth 1930–2000

Source: http://www.gothamgazette.com/article/demographics/20060627/5/1894

New York City Justice Morris Ploscowe wrote that "during the 30s only 418" crimes of "forcible rape" were reported in New York City (averaging thirty-five per year).[809] By 2004, the city recorded 1,740 *forcible* rapes.[810] So while the New York City population grew roughly 16 percent from 1930 to 2000,[811] its reported rape rate grew 4,871 percent.[812] And THAT is not JUST "better reporting."

Of course, Ploscowe's 1930 rape data included statutory rape (removed from the FBI uniform crime reports in 1957–1958), so this data therefore counted all female victims, including those under twelve years of age. Today though, rape data reported to the public does not include rapes of children under age twelve.

From 1950 to 2004, based on a "body count," the DoJ identified a shocking 19.6 percent increase in homicide nationwide; with 16,137[813] homicides reported in 2004.[814] (Remember, due to modern medical and emergency services that were not available decades ago, homicide rates are significantly *lower* than they would have been with 1950 medicine.) Absent similar physical proof of rape, 94,635 forcible rapes were reported in 2004,[815] with 20 percent estimated as "forcible rapes."[816] Even using this data, the DoJ data found forcible rape by men in 2004 was roughly 540 percent higher than homicide (commonly by men)—a 5:32 ratio.[817]

In 2007, the American Medical Association (AMA) cited sexual assault, often unreported and unrecognized, as a "silent-violent epidemic" and "the most rapidly growing violent crime in America, claiming a victim every 45 seconds."[818] Finally, the racial side of this epidemic deserves attention, indeed. White pornography has devastated the black community, the black family, and, of course, the honor due to black women and children.[819] Moreover, according to a recent task force:

> Native women are victimized at rates higher than any other population in the United States. It is estimated that in their lifetime 1 of 3 Native women will be raped and 6 of 10 will be physically assaulted.[820]

Despite the statistics, questions remain about their veracity. One moment the FBI announces that rape was disappearing. Fourteen months later, they announced that the purported respite was over: Rape numbers were heading up. A couple of years later, in 2004, the FBI said "violent crime" was down again—though one category of violence was up: rape. They reported a 1.4 percent increase in rapes over 2003, which had increased over 2002. By 2006, though, some law "professors" were charging that the FBI data again reflected a radical reduction in rape, *this time by a fantastic 85* percent. Citing to a *Washington Post* report, that "The number of rapes per capita in the United States has plunged by more than 85 percent since the 1970s" even though "other violent offenses increased, according to federal crime data."[821] Wow! Good news!

Kinseyan lawyers touted this nationwide; porn was up and rape was down, they cheered.[822] But the FBI "United States Crime Rates 1960–2005" data listed *not an 85* percent *decrease but an 8.6* percent *increase*, the Kinseyan liberals were speechless. This report also showed that, well, forcible rape had increased 230.2% from 1960 to 2008.[823]

Frankly, for rape statistics to be down at all, lying statistics have to be up.

In fact, a 2000 *U.S. News & World Report* article reported that "facing political heat to cut crime in the city, investigators in the New York PPD's Sex Crime Unit [Police Department] sat on (thousands of) reports of rapes and other sexual assaults."[824] A police commander said, "The way crime was solved was with an eraser." In one district, police "failed to report between 13,000 and 37,000 major crimes." "A 2000 *Philadelphia Inquirer* report found" that, from 1997–1999, of 300,000 sex crime reports, officials had *downgraded* thousands of rapes to "investigation of persons" or "investigation, protection, and medical examination"—codes for non-crimes. "This put one in four rapes in a non-crime category."

Debbie Goldberg reported in a 1998 *Washington Post* article that the crime-fighting method favored by the Philadelphia Police Department was reducing crimes:

> "It's been an accepted practice over a long period of time," said a twenty-five-year Philadelphia police veteran who spoke on condition of anonymity . . . "There's pressure to keep crime statistics down, and captains are held responsible for what goes on in their districts."[825]

"Date Rape" Skyrockets

Today's college co-eds, who must arm themselves with mace and rape whistles when they walk to the campus library believe they have more freedom than any young women in history. But pre-Kinsey college girls didn't need rape crisis centers or rape whistles, and parents did not fear sending their precious lambs to any American college or university. In past generations, men were expected to carry any nubile, errant young drinker to her bed, remove her shoes, cover her gently, and leave her unmolested. Young men did so.

Times change.

Current rates of "co-ed" sexual assault cites roughly 25 percent of college women.[826] Despite the controversy about the rate of rape, the fact that most colleges now supply "rape whistles" to their co-eds does suggest a change in college courtesies from pre-Kinsey days. Joe College no longer saves himself for his bride. With everyone encouraged to drink to excess and "hook up," rape is identified as the most common violent crime on U.S. college campuses today (this is *reported* rape; most rape goes unreported):

> College women are more at risk for rape and other forms of sexual assault than women the same age but not in college. It is estimated that almost 25% of college women have been victims of rape or attempted rape.[827]

Most respected colleges have become sexual war zones. The Harvard University Police Department reported that fifty-two sexual offenses . . . on the Cambridge campus . . . were reported to the police in 2004, and sixty-one Harvard students sought assistance from the Office of Sexual Assault Prevention and Response after experiencing a rape or sexual assault.[828]

Although they suppress findings of pornography's central role in rape, college administrators do admit that alcohol and drugs (including date-rape drugs) feed this culture. So did Kinsey.

Kinsey directly counseled states' law committees to destigmatize *all sex acts* that society previously had understood to be pathological, socially harmful, and (some said) even sinful. The Kinsey/Guyon legal theory held that *only* marks of violence *and* vehement physical resistance proved rape had occurred. Victims, *seduced* (once illegal and a felony in California), enticed, tricked, or drugged by a sexual predator (or a gang of predators) were no longer viewed as rape victims. And increasingly in the "hook up" culture, victims *are* "collaborators." Even if authorities charged and convicted such a predator(s), punishment would likely be drastically reduced—or even set aside. This philosophy then showed up especially in statutes and legal theory on what became commonly called "date rape." This new defense had defendants arguing that the victim should have known sex was part of the date. Kinsey's image of promiscuous females became a reality as boyfriends, professors, and feminists encouraged girls to be "modern" and "cool" with alcohol, drugs, and sex.

College coeds were secretly drugged at parties, then raped while unconscious. Often they were labeled "racy." With new rules about sex, girls who had been gang-raped by athletes or fraternity members regularly and humiliatingly lost in court, leaving the college to struggle with the emotional aftermath of the physical assaults, the self-blame, and humiliation. Not so for the rapists who generally remained on campus, graduating untainted. DoJ statistics confirm the presence of sexual sabotage and the absence of "justice" in rape cases:

> [A]mong all women who were raped since age eighteen, only 7.8% said their rapist was criminally prosecuted, 3.3% said their rapist was convicted of a crime, and a mere 2.2% said their rapist was incarcerated. . . . Thirteen percent of the women who were raped since age eighteen said they obtained a restraining order against their rapist. . . . Of these women, 65.9% said their rapist violated the order.[829]

In "Fraternities and the Rape Culture," Chris O'Sullivan reported that fraternity houses often display pornographic pictures and magazines, and the members eagerly watch pornographic films and videos.[830] Some frat brothers engage in sex with a young female student whom the boys consider unattractive as part of a "pig" or "hog" contest; after the "act," they discard the naïve victim. The girl is often a staple for ongoing frat "humor" as the men often video-record the events for posterity. One woman reported "fraternity brothers actively plotting to get first-year girls drunk and rape them, and . . . sorority sisters actively plotting to have other women taken advantage of ('tag rape')."[831]

Millions of girls paid a high price for the Rockefeller funded Kinseyan black propaganda that Hugh Hefner mainstreamed. For most, absent broken bones, black eyes, and *inappropriate* blood (vaginal blood would not count), there was no crime.

Culture of Implicit Consent

What happens when fraternity gang rapists graduate?

They become our professors, social workers, doctors, research scientists, filmmakers, executives, bureaucrats, reporters, penologists, teachers, judges, and lawyers, and even very powerful politicians and legislators. They become predators in power—like President Bill Clinton.

High education, wealth, and prestige do not protect against predatory intent. Remember, Nobel Prize winner Carleton Gadjusek, PhD; American University president Richard Berendzen, PhD; American University psychology department head Elliot McGinnies, PhD;[832] and University of Southern California's "father of gene therapy," William Anderson, MD.[833] All have all been arrested in pedophile/pederast-associated felonies. Such high profile trials will not escape some mass media attention, but if the predators are homosexual, the "gay lobby" will immediately launch damage control.

For decades, Kinsey's supporters and the ALI-MPC "blamed the victim," until an army of largely female lawyers (many of whom, like Susan Estrich, had been raped) began forcing legal change. The need to corroborate rape was allegedly abolished. As I touched on earlier, rape shield laws now often protect the victim's sexual history. Judges may no longer instruct juries to remember that the victim might be lying. And victims now have more time before they must report a rape to the police.

However, these are largely empty victories. Rape convictions are typically plea-bargained down to misdemeanors. At a cost of billions of tax dollars and immeasurable heartbreak, pandemic rape of women and children reigns unchecked. We try to educate our schoolchildren to make *them* responsible for protecting themselves. Adults in our society have abdicated the responsibility to secure tough penalties and a clean media to protect the most vulnerable of us.

Leading us into Sexploitation

Grinning, well, demonically, Alfred Kinsey "loved these films and often watched and showed them," said his biographer, Gathorne-Hardy. Kinsey leers as several young children are forced to watch a violent, scatological porcupine "mating" film. Consider their deeply troubled expressions, as Gathorne-Hardy described the film:

> The foreplay—standing on hind legs . . . the male pressing the female down, at which she dramatically and completely opened up all her quills and the male descended over her, entered with a number of rapid strokes, jackknifed over to suck his penis clean, and relaxed. . . .

Six adults are in the room with Kinsey. Clara and Cornelia Christenson (on the far right) look excited. The other adults look distressed. A dark-haired girl on the far right gasps and the boy at right front is clearly traumatized.

Prostitution and Sex Trafficking

As divorced mothers sought new partners to father their children, child neglect and sexual abuse increased. Physical and sexual abuse of children, including child murder, is especially linked to the mothers' boyfriends and new husbands.[834] When divorce skyrocketed, children were in a no-win situation. Whether their mother stayed with or left a violent husband, children got beaten and too often, suffered sexual assault. Daughters of batterers are 6.5 times more likely than other girls to become victims of father-daughter incest.[835]

When our "scientists" jettisoned God, as Voltaire warned, with him went the ideas of sin and guilt, men no longer condemned the man who dumped the wife of his youth for a "trophy wife." Few men no longer ostracized sexually exploitive male colleagues. And more and more men mistreated women, girls, and boys. Kinsey's effect on the sexual abuse of children was profound and far-reaching.

Kinsey gloated that he commonly asked a girl, "how old she was when she turned her first trick."[836] Although Kinsey interviewed a huge prostituted population, he hid the "data" on all prostituted women. He certainly hid the data on the age of initial prostitution. The Kinsey Institute in its reprint of Kinsey's key data reiterates his fraudulent *Male* findings:

- 69% of white males have had at least one experience with a prostitute;
- Among unmarried males, sex with a prostitute was about 10% of the total premarital intercourse.[837]

During World War II, the Kinsey team interviewed hundreds if not thousands of prostitutes and spent a massive amount of time discussing men's use of prostitutes. Yet, in their tomes alleging to report *all* the vital data on sexual behavior of men and women, the team censored all information on the origins or consequences of prostitution. In doing so, they made it another "victimless crime."

In 2008, Edwin Shur's 1963 book *Narcotic Addiction in Britain and America* (first published by the infamous Tavistock, London) was republished. In 1965, the influential sociologist and lawyer wrote one of a series in his far-left books on gender, deviance, the family, the sexual revolution, and crime. This earth-shaking treatise he called *Crimes Without Victims*. Here, Schur quotes Kinsey more than any other "sexpert," to explain that abortion, homosexuality, and drug use are consensual, therefore harmless, and should be legal. This argument is used to justify legalizing prostitution as well as pornography, polygamy, incest between "adults," and all manner of social crimes. Scores of social scientists and criminologists followed Schur, citing him and calling for legalization of any allegedly "consensual" vice as without victims.

But the public, the unorganized polity, began to organize to counter the crippling influence of these educated elitists, noticing that there *were* "secondary victims" to consensual adultery (the betrayed spouse and children!), to drug use, and even sodomy (venereal diseases, dead unborn babies), abandoned and impoverished single mothers, prostitution (diseases and even community blight).

Since prostitutes rated no Kinsey data, neither did their drug and alcohol abuse. Prostitutes, by definition are the most sexually active persons. They are also major drug and alcohol addicts with high rates of abortions and illegitimate babies. Both male and female prostitutes have commonly endured early sexual abuse and/or incest, and suffered STDs, battery, homicide, and suicide.

Kinsey obviously did not want to know that early sexual abuse is a chief cause of girls and boys entering prostitution, with high rates (65–90 percent) of incest among girls, according to the Council for Prostitution Alternatives in Portland, Oregon. Their 1991 annual report found that 85 percent of their prostitute clients reported history of sexual abuse in childhood; 70 percent reported incest.[838]

Homosexual academician Donald West's study of English male prostitutes confirmed early sexual abuse; incest was less common. West viewed *"sex abuse in childhood as a cause of male prostitution"*[839] and said, *"the perpetrators are nearly always men."*[840] However, characteristically, West insisted that the abused, violated, and betrayed boys were innately "gay" and so they largely "consented" to their continued abuse.[841] Despite this justification, West still admitted the brutality of both prostitution and what he calls "some gay male lifestyles."

Kinsey carefully ignored and discarded any such data among *his* specimens—data that obviously did not further his agenda. While he dispassionately examined prostitutes as scientific specimens—like the gall wasps he nailed to little bits of cardboard—he cherry picked the information that suited his agenda.

Sexual freedom advocates Harry Benjamin, MD, and R.E.L. Masters showed somewhat more compassion in describing the horrors of prostitution. Citing extensively from Kinsey's *secret* interviews with prostitutes, they trivialized prostitutes' drug and alcohol use and vigorously hid all data on homosexual abuse of boys, and then boldly called for legalizing prostitution as an outlet for men. Yet, they did describe what the Kinsey team knew from interviews with prostitutes:

> An unknown number of the drug addicts [prostitutes] are murdered by "pushers" by means of . . . an overdose of heroin, or narcotics laced with strychnine or some other lethal poison. According to addicts, such murders are numerous.[842]

Legitimizing Prostitution Normalizing Incest

As is clear from the effort by Georgia legislators in 2010, important sexually disordered people are always seeking to legalize prostitution of women and children. Kinsey, like most legalization advocates, ignored such murders in "the trade," censoring them from his reports. While he specialized in collecting stories from prostitutes in poverty-ridden urban areas—and bragging about measuring their clitorises for "science"—he hid what he knew about their tragic lives. Clearly he had contempt for the suffering of the "victimless" prostitute as he sought legalization of prostitution as a "job".

Touring Italy in 1955, Kinsey was oblivious to the postwar poverty and suffering around him, so obsessed was he with prostitution—namely the child-sex traffic. Like most pederasts, Kinsey viewed the boy prostitutes as "handsome young Italian boys" who, victimless, he argued, were engaged in sex *for pleasure*.

In the world according to Kinsey and Pomeroy, prostitution—even child prostitution—was neither wrong nor exploitive. In fact, Pomeroy's Institute for the Advanced Study of Human Sexuality (IASHS) has long advocated legalizing child pornography and prostitution by persons of any age. The IASHS, the "Harvard" of human sexuality credentialing and curriculum design, seeks to legalize prostitution for all "those disadvantaged *because of age*. . . ." Indeed, they "would legalize adult child sex, incest, child prostitution, and child pornography—providing that such practices are "consensual."[843]

Of all the horrors of child prostitution, most troubling is the fact that these young people are prey for sex traffickers. Indeed, even children from normal, healthy homes are stalked, abducted, murdered like Johnny Gosch and/or sold into prostitution (trafficking). The U.S. Department of State defines "sexual trafficking" as "the recruitment, harboring, transportation, provision, or obtaining of a person for the purpose of a commercial sex act."[844] Shared Hope International reports, "familial prostitution—the selling of one's family member for sex in exchange for drugs, shelter, or money—is a large and overlooked problem in the United States."[845]

Recovering prostitute and pornography "star," Shelley Lubben reports extensively on the batteries, murders, suicides, alcoholism, venereal diseases, forced operations, rapes, drug overdoses, etc., common to those victimized in these "businesses."[846] Since roughly 1981, the press occasionally has covered traffic in juvenile girls and now often covers the massive child sexual slavery trade. However, they deliberately ignore the thriving traffic in *boys*. The first and last major expose of homosexual boy abuse was in 1976, when investigative reporter Robin Lloyd reported in *For Money or Love: Boy Prostitution in America*[847]:

> Perhaps half of the million runaway boys in this country (aged ten to sixteen) are peddling their bodies . . .[848] There are tightly run organizations. . .geared to provide wealthy clients with . . . boys who [will] entertain movie stars, prominent athletes, *politicians*, and in some cases, *heads of state* (emphasis added).[849]

With roughly one to two million homosexual American males,[850] Lloyd's estimate of 500,000 prostituted boys means there is one boy victim per two or three "gay" men.[851] The data also find roughly one in six *other* (*nonprostituted*) boys are forcibly molested.[852] In fact, anything even vaguely near such numbers constitutes *a growing boy abuse culture* since the 1970s.

Sustaining Lloyd's numbers, liberal psychologist Gene Abel[853] recorded over one hundred fifty boy victims per male pederast offender. Obviously, males can access boys more easily than they can girls, so bisexual and homosexual predators harm even more boys than heterosexual predators could harm girls.[854]

The Next Step: Legitimizing Incest

> Actually, Kinsey was the first sex researcher to uncover evidence that violation of the [incest] taboo does not necessarily shake heaven and earth . . . Pomeroy reports many beautiful romances between father and daughter [participants].
>
> —*Penthouse* magazine, "Incest: The Last Taboo," December 1977

Strangers are not the only perpetrators of sexual assault.

In fact, the legitimate and growing sense of "stranger danger" has drastically restricted children's freedom of movement, and parents are keeping their kids closer to home. But it appears many sexual predators are known to the victims. With increases in divorce and fewer really protective dads in the home, more child predators are emerging—and abuse occurring—at the hands of "parent substitutes" or "caretakers"—as discussed earlier, teachers, family acquaintances, clergy, and others with direct access to and the trust of their hapless victims and their mothers.

Many studies claim fathers are the common child offenders, but to validate that as a scientific finding, researchers willingly lump nonbiological household molestors with biological fathers. It is agreed, however, that biological incest *is* increasing, particularly in dysfunctional families.[855]

Kinsey detonated his enemy-propaganda missile into the very heart of the family, creating the justification for incest along with euphemisms to blur its harm.

In 1980, John Leo wrote "Attacking the Last Taboo" for *Time*. Daring to expose bogus sex educators who were leading a "reprehensible" trend to undermine "the taboo against incest,"[856] Leo uncovered some of the key sex educators who doubled as pedophile advocates. He quoted Kinsey co-author Wardell Pomeroy. "It is time to admit that incest need not be a perversion or a symptom of mental illness," Pomeroy said. "Incest between children and adults . . . can sometimes be beneficial."[857]

Beneficial for whom?

Kinsey and his followers actively promoted incest, deliberately hiding its physical and emotional fallout, which includes promiscuity, frigidity, depression, suicide, homosexuality, prostitution, substance abuse, and more.[858] Among those followers, University of Utah anthropologist Seymour Parker viewed the incest taboo as undermining "the affectionate kiss and touch between family members."[859] The Sex Information and Education Council of the United States (SIECUS) attacked the Judeo-Christian incest taboo "as mindless prejudice." SIECUS educator, James Ramey, said incest laws were "a peculiarly American problem—the withdrawal of all touching contact"; Ramey recommended that more home "touching" could reduce "the present rash of feverish adolescent sexual activity outside the home." Euphemisms such as "home sex" began to multiply.[860]

Claiming to report Kinsey's incest data, Pomeroy, Kinsey's co-author and director of the IASHS, repeated the Kinsey team's claim that they had examined "a cross-section of the population," saying that the Kinsey team found "many beautiful and mutually satisfying relationships between fathers and daughters. These may be transient or ongoing, but they have no harmful effect."[861] On what did Pomeroy base this absurd claim? Pomeroy's "cross-section," like Kinsey's, was, in fact, as fictitious as his allegation that incest was harmless. Their "methodology" was modeled after their own pathologies: sexually deviant, political, implicitly incestuous. Pomeroy and Kinsey both said they interviewed about 1,400 sex offenders, including prisoners who were child rapists. But then-Kinsey Institute director Paul Gebhard, speaking of the "incest material," wrote in his letter to me that there were "too few cases" to count so "we omitted incest, except for one brief mention"[862] in the *Female* volume. Kinsey listed the word "incest" only once in his *Male* volume, and omitted it entirely from the *Female* volume's 4,300-entry index.

Thus, Kinsey hid incest in order to legitimize his call for *full sexual liberty*, portraying children as just having sex with "relations"—"adult partners, uncles, fathers, brothers, grandfathers, other relatives," using biased terms that favor child sexual abuse.

In the 1981 letter from Gebhard to me, it turned out that Kinsey found homosexual boy incest was double that of heterosexual incest. Gebhard said Kinsey's research "sample" had "47 white females and 96 white males" who were incest victims.[863] The boys would have been largely homosexual victims. Because Kinsey and his associates made no attempt to suggest that they ever found boys abused by women (a modern epidemic), these boys were incestuously victimized by male relatives.

Academic training and publications on "positive incest" led inexorably to changes in American law and public policy, all based on Kinsey's mad black propaganda. In their quest to have free sexual access to children, Kinsey and co-conspirators, Paul Gebhard and Philip Nobile, published villainous fantasies including:

- Kinsey, Gebhard, and Nobile found no trauma from incest;[864]
- Kinsey said children seek out incest experiences;[865]
- Kinsey said incest is beautiful and mutually satisfying,[866] Pomeroy adds it can be "enriching";[867]
- Gebhard said a tiny percentage of cases were reported because of its harmlessness;[868]
- Gebhard and Nobile renamed incest perpetrators and their victims as "participants";
- Nobile says to revisit laws: "Maybe this [incest] needs repressing, and maybe it doesn't";[869]
- Pomeroy says Kinsey was right that incest would lead to genetic improvement;[870]
- Like Kinsey, Pomeroy assured boys that sex with animals is "potentially joyous."[871]
- Kinsey said male incestuous lust is common, but only between children.[872]

Such outrageous lies were repeated frequently enough that policymakers began to respond with change: lighter legal penalties as Kinseyan clinicians and social workers made light of child molestation, including incestuous child abuse. For children, the outcome was disastrous.

Larry Constantine, PhD, then of Tufts University, spoke at the British Psychological Association's International Conference on Love and Attraction in Swansea, Wales in 1977. The symposium theme was "Infant and Child Sexuality."[873] Constantine spoke on "The Sexual Rights of Children," saying "professionals . . . accept that children are sexual beings from birth" and that they have "the right to behave sexually."[874] The father of at least four children, Constantine demanded children's "right" to sex with adults—for incest and for child pornography. He likened forbidding adult sex with children to oppressing "women and racial minorities." Constantine recommended that children "willingly" work in pornography under "monitorable conditions." Of course, no sane child would *willingly* do this. In our history, only tough laws banning public child begging and child labor stopped such adult exploitation. These are dangerous, self-serving falsehoods.

Kinsey's efforts to downplay the consequences of incestuous abuse showed up in psychiatrist Judith Herman's *Father-Daughter Incest:*

> Kinsey himself, though he never denied the reality of child sexual abuse, did as much as he could to minimize its importance. Some 80 percent of the women who had experienced a childhood sexual approach by an adult reported to Kinsey's investigative team that they had been frightened and upset by the incident. Kinsey cavalierly belittled these reports. He hastened to assure the public that children should not be upset by these experiences. If they were, this was the fault not of the sexual aggressor, but of prudish parents and teachers who caused the child to become "hysterical."[875]

Well said, but it puzzles as to why a fine feminist scholar like Herman missed Kinsey's brazen data that proved him, if not a child rapist himself, *at best* an academic pimp and procurer of mass child rape. Herman also missed Kinsey's claim that he interviewed 4,441 women and *none* had *ever* been harmed by a sexual encounter. Finally, once again, we see a reiteration of Kinsey's diagnosis that children suffered more harm from reactions of repressed or hysterical parents than from the abuse itself. Thus, Kinsey neatly converted outrage over child abuse into "hysteria" by child protectors. To Kinsey, then, *protectors* were the molesters, *protectors* were bad for children.

Only Widespread Male Morality Protects Children

Over the years, Big Sexology repeated this mantra endlessly. Parents and professionals, of course, fell for the ploy, strongly modifying their responses to assaults by not believing children and/or trivializing their pain. And offenders went free.

Lloyd DeMause, the most well-respected researcher addressing the cross-cultural history of child abuse, documents "The Universality of Incest." In Part I of this monograph, DeMause acknowledges that establishing rates of child sexual abuse depended on those who were often too emotionally traumatized to report.[876] Outlining problems of research into sexual abuse of children, DeMause concluded, "The best estimates for memories of childhood sexual abuse we now have for the United States are 40% for girls and 30% for boys." Almost half of the abuse of girls, he argued, was incestuous and about "a quarter" of the abuse of boys was incestuous.[877] These data did not reflect the most abused populations, "institutionalized criminals, prostitutes, juveniles in shelters and psychotics."

I, too, found pandemic incest and child sexual abuse, bred by Kinsey's cult of elitist pedophile and pornography addicts and advocates in academia and the law. Penalties are practically nonexistent for incest because offenders commonly receive so-called therapy in lieu of prison. In fact, even the DoJ National Incident-Based Reporting System (NIBRS) has demoted "incest," commonly by the adult provider, to "nonforcible sexual intercourse"[878]—more doublespeak.

A Legal Loophole: The Incest Exception

Under common law, adultery, battery, and incest were clear grounds for divorce and for significant alimony for the aggrieved party. But the Kinsey, ALI-MPC lobby soon bumped the healthy family unit's standing in law, with the "incest exception." Adding another notch on his belt, this legal loophole goes directly back to Kinsey and his collaborators. The ACLU and ALI-MPC won the "incest exception." If, as Kinsey said, children seduced their fathers, stepfathers, and uncles, those adults were not to blame. With the fiction that sex offenders—pedophiles—could be "cured" by therapy, the courts followed the legal policy of "reuniting the family."

Kinsey and his expert witness followers, such as Johns Hopkins pedophile advocating professor John Money and longtime Kinsey collaborator Hank Giaretto, PhD, (both deceased) of Parents United, saw to it that most states instituted the "incest exception." Money and Giaretto claimed to cure pedophiles, with Giaretto saying his treatment cured 95 percent of incest offenders.[879] Giaretto's "treated" incest abusers were then diverted from jail or prison and returned to the bosom of their families. In California, the treatment preference took the form of the infamous California Penal Code Sections 1203.066, 1000.12 and 1000.13.

Despite Giaretto's unverified 95 percent treatment success rate, the California Protective Parents Association reported quite the opposite. After reunification, "children quit reporting their abuse since they were locked into the barn with the wolf."[880] There was no long-term follow-up study once the wolf was home. How did they react to, once more, living in fear of daily rape? What were their lives like as adults? Said child trauma expert Bruce Perry, MD:

> Incest effects include terror, shame, depression, humiliation, but most typically it is a smoldering fear, ever present, and avoidable only by using maladaptive defenses such as drinking, cutting, dissociating by using drugs.[881]

Horribly, since potential victims were divided into two legal tiers, pedophiles quickly understood the incest loophole implicated benefits of growing their own victims.[882] In 1980 and 1981, state legislatures held hearings on child molestation. Legislators who believed the Kinsey lobby voted to preserve the "incest exception," creating outrageous loopholes for incestuous child rapists.[883]

Grier Weeks, of the National Association to Protect Children (PROTECT), now testifies in state legislatures across the country to repeal the incest exception. In a typical experience, then-assemblyman (now state senator) George Runner tried to rid California of the incest exception; his effort was beaten by what looks like a strong pedophile lobby. In April 2003, PROTECT representatives and Dr. Perry testified for California state senator Jim Battin's bill to protect children from incest. This, too, ended in failure. An outraged grassroots coalition of incest survivors, child protection groups, and women's organizations gathered to support a second Battin bill, insisting that California protect children equally from familial and stranger rapists. Finally, in 2005, Governor Arnold Schwarzenegger set the precedent for other states, signing SB 33, the Miracle Bill, into law to eliminate the Kinsey cult's incest exception in California.[884]

New York soon followed. With the help of children's advocate attorney Andrew Vachss and PROTECT. By July 2006, the New York State Senate passed the bill 60–0, and the State Assembly passed it

141–0. While this is a victory over the bad guys, terrible problems remain. In addition to widely available child pornography, activists incessantly promote legislative initiatives, such as California's new law requiring that homosexuality be taught throughout the entire Kinseyan educational system, while our systems to protect children have, says Vachss, become largely business enterprises and not child protection agencies. Vachss has been a whistleblower on failed government efforts to protect children and to find abducted children. PROTECT, revealed:

> In 2008, the latest year for which records are available, [Ernie] Allen made $511,069 as head of the U.S. National Center for Missing and Exploited Children and its international affiliate. He also received $787,126 in deferred compensation and underfunded retirement benefits, as well as $46,382 in nontaxable benefits—a total of $1,344,567.[885]

This suggests the disinterest of the government, despite its political party, in carrying out forthright persecution and protection of children, says PROTECT. If "follow the money" continues to be a logical maxim, this also is evidence for the unparalleled growth of child and adult pornography nationwide.

Using the First Amendment to Rape Children

Discussed earlier, in 1981, the New York Court of Appeals ruled that a child under age sixteen could be used in child pornography based on First Amendment rights. The ruling covered "sexual conduct," which it defined as "actual or simulated sexual acts, sadomasochistic abuse, sexual bestiality or lewd exhibition of the genitals.[886] Children were paid as "actors," with overtime pay. In *New York v. Ferber,* five appellate court judges (Wachtler, Cooke, Jones, Fuchsberg, and Meyer) voted to legalize child pornography while two (Jason and Gabrielli) stood for protecting children.

A year later, the U.S. Supreme Court reversed the New York court, agreeing that the First Amendment did *not* apply since this was legalized child sexual abuse. For their part, the five New York

Appeals Court judges, whose egregious ruling was overturned, remained on the Court of Appeals. In fact, chief judge Sol Wachtler was once suggested as a New York gubernatorial candidate or U.S. Supreme Court justice before his own arrest. The *New York Times* had editorialized *in favor* of Ferber as New York's highest court sent a clear *pro-pedophile, pro-pornographer* message to all lower court judges and prosecutors.

In 2004, the U.S. Supreme Court ruled that nonobscene simulated or "virtual" images of rape, torture, and molestation of children (under age eighteen) are *harmless* to children and society.[887] Of course, a new growth industry soon emerged. Within two years, by 2006, Internet images of virtual and pseudo child rape and molestation became increasingly common, as did and real children in illegal child pornography.

In *The Marketing of Evil*, David Kupelian, WorldNetDaily author, warned that the campaign for "intergenerational" sex, as its fans call it, would be the next big "sexual liberation" movement. A reported 100,000 Web sites now offer illegal child pornography to a growing population of child-lusting deviates. Worldwide, reported Kupelian, "child porn generates a reported three billion dollars in revenues every year."[888]

Pedophilia and Pederasty: The Insider Lobby

> Gay liberationists in general, and boy-lovers in particular, should know Kinsey's work and hold it dear. . . . Implicit in Kinsey is the struggle we fight today."[889]
>
> —North American Man-Boy Love Association (NAMBLA)

All professions and political parties now host their share of closet sexual psychopaths.[890] Their covert political power too often determines who is hired and fired; who gets scientific funding; whose story is reported or spiked; what laws are passed or locked in committee; and whether police, prosecutors, or judges aid predators or their victims. The "new" breed of Kinseyan doctors, lawyers, judges, prosecutors, defense attorneys, and attorneys general set out to destroy the "old common-law idea" of innocence and of protecting children. Child molesters and other sexual subversives have a perfidious influence in the highest offices in our land, and our legal system is infected with *many* sexually deviant bureaucrats who seek to attain their "rights" by changing the legitimate American political system. Indeed, our children's lives and our nation's culture are increasingly held hostage to many thousands of closeted political operatives.

Statutory Rape and the Age of Consent

An early supporter of Planned Parenthood, I believed their arguments that we should not consider sex "dirty," that children should learn appropriate words for body parts, and that having better information would produce better marriages, fewer "illegitimate" babies, and fewer venereal diseases—opening wide the gates to the enlightened, humane utopia for which we all longed. It didn't happen that way. I was wrong. Planned Parenthood was wrong. But though I recognized my stupidity by the late 1960s, Planned Parenthood's Kinseyan leaders remained willfully blind to the worsening status of children.

A major turning point came in 1965, says STOPP, when the Supreme Court:

> handed Planned Parenthood the *Griswold v. Connecticut* decision . . . setting the stage for court decisions that decriminalized abortion and opened the door for children to engage in sexual activity without their parents' knowledge and with the help of Planned Parenthood's products.[891]

A consequence of Griswold has been that Planned Parenthood has had a role in hiding massive numbers of statutory rapes. Planned Parenthood has a long history of abetting child rapists by aborting their victims' babies. To be clear: If a minor "partner" has not reached the legal age of consent, the adult has committed a statutory rape—even if the minor willingly participates—because a minor cannot "legally consent" to "sexual intercourse" with an adult.[892] Planned Parenthood's complicity in statutory rape has finally grabbed the attention of several state attorneys general. In 2005, Indiana investigators subpoenaed Planned Parenthood's abortion records on minors;

Planned Parenthood sued to halt the investigation, citing privacy rights. A 2006 federal appellate court in Kansas ruled that, because sex is illegal for minors, Planned Parenthood must obey state laws that mandate reports of underage sex acts. Kansas Planned Parenthood alleged that this was "government meddling" in private sexual decisions, but the state attorney general argued that the activity involved criminal sexual abuse of children and that Planned Parenthood must report evidence of such.

In 2006, an undercover activist tape-recorded calls to more than ninety California abortion clinics, including Planned Parenthood. The caller, who pretended to be a thirteen-year-old girl, requested an abortion, asked how to keep it from her parents, and mentioned that her boyfriend is an adult. Clinic after clinic assured her that they would keep the abortion secret from Mom and Dad[893] and that her adult boyfriend could bring her in for the abortion—even though it was obviously statutory rape; under California law, workers are required to report this crime to the police or Child Protective Services. Tape recordings of many of these conversations are available on Pro-Life America's Web site, ProLife.com.

According to J.T. Finn of Pro-Life America, a study of 46,000 pregnant school-age girls in California found that 71 percent of the fathers were adults, averaging 22.6 years of age. "California law lets abortion centers cover up these girls' abortions," Finn says, "with the girls' parents never knowing about this dangerous assault on their daughter's health, their family's life and privacy by strangers." He adds, "In California, sex with a minor is still a crime, especially if the perpetrator is an adult. Yet Planned Parenthood and other abortion centers. . .hide these sex crimes."[894]

Planned Parenthood is not alone in giving predators unfettered sexual access to minors. In legal terms, they seem to be part of a concerted, high-stakes effort to cleave teenagers from parental controls.

Before Kinsey, women wanted and won the increase in the age of consent, from ten years to eighteen or twenty-one years of age. But in Kinsey's wake, state law journals, legislative commissions, and therapeutic publications campaigned to weaken such laws, primarily because adults wanted freedom to seduce children without having to bother with their protective parents.

In 1950, the Group for the Advancement of Psychiatry (GAP) argued that "full responsibility for sexuality" should begin at the "age of 7,"[895] which should be the age of consent! Who would demand such child access? Manfred Guttmacher, MD. The leader of GAP was a twin to Planned Parenthood's Alan E. Guttmacher, PhD.

The notion of lowering the age of consent found ready champions among the rest of the psychiatric profession. Just a few years later, Manfred Guttmacher was an adviser in the composition of the 1955 ALI-MPC. "Kinsey's findings were the points by which we steered. The debt that society will owe to Kinsey and his co-workers for their research on sexual behavior will be immeasurable,"[896] Guttmacher wrote. Armed with these points, the ALI-MPC and their allies began working to end child protection laws by lowering the age of consent.

Judge Morris Ploscowe "ridiculed the statutory rape laws," noting that in Tennessee the legal age of marriage was "twenty-one" and most other states between sixteen and eighteen. He argued that it was ridiculous to prosecute a man who had sex with a child prostitute or thought his "companion" was older. The judge was especially indignant because "in most states the unchastity of the girl is no defense to a charge of rape so long as she is below the age of consent." Judge Ploscowe thought such a law "does not make much sense and should be changed."[897]

Pretending to see no difference between a man who makes passing sexual use of a twenty-one-year-old and a man who legally pledges to love, honor, and protect a sixteen-year-old girl until death they do part, Ploscowe argued that laws designed to protect youngsters from predators were based on a fantasy of children's asexuality and vulnerability.[898] Ploscowe repeated Kinsey's sexual-from-birth mantra, just as elitist educators have regurgitated it in thousands of books and articles for sixty years.

Irate about statutory rape laws, Ploscowe said a man "who has a normal act of sexual intercourse with the consent of a girl who is below the statutory age" should not be penalized because, he opined, the "valid" age of consent should be *age ten or less*, as the ALI-MPC proposed. Ploscowe also thought jail time was unfair, "particularly in the statutory rape cases, where the girl is close to the age named in the statute."

Ten-Year-Olds as Sexually Mature!

Citing Kinsey's *"proofs,"* the ALI-MPC authors argued that, at age *ten*, a little girl's "seductive" conduct might lead men into what some viewed as a sex crime. But if children are sexual from birth, and *unharmed* by sexual intercourse with an adult, and *children* are the ones who initiate the sexual encounter, then such relationships should be legally acceptable. After all, according to Kinsey, sex with children is benign. Therefore, they argued, it was "wise" to consider ten-year-old children as sexually "awakened."[899]

Once the ALI-MPC advised lowering the age of consent, America's legislatures and courts liberalized state laws against rape, child sex abuse, and incest, and eased criminal penalties for sex offenders in more than two-thirds of U.S. states. *Kinsey was the scientific authority for these disastrous changes.*

Homosexual leaders had long campaigned for lowering—or eliminating—the age of consent. Arguing that boys (and girls) were fully capable of "orgasm" and, as one teacher (among many) in an all-boys' school said: "Well, look around. Ten percent of you kids are gay." Thus, all children, especially "gay" children, should be allowed full sexual "rights," including the "right" to have sex with adults.

Kinsey's quest for the Big "O" as the end-all, be-all of human experience

The 1979 anthology, *Lavender Culture*, edited by homosexual activists, Karla Jay, PhD, and Allen Young, includes Gerald Hannon's essay, "Gay Youth and the Question of Consent,"[900] which describes the desire to legalize sex with children. Writing of child sex with adults, Hannon explains, "The child is very likely to have initiated the event and may even want to continue it." Citing Kinsey, Hannon argues the age of consent laws, "The innocence of children, and the idea of the potential harmfulness of sex" are "archaic concepts." So, Hannon argues, we should legalize sex with children.

Describing the homosexual movement's strategy since 1979, Hannon said abolishing "age-of-consent laws must come from young people themselves," since we are seen as adults trying to get "a lot of hot, young bodies." Better to get some teenagers to bring "their" demands before the legislature.[901] Hannon would recruit and use youths so that "abolition of age-of-consent laws" would seem to be "the work of young people."[902]

Thus, homosexual activists use Kinsey's lies about the harmlessness of adult-child sex to substantiate their case to end the age of consent protections. Never mind that, before Kinsey we had *two* types of venereal diseases and now we have at minimum twenty-five—some fatal, like AIDS. In the book of psychopathic pederasts and pedophiles, there is *no* disease, *no* heartbreak, *no* suicide, *no* trauma, *no* abuse. Were it abusive, the perpetrators would merely need tax-funded counseling.

Based on Kinsey, the American Psychiatric Association (APA) removed homosexuality from its list of "disorders" in 1973. Twenty years later, in 1994, the APA dropped the sexual age of consent to twelve or thirteen. The APA does not define adults seeking to have sexual relations with children of fourteen or fifteen years. The group also provided a troubling definition of pedophilia:

APA DSM-IV Criteria for Pedophilia

- Recurrent intense sexual urges and sexually arousing fantasies involving activity with a *prepubescent* child or children (generally age thirteen or younger) over a period of *at least six months;*
- The person has acted on these urges, *or is markedly distressed by them*;
- The person is at least sixteen years old and at least five years older than the prepubescent child or children.

—The American Psychiatric Association Fact Sheet[903]

At this time, this is the bible of the APA and the mental health profession. In sync with the Kinseyan model, the APA diagnosis is used in courtrooms, eroding the laws that penalize child sex predators some sexologists euphemistically call "age-discrepant sexual intimacy." These criteria allow that adults' sexual urges for young children are normal enough and healthy enough *if they are sporadic and if the adult feels fine about their child lusts.* Thus, sexual urges for young children represent pedophilia *only if the adult is five years older than a prepubescent child, if the urges persist, and only if the adult acts on or feels "guilt" or anxiety about these urges.* How convenient: *no guilt, no disorder!*

The APA now views "mild" sadism and masochism to be normal.[904] So the psychiatric profession—our psychiatric experts—say that torturing others is fine—if the victim gives "consent"—even if that consent is from a child of "at least sixteen years old."

How in the world did we get here?

[CHAPTER 13]

Our Legacy Given Over to Barbarians

> [V]irtually every page of the Kinsey Report touches on some section of the legal code . . . . a reminder that the law, like our social pattern, falls lamentably short of being based on a knowledge of facts.[905]
>
> —Morris Ernst, of the American Civil Liberties Union (ACLU)

REALITY FINDS THAT, ONCE sex is trivialized between adults, children become victims of adults' sexual violence. This was particularly likely when Kinsey's tireless army of pedophiles and pederasts started in 1948 to focus on gaining legal protection for their child lusts.

Immediately after Kinsey's first report in 1948, hundreds of lawyers and judges flooded the legal world with law review articles demanding sexual "emancipation" for children. Their timing seemed ominously orchestrated. It started with Kinsey's attorney, Morris Ernst, a companion to President Franklin D. Roosevelt and friend of U.S. Supreme Court justices. Ernst parroted Kinsey in 1948, arguing that Kinsey's data should be the basis of sex crime "revision and improvement." Morris Ernst called upon "every bar association in the country" to use Kinsey's "data" to revisit its state's sex laws and "adjust our laws" to "scientific knowledge."[906]

In turn, a cadre of perverse leaders at bench and bar cited Kinsey's findings and sought ways to justify what certainly smacked of lawful sexual access to children on behalf of closeted heterosexual pedophiles and homosexual pederasts. In "adjusting" our laws, they induced

Americans into accepting legal precedents that endangered children and their sexual morality.

A member of the saboteurs was Judge Morris Ploscowe. In 1948, Ploscowe touted Kinsey's claims of promiscuity, jeering at the idea that rape of women and children caused any damage. Thus, he minimized sexual assault on underage girls:

> "If most rapes simply involve consensual acts of sexual intercourse with underage girls, they are not the products of degenerates and psychopaths who force their attentions upon unwilling victims."[907]

But Ploscowe was a judge. He knew that "statutory rape" did not mean the victim gave consent; since she was under the age of consent, she could not legally, logically, cognitively give consent. He simply maintained that all sex legislation violates the realities of life and, thus, is unenforceable based on "wide human need" for sex—even with children.[908] Here Ploscowe simply repeated Kinsey's "scientific" findings:

> These pre-marital, extra-marital, homosexual and animal contacts, we are told, are eventually indulged in by 95 percent of the population in violation of statutory prohibitions. If these conclusions are correct, then it is obvious that our sex crime legislation is completely out of touch with the realities of individual living and is just as inherently unenforceable as legislation that prohibits. . .an activity that responds to a wide human need.[909]

Based on the so-called orgasms that Kinsey's child rapists reported, a "peer sex play" vision, which Kinsey's operatives favored, soon dominated most sex-offender laws. Ploscowe initiated this pioneering defense. "Only *where the age disparity between the man and the girl are very great,*" said Judge Ploscowe, "is it possible to say that the rape may be the work of a mentally abnormal individual, a psychopath, or a potentially dangerous sex offender."[910] A peer-rapist, then, is not a "potentially dangerous sex offender." This interpretation effectively legalized rape of children and youths by anyone within three to five years of their own age.

How many rapists have been released into society because a pedophile judge, perhaps like Ploscowe, felt the "age disparity" was fine?

In fact, today many states define the rape of a ten-year-old child by a thirteen-year-old boy as a form of "peer sex play." *But why should rape hurt less if the rapist is sixteen or thirty?* How many children have to return to school to sit in the same classroom with their teenage rapist—or rapists? This is a brutal legal legacy, indeed.

Ploscowe sought to correct the outdated prejudice that protected young girls, and to excise the "old common-law idea" about maidens. Within seven years, the legal profession accepted Kinsey's lies as "facts" that dominated the "Sexual Offenses" section of the 1955 Model Penal Code. (The "Frequency of Sexual Deviation" section quotes twenty-one legal "proofs"; nineteen of them are straight from Kinsey.) The section, "Sodomy and Related Offenses," proposed that men who have "consensual" sodomy with an "actor" ten years or older be reclassified as committing a misdemeanor. *This was a major step toward full legalization of homosexual assault on ten-year-old boys.*

By 1962, Ralph Slovenko, a prolific law, psychiatry, and sexology author, took Ploscowe's "wide human need" theory down a step:

> Even at the age of four or five, this [female] seductiveness may be so powerful as to overwhelm the adult into committing the offense. The affair is therefore not always the result of the adult's aggression; often the young female is the initiator and seducer.[911]

An *"affair"?* Between an *adult* and a *four- or five-year-old child?* Did Slovenko practice what he preached? Using Kinsey's predatory "data," then, our laws came to fit the "wide human need," arguably penned by the lowest of the low.

Pathology Runs Amok on the Bench

In 1973, in his book *The Finest Judges Money Can Buy and Other Forms of Judicial Pollution,* constitutional law professor Charles Ashman reveals shocking stories of judicial aberrations—sexual encounters with defendants, pimping, showing pornography, and, of course, taking bribes.[912] Our news media often miss such weighty reports, yet the sexual views and sexual morality of prosecutors, judges, and other legal bureaucrats can be a matter of life or death for children. Consider these developments, which Linda Jeffrey, PhD, located[913]:

- 1969 The Georgia Law Review, advised by Kinsey: Child molestation is a "relatively minor crime . . . [the] absurdity of enforcing most of our sex laws . . . should be obvious, even to the most prudish Neo-Puritans";[914] "Pedophiles comprise the largest class of sex offenders"; The Georgia Law Review also recommended that child molesters "should be released on probation" or after paying "a small fine" if they didn't use "physical force."[915]
- 1973 Missouri Revision Commission: Rape and child abuse "carry extremely severe punishment. . . . Those few who are punished are dealt with cruelly, to the satisfaction of no one. . . .";[916] "the label rapist should not be used in the statutory non consent cases. . . . The Code reserves that term for the most heinous sexual offender. . . . For, one may have sex with a "fully consenting . . . social companion . . . of twelve years of age" (The last Missouri review found consent at age fourteen).[917]
- 1976 Maine Law Review: "Only threats of serious bodily injury, kidnapping, or death will suffice to make out the crime of rape."[918]
- 1983 The New Jersey Law Journal: "[T]he older term "rape" was fraught with negative emotion and unrealistic for this era. . . . There is no justification for the perception that the female is a unique creature, harmed in some unique way by untoward sexual behavior."[919]
- "Current rape penalties are often trivial. In complex, graduated laws on "age of consent" even the youngest victims (age four in Georgia) are on trial. To prove an authentic rape, a child must often substantiate additional proofs of "force."[920]

The practical results? In 1990, the American Bar Association reported 80 percent of convicted child molesters plea-bargained and served no prison time! To the satisfaction of the deviant legal elite, the pedophile typically received taxpayer-funded "treatment for his sexual orientation to children."[921]

In 1993, openly homosexual Oregon Democrat Mark Kramer introduced a state bill to allow Oregon courts to transfer children from competent biological parents to nonfamilial "affectionate" adults. This bill did *not* require that parents be adjudicated as unfit in order to have their children transferred to dangerous predators, *nor* did it stipulate legal requirements for the new guardians. It said anyone "may petition or file a motion for intervention with the court."[922] An "affectionate" judge could award a child to someone who provides the fun and games that parents would not allow. The basis of this legislation? Kinsey. (The bill was apparently rejected.)[923]

After six decades of propaganda for sociopolitical revolution, the ACLU is flying in on Kinsey's wings and adding a pedophile revolution to its repertoire by defending the North American Man-Boy Love Association (NAMBLA). NAMBLA got headlines in 1997 when pederasts Salvatore Sicari and Charles Jaynes abducted a Boston fifth grader, Jeffrey Curley, age ten. Sicari and Jaynes took Jeffrey to the Boston Public Library and logged onto the NAMBLA Web site, which champions the seduction, abduction, and rape of boys. Then they took Jeffrey home and sodomized and murdered him. After they were caught, Sicari was convicted of first-degree murder and Jaynes of second-degree murder and kidnapping.[924]

In 2000, Jeffrey's parents filed a $200 million dollar suit against NAMBLA, claiming the "educational" content of the site played a role in the death of their son. Jaynes argued the NAMBLA site gave him "psychological comfort." One NAMBLA publication is, *The Survival Manual: The Man's Guide to Staying Alive in Man-Boy Sexual Relationships*. Fox TV anchorman Bill O'Reilly noted that the NAMBLA site included "techniques designed to lure boys into having sex with men."[925] Trivializing the NAMBLA Web site's sinister program and intent to seduce, abduct, and sodomize boys, ACLU lawyers eagerly sprang to NAMBLA's defense—against Jeffrey's parents. The ACLU argued that "holding the organization responsible for the crimes of others. . .would gravely endanger first amendment freedoms."[926]

This ACLU *policy* in action, representing the views of its leaders and most of its member states: "There should not be a variable standard of obscenity for minors"[927] lest we allegedly violate the First Amendment.[928] According to the ACLU, NAMBLA was a legitimate group, with both educational and legal pornographic rape materials that are part of "traditional" speech, even if they are pictorial pornography and obscenity.

A full-service predator-protector, the ACLU *defends* predators and *fights* protectors. Despite ACLU rhetoric, the organization is paid by Big Pornography—and that's who they serve, naturally campaigning to end child protections. For example, it fought AB 2893, the 2006 California bill, that:

> seeks to prevent a child from being placed in a home with a registered sex offender whose victim was a minor, or have unsupervised visitation with that offender, when a court fails to state its reasons for finding no significant risk to the child in writing or on the record.[929]

Though the ACLU and the California Attorneys for Criminal Justice (CACJ) fought the bill, it was signed into law in 2006. It protects minors who are *not* mature enough to provide *valid* assent to adult sexual lures. Still, the ACLU wants to erase any legal distinction between adults and children and has sought, when it could, to eliminate statutory rape laws.[930] Since "age of consent" determines statutory rape, this has been a prime focus.

Remember, eliminating *seduction* as a crime weakened the State's power to protect the young and the vulnerable. Lowering the age of consent multiplied this initiative, freeing many more young people for sex—and reducing or eliminating the penalties on those who prey on them. And this was not the doing of the World War II generation.

Normalizing Pedophilia and Pederasty

Increasingly, litigators and legislators have aided sophisticated and active pedophile advocates. To this lobby, we can trace the historical sex-law changes that altered our nation's character by lowering the age of consent and arguing that children are acceptable pawns in freedom of speech and art—despite abuse and torture. The pedophile lobby endangered and preyed upon our children, and they continue to do so. As they make our language increasingly pedophile-friendly, they integrate the psychopathic enemy's black propaganda into our entire social fabric. Their success is our demise.

Arguably, the most important—and devastating—outcome of Kinsey's attack on America is its effect on children's well being. Of nearly 2,000 pages of his reports, the most stunning items are Tables 30 to 34 in the *Male* volume. These tables record Kinsey's brutal sex experiments on very young boys—by him and/or his "team." *Unquestionably, these tests meet the definition of pederasty, the homosexual abuse and rape of boys.*

During a sexology conference, Paul Gebhard, co-author of *The Ethics of Sex Research*, told assembled "experts" that it was ethical to use the "normal" child orgasm data they obtained from child rapists. No "expert" at the seminar indicated outrage or even disagreement with this assertion. Nor did any protest when Gebhard revealed that the Kinsey team had covered up for his Nazi serial pedophile accused of murder and convicted of massive child sexual abuse. Gebhard admits as much:

> We [were] amoral at best and criminal at worst . . . . An example of our criminality is our refusal to cooperate with authorities in apprehending a pedophile we had interviewed who was being sought for a [child] sex murder.[931]

Even today, sexologists refuse to refute Kinsey's "child sexuality data," or Kinsey. Trained in Kinsey's image, they ignore the facts about the real damage of child victimization and believe, instead, Kinsey's pseudo-scientists.

World-famous "sexologist" Edward Brecher, who wrote *The Sex Researchers*, said the "stereotype of the lust-crazed sadist appears to be a relatively minor risk to American little girls."[932] According to Brecher, "little girls were erotically aroused, the Kinsey report adds." Moreover, these "contacts had often involved considerable affection and [some of] the older females in the sample felt that their preadolescent experience had contributed favorably to their later sociosexual development."[933] Future research proves such statements are dead wrong.[934]

After Alfred Kinsey, we experienced a paradigm shift, a sea of change that took us from the Greatest Generation to a coarsened, anti–Judeo-Christian culture. In the twentieth century, Kinsey dismantled and reversed the patriarchal era of protecting our most vulnerable members—our women and children. He denied the existence, meaning, and value of both innocence and shame. The madman had an agenda. He and his co-conspirators wanted to abuse children, especially boys, so their "research" focused not only on their own sadistic sexual gratification, but on the destruction of children, families, and the civil society into which we were privileged to be born.

We should not be surprised, then, that after six decades of legal support for Kinsey's pedophilia, children are now the primary targets of sexual assault. But we are. We have lost the voice of the Greatest Generation, committed to God, responsibility, self-restraint, sacrifice, and protection of women and children. Instead, America's sexual learning and conduct reflect Kinsey's pathological, abnormal, violent, and criminal values. A psychopathic, dirty old man's sexual deviance was imposed on an entire nation. As a result, we swim in a post-Kinsey sexual sewer. Indeed, in the years since Kinsey, America has been victimized by a horrifying surge in sex crimes, even against *infants.*

Legalization

Relying almost exclusively on Kinsey for "scientific" justification, the U.S. Supreme Court finally legalized homosexual sodomy in *Lawrence v. Texas* in 2003. Among other fallouts, the decision further demeaned the marital bed and the concept of eye-to-eye, lip-to-lip sex as the humane, interactive form of lovemaking. Worse, it further eroded protections for schoolchildren against pornographic "sex education," gave leeway to sodomy in mainstream entertainments, and put more boys at risk of sexual recruitment. And the results have been catastrophic in increases in the spread of AIDS and venereal diseases.

According to law professor Jonathan Turley, it "should be obvious that such laws governing private, consensual acts are no longer valid after the Supreme Court [sodomy] decision in *Lawrence v. Texas* in 2003."[935] Turley remarked that Justice Antonin Scalia wrote in his dissent [in *Lawrence*] that the U.S. Supreme Court "should not impose foreign moods, fads, or fashions on Americans."[936] Unfortunately, in fact, the entire Lawrence sodomy decision stood on Alfred Kinsey's fraudulent World War II homosexuality data.

The evidence shows that Justice Kennedy genuflected to "facts" about sodomy as documented by the American Law Institute's Model Penal Code (ALI-MPC) of 1955. Yet the primary source for the sodomy "data" codified as "fact" by the Court in the ALI-MPC was Kinsey alone. Tracing Kennedy's *majority opinion* to its origin reveals that *the majority of the justices* relied on one sex "science" resource as the Court's primary authority on sex and sodomy: the fraudulent, bi/homosexual, sadomasochistic American professor, Alfred C. Kinsey.

Of course, the Supreme Court majority were not the only ones to rely on Kinsey as the definitive authority on American sexuality. The "gay studies" historical revisionists, whom the majority cited, also relied on Kinsey as their primary sex science resource.[937] In the subsequent march to legitimize homosexuality, Kinsey led the parade.

Be clear: Kinsey's foremost aim was to legitimize widespread, unlimited sexual promiscuity *of any and all kinds*. Legitimizing bisexuality and homosexuality—his own preferences—were a natural means toward that end.

Again, historically and legally, before Kinsey, Americans empirically understood homosexuality and bisexuality as *largely due to early childhood sexual trauma and/or family disorders*.[938] Promiscuous heterosexual *or* bi/homosexual youths commonly share backgrounds in childhood trauma (e.g., parental neglect, violence, alcoholism, sex abuse, and/or other dysfunctions).[939] Then, Kinsey published his world famous "scale" claiming that his bogus "data" proved that there was a normal "sexual continuum."

To "prove" this, Kinsey cited his alleged scientific rating scale[940] for male sexuality, perhaps the most infamous and influential diagonal line ever drawn in human history. Kinsey's diagonal line charts exclusive homosexuality at the top of the sexuality ramp; a "6" on his scale, homosexuals represented at least 10 percent of the males Kinsey interviewed. From there, many males slide down to average sexuality at a "3," so he claimed that most men were bisexual. At the heterosexual end of the slide, "0" defines exclusive heterosexuality, which, not coincidentally, suggests no one. Claiming that children were sexual from birth, Kinsey however admits that early sexual experiences largely shape "orientation:"

> [P]atterns of heterosexuality and patterns of homosexuality represent *learned behavior* which depends, to a considerable degree, upon the mores of the particular culture in which the individual is raised. . . .[941] Learning and conditioning . . . the first experiences, the most intense experiences . . . effect an individual's subsequent behavior . . . bodies, are modified by their experience . . .[942] In general, males are more often conditioned by their sexual experience . . . than females . . .[943]

If the previous experience was with an individual of their own sex, they are, because of the association with the previous experience, more likely to respond again to individuals of their own sex . . .[944]

FIGURE 21

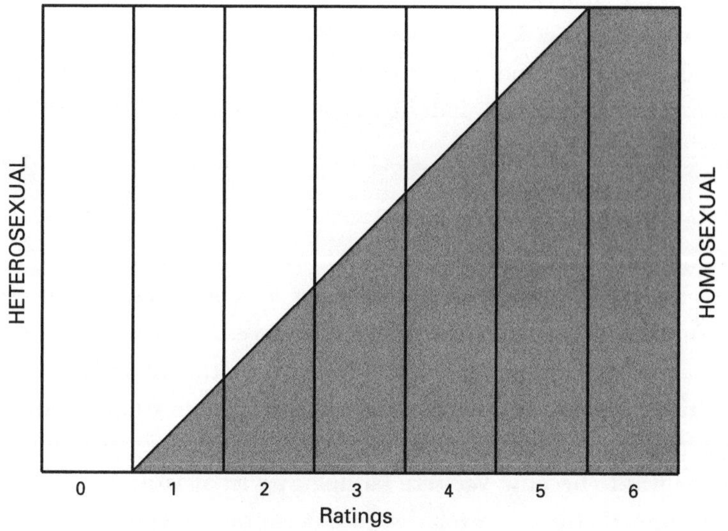

Figure 161. Heterosexual-homosexual rating scale
Source: Kinsey, *Male*, p. 638

Based on both psychologic reactions and overt experience, individuals rate as follows:

0. Exclusively heterosexual with no homosexual
1. Predominantly heterosexual, only incidentally homosexual
2. Predominantly heterosexual, but more than incidentally homosexual
3. Equally hterosexual and homosexual
4. Predominantly homosexual, but more than incidentally heterosexual
5. Predominantly homosexual, but incidentally heterosexual
6. Exclusively homosexual

Here, Kinsey speaks from personal experience! He actually writes as though he were warning millions of readers worldwide, hoping someone would catch on! A closet sadomasochistic, bi/homosexual, pederast panderer, and pornography addict, Kinsey actually admits, "[f]lagellation, masochism, transvestism, and the wide variety of fetishes appear to be products of conditioning" (emphasis added).[945]

Many scholars, he says, correctly emphasized the importance of one's early experience. Repeatedly citing early "conditioning" for later sexual "choices," Kinsey quite candidly adds that one can be conditioned to "un-natural and abnormal" or "bizarre, perverse, or unthinkable" sexual activity.[946] Kinsey even admits to the effects of "watching" sexual conduct! He says worldwide laws prohibiting public sex—as in pornography, erototoxins, and "erotica"—were all likely "an attempt to control the sympathetic response of the bystanders and the social consequences of group sexual activity."[947]

I interpret these as Kinsey's "true confessions." He admits his early conditioning in black and white. Someone, or some people, conditioned him early into lifelong—indeed *fatal*—sexual psychopathology.

Kinsey's Revenge

With no one recognizing Kinsey's confessions or "rescuing" him from his pain, Kinsey exacted revenge for his own early sexual conditioning (aka: abuse) seeding his own pathologies onto the generations. As he prescribed eliminating society's "moralistic classifications" and, thus, legal punishments for sexual deviance,[948] Kinsey's youthful sexual trauma was to become Western pathology writ at large.

His remarkable self-revelations are borne out by empirical observation and reliable research that biological evidence for genetic homosexuality does not exist. "Survival of the fittest" is a metaphor for Darwin's theory of "natural selection." English biologist Thomas Miconi explains Darwin's theory: "Survivors survive, reproduce and therefore propagate any *heritable* characters which have affected their survival and reproductive success."[949]

Natural selection requires that, if homosexuality were genetic, inherited homosexuals would have to reproduce themselves. If reproduction is impossible, that "group" will increase or decrease based on cultural "conditioning" or recruitment. It is not possible for children to inherit a "gay gene" from a non-reproductive gene pool unless one is not biologically *only* homosexual but capable of heterosexual reproduction.

Even Kinsey conceded that homosexuality was not genetically passed on.[950] Despite multiple "studies" of dead men's brains, of tears, fingerprints, twins and such, homophile researchers cannot locate a genetic path by which nonreproductive homosexuals reproduce "their kind."[951]

Indeed, biology, cross-cultural history, literature, animal and probability studies, empirical observation, and common sense all confirm that homosexuality commonly results from "learned behavior"—from "nurture," not "nature." As two medical researchers reported in the *Journal of the American Medical Association* in 1998:

> Abused adolescents, particularly those victimized by males, were up to 7 times more likely to self-identify as gay or bisexual than peers who had not been abused.[952]

The Fifth Column: A Controlled Mass Media

Kinsey conceded sexual identity as commonly a product of what he euphemistically called early "learned behavior." If such "learned behavior" is commonly early sexual abuse, parental neglect, etc., this negates Kinsey's "normality" agenda and the effort to legitimize homosexuality. The homosexual lobby, led by two brilliant strategists, Kirk and Madsen, would need to create an alternate "normal" reality that would slowly become part of the public's understanding of normality.

> [I]t makes no difference that the ads are lies; not to us, because we're using them to ethically good effect . . .[953] In the early stages of the campaign, the public should not be shocked and repelled by premature exposure to homosexual behavior itself. Instead, the imagery of sex per se should be downplayed, and the issue of gay rights reduced, as far as possible, to an abstract social question.[954]
>
> —Homosexual marketers Kirk & Madsen in *After the Ball*

According to Britannica.com, a fifth column is a secret group of subversives who work "to undermine a nation's solidarity by any means at their disposal." Further, they say:

> A cardinal technique of the fifth column is the infiltration of sympathizers into the entire fabric of the nation under attack and, particularly, into positions of policy decision and national defense. From such key posts, fifth-column activists exploit the fears of a people by spreading rumors and misinformation, as well as by employing the more standard techniques of espionage and sabotage.[955]

In the last fifty years, Americans went from priding themselves on their honest, religious lives to "sex, drugs, and rock 'n' roll!" Rockefeller, Ford, and other major philanthropies knowingly hid Kinsey's frauds and crimes, and continue to fund the Kinsey Institute and other Kinsey-based university departments that award "human sexuality" degrees.[956] By now, hundreds of thousands of Kinsey-cloned sexual saboteurs have redefined right and wrong, good and evil, normal and abnormal for billions of Americans—and the public policies that govern them.

Our Constitution grants the American press with "free speech" privileges so it will provide a "window to the world." The Greek philosopher Plato said the truth needed to be known so that the polity could keep society straight. The free press was not to be a tool of special interests, elite bankers, owners, unions, religions, or cults. Were the press serving unelected power lobbies, the fourth estate (the media) would be a "fifth column": "a group of people who, although residing in a country, act traitorously out of secret sympathy with an enemy."[957]

In 1978, Aleksander Solzhenitsyn outraged his Harvard audience when he said:

> The press can both stimulate public opinion and miseducate it . . . The press has become the greatest power within the Western countries, more powerful than the legislature, the executive, and judiciary. One would then like to ask: By what law has it been elected and to whom is it responsible?[958]

As mass media controls our information—our "window to the world"—it shapes the public mind, behavior, laws, and policies. We can judge who is in control of the press by studying the health and welfare of our people. Pre-Kinsey, mass media commonly reflected the sexual morality of the Greatest Generation. Looking at the hard data on violence, rape, child abuse, venereal disease, divorce, and more, we find the sexual health and welfare of our citizenry was relatively excellent. Post-Kinsey, despite astounding advancements in science and medicine, we have epidemic rates of rape, violence, child abuse, divorce, sexually transmitted disease, illegitimacy, and more.

Even before Kinsey's *Male* volume appeared, the media blitz splattered Kinsey's false data across the country. Sixty years later, media saboteurs continue to bombard us with false information that produces disease and social breakdown. How has the media defrauded us?

FIGURE 22
THE MECHANICS OFTHE SHIFT

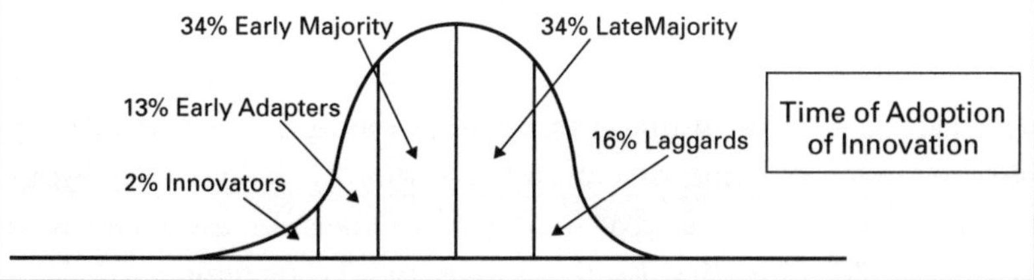

Phillip Kotler (1986) *Marketing Management* "Theory of Diffusion of Innovation"

Philip Kotler's famous book, *Marketing Management*,[959] documents how a controlled media can "stimulate public opinion and miseducate" it. Kotler demonstrates how 2.5 percent of social leaders—carried forth on the shoulders of the mass media—can rapidly sway roughly 13 percent of the public into adopting a new innovation, belief, or product. Supported by the mass media, this influential group sways another 34 percent. The process continues until a majority of people are onboard.[960] Based on this model of the "diffusion" of new ideas, nations often radically change their belief systems.

Kinsey's fraudulent claims about homosexual normality in 1948 and 1953 began to shift public views on homosexuality. Following Roger's model popularized by Kotler, gullible and/or predatory professors in major universities were quick to report Kinsey's "findings" to their naïve students. This 2.5 percent or so of leaders—fueled by the heroic Kinsey in newspapers and television—began the climb up the bell curve.

Even Kinsey could not cook up enough sodomy data to convince the public of its commonality, though the media, using advertising and organizational psychology, caused an "adoption of innovation" that led to our current sodomy crusade. The allegation that over 50 percent of "teenagers aged 15 to 19" had oral sex[961] is an excellent example of Kotler's "Adoption of Innovation Curve." "This is a point of major social transition," says James Wagoner, president of Advocates for Youth, especially as girls are often the "hunters" and boys the prey.[962]

However, the resulting pain, trauma, sickness, and heartbreak among our youth who have lost their hold on intimacy does not follow a curve. Such harm is exponential—a diagonal line slanting straight up.

Pedophilia and Pederasty—The Truth

Refuting blatant facts, sexologists argued that there *isn't* more child sexual abuse—we are just more *aware* of the crime. While they *do* accept statistics that show more divorce, robbery, murder, and venereal disease, stunningly they maintain that similar statisticians are just wrong about rape and child abuse. But it is the sexologists who are wrong. Yes, let us hope that we *are* more aware, and that more children *are* able to report their abuse. But we must also face the fact that sex crime like sex, is more prevalent today than at any time in American history.

In 1950, two years after Kinsey's *Male* volume, the FBI's craggy director, J. Edgar Hoover, announced a "terrifying increase in sex crimes."[963] Hoover advocated tough laws against sex offenses to help law enforcement wage "war on the sex criminal who Hoover viewed as a sinister threat to American childhood and womanhood."[964]

Kinsey detested Hoover. Wardell Pomeroy bragged that Kinsey ridiculed "what the nation and the FBI were calling heinous crimes against children,"[965] and Kinsey publicly sneered at two Hoover-approved pamphlets warning parents about child molesters.[966] But secretly Kinsey was terrified. What if Hoover discovered that he had hired men to seduce, rape, and abuse children? Would Hoover charge Kinsey himself? Kinsey and his team could have gone to prison and even faced capital punishment. Certainly, if people learned that Kinsey and his clan had refused (as they did!) to help Hoover's FBI find a child's sex-murderer—and if they doubted Kinsey's "data" and assertions about the insignificance of sex crimes—the legal momentum to weaken sex laws would stall, even fail. So to hide the truth—all of the truths—they had to protect their image and insulate themselves from Hoover's scrutiny. Thus, the Kinsey cult of pedophile protectors traveled far and wide to popularize their propaganda—that they were objective, conservative "scientists," *and* that children did in fact sexually seduce adults. In fact, years later I interviewed a prosecutor who confessed he and his colleagues were forced to be trained by John Money at the FBI headquarters.

But we *know* that the Kinsey Institute protected child sex predators and even Gebhard said "a pedophile we had interviewed [who was] being sought for a sex murder."[967] Nice guys!

In 1981, the National Study of the Incidence and Severity of Child Abuse and Neglect reported a *massive* increase in child sexual abuse, as reported to child protective service agencies, police, social services, and other treatment facilities:

> [I]n 1976, the first year for which data from all 50 states were available, 416,033 reports were documented; by 1979, the number had jumped to 711,142, an apparent increase of 71% over a three year period.[968]

Twenty years later, we saw irrefutable evidence of sexual abuse on boys, as 7,166 boys were infected—actually killed—by AIDS-infected men (Figure 23). The inexcusable cover-up of boys killed by men with AIDS jumped out from a radical 1995 "Advocates for Youth" report. The agency announced an increase in child molestation *by* adolescents, though the article also ducked the obvious fact that sexually abused children often turn their abuse on other boys and girls.

FIGURE 23
1991 EARLY YOUNG AIDS VICTIMS

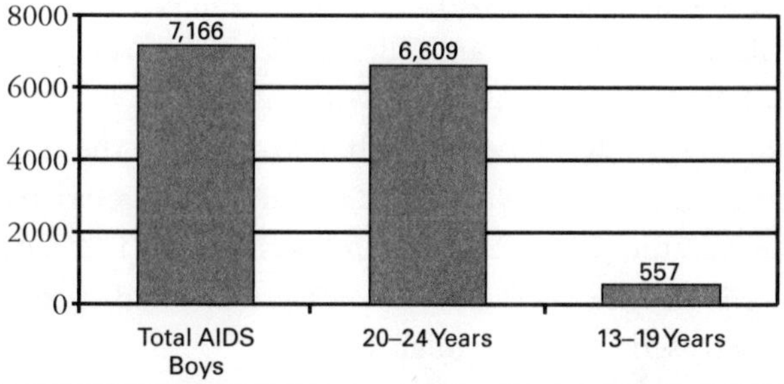

October 1991 CDC data reported in *The Advocate*, March 24, 1992

The Advocate's story also said the CDC, in 1991, identified 537 girls with AIDS. Again, the girls were likely infected by bi/homosexual boyfriends. Where are the arrests, the media outcry, the congressional investigations? Remember the ancient Greeks celebrated "pederasty," male sexual desire for boys more than pedophilia, opposite-sex child lust.

Traumatized, confused, and despairing, most child abuse victims believe the lies adult predators tell them about their "sexual identity." Labeling boys "consenting gays," places responsibility for their deaths *on the children*.[969] Citing the rates of young "gay" deaths, then, the gay lobby justified government funding increases, which, in turn, enabled them to indoctrinate more children via pro-homosexual school "sex education" about "AIDS," "diversity," "bullying," and "hate crimes." Sexual sabotage can be fatal.

Though information from local "Child Protection Services" (CPS) agencies was hotly contested and largely discredited, subsequent statistics validated the increasing numbers of child sexual abuse charges. Indeed, some child abuse reports jumped 348 percent in 1996 over 1976. The American Health Association estimated that Americans reported 669,000 abused children to CPS agencies in 1976. Fast forward: Data from the National Child Abuse and Neglect Data System (NCANDS) say that, in 1996, more than *three million abused children were reported*.[970] (During this time, the child population increase was miniscule.) Moreover, CPS agencies were unable to keep up with the volume of calls and simply did not investigate all of them. Rather a different story than the FBI is telling about "better reporting."

Remember, data from the DoJ show that *non-family members* abducted 58,200 children in 1999. Though these children returned home within twenty-four hours, *roughly half had suffered sexual molestation*.[971] As Orwell said, despite what we see with our own eyes, the "experts" tell us that gutting laws that favored the family and restricted divorce brought us greater peace, civility, and wellbeing. The truth is that these changes, and the prevalence of pornography and "sexology," dramatically increased criminal violence rates.

The Numbers Game

America, the government asserted, was no better and no worse than ever before. What choice did we have but to accept this status quo? As the experts insisted that the nightly news of heinous cases of sexual crimes against children were "just" isolated incidents—sensationalized and blown out of proportion—we questioned our own powers of observation. We tried to convince ourselves that such cases really were quite rare, even if we *did* hear about them happening all the time, all over the country: *Please, God, let it be my imagination.*

It wasn't.

Government agencies skillfully and systematically covered up the terrifying ongoing increase in sex crimes against children for decades. Though we continued to believe our venerable justice agencies, they did not warn us that something was—and is—very, very wrong.

How and why have they hidden this truth?

The information they released—and continue to release—does not include sexual crimes against younger children and, therefore, does not reflect true rates of even more predatory crimes against children.

Shortly after Kinsey published his *Female* volume, the FBI began covering up child sexual abuse. In 1957–1958, the FBI *dropped child victims under age twelve*—the age group most susceptible to sexual violence—*from rape reports*. Guided by an anonymous group of outside "experts," the FBI excluded all data on incest, sodomized boys, rapes of girls, and plea-bargained cases of child statutory rape, purging data of such crimes against children under age twelve from its Uniform Crime Reports (UCR). Though the UCR includes reports from the FBI, Health and Human Services, and the DoJ's Office of Juvenile Justice and Delinquency Prevention, academic researchers and government oversight agencies did *not* include statutory rape, child sexual abuse, or incest assaults on children under age twelve in the UCR sex-crime data from 1958 to the present day.

In July 2000, the FBI's National Incident-Based Reporting System (NIBRS) acknowledged this decades-long "flaw" in national sexual-abuse data collecting, saying that the "only existing national data collection effort that explored the incidence of sexual assault *ignored crimes against young victims*."[972] The NIBRS reported the shocking, first-ever nationwide statistics on child abuse, including forcible rape and victims *under twelve years old*: (Figure 24)[973]

- 67% of all sex abuse victims were under 18.
- 34% were under 12.
- 14% were under 5.

FIGURE 24

67% OF REPORTED SEX ASSAULT VICTIMES ARE UNDER AGE 18

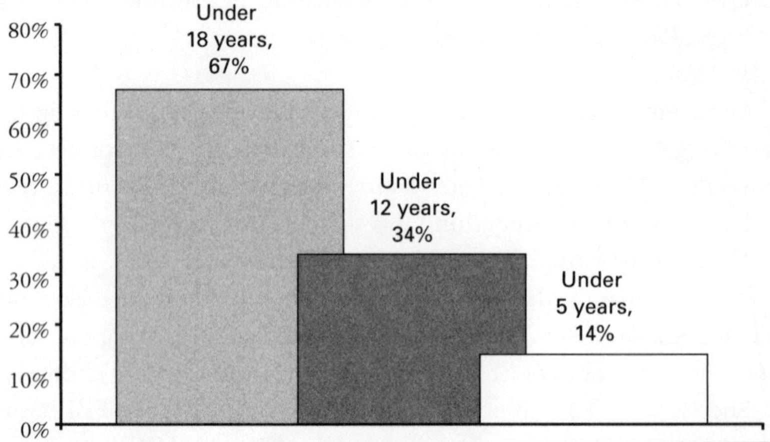

(NIBRS "Sexual Assault of Young Children . . ." July, 2000, NJC 182990, p2)

So in the post-Kinsey sexual revolution, almost seventy out of 100 sex-crime victims were minors, and a third of all child sexual abuse victims were under twelve. Gang rapes and racially tainted rapes were all hidden away in complex statistical analyses. Explosive NIBRS data in FBI "forcible rape" statistics shatter the rosy illusion that our highly eroticized society is a nice, safe, and free society. Even *Frontline's* report, "The Adjustment Difficulties of Boys and Girls in the United States" documents the effects of our newest cultural contagion while refusing to identify its critical cause.

- In 2001, 4,126 boys between 5 and 24 *committed suicide*.[974]
- 433,108 boys were victims of child abuse or neglect in 2001.[975]
- Juvenile girl delinquency increased 182% in nine years (1987–1996).[976]
- More than 2.7 million children were victims of criminal attacks in schools in 1997.[977]
- "Every day between 1.3 and 2.8 million runaway and homeless youth live" on our streets[978] (roughly half of whom enter prostitution).[979]
- Since 1999, foster care has held 550,000 children, often abused.[980]

Credibility of FBI Statistics

In October 2000, the FBI's UCR claimed a nine-year decrease in violent crime. In January 2001, the Office of Juvenile Justice and Delinquency Prevention declared that sexual abuse of children had nose-dived 31 percent from 1992 to 1998. In 2003, the DoJ asserted that there is "progress" in the area of child sexual abuse and that things are "getting better." And recall that, in 2006, the *Washington Post* quoted an FBI report that, since 1979, rapes had plummeted by 85 percent.[981]

However, reading the small print, we find *no* evidence of decline, just "research" to cover up the shameful, visible truth. Even the *Washington Post* FBI report *appears to have slipped a decimal*: The official "United States Crime Rates 1960–2005" find 34.7 forcible rapes per 100,000 in 1979, "dropping" to 31.7 in 2005, an alleged *8.6 percent decrease*—a far cry from 85 percent! And even the alleged 8.6 percent "decrease" is reprehensible statistical gamesmanship, negated by *a 231 percent forcible rape increase* 1960 to 2005.[982]

One of Kinsey's academic disciples is David Finkelhor, PhD, the primary child abuse researcher at the DoJ's Crimes Against Children Research Center (CACRC). Also a member of a Kinsey Institute "child sexuality" study group, Finkelhor has chosen not to reveal or criticize Kinsey's sex crimes against children.

Finkelhor's office is funded by the DoJ's Juvenile Justice and Delinquency Prevention office in an effort to "solve" our child-abuse problems. In 2003, Finkelhor's team reported that crimes against children declined. To make that stick, his team ignored data that would compromise the "good news." These highly sophisticated researchers simply bypassed child sexual abuse among:

- Roughly 58,200 children abducted annually by non family members, at least half sexually molested
- More than 350,000 prostituted children, runaways and "throwaways"
- All sex abuse victims under age twelve
- Roughly 16,000 estimated statutory rape victims (*over age seven*)
- 500,000 foster children (this doubled from 1995 to 2000)

According to a 2005 DoJ report, *Statutory Rape*, by K. Troup-Leasure and H. Snyder, the "incidence of statutory rape is relatively unknown" at the national level. According to this report, the FBI's UCR "maintains national data on forcible rape and other sex offenses but does not isolate statutory rape crimes in its annual *Crime in the United States (CIUS)* report." The report further elucidates that the Office of Justice Programs Office of Juvenile Justice and Delinquency Prevention Bulletin defines statutory rape as "nonforcible sexual intercourse with or between people who are younger than the age of consent." (Of course, the word "nonforcible" in that context is an oxymoron.) Furthermore, according to the DoJ report, the juvenile justice bulletin *excluded victims under age seven*.[983]

While sexual victimization soars,[984] government reports hide these facts and suppress critical real-world data. As with other crime statistics—including rape—some of the numbers game happens at the local level, within police departments.

One heroic whistleblower is Denver Police Lt. James D. Ponzi, a professor at Regis University and author of the 2005 "Compstat Revealed: CompStat or CompScam."[985] Ponzi wrote that a lawsuit regarding a rape and murder revealed the practice of downgrading sexual crimes. Using the Compstat and then Compscam systems, police departments "cooked the books to lower crime rates." This system of lowering crime rates is supported by Lt. David Grossman, PhD:

> The "CrimeStat" program made cops accountable for bringing down crime . . . When the NYPD police union went over the data, the crime rates doubled in NYC if the proper classifications were applied.[986]

Except for murder statistics (which new emergency medical technology reduces), the pressure on the cop on the beat means "police artificially 'bring crime down' and the root causes of the crime get off scot-free, because we cook the books." For example, Officer Ponzi says some high-crime public schools define "assaults" as "scuffles." And they do not report scuffles.

In an email to me, Officer Ponzi wrote that after his "Compstat" article, he got "emails from different departments all over the country confirming statistics being altered in their cities":

> You are right on target in your article about the rape of children [being downgraded and not counted if the victim is under age twelve]. The crime category that you want to lower [is put] in another category that is not counted by the National Incident-Based Reporting System [NIBRS] or is not in the public eye at that moment.[987]

Ponzi opined that Tennessee law professor, Glenn Reynolds, PhD, "used statistics that don't reflect what is truly happening in sex-related crimes." According to Officer Ponzi, while police try to do their jobs, some feel-good administrators handcuff them, refusing to back the cops on controversial issues.[988] Although New Orleans fired five officers in 2003 for downgrading violent crime stats, in 2004, the Policeman's Benevolent Association in New York City revealed that officials there were "cooking the books"—classifying felonies as misdemeanors and rapes as "inconclusive incidents"—to lower crime statistics. In 2005, the Los Angeles Police Department reported a 28 percent drop in violent crime after they reclassified domestic assaults in which victims were not injured—or at least not *seriously* injured.[989] Officer Ponzi *reported that Atlanta crime reports omitted 22,000 crimes*. In New York, when the police union applied proper classifications, precinct crime rates doubled since sometimes a suspect would admit to dozens of crimes but only be charged with one.

The list goes on.

We are indebted to *real men* like Lt. Ponzi, Lt. Grossman, Detective Vernon Geberth, their colleagues, and thousands of unsung police on the beat who are still on the job, trying to protect women, children, and our nation!

Recidivism: Fraud and Truth[990]

Politicians, who felt public resentment over the failed Kinseyan justice system, sought political cover behind parole, rehabilitation, and sex-offender registries. But upon release, parolees frequently repeat and accelerate their crimes. Unfortunately, offenders—especially pedophiles—can never be safely or ethically released. Still, all Western nations accepted Kinsey and the ALI-MPC recommendations for leniency and parole. And all of these nations felt the vile effects.

Canada was typical of that Western fall. Even more liberal and liberated than the United States, Canada "therapeutically" treats brutal sex predators and then quickly releases them. During the thirteen years from 1959 to 1972, the rate of Canadian prisoners serving most of their sentence plummeted.[991]

The roots of our leniency to convicted predators, of course, date back to Kinsey and his cohorts. His colleague, Manfred Guttmacher, for example, of the Group for the Advancement of Psychiatry (GAP), which advocated a therapeutic solution for criminal conduct, absent any proven success of such therapy. Today, many of our elitist judiciary, ignore public safety, continue to elevate the futile and failed solution of "therapy" for sex offenders.

Based on sexpert testimony, courts and parole boards have increasingly recommended treatment and, thus, released convicted sex offenders—giving them pills, strapping them with ankle bracelets or otherwise "monitoring" their activities. But consider the 1988 case of Jim and Anna Stephenson, whose eleven-year-old son, Christopher, was "grabbed at a shopping mall, sexually assaulted" and brutally murdered by a "convicted child sex offender who had been released on supervision." According to California State Senator Dennis Hollingworth, though:

> [A] team of police officers tried monitoring offenders who had been released into the public. For 20 days the police kept close watch on 12 high-risk sex offenders to see if they stayed away from children, playgrounds and schools as promised. The police were shocked with what they found. One man used his girlfriend to lure a child to a hotel. Two others were volunteering at a church-run daycare. Seven of the 12 offenders were re-arrested on a number of charges.[992]

Naïve "sex therapists" naturally want to believe in the efficacy of what they believe to be their curative powers, and they are easily conned by predators. Along with malevolent therapists, these credentialed sexperts argued that such offenders would never rape again. But millions of victims attest to the fact that paroled sex predators *commonly rape again*. The dead, too, could speak, if the DoJ released the number of paroled offenders who committed murder. The fact is that, just as pornography must provide increasingly shameful or violent images to produce the same "thrill," so it is with sexual violence; "high" on violence, offenders resist "treatment," and instead, increase their brutality.

Professors Seth LaFond and John Winick were surprised to note that, once released, violent offenders relocated to other states and were "hard to trace."[993] Still, these elitist law professors viewed prison as unfair to rapists, since the legal view *in vogue* was that sex predators had low recidivism rates and, after serving some jail time, they "fulfilled their debt to society."

But the truth about sex offender recidivism is chilling. In 1997, DoJ research[994] shows that:

- "Sex offenders were about four times more likely than non-sex offenders to be arrested for another sex crime after their discharge from prison."
- In 1991, an estimated 24% of rapists and 19% of men convicted for sexual assault were on probation or paroled when rearrested for another sex offense.
- 40% of released sex offenders who allegedly committed another sex crime were caught on a new offense within a year or less of release.
- "About 8 in 10 inmates serving time in state prison for intimate partner violence had injured or killed their victim."[995]

Of 272,111 prisoners released from U.S. prisons in fifteen states in 1994:

- 67.5% were rearrested for a felony or serious misdemeanor within 3 years.
- 46.9% were reconvicted.
- 25.4% were re-sentenced to prison.[996]

These data support a Government Accounting Office (GAO) report that examined 500 sex offender therapy programs over fifty years. The 1996 GAO report found *none of the 500 sex offender therapy programs produced any evidence of success in curing sex offenders—with pedophiles especially incurable.*[997]

Validating the 1996 GAO report, a 2004 report on 724 Canadian sex offenders looked at 403 prisoners who received treatment in prison and 321 who did not. After twelve years, the rate of sex crime recidivism for each group was nearly identical:

- 21.1% who *received treatment were caught* for another sex crime.
- 21.8% who were *not treated were caught* for another sex crime.[998]

Why, then, does the September 6, 2006, DoJ report on "Criminal Offenders Statistics" claim only a 3.3 percent re-arrest rate within three years among 4,300 released child molesters? First, most child molestation data are unreported. Still, even if we accept these sanitized data, released predators violated roughly 129 *more* children in three years—forty-three sacrificial lambs a year to freed criminals. But much is hidden here. These data only include offenders who were *captured within three years* for yet another sex crime. And there is no way to tell *who* will re-offend. So paroling sex offenders—treated or not—are more dangerous than Russian roulette.

The fact is, post-Kinsey states parole even three-time convicted rapists *and murderers.* And even the 2007 KIDS ACT allows parole of child sexual predators. This is a *state guarantee* that more children will be raped and killed by the parolees.

Is one child's life worth that of a single paroled offender?

Today, just in California, lawmakers and judges have paroled more than 100,000 convicted, registered sex criminals. These predators allegedly must live in California neighborhoods, though tens of thousands of them *are missing*. This is typical of the rest of the nation. California Senator Dennis Hollingsworth reported that "33,000 of 76,000 sexually violent offenders required to register under Megan's Law in California are missing from the system."[999] These predators could be anywhere. *Notably, the Associated Press—not the DoJ—reported this to the American public.*

The KlaasKids Foundation (named for twelve-year-old Polly Klass, one of thousands of abducted, violated, and murdered children in the last decade), created the "Megan's Law" color-coded map, which is available on the Internet at http://www.klaaskids.org/pg-legmeg.htm. This interactive map reports each state's laws under the "Sex Offender and Community Notification Act."[1000]

Statutes, such as "Megan's law," supposedly track violent child abusers who "reintegrate into society" after vicious sexual attacks. But why should this be acceptable? Only permanent incarceration guarantees public protection from sex offenders. The only known—and validated—solution to repeated crime is to remove molesters, rapists, mutilators, and murderers from the pornographic environment that breeds them. The only guarantee that a child sexual predator will never harm another child is by life in prison. Humane treatment within prison walls should be a lifetime effort. One strike and you're in.

Instead, the State frees sex offenders by the millions.

Sadism in Kinsey's Image

According to the Tacoma *News Tribune*, seven-year-old Ryan Hade was riding his bike when a paroled sex offender and murderer abducted, raped, stabbed, and mutilated the boy, leaving him for dead.[1001]

Ryan's attacker had done time for savagely molesting seven children. Authorities paroled him because he "successfully" completed therapy. Then he murdered a fifteen-year-old girl. He was convicted and imprisoned for several years, until the authorities felt *he was really sorry for the child's murder*. Though the killer announced he planned to build a "death van" equipped with shackles and a cage for capturing, sexually torturing, and mutilating children, the prison authorities cited psychological evaluations and paroled him anyway. Loosed upon society, he moved in next door to an elementary school. Local police often questioned him about various sex assaults upon children.

So after brutalizing seven children and murdering (at least) one girl, this man was *legally* free when he attacked seven-year-old Ryan. Kinsey-trained "sexperts," psychologists, and courts insured this psychopath's repeated release, child rapes, mutilations, and murders.[1002] The brutal attack on Ryan finally forced the establishment of a Washington State "task force on sexual predators," which called for life imprisonment without parole for any violent sexual act against a child.

Despite state and media propaganda, America has *never* before been a culture of such sexual violence. What's more, from the Greatest Generation to the Hate America "Me" generation, we have seen a 6,371 percent increase in serious juvenile crime and, in roughly thirty years, the United States averaged over 200 percent more violent juvenile crime annually. Again, we find the origin of sexual violence echoes Kinsey's sexual psychopathology.

FIGURE 25

THE ADVOCATE LOWEST SELF-REPORT DATA ON SADISM/SELF-ABUSE

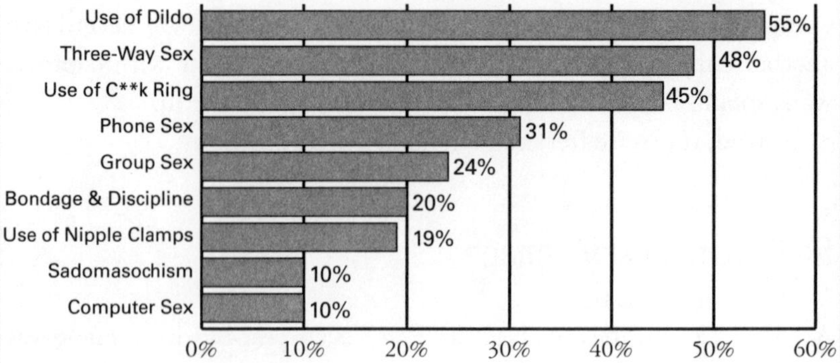

August 23, 1994: "Percent who [admit they] engaged in these acts in the last five years."
[*This graph is an exact replica of *The Advocate* graph except for the use of ellipsis]

In 1973, Pomeroy told *Playboy* magazine that he found sadism is often "loving." No one normal considers sexual torture to be *loving.* Since 1973, countless millions of men and boys, even women and girls have accepted sadomasochism as a sexual "high," buying steel handcuffs, silk four-poster bed ties, and even sadomasochistic whips and clothing on the Internet and at local stores like "Spencer's Gifts." Millions now obsessed by Internet pornography have become "excited" rapists who violate women and children. In groups, in gangs, and singly, they violate those who are weaker than they. Victims' cries bring only more arousal, more violence, and even death.

The August 23, 1994 *Advocate* self-report finds at minimum, 55 percent of upscale "gay" respondents assault themselves with an insertive instrument ("dildo"); 45 percent abuse the phallus with a clamping instrument ("cock ring"); 20 percent admit to sadism they define as "Bondage and Discipline" (commonly being or making others ones "slave"); 19 percent inflict pain on the nipples with metal clamps; and 10 percent practice sadism they call sadomasochism. That 100 percent of *Advocate* respondents combine these violent acts is highly probable.

After Kinsey "had his way" with our culture, deviants began openly promoting sexual cruelty. Internet sales and mass media, retailers like "Spencer's Gifts" in upscale malls, feature designer torture materials, for what is euphemistically called "bondage and discipline," the kind of debasing and humiliating paraphernalia and behavior displayed at Abu Ghraib in 2009 on Iraqi prisoners. The pornographic, dehumanizing Abu Ghraib assaults are precisely the kinds of acts sexologists commonly recommend as "sex play" to jazz up disabled—or merely disappointing—sex lives. Of course, unlike Abu Ghraib, in "bondage" "play" the domestic torturers allegedly cease their brutality at the subtlest signal from their victims. My interviews with such victims confirms that the fantasy game too often disintegrates into torture.

An analysis of Everett Rogers, PhD's, marketing "diffusion of innovation" law predicts that as important leaders accept a new idea or product, eventually much of society adopts this idea or product. Accordingly, society increasingly adopts retailed sexual aberrations, including Kinsey's homosexual deviancies.

Consider the results of a 1994 survey by the premier homosexual magazine, *The Advocate.* The self-reports of two thousand five hundred *Advocate* readers logically minimize their involvement in sadistic behavior, but still the results are shocking. Like other homosexual publications, *The Advocate* acknowledges staggering levels of inter-homosexual violence. At least 75 percent of these readers confess they enjoy violent sex; 55 percent used painful objects on one another; and 20 percent admit to sadistic "bondage and discipline."[1003] These revelations preceded the modern flood of television dramas that depict handcuffed sex as exciting as well as the fallout in real-time sexual violence.

The Extreme: Sado-Sexual Pedophile Homicide

If males welcome sexual violence to one another, this creates a logical trail to violence against their intimates, including children. Consider the general rate of child homicide:

> In the U.S., one of the leading causes of death for juveniles is homicide. . . . [It is] the fourth leading cause of death for children ages one to four, third for ages five to fourteen and, second for ages fifteen to twenty-four.[1004]

While heterosexual males figure large in the abuse of girls, homosexual predators figure large in the abuse of boys. Men and older boys often initiate younger boys into the affluent lifestyle of homosexual pornography and prostitution. Victims include runaways, boy "prostitutes," boys who advertised in the homosexual press, boys picked up in homosexual bars, as well as kidnapped boys. Robin Lloyd provides a litany of police-blotter cases of boy sex murders, "common place" in the gay world.[1005] A report in the *Washington Times* said that the 1980s saw numerous homosexual kidnap-rape-castrations of boys.[1006]

However, the mass media typically hides such disturbing news from the public. That said, in 1984, shortly before the onslaught of gay power, the *New York Times* did publish such a report: "Officials Cite a Rise in Killers Who Roam U.S. for Victims."[1007] This in-depth article profiled the killers of women and girls and also noted the high percentage of homosexual boy killers: "Many of the most violent recent multiple murders have been committed by homosexual males."[1008] In fact, homosexual boy assault and murder is often very brutal, including torture and maiming. Mutilation and castration are common features.

Vernon J. Geberth, M.S., M.P.S., Former Commander, Bronx Homicide, NYPD's "Homosexual Serial Murder Investigation," summarizes "gay" sexual murders. "Homosexual related homicides [involve] acts of sexual perversion, and serial killings."[1009] The most frequent motivation, he wrote:

> was sadomasochistic sexual acts followed by male pedophilia. Lust murders and robbery accounted for the balance. Twelve pedophile homosexual serial killers were suspected in the deaths of 126 young males and boys.[1010]

The National Center for Prosecution of Child Abuse reported 1,490 American children "died at the hands of their caretakers" in 2004.[1011] The official definition of "caretakers" is so broad that it might include a single mother's boyfriend or a babysitter. No state agency lists the thousands of sexually violated child murder victims, but untold thousands of toddlers and children have been raped, sodomized, mutilated, and murdered in the last decade. *We know that this is not normal American behavior!* The unspeakable deaths of thousands of children are the direct result of aborting Judeo-Christian judicial policies and mental health training by the sexual saboteurs in Kinsey's wake.

What does the following tell us?

19 State Bills/Acts in 13 Years:
Commonly Named for a Raped/Murdered Child

2007: The federal *KIDS ACT of 2007* establishes a registry of sex offenders mail addresses (generic victims).

2006: The federal *Jessica Lunsford and Sarah Lunde Act*, "Sexual Predator Monitoring Program."

2006: The federal *Jeremy Bell Act of 2006* penalizes the "Interstate Transfer of Child Sex Offenders."

2006: The federal *Adam Walsh Child Protection and Safety Act* includes other acts punishing offenders.

2005: Wisconsin's *Amie's Law* releases information on juvenile sex offenders who may re-offend.

2005: The federal *Christy Ann Fornoff Act* limits habeas corpus for killing of a person under age eighteen.

2005: The federal *Jetseta's Bill* strengthens the Prevention and Deterrence of Crimes Against Children Act.

2005: Florida's *Jessica Lunsford Act* imposes twenty-five years to life for some first-time child sex offenders.

2004: Florida's *Pending, Carlie's Law* for Carlie Brucia considers parole revocation if felons violated children under sixteen.

2003: The federal *Protect Act of 2003*, for Elizabeth Smart, toughens punishments and enacts Amber Alerts.

2003: California's *Pending "Danielle's Law"* for Danielle van Dam "anyone who kills a child in the home eligible for the death penalty."

2002: The federal *Amber Alert* for Amber Hagerman, requires media, business personnel, and police to speedily locate abductees.

2002: The federal *Levi's Call* for Levi Frady requires action when an abduction is confirmed.

1996: The federal *Megan's Law*, for Megan Kanka, amends the Wetterling Act and requires a community notification system.

1996: The federal *Pam Lychner Sexual Offender Act* requires lifetime registration for certain recidivists.[1012]

1995: The Florida *Jimmy Ryce Act* reviews inmates for probability of re-offence.
1995: The Arkansas *Morgan Nick Alert* is a cooperative effort of 250 radio stations in case of abduction.
1994: The federal *Jacob Wetterling Crimes Against Children and Sexually Violent Offender Act* provides stronger penalties.

In the past few years, the media has given national coverage to a number of sex crimes perpetrated by strangers against children, including those against Jetseta Gage of Cedar Rapids, Iowa (2005); Jessica Lunsford (2005), Sarah Lunde (2005), and Carlie Brucia (2004) all of Florida; Elizabeth Smart of Utah (2002); and Samantha Runnion of California (2002). In addition, two notable sexual assaults by repeat sex offenders against young adult women, Dru Sjodin in North Dakota (2003) and Alexandra Nicole Zapp in Massachusetts (2002), were widely reported. Both federal and state governments have enacted laws with provisions that allegedly increase penalties for crimes against children, require sex offenders released from prison to register, and require law enforcement to monitor them.[1013] The only sure protection from offenders remains permanent incarceration and capital punishment.

[CHAPTER 14]

The Sex Industrial Complex

Commercial opportunities for sex-enhancing drugs have exploded, and sex researchers are eagerly sought for help in commercial ventures. Our dance cards are no longer empty.

—Sexologist Leonore Tiefer[1014] *SALVO,* An Interview with Dr. Judith A. Reisman, by Bobby Maddex, Spring 2007

In the course of producing my documentary *Kinsey's Paedophiles*, it became clear that every substantive allegation Reisman made was not only true but thoroughly sourced with documentary evidence—despite the Kinsey Institute's reluctance to open its files.[1015]

—Tim Tate, Yorkshire Television, UK, Producer, *Kinsey's Paedophiles*, 1998

MAKE NO MISTAKE: ALFRED C. Kinsey was the most effective and deviant sexual philosopher in human history. He was the first acclaimed American scientist to insist that virginity is unhealthy, promiscuity helps marriages, pornography is constructive, obsessive masturbation and bestiality are never problematic, bi/homosexual sex acts are normal, and children are "sexual from birth" and appropriate sex partners for adults. On and on, for sixty years.

It has not always been smooth sailing. In 1964 the "erotica" bibliographer for the Kinsey Institute (now the Kinsey Institute for Research in Sex, Gender and Reproduction), Gershon Legman wrote in *The Horn Book* (1964) that Kinsey's studies were "statistical hokum" with data designed to "disguise" Kinsey's "propagandistic purpose of respectabilizing homosexuality and certain sexual perversions."[1016] Legman was correct. Sexologists called him disgruntled.

In 1976, Stanford University historian Paul Robinson, observed in *The Modernization of Sex* that Kinsey's statistics were designed "to undermine the traditional sexual order"[1017] and that paying heed to Kinsey would gut all sex laws, including age of consent.

The sexologists always fought back, since the notion of infant sexuality is powerfully entrenched in sexology. We see this in statements by Mary Calderone, MD, past president and co-founder (with Lester Kirkendall) of the Sex Information and Education Council of the United States (SIECUS), and past medical director of Planned Parenthood. Speaking before the 1980 annual meeting of the Association of Planned Parenthood Physicians, Calderone said the primary goal of SIECUS was teaching society "the vital importance of infant and childhood sexuality."[1018]

Infant sexuality?

This theory, that sexualized children are prey for pedophiles, is staggering. Children's "sexuality," she said, should:

> be developed in the same way as the child's inborn human capacity to talk or to walk, and that [the parents'] role should relate only to teaching the child the appropriateness of privacy, place, and person—in a word, socialization.[1019]

To sexualize an *infant* before his or her ability to walk or talk, never mind before their developmental maturity and reproductive readiness, is criminal—a cruel torment that interferes grotesquely with children's natural developmental sequence and produces unnatural behavioral, psychobiological, and psychological deviance. Not to be outdone, in a legal deposition, June Reinisch, as Kinsey director, claimed children were masturbating in "the womb."[1020]

Bruce D. Perry, MD, of the Child Trauma Academy, said sexually abused children easily become hypersexualized; promiscuity is reported in 38 percent of victims.[1021] Ignoring myriad other responses, from depression to self-mutilation to suicide, Kinsey and his followers cited children's subsequent promiscuity as *proof of the "pleasure" they got from their violation*. Such twisted interpretations support the pedophile agenda, which argues that premature sexualization and even sexual trauma are *good* for children. The Kinsey Institute, SIECUS, Planned Parenthood, and others serve pedophiles well.

The Kinsey crimes should have a grand jury and congressional and mass media investigation to overshadow Watergate. After all, allowing the Kinsey crimes to go unpunished has brutalized and dehumanized every western nation. Within the last ten years, though, we have seen a small chink in the armor. As sex addiction spiraled out of control, Christian sex addiction therapists have begun to challenge the premises of modern sexology. Predictably, therapists today face a growing victim population. Sex-addiction therapists see pornography-addicted patients who suffer myriad fallouts—divorce, impotence, homosexual ideation, sex crimes, and more.[1022]

Some of the Christian therapists understand that the origin of these problems is in Kinsey. Beyond biblical counsel and support, some of these groups teach students and survivors about sexology's Kinseyan foundation and how it has lied, entrapped, and debauched them and the entire Western world. Knowledge is power. Unfortunately, most sex-addiction therapists today, co-opted by the Kinsey mentality, continue to recommend the benefits of sexual fantasy, for example, as though this were healthy and harmless, which it is surely not.[1023]

Sexologists know that they must protect Kinsey and his data. Despite the fact that his twisted data remain hidden by the Kinsey Institute, his disciples cling to his prescriptions as gospel. And though Kinsey's sadomasochistic psychopathology, criminal sex experiments on children, and eugenicist ideology are well documented, his followers ignore or discredit the hard evidence. Try, they must. For Kinsey's "biography is the battleground," said sadosexual advocate lesbian anthropologist Carol Vance, PhD. If Kinsey is discredited, "fifty years of sexual progress is undone."[1024]

That depends on your idea of progress.

The Sex Industry Complex

As sexologist Tiefer gleefully notes, the massive sexual dysfunctions dominating our culture mean that our "dance cards are no longer empty." Big money flows from big sexual despair! The chart, "Scientific Authority for the Sex Industry Complex," describes how the Kinsey

FIGURE 26

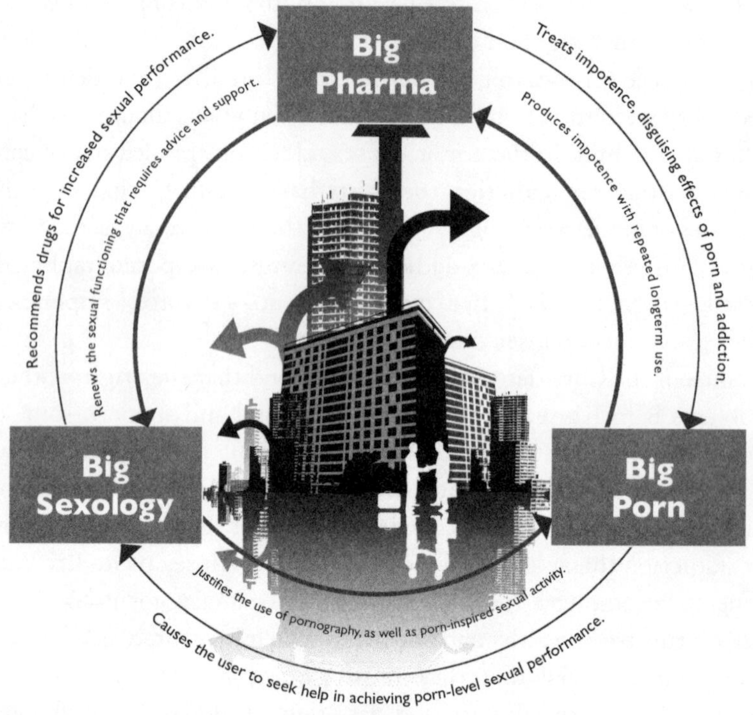
Big
Pharma
Big
Sexology
Big
Porn
Recommends drugs for increased sexual performance.
Renews the sexual functioning that requires advice and support.
Treats impotence, disguising effects of porn and addiction.
Produces impotence with repeated longterm use.
Justifies the use of pornography, as well as porn-inspired sexual activity.
Causes the user to seek help in achieving porn-level sexual performance.

Bobby Maddex, "An Interview with Dr. Judith A. Reisman," *SALVO*, Spring, 2007, p. 33.

Institute sabotaged the Greatest Generation and paved the road to today's national sexual pathology. This chart is a road map from the Kinsey reports to today's society, even to kindergartens, governed by what I call the Sex Industry Complex (SIC).

To understand the relationship between Kinsey, modern sexology, and the SIC, we need only follow the gold. The Kinsey Institute receives millions of dollars in state and federal funds, plus investments from Big Pharma and Big Pornography. Today our lives and culture are under the influence of Big Sexology—a multimillion dollar industry.

Consider the résumé of the Kinsey Institute's current director, Julia Heiman, PhD, paid by the U.S. Natural Institute of Health and the Sinclair Institute, an Internet pornography trafficker.[1025] The Sinclair Institute sells pornographic media, sexual torture equipment, and "anal fun" kits for all. Thus, Heiman peddles and

FIGURE 27

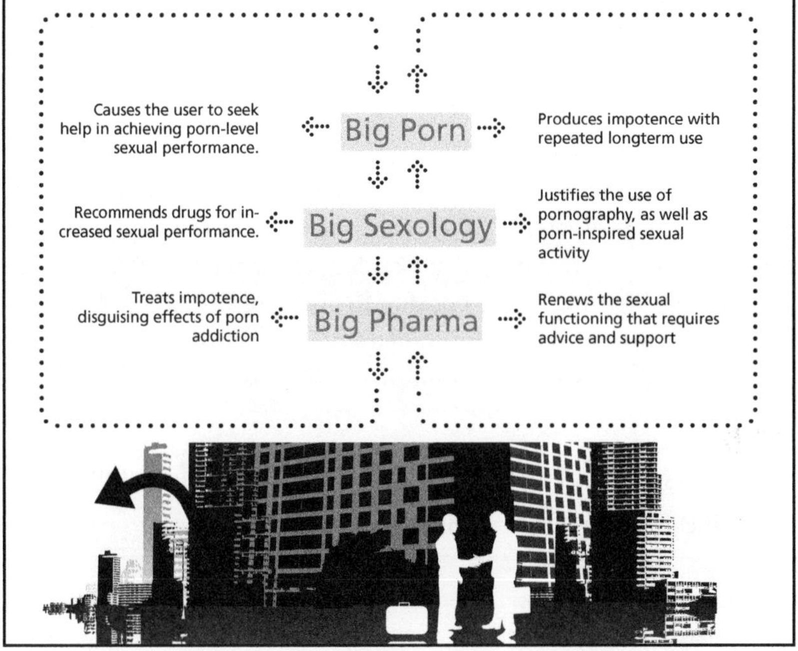
Causes the user to seek help in achieving porn-level sexual performance.
Big Porn
Produces impotence with repeated longterm use
Recommends drugs for increased sexual performance.
Big Sexology
Justifies the use of pornography, as well as porn-inspired sexual activity
Treats impotence, disguising effects of porn addiction
Big Pharma
Renews the sexual functioning that requires advice and support

Post *SALVO* reference to Spring, 2007 interview, p. 33.

panders pornography and anal sodomy, which is directly linked to spreading AIDS.

In her previous position at the University of Washington, Heiman headed a series of studies to find a female Viagra pill while exposing female volunteers to pornography. Heiman called these studies "clinical" and "reproductive," though they were clearly sex experiments to profit the pharmaceutical industry. Reporter Cynthia Gorney of the *Washington Post* wrote that "the goal, the anticipated source of these staggering sums of money, is a women's equivalent to Viagra."[1026] "[S]cientists and capitalists dream of finding a drug that could boost female sexuality."[1027]

One Heiman aide said selecting pornography films was "the worst two weeks of my life." A coarsened Heiman dismissed the visible distress of her aides and subjects. "You sell things off insecurity," she said.

Multiplying and marketing women's insecurity is money in the bank. Indeed, Big Pharma has invested *billions* of dollars in encouraging women's sexual *ab*normality. Lonely people create the market for

Big Pharma and Big Pornography, selling chemical and media "love" products. Thus, Heiman's hands were in the pockets of Big Pornography and other SIC funders.

Then Heiman moved on to control research in a bigger pond—at the Kinsey Institute, where she took Indiana University's prestige to the bank. Such well-placed sexologists have longstanding profit-sharing arrangements with the SIC. Pandemic promiscuity creates profitable pornography addictions, and a subsequent mass market for pharmaceutical impotence "aids" and vaccines to retard and treat sexually transmitted diseases. Big Sexology benefits Big Porn, which benefits Big Pharma, which benefits Big Sexology. It would be a perfect system, if it weren't so fatally flawed.

Where is the Sex Industry Complex taking us?

"Restless Vagina Syndrome": Big Pharma's Newest "Be Like a Porn Star" Disease

November 3, 2009. Terry Allen, senior editor of *In These Times*, wrote, "The pharmaceutical industry wants you to think that if you don't have sex like a porn star, you're in need of their drugs." You, like 43 percent of other women, have female sexual dysfunction (FSD) and they want to help.

The Journal of the American Medical Association article said you need help if lack of porno libido gives you "personal distress." "So, convincing women to feel distress is a key component of the drug company strategy to market a multi-billion-dollar pill that will cure billions of women of what may not ail them."

By pushing the idea that "normal" women have explosive sex all the time, "BigPharma helped launch the disease." Absent orgy pills she can try the Orgasmatron: a spinal implant that risks "infection and paralysis." Or at $60 a month, one can buy "horny goat weed extract" to "feel like a real woman." The shaved, bare pudenda (like a baby), and the vaginal surgery to be "tighter," (like a baby) is increasingly accepted, even by educated and intelligent women. Allen says companies and clinics that push pornography standards "concoct illnesses and then develop drugs to treat them, and vice versa. Either way, the syndrome" makes a profit.

Dr. Jennifer Berman now heads a Beverly Hills FSD clinic and appears on *Oprah*. She was also on a panel sponsored by Big Pharma and helped define female sexual dysfunction; "22 drug companies, including Pfizer, had paid off 18 of the 19 authors of that panel's report, the BMJ revealed."[1028] Yep there is big money in the collaboration of Big Pharma, Big Pornography, and Big Sexology.

Kinsey Institute: The Epicenter

Millions of "normal" males (and females) can no longer achieve orgasm without taking a pill or viewing pornography or fantasizing about it. Profiting from—and masking—the grotesque increase in young, healthy men with pornographically-induced impotence, Big Pharma is marketing new libido drugs and perfumes. The research that uses pornography to test sexual response arguably will addict some subjects to these erototoxins. That's just fine with the sex industry, so sexologists have used and prescribed pornography for decades.

Not coincidentally, big-business abortion funders (Rockefeller) and pornographers (*Playboy* and Rockefeller) initially financed the sexology "field." Sexologists, in turn, produced, sold, and contributed their own "academic" pornography and advice to *Playboy, Penthouse Forum, Playgirl, Hustler*, etc., and served as expert witnesses in all major pornography trials.[1029] No conflict of interest there.

Today, Big Sexology receives millions of dollars to search for that magic drug, smell, or image that will kick-start a sexual climax—with or without a partner. Soon, they will no doubt mass market a full-service arousal-and-climax pill, a "medical advance" for men. Sexology is working on the challenge of doing the same for women. Just as the media have taught women that they "need" hair color, facelifts, and breast implants, sexologists are teaching them that they "need" heightened lust, an entirely new concept. Until now, women's identity has not depended upon *her* sexual virility. A new pathology: American women—trying to please pornographically imprinted men—are now paying for dangerous surgeries to tighten and resculpt their genitalia to resemble pornographic models.[1030]

Big Pornography and Big Pharmacology *paid* Big Sexology to create and legitimize such "needs" by increasingly eroticizing females. In turn, a female libido pill will mean meteoric profits for the SIC.[1031]

But they need women to believe that they "need" a hot libido. Working together, the SIC both creates and fulfills that "need."

On the other side of the equation, the SIC largely victimizes men. Kinsey Institute associate scientist Erick Janssen explained in *Frontline* that regular pornography, which male subjects had found exciting, no longer stimulated them. To arise to the same arousal state, the researchers had to increase the men's "dose" to sadistic pornography. Janssen said:

> [These] *highly sexually active men did not respond to porn clips that had proven successful in eliciting sexual responses in earlier studies*. It was not until we provided them with a wide variety of porn clips to choose from, depicting anything from group *sex to sadomasochism (S&M) that we started to obtain clear signs of arousal* (italics added).[1032]

Thanks to Kinsey, the industry continues to normalize its gateway drug—pornography—and legitimize pharmaceutical arousal and climax. In the end, the bizarre Woody Allen's "virtual sex . . . Orgasmatron," made famous in his 1973 film *Sleeper,* will not be comical science fiction.[1033] It is becoming our reality—and it isn't funny.

It seems eerie that Alfred Kinsey and his saboteurs launched this brave new world in 1948, the year of Orwell's *1984*. Now, it is in full gear and fully financed—by Eli Lilly, Pfizer, Ford, Rockefeller, the pornography industry, and State-supported research, schools, and libraries. Thus, the SIC is entrenched in our society.

Big Pharma

Pleased that sexology is no longer a stepchild of the health field, even sexologist Lenore Tiefer worried about "industry giants with the resources and determination to create multi-billion dollar blockbuster [sex] drugs." Tiefer said that it puts public safety at risk when sex researchers are commonly unable to reveal the downside of the libido drugs they help create.[1034]

Especially worrisome, the use of these drugs is escalating. Whatever the benefits, the media skirt the drawbacks of impotence drugs such as Viagra, largely ignoring disturbing data implicating Viagra in heart attacks,[1035] and the role of these drugs in sexual assaults by chemically aroused satyrs, old and young.[1036] One new study confirms what college kids have been saying:

> From 1998 to 2002, the use of Viagra in men under forty-five tripled . . . Viagra is being used as a recreational drug . . . Thus, it belongs more in the category of pot, crack, heroin, or meth rather than being a medicinal pharmaceutical.[1037]

"The very fact that young males actually think they need this drug is all by itself alarming," adds reporter Mike Adams. "But it's even more alarming to realize that Pfizer appears to be doing very little to restrict the sales of Viagra for recreational use." Independent research confirms that "pharmaceutical companies don't care how their drugs are sold or who uses them, even if there's no justified medical use whatsoever . . . to fatten up their own bank accounts."[1038]

Profiteering from Child/Adult Sex

The Kinsey Institute's claim that children are sexual from birth helped create libertine sex laws that legalized "adult" pornography, which putrefied into child pornography. Pedophiles, pornographers, and most sexologists and sex educators argue that once Big Pharma immunizes children against venereal diseases and pregnancy, kids can have sexual relations—hetero/homo/bi/group/oral/anal—without consequence.

To unravel the agenda and outcomes of the pedophile lobby, again, "follow the money." In 2003, the Kinsey Institute built on tortuous child sexual experiments published *Sexual Development in Childhood*,[1039] a product of the pornography-pharmacology connection. The marketing strategy of this deadly collaboration is to give children legal access to pornography (as in some "sex education" classes today), so they will have sex with each other and adults, then to vaccinate children for venereal diseases and even pregnancy, thereby preventing unfortunate consequences of such abnormal behavior. This was—and *is*—a business partnership made in hell.

The Kinsey Institute's libido experiments and its *Sexual Development in Childhood* book are allied marketing tools for pedophiles and the

SIC. Both would retail children's sexuality on the open market. Both would seek to lower the age of consent and increase pornography addiction. SIC libido traffickers are profiteers, whose promiscuity "sex ed" programs dangerously exploit (even kill) children via resulting abortions, STDs, HIV/AIDS, pregnancy, and dangerous vaccinations against venereal diseases (VD).

Raking in huge profits, the VD vaccines are known to increase neurological impairments in some children that require pharmacological intervention for life. Though few parents knew the need for hepatitis B vaccines in their lifetime, these shots are already mandated for vulnerable infants and children. Many more STD vaccines—for genital herpes, syphilis, and gonorrhea—are moving down the pipeline for children.

For years, the SIC hid the fact that multiple-partner sex breeds the human papilloma virus (HPV) and most sexually transmitted viruses, which cause about 70 percent of cervical cancers and painful, contagious genital warts. About twenty million Americans have some form of HPV. Merck pharmaceuticals, in fact, in 2005 announced Gardasil, an HPV vaccine that is "100% effective in the short term at blocking the HPV and lesions likely to turn cancerous."[1040]

"I see this as a phenomenal breakthrough," said Gloria Bachmann, MD, director of The Women's Health Institute at Robert Wood Johnson Medical School in New Brunswick. "You have to get students in grammar school, middle school, high school [vaccinated] before they become sexually active," she said.[1041] Indeed, Merck would inoculate babies and children against diseases that would shortly be inflicted on them by pedophiles? Unfortunately since the fanfare heralded during a mass media blitzkrieg for "Gardasil," there have serious side effects laid at the feet of the vaccine. By 2009 there were nearly six hundred serious events reported including twenty deaths attributed to Gardasil.[1042]

Federal Government Gives Millions to Kinsey Institute and Thus to Planned Parenthood and Sexology

If sexology's "dance cards are no longer empty," the Kinsey Institute is the most popular partner at the dance—its dance card overflows with names of government and corporate suitors. A preliminary study of the Institute reveals that roughly 90 percent of its federal, state, and corporate research grants involve uncovering hotter sex through chemistry—both the exogenous chemistry of Big Pharma and endogenous brain chemistry stimulated by seeing and hearing pornography. Pornographers, sex-pill pushers, and state and federal budget appropriators are lining up to cut a rug with the Kinsey Institute swingers.

Sexologists, who credentialed themselves as "health professionals," have become the "scientific" authorities for all scholarly information about the libido. Thus, they control virtually all sexuality research and information. In their pseudo-science—say, arousal experiments—toxic pornography is the methodology of choice. But we know, by definition, that Kinsey Institute and other "sexology" professionals are clinically conditioned by pornographic stimuli and its triggers. "Addictive" sexuality commonly stems from this insult to the brain.

Considering their early and ongoing pornographic conditioning, it is not surprising that many if not most of today's sexperts also work for pornographic and/or pedophile magazines, and several, like John Money, Wardell Pomeroy and the IASHS and their graduates, have publicly advocated for early promiscuous sex for and with children.[1043] Such *deviants* are deeply involved in the business of marketing child sex. The scientific basis for this business was Kinsey, whose frauds expressed only his psychopathology.

To study women's arousal to pornography, the Kinsey Institute eagerly hijacked roughly $711,000 from *the National Institute of Child Health and Development (NICHD)*. Though the Institute's original abstract cited the sexual nature of this grant, they later deleted language about sexual arousal and pornography from the grant application. By deliberately falsifying both its research methods and its purpose, the Kinsey Institute got the better part of $1 million from the federal government—*monies that should have gone to children's health.*

Eventually, it came to light that the sexologists had hijacked the children's health money to profit the SIC. Angry that the National Institutes of Health (NIH) granted $263,038 to the Kinsey Institute over the past five years, Representative Mark Souder (R-IN) said:

> Kinsey and his associates, at the very least, encouraged the rape and molestation of children under the guise of "science." I would hope that an institute dedicated to child health would be primarily focused on protecting children from sexual abuse, a mission inconsistent in

my opinion with providing support for any institution built upon Kinsey's hideous legacy.[1044]

Reporter, Robert Stacy McCain reported legislators' protests over SIC grants In the *Washington Times*:

> Representative Dave Weldon (R-FL) denounced the NICHD's decision to fund a Northwestern University study to determine "what types of audiovisual erotica women find sexually arousing."
>
> A House subcommittee demanded information about an NICHD grant of $137,000 for a study to "provide the most comprehensive picture to date of the sexual behavior of aging men"; House members asked Health and Human Services Secretary Tommy Thompson to explain how the study will benefit "children afflicted with pediatric diseases."

House Republicans complained about a $26,000 NICHD grant for a sexual arousal conference at the Kinsey Institute. Reporter McCain quoted Representative Jeff Flake, (R-AZ) saying, "If this conference needs funding, they ought to hit up {pornographer} Larry Flynt, not taxpayers."[1045]A list of direct public funds 1986-2004 totaled $5,396,338. Public monies continued to flood this disgraceful institution after 2004. Congressional investigators disclosed that NICHD fleeced $263,038 in research grants from deserving children, to give to the Kinsey Institute in five years.[1046] Regarding one NIH study of women's responses to pornographic videos, Representative Dave Weldon (R-FL) said he asked NICHD three years ago to study whether the measles, mumps, and rubella (MMR) vaccine was associated with autism. Weldon said: "The NIH couldn't find the money to look into this relationship between kids with regressive autism and the mandatory MMR vaccine, but they can pay people $150,000 to watch pornography."[1047] While the NIH serves the Kinsey clique, the NICHD pilfers children's funds for favored libidinous nihilists. From 1981 to 1989, former Kinsey Institute Director June Reinisch received three grants for over $3 million[1048] from the NIH, and she, too, got money from the NICHD.[1049] In 1989, the *Chicago Tribune* reported that an NIH investigation found the use of the NICHD funds to be "highly questionable."[1050] Reinisch's bank account was seized and closed "as a result of the initial internal review conducted by the University." As of the date of this writing, there has been no subsequent information released.[1051]

When a federal committee challenged the Kinsey Institute's funding, the Institute responded saying it was studying women's "mood" during arousal by pornography. Though no scientific trial can adequately assess a "mood," the bogus study *passed* the scrutiny of Indiana University's Internal Review Board (IRB) for human experimentation and the peer-review process. Since the sexology "field" is built on Kinsey, the sexperts who do "peer reviews" for grants and publications tend to be SIC lackeys. Congress would never give tax money earmarked for children's health to sex "research," unless the sex lobby was as powerful as it is. So IRBs approve the plunder, as Big Sexology steals taxpayers' money from children to create private profits from pills and perfumes that can abnormally heighten arousal in females exposed to pornography.

Even legitimate science (which this is not) too often bears the taint of bias, personal agendas, and special-interest financing. For example, Martin Sturman, MD, reported on university researchers and educators sabotaging for Big Pharma:

> 94% of the more than 5,000 scientists at NIH were engaged in lucrative conflict of interest activities, and that top officials had received over $2.5 million in fees and stock options from drug companies over the past decade. In 2002, the pharmaceutical industry spent $91.4 million on federal lobbying activities, and at least another $50 million was spent to "influence Congress and others through advertising, direct mail, telemarketing, and grants. Drug companies had 675 registered lobbyists and 26 of these were former members of Congress."[1052]

Built on Kinsey's frauds, most of Big Sexology's human sexuality "professionals" are irreparably compromised. Beyond their individual histories, experiences, and pathologies, they are beholden to a very powerful lobby in Big Pornography, Big Pharma, and Big Sexology. *Riddled* with lucrative, congruent interests, the SIC clearly faces a "conflict of interest" between its own greed and the public welfare.

Should State Funding of the Kinsey Institute's Sexual Research End?[1053]

YES! A proper American investigation should finally take place, a congressional and grand jury investigation to examine the evidence of deliberate sexual sabotage and child torture.

Although taxpayers fund the Kinsey Institute at more than $750,000 a year (plus salaries and added resources), the Institute is cloaked in secrecy. VIP tours are squired by a Kinsey watchdog. Indiana State Senator John Waterman was banned from viewing Kinsey's Morrison Hall. He and Representative Woody Burton called for defunding the Kinsey clan: "No public funds should be used to operate or support institutions that further the claims made by Alfred Kinsey's research." To date, the power behind the Kinsey sabotage has managed to forestall defunding and public condemnation.

> [I]n 1930 [Morgan and Rockefeller] had greater assets than the total wealth in twenty-one states of the Union. [Their influence] was so great that the Morgan and Rockefeller groups acting together . . . could have wrecked the economic system of the country . . . [They] could almost control its political life, at least on the Federal level.
>
> —Caroll Quigley, *Tragedy and Hope* (1966),[1054] 71–72

With powerful foundation allies like Rockefeller and Ford, the Kinsey Institute was insulated from investigation and exposure for over half a century. In a 1988 interview with E. Michael Jones, Paul Gebhard said "anything that was confidential"[1055] is hidden, even from friendly researchers. But what material is so "confidential" that it must be hidden? Does Kinsey describe his own pederasty or pedophilia? Does he reveal his Nazi sympathies and his eugenicist agenda? What is in the thousands of letters to and from Kinsey mentioned by James Jones?[1056]

Nonchalantly, fearlessly, the Kinsey Institute published lies disguised as "science." Nonetheless, the Institute, Indiana University, and the Boards of Directors of both persevere, fully aware of Kinsey's addiction to sadomasochism, pornography, the bogus data, and the child sex crimes of his studies. It makes sense that the "mad scientist" of Big Sexology leads the sex research race; this is in keeping with its long history of lust and crime, its mass child sexual abuse, and its unapologetic cover-up of atrocities. For example, Dr. Alveda King's "Black Prolife Movement" says Planned Parenthood panders promiscuity "to support their agenda of murder," "abortion dynasty" profits from "killing black babies." My earlier book documents Kinsey's eugenic attack on the black community.[1057]

Kinseyan Experiments

The "work" of Kinsey continues undeterred, funded by federal and state agencies and conducting sex, drug, pornography, and libido experiments. Add the SIC profits from any "erotic" discovery—a conflict of interest for any research institution. Tax-funded universities are mandated to serve public health. But Indiana University's Kinsey Institute, like many others, uses pornography on volunteers who cannot give informed consent to the research, because neither the volunteers nor the "researchers" really understand what they are doing. Nor can their alleged studies be guaranteed if senators are banned from the premises. Tainted, presumably addicted by their own long-term pornography exposure; these "scholars," are additionally unable to warn their subjects of the erototoxic/neurotoxic effects on the brain.

Who Sends Rape Records to the Kinsey Institute?

The 2004 Fox film, *Kinsey,* yielded a fresh twist. Following the movie, the Kinsey Institute's Liana Zhou, in charge of the Institute's collections, announced that a ninety-one-year-old woman, one of Kinsey's subjects fifty years earlier, had mailed in another of her sex records. "When he interviewed people he encouraged them to record their subsequent behaviour: self-stimulation, any kind of sexual contact," Zhou told the Kinsey filmmakers. "For 50-some years, ever since she was interviewed, she's been reporting."[1058]

But who else has been "reporting"? Zhou admitted that other Kinsey subjects still send records of their sex acts to the Institute. Kinsey encouraged them to send photographs and cinema—to aid "science," of course. But these "encouraged" participants include rapists, incest offenders, pedophiles, pederasts, and even sex murderers!

Kinsey said he interviewed 21,000 people. Although he trashed all but 4,500 of his specially selected subjects' interviews, many thousands of "encouraged" psychopaths likely continued to mail records of their criminal "sexual contact." Indeed, incestuous predators are often generational, passing on their "traditions" through their damaged progeny. Despite the smoke screen that continues to obscure the real Kinsey from public understanding, even Indiana University[1059] admits that the sex-industry's hero used pedophile rapes for his data. *Rapists must be still sending their diaries and data to the Kinsey Institute!* Their behavior is addictive. It does not stop. Perhaps they even passed on the Kinsey torch to other predators, even to their own progeny, since pedophile devotion to self-serving science knows no bounds.

In the British documentary, *Kinsey's Paedophiles*, Jonathan Gathorne-Hardy said Kinsey received accounts of sex abuse from "five headmasters of boy's schools in the Princeton, New Jersey area." These headmasters, who sodomized students, claimed the boys definitely "enjoyed" the experiences.[1060] How long were *these* records sent to the Kinsey Institute and filed away for future use? Are they still?

Without a doubt, the Kinsey cult encouraged and covered-up sex crimes—from rape and incest to sadistic murder—for decades. How many sex crimes does the Kinsey Institute keep on file as evidence? Hundreds? Thousands?

Mad Academic Writers of Kinsey's *Sexual Development in Childhood*

As noted earlier, not only did the Kinsey Institute republish both Kinsey books in 1998 without apology or admission of crime, in 2003—after five decades of spewing its black propaganda—the Kinsey Institute published its seminal work of propaganda: *Sexual Development in Childhood.* The sinister plan was clear: Children are sexual from birth.

Some of the sexpert authors of *Childhood* were openly pro-pedophile.[1061] Almost uniformly, they scorned traditional American morality, normalcy, and childhood sexual innocence. The foundations for the frauds in the Kinsey Institute's new, influential publication had not changed in fifty years: The sexperts covered-up Kinsey's pornography addiction, sadism, and child sex crimes, and rejected the premise of puberty as the natural time of normal sexual awakening.

A teaching text, Sexual Development in Childhood promotes the harmlessness of "childhood sexuality." Yet even the term is an oxymoron, a political ploy to lull the populace into believing that these two words belong in the same sentence, much less paired together. The evidence to date finds for childhood to include sexuality, someone must intrude upon childhood innocence. Since absent sex hormones, child sexual behavior before puberty is entirely unnatural, even the book's title is propaganda.

The WT Grant Foundation funded a special conference[1062] for the then Kinsey Institute director, John Bancroft, MD, who recruited forty-five like-minds to contribute to *Sexual Development in Childhood.* In a choice that reveals his stance of aggressive pedophile promotion, Bancroft selected several pedophile activists for the book. In his Introduction to the *Childhood* volume, Bancroft attacked Congress for condemning a brazenly biased study that concluded with a "harmlessness" assessment of child sexual abuse.[1063] Interviewed for the Yorkshire Television documentary, *Kinsey's Paedophiles*, Dr. Bancroft argued that to avoid "ignorance," some child sexual abuse could be scientifically acceptable.

Of the book's assorted Kinsey invitees, none condemned or questioned Kinsey's child sex abuse "methodology" nor any other aspect of the original reports. None asked that the child victimization be publicized so that survivors could seek redress, compensation, therapy, or even simply notification to help them clear up mysteries about their pasts. Indeed, the authors were in lock step, except for one.

Dennis Fortenberry, MD, a professor of pediatrics and medicine, tried to rein in the group's narcissistic delusions. "Our history as professionals over the past 100 years has been to be wrong more often than we've been right," he pointed out. "I'm just very nervous about succumbing to the temptation to speak as arbiters of normalcy.[1064] But he was alone. All agreed that *all* sexual "varieties"—except abstinence—are "normal." They ignored Fortenberry's counsel and proceeded.

Bancroft allowed no criticism of past errors by sex "experts," so all of the contributors participated in covering up Kinsey's crimes against children. While conference attendees were concerned about "the current hysteria over sex offenders," this concern was about *protecting* criminals, not preventing or *catching* them. We know that some of the attendees—the authors of *Sexual Development in Childhood*—committed crimes of their own. Those with particularly egregious backgrounds, who revealed their own sexual disorders, or committed crimes, deserve special notice.

John Money, of the *Journal of Paedophilia*, stands out as the main proponent of juvenile "sex change" operations. Indeed, the ghoulish cut-n-paste operations continue based on the notion that one's biological sex can be altered at will. On January 24, 2010, the British *Daily Mail* reported that the British health services will pay for a sixteen-year-old boy to get a £10,000 sex change operation. The lad, who just turned sixteen, was approved by a "psychologist" for surgery to remove his sexual organs followed by hormonal treatments. My, my. The TaxPayers' Alliance did protest that the "cost cannot be justified while other patients are denied life-saving cancer treatment." They have a point. Also, other "sex change patients warned" the boy was too young for this "irreversible procedure."[1065]

Moving right along, other attendees included, Julia Heiman, PhD, mentioned earlier as the current Kinsey Institute Director, who continued as a sexpert for the Internet Sinclair Institute pornography. The products for which Dr. Heiman served as a spokeswoman included sadomasochistic videos and bondage equipment, including handcuffs as well as pornographic materials promoting anal sodomy.[1066] (As of the date of this writing, the Sinclair Institute had removed its "expert advisors" list. However, Heiman's Kinsey Institute vitae still read, Professional Advisory Council, 1993–present."[1067] Philip Jenkins, PhD, Anglican scholar and historian, whitewashed Kinsey for the history books. PhDs Anke Ehrhardt and Suzanne Frayser, were students of the cited pedophile lobbyist, John Money.[1068] NIH director Duane Alexander, MD used his children's funds to support Money's ghoulish sex change operations.[1069] Money has a special room devoted to him at the Kinsey Institute. They all would have known that Money forced a boy to perform homosexual acts on his twin brother, that he filmed; that he wanted to eliminate age of consent laws, and that he said if a boy dies in a sadomasochistic "ritual," the killer should perhaps be free if there was "consent" to a ritual death pact.

Money's disciple, Anke Ehrhardt, PhD, HIV Director, Behavioral

Studies, NY State Psychiatric Institute was a *childhood* contributor. She said there is no genetic gender and sexologists must decide the "facts" of child sexuality and instruct the public. Suzanne Frayser, PhD, past President of the Society for the Scientific Study of Sexuality thought *without early sex* children are likely to be sexually and emotionally disordered. "Childhood innocence" was a fable. Auspiciously children are free to enjoy "[m]asturbation, oral sex, and sexual desire or activity," says Frayser.[1070]

Gilbert Herdt, PhD, Anthropologist, Director of Human Sexuality Studies, San Francisco State University, a public pedophile advocate and lobbyist for the *Journal of Paedophilia*, said "child or childhood . . . should be resisted at all costs," since child sexuality was normal.[1071] In the *Journal of Paedophilia,* Herdt said the age of consent should be "six or seven" to "nine-and-a-half;[1072] in *Gay and Lesbian Youth* he said childhood sex with adults is helpful. For that reason he was pleased homosexuals have been "institutionaliz[ing] 'socialization' techniques for the transmission of its cultural knowledge to a younger generation."[1073]

Michael Bailey, PhD, psychologist, head of the Northwestern University psychology department, got NIH pornography funds and was caught in exploitive sex with a transvestite subject used in his book—absent the subject's informed consent.[1074] In *Childhood,* Bailey largely debunked the notion of child sex trauma. He said "gay" boys of twelve and thirteen *wanted* "sex" (sodomy) with adults because the boys "would become gay anyway."[1075]

Erick Janssen, PhD, an Indiana University sexuality professor, organized a four-day Kinsey Institute conference in 2003 funded by NIH at which Janssen honored two *Journal of Paedophilia* editors/lobbyists, Theo Sandfort and Vern Bullough, as lead speakers. Janssen reiterated the Kinsey dogma that there exists no such thing as "normal," so children's rejection of sexual abuse may just reflect adult repression. Like others in the organized pedophile lobby, Janssen opined that children could not really be sexually abused because "we" don't know "what makes a sexual action wrong."[1076] True indeed! How could these corrupt Caligulas and Neros know wrong or right, normal or abnormal?

Jerome Cerny, PhD, an Indiana University Psychology Professor, fired for molesting male students while showing them his NIH-funded pornography, later worked for the Kinsey Institute where he conducted more pornography "studies". Cerney was convicted of felony abuse, "lewd or immoral conduct" during homosexual pornography experiments on vulnerable students at Indiana University, when he was welcomed by the Kinsey Institute as a premier sexologist.

More Mad Modern Sexologists

Since Kinsey, sexology has become a hugely popular academic "discipline." Hundreds of thousands count themselves as professional sexologists—therapists, educators, researchers—and scores of American and international academic institutions offer sexuality degrees.

What does one do with a degree in sex? Well, that depends. Some publish papers and books on topics such as "A Telemetric Method for Registration of Vaginal Sexual Response." Some travel the speaking circuit to promote the "loving nature" of "most" father-daughter incest. Some teach about sex in colleges, high schools, and grammar schools under the guise of "AIDS prevention," "tolerance," or "hate crimes." Some are sex-addiction or relationship therapists. Some merely help develop sexual stimulation aids such as the Clinical Perineometer, which strengthens the muscle that tightens the anus. And some work for the Sex Industry Complex as consultants, lobbyists, advocates, and expert witnesses.

Regardless of the specialty, sexologists commonly shill for pornography, bisexuality, bestiality, fisting, all sodomies, homosexuality, transvestitism, sadomasochism, prostitution, pedophilia and pederasty—all while performing Kinsey's no-harm mantra. Aside from their value as endorsers of the SIC, the thing that keeps sexologists in business is that they legitimize sexual deviancy. So the field, led by mad sexual psychopaths, continues to seek nothing less than *absolute sexual license*—the normalization and legalization of *all* allegedly "consensual" sex acts—though the media rarely reports on such aims.

The truly scary part? Most of its efforts have been successful. They have gutted or dramatically relaxed the laws that required men to behave honorably, protecting women and children, and that actually permitted women thereby to be women. School curricula commonly condone "therapeutic" porn, homosexuality, transvestitism, and oral and anal sodomy. Infants and children receive STD vaccinations. Pornography has spawned a child pornography avalanche. Children produce *their own* pornography, sending nude pictures of themselves over cell phones and the Internet. And in an economic downturn, we see youngsters "voluntarily" selling their bodies, which have significant worth on the open market. In such a climate, the sex slave trade of yesteryear has made a frightening comeback. The ostensibly scientific judgments of sexologists have justified *all* of this.

This, of course, begs the question: How in the world has this ridiculous, pseudo-scientific "field" achieved even a modicum of authority, let alone a place in the modern university?

Despite Kinsey's Madness, Authorities Cite Him—Widely

That Kinsey was a pathological "voyeur, an exhibitionist, and a sadomasochist, descending at times in his masochistic moods into outright lunacy"[1077] is no longer open to dispute. Yet, as mentioned earlier in 1998, Indiana University and the Kinsey Institute, backed by the Ford and Rockefeller Foundations, republished Kinsey's two original reports—without corrections, disclaimers, or warnings. Fearing nothing, the Kinsey lobby has a solid lock on academic publications, mass media, and, therefore, the national mind. So *thousands* of history, sociology, anthropology, law, health, medical, education, psychology, and sexology textbooks and professors *still* regurgitate Kinsey's frauds and allegations as gospel.

An analysis of the *Social Science Citation Index* and *The Science Citation Index* (1982–2006) reveals that Kinsey has more than double than *any other luminary* in the relevant fields. Sigmund Freud, Abraham Maslow, Margaret Mead—none of them compare. *Westlaw*, the most widely used database for law review journals and cases, began recording in 1982. A preliminary search in Westlaw from 1982 to 2000 yields over two thousand citations to "Alfred Kinsey." *No* sexperts compare while the *Social Science Citation Index, the Science Citation Index* and *Westlaw* also find double Kinsey cites to those of Masters and Johnson.

Remember, computerized records began only in the early 1980s, whereas Kinsey's initial impact on our laws and social conduct occurred between 1948 and 1960. An educated guess is that Kinsey's fraudulent data control 95 percent of all college texts, reports, essays, and opinion on sexuality from 1948 until today.

The Literature of Modern Sexology

Briefly, Ed Brecher, PhD, lead author of the influential *Consumers Union Report on Licit and Illicit Drugs* (1972), cheerfully repeated in 1969 that Kinsey's "affectionate" child molesters often contributed "favorably" to their victims' later "sociosexual development."[1078] Brecher regurgitated that popularized Kinseyan phrase and its attendant dogma: that the child predators are *not* the problem; parents' *overreactions* are the problem. Further parroting Kinsey, Brecher wrote:

> [T]he emotional reactions of the parents, police officers, and other adults . . . the current hysteria over sex offenders may very well have serious effects on the ability of many of these children to work out sexual adjustments some years later in their marriages.[1079]

The famous team of Masters and Johnson said they "stand on Kinsey's shoulders," wrote Ira Reiss, University of Minnesota sociology professor in his college textbook, *An End to Shame: Shaping our Next Sexual Revolution.* adding that Kinsey "shocked this country" with his amazing find that "erection and lubrication" occurred "even in newborn infants."[1080] Endorsed by SIECUS, the *Journal of Sex and Marital Therapy,* and popular child-sex propagandist Sol Gordon, PhD, Reiss cited "social scientists like Boston therapist Larry Constantine, PhD, and Minnesota sociologist Floyd Martinson, PhD, both pedophile advocates demanding legalized incest and child pornography.[1081] Like other "sexologists," Reiss did not disclose his real reason for sexualizing children.

Martinson repeats the "sexologist's" mantra that a girl infant's lubrication at signs of a baby boy's erection, is a sign of sexual readiness.[1082] But in girls, all bodily passages are naturally lined with mucosa, including the nose and vagina. And in boys, the reflexive nervous and vascular reactions of the penis respond to many biological stimuli—such as urinary buildup, friction, infections, and especially fear and terror. These are biologically natural and non-sexual states. But sexology-trained people sexualize everything, at the same time that they deliberately ignore that frightening sex stimuli, such as sex abuse and pornography, can prematurely disturb, emotionally arouse, and physiologically traumatize children.

Could these sociologists truly have been ignorant of such basic biological facts? Or are Reiss and his colleagues simply captives to the same pedophile lusts? Like Kinsey, to fulfill their own deviant agendas, they wanted to prove infant sexuality, and erroneously used infant erection and lubrication to do so.

If you repeat a lie often enough, people will believe it, no matter how big it is. English professor James Kinkaid, PhD's book, *Child-Loving,* reiterates Kinsey's straight line between childhood and adult sexuality. "Alas," says Kinkaid, Kinsey's "brilliance and clarity" are not sufficiently honored.[1083] Hence he quotes Kinsey as a critic and reformer, "it is probable that half or more of the boys in an uninhibited society could reach climax by the time they were three or four years of age, and that nearly all of them could experience such a climax three to five years before the onset of adolescence." He adds that Kinsey has a great deal of sympathy for this "uninhibited society" and "an equal amount of scorn for the one around him."[1084] That's it for Kinkaid as a sexology critic.

Lenore Bauth, PhD, Paul Cameron, PhD, and other "Christian" Sexologists sing from the same Kinseyan hymnal as the group above. In *How to Talk Confidently to Your Child About Sex, for Children are Sexual Beings, Too*, Lenore Bauth regurgitates Kinsey's fundamental lie:

> It may be surprising to realize that our children are sexual beings from birth. For instance, a parent changing a male infant's diaper may accidentally stimulate the child and be shocked to realize the child is having an erection. Similarly, researchers tell us that baby girls have vaginal lubrication regularly. In fact, a little girl being bounced on her parent's knee may feel pleasant sensations and begin to make natural pelvic thrust movements.[1085]

Again, Bauth eroticizes infants' physiological mucosa and erectile tissue, that clearly reflect her study of pro-pedophile essays, written by mad sexologists, to further molesters' sabotage. In his 1978 book *Sexual Gradualism*, "Christian" sex educator Paul Cameron, PhD, directed parents to have their young children bring current lovers home. Parents should "allot a room, privacy, access to a bathroom, a [TV], and snacks for their teenagers to practice gradualism . . . without fear of adult interference."[1086] What was "gradualism"? Cameron spelled it out:

Parents should have their children commit escalating "levels" of sex acts. For early levels, kissing, hugging, and so on are fine. By age thirteen, "Breast fondling, manipulating, sucking" are appropriate. By age fourteen, children begin "Mutual hand exploration of genitals, mutual masturbation, fingering . . . rubbing." Then comes "Total nudity." Next comes "Oral sex." Anal sodomy is also okay, but sexual intercourse is a no-no. After engaging in various perverse acts for years, children must save intercourse for the marriage bed—as if they would or could "naturally" refrain from intercourse after everything else—since adolescence—was A-okay! So much for *Sweet Sixteen* and *Never Been Kissed.* One does wonder about Cameron's own experience with intimacy avoidance.[1087]

Scientific Fraud Is Socially Destructive

Kinsey's biographers and filmmakers tried to make him a tragic figure who sought only to spread tolerance—a high-minded, ethical scientist, with no "prurient" interests of his own. Therefore, they brand those who pull back the sheets and expose the real Kinsey as religious zealots, bigots, and sexually repressed fanatics. But this no longer works. We know too much about Alfred Kinsey now. We know that Kinsey slyly and heinously used the sex habits of deviants to paint an ugly portrait of our Greatest Generation. Although delusionary, Kinsey cultists still deny the truth about Kinsey's distortions. But we know the truth.

The high purpose of science is to discover facts to improve society, especially to help inform our laws. But beyond exploiting the data-collection process for his books, Kinsey made no scientific use of his child pornography, the financial cost of which was borne primarily by the Rockefellers and Indiana University, thus by taxpayers. Kinsey's attic scenes were never available to other researchers because he, his wife, and followers were recognizable. Blackmail, of course, likely aided Kinsey's agenda for years. Wardell Pomeroy wrote:

> The public would have been astounded and disbelieving to know the names of the eminent scientists who appeared at the Institute from time to time to examine our work and talk with Kinsey, and who volunteered before they left to be photographed in some kind of sexual activity.[1088]

Indeed—as in Tuskegee, the LSD experiments, the Willowbrook scandal, and on and on—we know that too many psychopaths are passed off as "eminent scientists." Indiana University and its public relations apparatus has always protected Kinsey's aggressive, illegal conduct, and many other officials and scholars covered up his crimes during his lifetime. The Kinsey Institute, Indiana University, and other academic institutions, they continue to do so.

In 1987, writing in the journal *Science*, then-editor Daniel E. Koshland, Jr., argued that fraud is "unacceptable." All of science, he said, is "based on trust." Koshland said any important fraud "will become exposed." Yet, my scores of letters, phone calls, and faxes to Koshland and *Science* about Kinsey's fraud—the greatest criminal scientific scandal of all time—have yielded only silence. It means that objective, thoughtful scientists should be on inquiry as to how deep the pedophile cover up really is.

The Office of Scientific Inquiry at the NIH reviewed nearly 100 cases of alleged fraud or misconduct. In 1988, Stephen Breuning, MD, was convicted of a crime and punished for scientific fraud because, the prosecutor argued:

> His well-established reputation was considered instrumental in forming public health policy nationally. . .several states amended treatment practices as a result. . . . There was no evidence presented in the indictment that the therapy advocated by Breuning actually helped or hurt the children . . . just that the research wasn't done. . . .[1089]

Promulgating a great fraud, Kinsey and his Institute committed much worse crimes. Kinsey's pedophile team deliberately and sexually tortured children. In their grander abuse, they pandered theories that changed human life, behavior, and culture in the most intimate, personal, and important ways. State and federal funds financed these frauds and crimes, violating the public trust. And, despite decades of cover-up and exposure, the Kinsey Institute continues to receive government monies to perform "research" today.

Newton's *Principia* launched modern science as the new religion. In 1986, celebrating *Principia's* three-hundredth anniversary, the illustrious Sir James Lighthill lectured the Royal Society, lamenting the arrogance of modern science in misleading the world about

Newton. Lighthill apologized over the angry protests from many of his colleagues:

> [O]n behalf of the broad global fraternity of practitioners of mechanics. . . . We collectively wish to apologize for having misled the general educated public by spreading ideas about the determinism of systems satisfying Newton's laws of motion that, after 1960, were to be proved incorrect [and] uncovered so late."[1090]

Sexology's "broad global fraternity of practitioners" certainly owes the world such an apology. No other scientists have so misled "the general educated public" with lies that have been proven fatally incorrect, deliberate and socially catastrophic.

It is time to stop the fraud, to correct the record, to amend the law. It is time to stop the flow of funds. *It is time!*

[CHAPTER 15]

Yes, Recovery Is Possible!

[M]odern science . . . now tells us that there is little difference in the physical or chemical changes in the pleasure and control centers of the brain regardless of whether the addiction is "from a chemical or an experience," as stated in the journal *Science.* It is imperative that we treat pornography and sexual addiction with the respect accorded any drug addiction, for, as we shall see, that is precisely what it is.

—Donald L. Hilton Jr., MD, *He Restoreth My Soul* (2009)

If thine *eye* offend thee, *pluck* it *out*: it is better for thee to enter into the kingdom of God with one *eye*, than having two *eyes* to be cast into hell.

—Mark 9:47

Action Item One: *Support from the Brain Sciences*

Science is now catching up with biblical truth for "neurons that fire together wire together." When we have an "eye" experience, it is wired into our brains. Eventually, whether we want to or not, when we think about or revisualize an event our memory, our wiring is strengthened. For good or ill, this is the road to sex addictions. The "wiring" of neurons cements memories together with the facts or details related to that memory.

In his Sonnet 129, Shakespeare warns that lust "leads men . . . to . . .

hell." What we see, do, think, and dream, alters our brain. Hence, people who view pornography continue to "see" images embedded in their mind's eye. The images link to, and network with, motoric, bodily arousal.

The problem has been that, seeking freedom *in* pornography, users instead became enslaved by pornography, by the "drug." Mainstream media spreads degrading images and stories of hatred and humiliation, blending these with sexual arousal, 24/7. So-called soft pornography does the same thing, burning and mirroring images into the brain. High-speed Internet pornography especially triggers a dopamine, natural poly-drug high. *All such experiences create neuroplastic changes in the brain.*

Until the 1980s, most neurologists believed the brain was hard-wired, unable to replenish neurons or create new neuronal networks after emotional or physical trauma. But the *Wall Street Journal* science editor, Sharon Begley, reported on the neurological studies that show that the "brain can change, and that means we can change," with "attention and mental effort."

In *Train Your Mind, Change Your Brain: How a New Science Reveals Our Extraordinary Potential to Transform Ourselves*,[1091] Begley cites some ways the human brain rewires, expands, and shrinks different areas to make new connections and eliminate others. One reader says the brain can "run new cables like an electrician bringing an old house up to code, so that regions that once saw can instead feel or hear." Circuits that were damaged by aberrant activity like "depression, obsessive-compulsive disorder and sexual pathologies *can be rewired*." Great news!

Columbia University neuroplastician Norman Doidge, MD, documents brain rewiring in adults and children in *The Brain that Changes Itself*. Doidge says the pornography epidemic proves "sexual tastes can be acquired"[1092] by those driven to exert the mental discipline to "re-wire" the brain. Users, writes Doidge, are "seduced into pornographic training sessions," wiring the sex and other images they see "into the brain's pleasure centers and changing their brain maps."[1093]

According to Doidge, "The discovery of neuroplasticity, that our thoughts can change the structure and function of our brains, even into old age, is the most important breakthrough in our understanding of the brain in four hundred years."[1094] NIH researchers trained rats to press a bar until they got a shot of dopamine, the endogenous reward transmitter. The dopamine system is our brain's pleasure center. By hijacking the dopamine system, we get a pleasure "hit" without working for it! One dose of some addictive drugs produces "a protein, called delta FosB that accumulates in the neurons." In the same way, sex images would throw a genetic switch, "leading to irreversible damage to the brain's dopamine system and rendering the animal far more prone to addiction."[1095] Doidge says that men, using pornography at their computers, "uncannily" resemble caged NIH rats, pressing the bar to get their dopamine or equivalent high.[1096]

Like rats pressured by intense competition, pornography Web sites produce increasingly shameful, cruel scripts that change users' naïve brains. As the brain rewires for novelty, it ignores and bypasses the familiar. As wives and lovers lose their appeal, users lose their natural potency. They need new pictures to trigger that appetitive, hyperactive, dopamine spritz.

Doidge's research supports survey findings that pornography users increasingly lose relationships and jobs, withdrawing from the world to live with their pornography collections. Says Doidge, what commonly began as a lark now leaves them impotent until they fantasize themselves into "a porn script." Impotence, impotence, impotence, says Doidge. Young, healthy males now use Viagra-type "medicine developed for older men with erectile problems related to aging and blocked blood vessels."[1097] Impotence means "without power," without one's natural potency. If one needs the pictures in one's head, the story, and one's lover doesn't satisfy, one is impotent, without natural power.

Our excitation system from coitus is designed to be consummatory, producing "calming, fulfilling pleasure," releasing endorphins, including oxytocin, which is related to opiates, causing "a peaceful, euphoric bliss." But pornography, says Doidge, "hyperactivates the appetitive system. Porn viewers develop new maps in their brains, based on the photos and videos they see." With a use-it-or-lose-it brain, we tend to keep the brain systems that were intensely activated.

The human brain can attach sexual arousal to our pain systems. Severe sadomasochists, like Kinsey, would have wired painful sensations to their sexual excitatory systems for "voluptuous pain." Like Kinsey, some sadomasochists suffered early childhood medical trauma that would have "occurred during the critical periods of sexual, neural plasticity."

Perhaps science may yet catch up with the hope found in religious faith, that "With God, all things are possible" (Matthew 19:26).

It turns out that the same laws of neuroplasticity that allow us to acquire problematic tastes also allow us, *in intensive treatment*, to acquire newer, healthier tastes and desires, and in some cases, even to lose our older, troubling ones.

Sex and pornography addictions are addictions. Since the brain operates in use-it-or-lose-it mode, where lust is concerned, total abstinence from exterior "lust" imagery can begin the long voyage to health and wellbeing. Like all other twelve-step addiction recovery programs, for most people who have successfully overcome obsessions, this also appears to require a commitment to God, to a "higher power," to relevant others, perhaps even meditation. Addicts have not been known to gain sobriety alone.

Action Item Two: *Challenge the Sexology Status Quo*

Despite the revelations about Kinsey's incalculable impact on our daily lives, many questions remain. These questions are legitimate and important, and we need to ask them and to demand answers. Pressing for a discussion of the foundations of modern sexology is one way to unravel its grasp on our lives. I encourage you to challenge our doctors, courts, legislators, teachers, mass media, clergy, and others with questions.

Action Item Three: *Correct the Legal Record!*

Certainly ample evidence indicates that Kinsey's fraud actively harmed both children and society and was "instrumental in forming public health policy nationally," as the NIH prosecutor alleged in the case of Dr. Breuning. Therefore, the Kinsey Institute and Indiana University *must be held similarly accountable* for their actions and omissions, for their willful cover-up of scientific fraud, for their protection of pedophiles, and for their criminal employment of child molesters. If a cadre of true patriots can be awakened to organize and lobby for the Greatest Generation, all things *are* possible!

1. We can demand that an honest judge subpoena the Institute's records and investigate these crimes. Simultaneously, we urgently need to recall all victimized test subjects and their family members to contact the court.

2. We can demand that the American Law Institute (ALI) revisit all legal precedent that relied on skewed Kinseyan "data." Hundreds of decisions in the ALI-Model Penal Code turned on Kinsey Institute lies. The ALI, the American Psychiatric Association, the American Psychological Association, and our law schools have a clear moral and legal obligation to revisit and revise (or abolish) all policies and laws that are based on Kinsey's frauds.
3. We can demand that Congress investigate the Kinsey Institute and its funders—both philanthropic organizations and government agencies—that supported his frauds. Clearly, Kinsey—and his successors—violated grants and the public trust, working with systemic financial, political, and personal conflicts of interest; colluding with lobbyists and advocates, for example Big Pharma and Big Pornography, which also donate to the Institute. Further, the Institute used medications, pornography, and other substances in violation of grant terms.
4. We can demand that our elected representatives divest from funding schools *at any level* if their curricula includes Kinsey-based sex education or "sexuality" courses, including those conducted by Planned Parenthood and SIECUS.
5. We can demand that Kinsey-type sex-ed be eliminated from our schools, churches, and temples. We can write letters to our newspapers about Kinsey's influence. We can call radio talk programs and TV talk shows. We can join political, religious, community, national, and international organizations that work to reestablish the values of the Greatest Generation.

Qui Tam Lawsuits: "Lincoln's Law," On Behalf of the State

Egregious frauds perpetrated by the Kinsey Institute—as well as Planned Parenthood, SIECUS, and others—make these organizations vulnerable to class action lawsuits and to legal action under provisions of the Whistleblowers Act. Bolstered by congressional amendments in 1986, this law arms private citizens with a weapon to prosecute contractors who defraud the government. It was signed into law by President Abraham Lincoln during the Civil War. *"Qui Tam"* lawsuits allow citizens who have independent and direct knowledge of such fraud to sue *on behalf of the government*. The citizens who sue share in the financial recovery. The 1986 Amendment defines a "claim" as:

> any request or demand which is made to a contractor, grantee, or other recipient if the United States Government provides any portion of the money or property which is requested or demanded, or if the government will reimburse such contractor, grantee, or other recipient for any portion of the money or property which is requested or demanded.[1098]

Qui Tam cases generally involve accusations of false claims that someone directly or indirectly presents to the government for "payment or approval." Examples of false claims include submission of false records, statements, or other fraudulent representations. The Kinsey Institute, Planned Parenthood, SIECUS, and others, for example, generated false claims by holding themselves out to the State as experts, and then obtaining federal and state funds based on their submitting false data, information, records, statements, and other representations about their aims, missions, and accomplishments.

The Kinsey lobby, which has committed egregious fraud for sixty years, is certainly vulnerable to "grassroots" lawsuits under the False Claims Act and *Qui Tam* provisions. Consider that:

- $667 million in the fiscal year 2004 was recovered under the False Claims Act.
- This was down from more than $2 billion recovered in fiscal year 2003.
- The total amount recovered in 2004 by plaintiffs for malpractice under *Qui Tam* provisions of the False Claims Act was $554 million.
- In cases that the Department of Justice entered or otherwise pursued, the amount recovered by the DoJ was $8 billion.
- 4,704 *Qui Tam* cases have been filed, to date.
- Total awards to individuals when government declined to intervene in a case was $92.15 million.[1099]
- You can learn more about whistleblower victories and *Qui Tam* law at www.governmentfraud.us/cases.html and www.governmentfraud.us/contact.html.

Action Item Four: *Resurrect the Kinsey Bill*

A fair and impartial investigation of the Kinsey Institute—at local, state, and federal levels—would lead to ending government funding of *all* Kinsey-based institutions, from the Kinsey Institute to "research" entities in higher education and from Planned Parenthood, SIECUS, and their ilk to "sex-ed" in local classrooms. Further, such an investigation would also lead to prosecutions for defrauding the government, taxpayers, and the general public.

I encourage you to pressure your legislators to support formation of such an investigative body.

Action Item Five: *Call a Traitor a Traitor*

On June 3, 2005, *Human Events*, the nation's oldest conservative weekly, asked a panel of fifteen conservative scholars and public policy leaders to list the ten most harmful books of the nineteenth and twentieth centuries. Their first three picks were the work of infamous, psychopathic, foreign tyrants who penned secularist, statist books in order to change the world. They were *The Communist Manifesto* by Karl Marx (1848), *Mein Kampf* by Adolf Hitler (1925), and *Quotations from Chairman Mao* by Mao Tse-Tung (1967). Their fourth selection was *Sexual Behavior in the Human Male* (1948), the foremost *American* book written to alter the world—drastically.

Kinsey, like Marx, Hitler, and Mao, sought to deliberately destroy a nation's moral and religious inheritance. All four men attacked marriage and the family; the authority of a protective, providing father; and a (married) mother. Only Kinsey additionally attacked the sexual innocence and sanctity of childhood. All four books are anti-parent, anti-God manifestos. But foreign-born Marx, Hitler, and Mao at least railed against their nations' misery and corruption. Kinsey and his co-conspirators, on the other hand, conspired to destroy the most successful and prosperous republic in human history, to turn the American people against themselves and their own stabilizing institutions of family and church by libeling the Greatest Generation and its priceless historical legacy.

CUT OUT AND SEND TO YOUR REPRESENTATIVES

Create an Act with Legislative Supporters

Title: To determine if Alfred Kinsey's *Sexual Behavior in the Human Male* and/or *Sexual Behavior in the Human Female* are the result of any fraud or criminal wrongdoing.

SUMMARY

This Act Directs the Comptroller General to conduct a study to determine whether programs, lectures, texts, or other pedagogical materials involving sexuality used by agencies, universities, or elementary and secondary schools (institutions) that receive federal funds for educational purposes significantly or particularly rely on the scholarship of, directly or indirectly consisting of, or based on the studies entitled *Sexual Behavior in the Human Male* and *Sexual Behavior in the Human Female* authored by Alfred Kinsey and his team of researchers, published in 1948 and 1953 (Kinsey reports). Authorizes the General Accounting Office to evaluate whether the contents of the Kinsey reports are erroneous, wrongfully obtained by reason of fraud or criminal wrongdoing (i.e., systematic sexual abuse of children), or both.

Directs: (1) the Comptroller General to complete such study and report to the Congress by {Date} and (2) the Secretary of Education, if the Comptroller General's determination is in the affirmative, to ensure that for this year and all subsequent fiscal years no federal funds are provided to any persons or institutions for any educational purpose which instruct in Kinsey's work, derivative Kinseyan scholars, or scholarship without indicating the unethical and tainted nature of the Kinsey report. Directs the chief executive officer of the State involved to certify to the Secretary which such agencies or school programs cite such materials.

To determine if Alfred Kinsey's *Sexual Behavior in the Human Male* and/or *Sexual Behavior in the Human Female* are the result of any fraud or criminal wrongdoing.

(SIGN UP YOUR LEGISLATORS)

Why did the fifteen *Human Events* scholars select *Sexual Behavior in the Human Male* to join Marx, Hitler, and Mao on this list?

As we now know, Kinsey's 1948 fraud-in-print hit like an academic H-bomb, spreading distrust, division, divorce, and degeneracy across America like radioactive dust. Firing his "data" at the nation less than three years after our GIs returned home, Kinsey's attack caught Americans totally off-guard and fueled a massive breakdown in faith, marriage, and family. It produced socio-sexual toxins in the body politic that spread virulently and poisoned the minds and bodies of American men, women and children, unto the current generation.

All normal people would consider Kinsey's grotesque self-abuses several degrees past abnormal, beyond even mild psychopathology. Yet academic, legal, and judicial America accepted this man as its hero. And then they followed him off the moral cliff, pulling the public over with them.

To engineer the destruction of one's country—to betray one's country—is to commit treason. Having witnessed it, understanding it now, we should demand correction of the historical record about Alfred Kinsey. I accuse Kinsey, the Kinsey Institute and Indiana University, and his co-conspirators of committing treason against the United States. They spread black propaganda, which they designed to undermine America's common law, sexual morality, and social fabric in the service of their mad eugenic vision of global control.

Though we know that the Kinsey Institute has censored all of Kinsey's correspondence, Kinsey almost certainly wrote *something* about World War II. If his letters reveal, as I believe they do, fascist sympathies, the Kinsey Institute certainly would have hidden or possibly destroyed them.

Paul Gebhard said of Kinsey's biographer:

> James Jones can see the stuff that's previously looked over. He got to see some of the correspondence, but I ran ahead of him and made sure to abstract anything that was confidential.[1100]

What exactly was the "confidential" material that Gebhard ran ahead and made sure to abstract? What did Kinsey really write in those hidden "thousands of letters"? Did materials implicate Kinsey in crimes and perfidy? What was the truth about Mike Mikshe,

Kinsey's sexual sadist partner, who committed suicide. Gathorne-Hardy speculated that "[Mike's] letters may have been too open about the filming."[1101] Or was Mike too open about Kinsey's crimes against children? What of the red binders that contain mega-molester Rex King's descriptions of sexually torturing children for Kinsey? The Kinsey Institute illegally covers up Kinsey's crimes. Until a judge finally slaps an injunction on the Kinsey Institute and we acquire the hidden files, we will not know what its present staff conceals.

James Jones made another revealing remark. Writing to Glenn Ramsey, then a reluctant soldier, Kinsey said the war was a total waste of time and "he paid it no mind."[1102] He *paid it no mind?* Only a pathological person would mock the entire world's suffering with such a remark. A eugenicist, Kinsey admired the notion of the "super man." Were there letters that exposed him as a Nazi sympathizer—or more? Where is Kinsey's correspondence with Rex King, his Nazi pedophile? When did it begin? He certainly was not a patriot!

Kinsey clearly felt disdain for our boys overseas—and for their loved ones at home. He cared not about their victories or defeats, casualties or deaths. He had no interest in soldiers, stranded in combat, without gasoline. Further, there is no record that anyone among his staff felt concern about soldiers or their families. And no one at the Kinsey Institute showed any desire for the defeat of the Axis powers or the victory of the Allies.

Was Kinsey, like his Rockefeller patrons, unsure which side would win? Could he have thought that, if Hitler won, his "work" would receive continued support, greater funds, and more opportunity? After all, psychopathic scientists, such as Kinsey, did well—unhindered—under Hitler. Additional information about Kinsey's links to fascists and Hitler's henchmen suggest much is hidden.

Jones says Kinsey's war interest was solely in ending American sexual morality. "While the free world fought to survive, he waged his own private war against Victorian morality. He put everything he had into collecting data, his weapon of choice in the great war he had fashioned for himself."[1103]

In their war, Kinsey and his cult set about to change the face of our nation, using their own covert but powerful weapons. They deliberately lied about and gutted the "common law" morals of the Greatest Generation, and plotted to replace those values with their own immorality, with deviant *anti*-values. They purposely undermined our nation's health, welfare, strength, and resolve.

That was Kinsey's betrayal, a violation of allegiance to his country. *And that is treason*, by definition.

Our God-Given Obligation and Privilege

Painting the Greatest Generation's traditional values as promiscuous depravity, Kinsey and his team defamed our moral heritage as sexual hypocrisy. We have watched as the children of our World War II heroes believed the Kinsey slander, revolted against all moral authority, and decayed into the "sex, drugs, and rock 'n' roll" generation of the 1960s. They went on to parent Shapiro's "Porn Generation," now steeped in adult and "kiddie" porn and now parenting the "Child Sex Abuse Generation."

Before Kinsey, Americans were normally sexually literate and aware of sex as belonging in love and marriage. Post-Kinsey, we are certainly sexually *illiterate* if we measure literacy by rates of illegitimacy, abortion STDs, sex crimes, and divorce. How can we say, with a straight face, that our pre-Kinsey sexual "repression" was harmful and our modern liberation healthy? Can we say, with a straight face, that our "health" is evident in promiscuity that knows no bounds, such that men and women of every socio-economic, irreligious, religious, political, racial and educational level are increasingly caught up in super sexual child sexual abuse? Indeed, we *are* becoming degenerate, perverse, and violent. We have lost our virtue.

The fact is that Kinsey's deviants and psychopaths betrayed our nation, seducing us into "hate America" and gutting a moral system that had brought our nation unparalleled health and prosperity, and into rejecting our traditional moral standards. With dishonest, mendacious research and a secret psychosexual agenda, Kinsey and his cadre of eugenicists led the sexual revolution—to eliminate babies, love, and family, to destroy our God-based morals, and to allow unfettered access to the bodies and minds of innocent children.

But take heart. Knowledge is power. We have it. We know the enemy, and we know what is right and true. We can use this knowledge to set the record straight—about Kinsey, about the sexologists, about the damage they've done to children and generations, to our parents and grandparents. We can use this knowledge—and we *should.*

This is our call, our obligation to the Greatest Generation, to the men and women who gave their lives that we might live in freedom.

Let's do it America!

ENDNOTES

[CHAPTER 1]

1 Tom Brokaw, *The Greatest Generation* (New York: Random House, 1998), xix–xviii.

2 Allan Bloom, *The Closing of the American Mind* (New York, Simon & Schuster, 1987).

3 See, "The War Mothers Flag," http://www.bluestarmothers.org/mc/page.do?sitePageId=64171&orgId=bsma.

4 Congressional Research Report—American War and Military Operations Casualties, updated June 29, 2007.

5 Andy Rooney, *My War* (New York: Public Affairs, 2000), 13. I have ellipsed the two offensive words.

6 Alfred Kinsey, June 23, 1894, Hoboken, New Jersey to Alfred Seguine Kinsey and Sarah Ann Charles, the eldest of three children.

7 Julia A. Ericksen, "With Enough Cases, Why Do You Need Statistics?" *Journal of Sex Research* 35, no. 2 (1998): 132ff.

8 Gertrude Himmelfarb, *One Nation, Two Cultures* (New York: Vintage Books, 2001), 13.

9 Morris Ernst and David Loth, *American Sexual Behavior and the Kinsey Report* (New York: Greystone Press, 1948), 81, 83.

10 "The League of Grateful Sons," 2005, http://www.leagueofgratefulsons.com.

11 Andrea Tone, *Devices and Desires: A History of Contraceptives in America* (New York, Hill and Wang, 2001), 6.

12 The Comstock Act, a U.S.A law made it illegal to send any "obscene, lewd, and/or lascivious" materials through the mail, including contraceptive devices and information. Twenty-four states passed similar prohibitions on materials distributed within the states. See http://www.absoluteastronomy.com/topics/Comstock_Law.

13 Tone, *Devices and Desires*, 7.

14 Leonard Leff, "Hollywood and the Holocaust: Remembering The Pawnbroker" *American Jewish History* 84, no. 4 (1966): 353–376. http://www.cmcdannell.com/HollywoodHolocaustReading.pdf.

15 Himmelfarb, *One Nation*, 10.

16 Cover, Kartes Video Communications, Inc, circa 2000, http://www.sparknotes.com/lit/ourtown/context.html.

17 Ibid.

18 Frederick L. Schuman, review citing to books by Ewald Banse, "Germany Prepares for War; and Nazi Means War by Leland Stowe," *American Political Science Review* 28, no. 3 (June 1934), 524–526.

19 Eugenia Kaledin, *Daily Life in the United States, 1940–1959: Shifting Worlds* (Greenwood Publishing, 2000), 42.

20 Kingwood College Library, *American Cultural History*, see 1930–1939 http://kclibrary.lonestar.edu/decade30.html.

21 Dr. Hjalmar Schacht became minister of economics in 1934, "with instructions to secretly increase armaments production." See Phil Stokes's excellent historical site, http://www.secondworldwar.co.uk/ahitler.html.

22 American Battle Monuments Commission, etc., see http://www.abmc.gov/home.ph.

23 Joseph Heller, *Now and Then: From Coney Island to Here* (New York, Alfred Knopf, 1998), 10–11, 17, 43, 170.

24 Ibid.

25 Phyllis and Eberhard Kronhausen, *Sex Histories of American College Men* (New York: Ballantine Books, 1960), 219.

26 Brokaw, *Greatest Generation*, 37.

27 Ibid., xx, 37, 55.

28 Ibid., 37.

29 Introduction of Bernard S. Sadowski, *Autobiography, The Greatest Generation*, http://www.geneabios.com/sadowski.htm.

30 Emily Yellin, *Our Mothers' War: American Women at Home and at the Front During World War II* (New York: Free Press, 2005), 39.

31 Ibid., 60.

32 Ibid., 13.

33 Ibid., 23.

34 Ibid., 30.

35 Ibid., 32.

36 Ibid., 33.

37 "Dwight D. Eisenhower, His Life and Times," *Infinite Mind*, Public Radio Series (New Hudson, MI, 2005).

38 Brokow, *Greatest Generation*, xviii.

39 See http://www.powells.com/biblio?isbn=0385334621.

40 See http://www.bookbrowse.com/reviews/index.cfm?book_number=128.

41 Tracy Sugarman, *My War: A Love Story in Letters and Drawings* (New York: Random House, 2000), 7–11.

42 Sugarman, "Experiencing War," Library of Congress, (March 3, 1944), http://lcweb2.loc.gov/diglib/vhp-stories/loc.natlib.afc2001001.05440/transcriptturner?ID=pm000200.

43 Brokaw, *Greatest Generation*, 48.

44 Read more about Lt. Col. Butler on, Spotlight On Marine Heroes #10, http://www.ww2gyrene.org/spotlight10_1.htm.

45 Brad Minor, *The Compleat Gentleman* (Dallas, TX, Spence Publishing Company, 2004), 16–18, 83–85.

46 Ibid., 83–85.

47 See http://www.brainyquote.com/quotes/quotes/v/voltaire169603.html.

[CHAPTER 2]

48 Thanks to SGM Herb Friedman (Ret.), for this well-documented Web site! http://www.psywarrior.com/PSYOPVD.html.

49 See http://www.chapala.com/chapala/columnists/insight/insighapril2002.htm.

50 Hear a recording of Axis Sally: http://users.rlc.net/catfish/liberatorcrew/11_Axis%20Sally.html.

51 See http://www.historynet.com/mildred-elizabeth-sisk-american-born-axis-sally.htm. (June 9, 2009).

52 Friedman, http://www.psywarrior.com/PSYOPVD.html.

53 Thanks to the well-documented *Grandboomers* Web site!, http://www.grandboomers.com/GB_love_letters_2.html. February 2, 2010 broken, check http://www.grandboomers.com/page/love-letters-from-wwii.

54 See http://www.grandboomers.com/GB_love_letters.html.

55 Henry J. Sage, *The U.S. After World War II: Domestic Issues*, 1996–2005, www.sagehistory.net/history122/ topics/PostWorldWarIIDom.htm.

56 Nina G. Seavey, *A Paralyzing Fear: The Story of Polio in America*, The Documentary Center, George Washington University, 1998.

57 Ibid., Seavey.

58 Ben Shapiro, *Porn Generation* (Washington, D.C.: Regnery Publishing, 2005), 20.

59 Charles Socarides, M.D., NARTH interview, *Homosexuality: A Freedom Too Far*, September 20, 2004, see NARTH. http://www.narth.com.

60 Judith Orr, "Judith Orr Takes On the Right Wing Moralisers—Review of *Kinsey*" *Socialist Review* (March 2005), http://www.socialistreview.org.uk/issue.php?issue=294.

61 "The Ten Most Harmful Books of the 19th and 20th Centuries," *Human Events*, May 31, 2005, http://www.humanevents.com/article.php?id=7591.

62 Clarence Tripp, "Incidence, Frequency, and the Kinsey 0–6 Scale," in *The Encyclopedia of Homosexuality*, New York, 1990.

63 See Kinsey Institute claims, http://www.kinseyinstitute.org/research/akdata.html.

64 See especially Kinsey's testimony in the Preliminary Report of The Subcommittee on Sex Crimes of the Assembly Interim Committee on Judicial System and Judicial Process, California Legislative Assembly, 1949 (Created by HR 232 and HR 43), 103, 105, 117.

65 Alfred C. Kinsey, Wardell Pomeroy, and Clyde Martin, *Sexual Behavior in the Human Male* [hereafter *Male*] (Philadelphia: W.B. Saunders, 1948), 677; see also Alfred C. Kinsey, Wardell Pomeroy, Clyde Martin, and Paul Gebhard *Sexual Behavior in the Female* [hereafter *Female*] (Philadelphia: W.B. Saunders, 1953), 79–81.

66 *Life Magazine*, August 24, 1953, 45.

67 Ibid., Kinsey Institute, supra, 55, "Kinsey said that good incidence data was not available," (585, *Female*).

68 American Law Institute, "207.1" Sex Offenses, Model Penal Code, Tentative Draft No. 4, April 25, 1955 (hereinafter "MPC"), 207.

69 Paul Gebhard, Wardell Pomeroy, Clyde Martin, and Cornelia Christenson, "*Pregnancy, Birth and Abortion*," in *Sex Research Studies from the Kinsey Institute*, ed. Martin S. Weinberg (New York: Oxford University Press, 1976), 102.

70 *The American Law Institute Model Penal Code*, Tentative Draft 9, (Philadelphia: American Law Institute May 9, 1959), § 207.11, n. 1. See also Samuel Kling, *Sexual Behavior & the Law* (New York, Random House, 1965), 9. See also Paul Gebhard, Wardell Pomeroy, Clyde Martin, Cornelia Christenson, *Pregnancy, Birth and Abortion*, the "Science Editions" (New York, John Wiley & Sons, Inc., 1958), xi-xiii (emphasis added). See extensive discussion in Judith Reisman, *Kinsey, Crimes & Consequences* (Crestwood, KY: Institute for Media Education, 2003).

71 *Female*, ibid., 122.

72 Ibid., 122, only "one clear cut-case of serious injury done to the child."

73 Ibid., 434, 326, 318, 345 (see cite to 333 pregnancies).

74 There are no references to children in these reports beyond their sexual or reproductive role.

75 Sarah Goode, *Paedophiles in Society: Reflecting on Sexuality, Abuse and Hope*, Chapter Four, "'Early Sexual Growth and Activity': The Influence of Kinsey" (UK, Palgrave Press), 2010.

76 *Male*, ibid., 176.

77 Ibid., 178.

78 J. Gordon Muir, MD, editor of Judith Reisman et al., *Kinsey, Sex and Fraud*, (Lafayette, LA, 1990), audio taped telephone interview with Paul Gebhard November 2, 1992.

79 *Male*, ibid., 179.

80 Ibid., 180.

81 Wardell Pomeroy, *Dr. Kinsey and the Institute for Sex Research*, (Harper & Row, 1972), 172.

82 Reisman, *Kinsey, Crimes & Consequences*, 137.

83 Paul Gebhard, in Masters, Johnson and Kolodny, Ed., *Ethical Issues in Sex Therapy and Research, Reproductive Biology Research Foundation Conference*, (Little, Brown and Company, Boston, 1977), 13.

84 "Scrapbook," *Weekly Standard*, January 31, 2005.vhttp://hnn.us/roundup/entries/9895.html, January 28, 2005 at 8:46 PM From the: He'd been involved in [Kinsey's research] project from 1948, "Kinsey Lives!" *Advocate*, November 23, 2004.

85 *Male*, ibid., 160–161.

86 Albert Jonsen and Jay Mann, "Ethics of Sex Research Involving Children and the Mentally Retarded," in William H. Masters, Virginia A. Johnson, Robert C. Kolodny, and Sarah M. Weems, *Ethical Issues in Sex Therapy* (Boston: Little Brown & Co. 1980), 71.

87 *Female*, ibid. 104.

88 Ibid., 105.

89 Pediatric Consult, Williams and Wilkins 1997, http://www.drgreene.com/qa/treating-pinworms.

90 Marjorie Greenfield, M.D. in Dr. Spock, http://www.drspock.com/article/0,1510,5888,00.html, and http://www.ehow.com/how_4484393_detect-symptoms-pinworms-children.html, November 16, 2009.

91 *Female*, ibid., 119.

92 Ibid., 118.

93 See Kinsey Institute "Data from Alfred Kinsey's Studies," http://www.indiana.edu/~kinsey/research/ak-data.html#analsex.

[CHAPTER 3]

94 James H. Jones, *Alfred C. Kinsey, A Public/Private Life*, (New York, W.W. Norton & Company, 1997), 22–23.

95 Ibid., 82.

96 Ibid., 81.

97 Ibid., 78.

98 Ibid., 82.

99 Michael B. Katz and Mark J. Stern, "School Attendance in 1910, America at the Millennium Project"; see *One Nation Divisible: What America Wants and What It Is Becoming* (New York, Russell Sage Foundation Publications, July 2008), "High school graduation leaped from 9% in 1910 to 40% in 1935," 58.

100 Wardell Pomeroy, *Kinsey and the Institute for Sex Research* (New York: Harper & Row, 1972), 21, 25.

101 Ibid., 26.

102 Ibid., 33.

103 Jones, *Alfred C. Kinsey*, 75.

104 Ibid.

105 Ibid., 29.

106 Pomeroy, *Kinsey and the Institute for Sex Research*, 32.

107 Ibid., 27.

108 James H. Jones, *The Origins of the Institute for Sex Research*, (UMI Dissertation Services, Ann Arbor, Michigan, 1973), 122.

109 Cornelia Christenson, *Kinsey: A Biography* (Bloomington: Indiana University, 1971), 25.

110 Ibid., 45.

111 American Philosophical Society, http://www.amphilsoc.org/library/mole/w/weir.xml.

112 James H. Jones, *Alfred C. Kinsey, A Public/Private Life*, (New York, W.W. Norton & Company, 1997), 809, fn. 78.

113 Legislators did not fully repeal Indiana's sterilization laws until 1974; see, http://www.kobescent.com/eugenics/timeline.html.

114 Pomeroy, *Kinsey and the Institute*, 9–10: "That was Kinsey, the mother superior keeping us within the strict boundaries of his schedule, yet we did not often resent it. . . . Kinsey was in fact an aggressive individual, and I think it was because of his hidden fear of failure. . . . He was aggressive, too, when someone attempted to 'get something' on him. Sometimes I might feel hurt by a remark he had made to me and after licking my wounds for two or three weeks I would make an attempt at revenge by trying to trap him in some inconsistency."

115 Pomeroy, *Kinsey and the Institute*, 38.

116 Jones, *Kinsey*, 604.

117 PBS, *American Experience*, Kinsey Timeline, http://www.pbs.org/wgbh/amex/kinsey.

118 James H. Jones, "Annals of Sexology, Dr. Yes," *New Yorker*, August 25 & September 1, 1997, 103–104.

119 Ibid.

120 Ibid. See also PBS, *American Experience*, Kinsey Timeline, http://www.pbs.org/wgbh/amex/kinsey.

121 Jones, "Annals of Sexology," 236–237.

122 James Jones, PBS TV interview on "The First Measured Century," http://www.pbs.org/fmc/segments/progseg10.htm; confirmed by Tim Tate interview in, the UK, Yorkshire Television's "Kinsey's Paedophiles." August, 1998.

123 James H. Jones, *Alfred C. Kinsey, A Public/Private Life*, (New York, W.W. Norton & Company, 1997), 280–281.

124 *American Experience*, Kinsey timeline, http://www.pbs.org/wgbh/amex/kinsey/peopleevents/p_circle.html. A doctorate commonly takes roughly five years after one has earned a Masters degree. Sexologists still commonly get doctorate degrees quickly from like-minded professors.

125 Pomeroy, *Kinsey and the Institute for Sex Research*, 62.

126 Jones, *Alfred C. Kinsey, A Public/Private Life*, 285.

127 Tim Tate, producer, UK, Yorkshire Television, "Secrets: Kinsey's Paedophiles," August 1998.

128 *American Experience*, Kinsey.

129 Pomeroy, *Kinsey and the Institute for Sex Research*, 150.

130 Ibid., 42–43.

131 Stephen Norwood, *The Third Reich in the Ivory Tower* (New York, Cambridge University Press), 2009.

132 "Lothar Machtan', *The Hidden Hitler* (New York, Basic Books, 2001), http://www.findarticles.com/p/articles/mi_m1571/is_7_18/ai_83553874.

133 Cornelia V. Christenson, *Kinsey: A Biography* (Bloomington: Indiana University Press, 1971), 97.

134 Clarence Tripp, "Incidence, Frequency, and the Kinsey 0–6 Scale," *The Encyclopedia of Homosexuality* (New York, 1990).

135 Jones, *Kinsey: A Public/Private Life*, 514–515.

136 Jones, *Kinsey: A Public/Private Life*, 514–515.

137 Ibid., 514–515.

138 Pomeroy, *Kinsey and the Institute for Sex Research*, 107–108.

139 Arno Karlen, *Sexuality and Homosexuality* (New York: W.W. Norton, Inc., 1971), 456.

140 Pomeroy, *Kinsey and the Institute for Sex Research*, 58.

141 James Jones, "The Origins of the Institute for Sex Research" (doctoral dissertation, 1997), 98.

142 Pomeroy, *Kinsey and the Institute for Sex Research*, 317.

143 This Kinsey victim eventually married into a famous Hollywood family, the stepson a wealthy film director. She recorded her life with her former husband as a household filled with pornography, his participation in sex orgies at Esalen and the Masters & Johnson sex surrogacy program her husband participated in, providing prostitutes at Hollywood hotels each weekend, etc. News flash. The marriage ended in a bitter divorce.

144 Judith Reisman, *Kinsey, Crimes & Consequences* (Crestwood, KY: Institute for Media Education, 2003), 80.

145 Ibid.

146 This begins the "academic pornography" that defines the sexology training field, and the subsequent pornography films made commercially in IU dormitories circa 2003.

147 Christopher Simpson, *Science of Coercion: Communication Research & Psychological Warfare*, 1945–1960 (New York, Oxford University Press, 1994), 29.

148 *International Encyclopedia of the Social Sciences* (New York: Macmillan, 1968), 389. Writing in *Twenty-Five Years of Sex Research, History of the National Research Council Committee for Research in Problems of Sex, 1922–1947*, Sophie D. Aberle and George W. Corner report that the Rockefeller Foundation helped organize and fund the American Social Hygiene Association in 1913 "for reconsideration of public attitudes toward prostitution," and to work for birth control and other social reforms. European and English sex studies

were fashionable, and a number of major treatises had been published by men (and a few by women) between 1885 and 1912.

149 MIT Alternative News, *The Thistle* 13, no. 2 (Dec. 2000–Jan. 2001), http://mit.edu/thistle/www/v13/3/oil.html#top.

150 Anthony Sutton, *How the Order Creates War and Revolution* (Phoenix, Arizona, Research Publishing, 1984), 86. See also William Stevenson, *A Man Called Intrepid: The Secret War* (New York, Ballantine Books, 1977), 65, 91, 307, 308, 311; see also Harry Truman, Congressional Record, March 27, 1942.

151 Cornelius Borck, *Mediating Philanthropy in Changing Political Circumstances: The Rockefeller Foundation's Funding for Brain Research in Germany, 1930-1950* (Berlin: Center for Humanities and Health Sciences, Institute for the History of Medicine, 2001), 1.

152 Judith Reisman, *Kinsey, Crimes & Consequences*, Chapter 10 on ties between WWII German interests and Kinsey/Rockefeller.

153 Dennis Cuddy, *The Indiana Connection*, http://www.newswithviews.com/NWO/newworld17.htm.

154 PBS TV, *The American Experience*, http://www.pbs.org/wgbh/amex/kinsey/timeline/index.html. See Sophie Aberle and George Corner, *Twenty-Five Years of Sex Research, History of the National Research Council Committee for Research in Problems of Sex, 1922-1947* (Philadelphia: W. B. Saunders, 1953).

155 Warren Weaver to CIB, *Subject: Kinsey*, The Rockefeller Archive Center, May 7, 1951, 7.

156 Private interview with W. Allen Wallis at his Washington D.C. apartment, circa February 1996.

157 James Jones interview on Yorkshire Television, "Secrets: Kinsey's Paedophiles," Channel 4, UK, August 10, 1998.

158 Pomeroy, *Kinsey and the Institute for Sex Research*. 101–103.

159 Ibid.

160 The *Kinsey* Fox Searchlight film (2004) describes Martin as a sexually experienced "pro" who seduced Kinsey. None of the biographies of Kinsey's fans and cult members even vaguely suggest that to be the case. Both Jones and Gathorne-Hardy admit that Kinsey, the elder, carefully groomed the virginal Martin and then seduced him. Film director Condon, realizing the public would react very badly to the notion of this older professor homosexually seducing his young student, simply made the film "biography" suit Condon's own sexual preferences.

161 *American Experience*, "Kinsey," transcript.

162 Pomeroy, *Kinsey and the Institute for Sex Research*, 87.

163 Jonathan Gathorne-Hardy, *Sex, The Measure of All Things*, (London: Chatto & Windus, 1998), 298.

164 Vincent Nowlis' admission on Yorkshire Television's documentary *Kinsey's Paedophiles*, August 1998, is available from the author's archive.

165 Ibid., Nowlis' admission.

166 Jones, *Alfred C. Kinsey: A Public/Private Life*, 489.

167 Pomeroy, *Kinsey and the Institute for Sex Research*, 83.
168 Ibid., 178.
169 Tim Tate, the youthfully handsome Yorkshire Television producer of *Kinsey's Paedophiles*, reported that Tripp had eagerly shown him sexual photographs of young boys he had photographed for Kinsey. In fact, it seemed the old fellow was "trying to hit on me!"
170 Pomeroy, *Kinsey and the Institute for Sex Research*, 172.
171 Ibid., 101.
172 Ibid., 101.
173 PBS TV, *The American Experience*, Kinsey, Time Line; http://www.pbs.org/wgbh/amex/kinsey.
174 James Jones, *Alfred C. Kinsey*, 604, 605, 607. Jones says he saw sex films of Mr. and Mrs Kinsey and others in the team as a student, etc., in Yorkshire's *Kinsey's Paedophiles.*
175 PBS TV, *American Experience*, "Kinsey."
176 Jones, *Alfred C. Kinsey*, 103, fn. 43.
177 Ibid., 474.
178 Ibid.
179 Gathorne-Hardy, *Sex, The Measure of All Things*; see also Yorkshire Television's documentary, *Kinsey's Paedophiles*, August 1998.
180 Jones, *Alfred C. Kinsey*, 474.
181 The author has done extensive work on Kinsey's influence on the military. When these data are included in court cases, they have been highly important to the repudiation of the homosexuality as a norm concept. See esMarc Wolinsky, Kenneth Sherrill, eds., *Gays and the Military* (Princeton, NJ: Princeton University Press, 1993), on *Joseph Steffan v. the United States, the book* citing to Kinsey 19 times, more than any other "scientist."
182 Jones, *Alfred C. Kinsey*, 475.
183 http://miscman.com/posters_graphics/details.asp?ID=305&CatID=40&PID=1.
184 Jones, *Origins of the Institute for Sex Research*, 244–245.
185 Ibid., 217.
186 Anna Malpas, "Exhibition reveals Stalin's 'nude drawings hobby," (AFP), December 18, 2009, http://www.nationalpost.com/scripts/story.html?id=2361850.
187 Jones, *Alfred C. Kinsey*, 602.
188 Ibid., 610.
189 Larry Layton on The People's Temple. Use of sex to control followers, http://www.skepticfiles.org/cultinfo/jones1.htm.

See also Jim Jones' use of sex to control followers, Pamela MacLea, http://www.skepticfiles.org/cultinfo/jones1.htm

190 http://en.wikipedia.org/wiki/Jim_Jones.
191 Robert Hercz, *Psychopaths Among Us*, http://www.hare.org/links/saturday.html.
192 Yorkshire Television, "Kinsey's Paedophiles," ibid.
193 Pomeroy, *Kinsey and the Institute for Sex Research*, ibid., 5–10. Emphasis added.

194 Ibid. 9–10.

195 Ibid. 5–10.

196 See Stanley Milgram's infamous "Obedience to Authority" experiments conducted at Yale University from 1961–1962, http://www.new-life.net/milgram.htm.

197 Jones, *Alfred C. Kinsey*, ibid. 607.

198 Jones, ibid. 607.

199 Pomeroy, *Kinsey and the Institute for Sex Research*, 235–237.

200 *American Experience* cites, "Paul Gebhard, a Harvard-trained anthropologist, joins Kinsey's research staff" in 1946. Two years later Kinsey publishes *Sexual Behavior in the Human Male*, by Kinsey, Pomeroy and Martin.

201 Pomeroy, *Kinsey and the Institute for Sex Research* ibid., 236–237.

202 Ibid., 236.

203 Ibid., 235.

204 Yorkshire Television documentary, "Kinsey's Paedophiles," transcript, in the author's archive.

205 Ibid.

206 *Time*, Aug. 24, 1953, http://www.time.com/time/archive/preview/0,10987, 818753,00.html.

207 James Jones, *The New Yorker*, "Dr. Yes," 103.

208 James Jones, *Alfred C. Kinsey*, ibid., 607.

209 Pomeroy, 175.

210 See Pomeroy, Yorkshire Television's *Kinsey's Paedophiles* and the several BBC Kinsey biographies.

211 In his 1973 dissertation, Jones revealed that the University board of trustees approved what they were told were Kinsey's sex survey questions and his sex lectures *prior to* his supposed initial yielding to the student calls in 1938. We know that Kinsey was taking "still" sex photos until Dellenback arrived with his movie camera in 1941, leaving roughly three years of photographic activity prior to the movie films.

212 Jonathan Gathorne-Hardy, *Sex, Alfred C. Kinsey, The Measure of All Things*, (Chatto & Windus, Random House, London, 2000), 98.

213 The British Broadcasting Company, Biographies, "Reputations," August 14, 1996, story of Alfred C. Kinsey. This video, a copy of which is in the author's archive, includes the testimony of such Kinsey colleagues as Paul Gebhard, former Kinsey Institute director and Kinsey co-author, and former Kinsey senior researcher John Gagnon. Also appearing are Kinsey's daughters, *Playboy* publisher Hugh Hefner, and this author. This BBC production, though designed to maintain the Kinsey myth, did document the first public admission that Kinsey's co-workers had performed in the pornography produced in Bloomington. The documentary was repeated in the U.S.A. as *Biography, Arts & Entertainment*.

214 Jones, *Alfred C. Kinsey*, 605.

215 Both Jim Jones and Gathorne-Hardy admit this in their biographies and in

the Yorkshire Television documentary, *Kinsey's Paedophiles*. This was a key method Kinsey had of controlling any possible leakage to the press or the authorities of their illegal activities. It seems logical that Kinsey made sure on interview that these staffers and their wives would participate and thus earn his trust.

216 Jones, *Alfred C. Kinsey*. 607. I interviewed one student from Pomeroy's "Institute for the Advanced Study of Human Sexuality" in San Francisco who reported that Pomeroy had a weekly liaison with one or another of his young students each week (illegal, of course) when Martha would obligingly go shopping. "It was well known around the place," the young man said, and "everyone just would wonder who he'd pick this week." The student—who refuses to be named, and who dropped out of the IASHS program—said he first met Pomeroy walking around the IASHS nude under a terry cloth bathrobe as he made his way to their "hot tub" for some student exchanges.

217 Ibid. See also "Kinsey's Paedophiles" for Jones's remarks in the second paragraph of quotes.

218 Ibid., 607.

219 *The Telegraph Magazine,* London. The bedroom and beyond, November 13, 2004 http://www.mask.org.za/SECTIONS/ArtsAndCulture/ac_new/film/kinsey report.htm.

220 See the 1998 Yorkshire Television transcripts in the author's archive.

221 Jones, *Alfred C. Kinsey*, ibid., 606.

222 Tim Tate, ibid. Tripp published *The Intimate World of Abraham Lincoln*, in 2004, claiming *Lincoln* was "gay."

223 Jones, *Alfred C. Kinsey*, 609–610.

224 Gathorne-Hardy, *Sex, Alfred C. Kinsey, The Measure of All Things*, 87–88. Also see Jones, *Alfred C. Kinsey*, 603.

225 Ibid., 604.

226 Ibid., 610.

227 Jones, "Annals of Sexology, Dr. Yes," 113.

228 Jones, *Alfred C. Kinsey* ibid., 604.

229 Jones, "Annals of Sexology, Dr. Yes," 113.

230 *Dorland's Medical Dictionary* (Phildelphia: W.B. Saunders, 1981), 933.

231 Donald (born 1922, died 1926), Anne (born 1924), Joan (born 1925), and Bruce (born 1928).

232 *The Telegraph Magazine,* London. http://www.mask.org.za/SECTIONS/ArtsAndCulture/ac_new/film/kinseyreport.htm. "The bedroom and beyond," November 13, 2004.

233 *The Telegraph*, ibid.

234 Statement by Bruce Kinsey to Kenneth R.R. Gros Louis, IU Senior Vice President for Academic Affairs, following the 2005 premiere at IU, as reported to Indiana Representative Cindy Noe, January, 2005, in Dr. Louis' office.

[CHAPTER 4]

235 UK data, http://www.telegraph.co.uk/technology/news/6698517/One-in-four-teenagers-admit-sexting.html, December 2, 2009.

236 Michael Alvear, *Salon*, October 19, 2000, http://www.salon.com/sex/feature/2000/10/19/peek/index.html.

237 *Life Magazine*, August 24, 1953, 45.

238 See writingstudio.co.za/page807.html, 2004.

239 "Biography, Alfred C. Kinsey," originally the BBC replayed in the U.S.A on A&E, 1997–1998.

240 Kinsey Institute publicity release, http://www.iub.edu/~kinsey/services/2003/media-reaction.html, May, 9, 2005.

241 Robert Cecil Johnson, *Kinsey, Christianity, and Sex: A Critical Study of Reaction In American Christianity to the Kinsey Reports on Human Sexual Behavior*, UMI Dissertations Services, Ann Arbor, Michigan 1973, 12–13 and Paul Dilbert Brinkman, *Dr. Alfred C. Kinsey and the Press: Historical Case Study of the Relationship of the Mass Media and a Pioneering Behavioral Scientist*, UMI Dissertation Services, 1971. This laudatory Indiana University dissertation is similar to virtually all dissertations on Kinsey, with little or no critical evaluation. It is therefore important to compare what the author wrote to what he ignored; what he perceived to what he avoided. For example, Brinkman, when focusing on the mass media, overlooked Johnson's report regarding the placement of advertisements in major press avenues, and especially the claim that the media blitz began gearing-up three years prior to the instigation of Kinsey's research.

242 Scott McLemee, "Alfred Kinsey and the Gall-Wasp of Desire," *Salon*, 5 November, 1997.

243 Author's conversation with Wallis in Washington, D.C., September 1, 1997, following his review of the authors' methodology Chapter addressing the bogus male sample.

244 *Colliers*, "Kinsey: On the Difference Between Men and Women," September 4, 1953, 19–21.

245 The Kinsey Institute, Indiana University, http://www.iub.edu/~kinsey/about/controversy%202.htm, November 16, 2009.

246 Kinsey publicity, ibid.

247 *Norman Podhoretz*, "Lolita, My Mother-in-Law, the Marquis de Sade, and Larry Flynt," *Commentary*, April 1997.

248 Wardell Pomeroy, *Dr. Kinsey and the Institute for Sex Research*, Harper & Row, New York, 1972, 29.

249 Vern L. Bullough, "The United States during and after Kinsey." *The Journal of Sex Research*. Volume: 44. 2. 2007.p: 2137, Society for the Scientific Study of Sexuality, Inc.

250 "Biography, Alfred C. Kinsey," originally the BBC replayed in the U.S.A on A&E, 1997–1998.

251 *Life Magazine*, "Incredible" in "Kinsey Report on Women," August 24, 1953, 60.
252 Joseph Epstein, *Commentary*, January 1998. see: www.Britannica.com, downloaded March 31, 2001.
253 Gertrude Himmelfarb, *One Nation, Two Cultures*, Vintage Books, New York, 1999 quotes the Harvard philosopher, "What used to be considered morally reprehensible is now . . . styled moral progress and a new freedom." 13–15.

[CHAPTER 5]

254 Sarah Goode, *Paedophiles in Society: Reflecting on Sexuality, Abuse and Hope*, Chapter Four, "'Early Sexual Growth and Activity': The Influence of Kinsey" Palgrave, United Kingdom, 2010.
255 Sarah Goode, ibid.
256 Kinsey, Pomeroy, Martin, and Gebhard, *Sexual Behavior in the Human Female*, W.W. Saunders, Philadelphia, 1953, 9.
257 C.F. Turner, H.G. Miller and L.E. Moses, Eds. *AIDS, Sexual Behavior and Intravenous Drug Use*, National Research Council, National Academy Press, Washington, D.C., 1989, 79.
258 McLemee, *Salon*, 5 November 1997, http://www.mclemee.com/id127.html, June 7, 2009.
259 Cornelia V. Christenson, *Kinsey: A Biography*, Indiana University Press, Bloomington, 1971, 97– 98.
260 See http://caosblog.com/archives/14479 for a video and full citations of the Boston reviews.
261 Ibid., see also, http://www.massresistance.org/docs/gen/09d/slutcracker/index.html, Dec. 2, 2009.

[CHAPTER 6]

262 Jones, *The First Measured Century*, PBSTV, "Social Science in America's Bedroom, Alfred Kinsey Measures Sexual Behavior http://www.pbs.org/fmc/segments/progseg10.htm.
263 Jim Jones, *Alfred C. Kinsey.* ibid., 604.
264 Jones, ibid., 604
265 Jones, ibid., 608.
266 Yorkshire Television, "*Kinsey's Paedophiles*" provides further detail on the filming.
267 Cornelia V. Christenson, *Kinsey: A Biography*, Indiana University Press, Bloomington, 1971, 97.
268 Phyllis and Eberhard Kronhausen, *Sex History of American College Men* (New York: Ballantine Books, 1960), 219.

269 Kronhausen, ibid.

270 *Abigail and John Adams*, letters, http://www.thelizlibrary.org/suffrage/abigail.htm.

271 The National Office of Vital Statistics during the 1930s revealed a birth-rate hovering at .98 (meaning that every 100 girls born in America would have only 98 daughters), http://www.msnbc.msn.com/id/9925897/site/newsweek.

272 CDC, http://www.cdc.gov/nchs/births.htm, see also, http://www.cdc.gov/nchs/pressroom/07newsreleases/teenbirth.htm.

273 *Changing Patterns of Nonmarital Childbearing in the United States*, U.S. Centers for Disease Control and Prevention, 2009, see, http://www.womenshealth.gov/news/english/627049.htm.

274 U.S. population in 1947 was 144,126,071, http://www.infoplease.com/year/1947.html#us and in 2007 was 302,200,000 (a 110% increase) http://www.prb.org/Publications/Datasheets/2007/2007WorldPopulationDataSheet.aspx.

275 Phillips Cutright, "AFDC, Family Allowances and Illegitimacy," *Family Planning Perspectives*, 1970, 4, see http://www.jstor.org/pss/2133830.

276 *Newsweek*, Web site: http://www.msnbc.msn.com/id/9925897/site/newsweek/ November 6, 2005.

277 Cutright, AFDC, ibid. 4.

278 *Newsweek*, ibid., Web site: http://www.msnbc.msn.com/id/9925897/site/newsweek.

279 Donald Porter Geddes, Ed., *An Analysis of the Kinsey Reports on Sexual Behavior in the Human Male and Female.* New American Library, New York, 1954, 134. Emily Mudd, PhD, was one of five consulting editors for the *Female* report. She was director of the Marriage Council of Philadelphia, Assistant Professor in Psychiatry at the University of Pennsylvania Medical School, and President of the American Association of Marriage Counselors. Yet Dr. Mudd never questioned Kinsey's methodology, where he got those "married women," why he combined all married women with prostitutes, etc.

280 *Male*, 40–41. "Payment," wrote Kinsey in the *Male* volume, "has been confined to prostitutes, pimps, exhibitionists or to others who have turned from their regular occupation and spent *considerable time* in helping make contacts." (Emphasis added)

281 Eugenia Kaledin, *Daily Life in the United States, 1940–1959: Shifting Worlds*, Greenwood Publishing Group no state given, 200, 109.

282 *The Illinois Commission on Sex Offenders* delivered its report to the 68th General Assembly of the State of Illinois, March 15, 1953, 8, 37, 36, Emphasis added.

283 Pitirim Sorokin, cited in Gertrude Himmelfarb, *One Nation, Two Cultures*, Vintage Books, New York, 1999, 13–15.

284 Jonathan Turley, "Of Lust and the Law," *The Washington Post*, September 5, 2004; B01.

285 A body of Muslim clerics in India has issued a marriage code that urges Muslim men not to use the so-called "triple talaq" method of divorce. However, the new code from the All India Muslim Personal Law Board stops short of banning the controversial practice of Triple Talaq, which allows a Muslim man to divorce his wife simply by saying "I divorce you" three times while she is in a state of purity, May 2, 2005. http://divorceinfo.com/blog/?p=203; See also, "Galloway's Muslim Wife Wants a Divorce: Galloway is being sued for divorce by his Palestinian wife http://www.littlegreenfootballs.com/weblog/?entry=15694.

286 David Allyn, "Private Acts/Public Policy: Alfred Kinsey, the American Law Institute and the Privatization of American Sexual Morality," *Journal of American Studies*, 30, 1996, 3, 405–428, see 425–427.

Citing 1955 transcript ALI draft committee meetings, 86–163.

287 Allyn. ibid.

288 The American Law Institute, *Model Penal Code, Tentative Draft No. 4*, "207.1" Sex Offenses, April 25, 1955, 208.

289 Kinsey et al, *Sexual Behavior in the Human Female* (1953) 53.

290 Morris Ploscowe, "Sexual Patterns and the Law," in Albert Deutsch (ed.), *Sex Habits of American Men* (New York: Prentice Hall, 1948), 126.

291 Morris Ernst and David Loth, *American Sexual Behavior and The Kinsey Report*, (Greystone Press, New York, 1948), 81, 83.

292 Ernst and Loth, ibid. 81.

293 Ronald Reagan, Preface to the *California Department of Justice, Crime Victims Handbook*, U.S. Dept of Justice, 1981.

294 Jonathan Turley, "When Lust And The Law Collide," (Editorial) (Column) *The Cincinnati Post* (Cincinnati, OH); 9/15/2004 Turley is the Shapiro Professor of Public Interest Law at George Washington University. This column originally appeared in the Washington Post 2004.

295 Nena and George O'Neill, *Open Marriage* (Avon Publishers, New York, 1972), 28.

296 O'Neill, ibid., *Open Marriage.*

297 Joseph Heller, ibid., *Now and Then* (Knopf, New York, 1998), 170.

298 Melanie Thernstrom, "Rethinking Matrimony," *The New York Times*, December 31, 2000, 40.

299 Nena and George O'Neill, *Shifting Gears* (Avon Publishers, New York, 1974), 19.

300 Ron Haskins, Brookings Institution testimony to the Committee on Appropriations, Subcommittee on the District of Columbia, *Trends in Family Composition*, May 3, 2006, 1.

301 Maggie Scarf, *Intimate Partners: Pattern in Love and Marriage* (Ballantine Books, New York, 1987), 136–137.

302 National Center for Health Statistics (NCHS), "Advance Report of Final Marriage Statistics, 1989 and 1990," July 14, 1995, Web site: http://www.cdc.gov/nchs/pressroom/95facts/fs_4312s.htm.

303 Scarf, *Intimate Partners* ibid., 136.

304 National Center for Health Statistics (NCHS), ibid., Web site.

305 Scarf, *Intimate Partners* ibid.

306 Arlene Skolnick, *Embattled Paradise: The American Family in an Age of Uncertainty* (Basic Books, New York, 1991), 91.

307 Scarf, ibid., 136–137.

308 http://waysandmeans.house.gov/media/pdf/greenbook2003/AppendixM.pdf.

309 Scarf, *Intimate Partners* ibid., quotes "conservative" "experts" such as Nass, Libby and Fisher for massive adultery. These "researchers" are directly associated with the sexual radicals' movement. Roger Libby created a open sex group for indiscriminate coupling while serving as a lecturer for the Kinsey-based Institute for the Advanced Study of Human Sexuality in San Francisco. These and scores of other "sexuality" researchers simply perpetuate Kinsey's successful fraud, to shape the nation in their own image.

310 http://www.profam.org/pub/fia/fia_1401.htm.

311 Rachel Wildavsky, "Sex, Lies and the Kinsey Reports," *Readers' Digest*, April 1997.

312 D'Vera Cohn, Pew Research Center, October 15, 2009, http://pewresearch.org/pubs/1380/marriage-and-divorce-by-state.

313 MSN *Encarta*, "Marriage," http://encarta.msn.com/encyclopedia_761574825_3/Marriage.html.

314 Hugh Hefner, *Sunday Plain Dealer*, Cleveland Ohio, January 11, 1976.

315 Judith Reisman, *"SoftPorn" Plays Hard Ball*, Huntington House, Lafayette, LA, 1990, 36–37, citing Thomas Weyr, *Reaching for Paradise*, (Times Books, New York, 1978), 195–196.

316 Ibid., 11.

317 Kathleen Tierney, "The Battered Women Movement," *Social Problems*, Vol. 29, No. 3, February 1982, 1.

318 *The Washington Post*, Parade, June 22, 1994.

319 Bob Just, "Son of divorce," *WorldNetDaily.com*, Saturday, March 12, 2005.

320 Ibid.

321 Runaways and Missing Children, see http://www.focusas.com/Runaways.html.

322 Runaways, ibid., http://www.focusas.com/Runaways.html.

323 Richard Gaines, "Sexual Behavior Problems and Psychopathology Symptoms in Sexually Abused Girls" *Journal of the American Academy of Child and Adolescent Psychiatry*, Farmington Hills, Michigan, August 1, 1995.

324 See also William Friedrich, Mayo Clinic, "Sexual Behavior in Sexually Abused Children," January, 1993.

325 Vincent Felitti, ACE study, San Diego Kaiser Permanente and Robert Anda, M.D. Centers for Disease Control and Prevention http://www.cdc.gov/nccdphp/ace/prevalence.htm.

326 *Time Magazine*, "Law: The Rough Sex Defense," May. 23, 1988, court records of the "rough sex defense."

327 See Master List of Missing Children, as of December 2009, ttp://www.pollyklaas.org.

328 Franklin Coverup: see http://educate-yourself.org/cn/franklincoverupexcerpt.shtml.

329 William Raspberry, *The Washington Post*, July 25, 2005, A19.

330 See http://ei.oxfordjournals.org/cgi/content/abstract/44/3/547.

331 Bryce Christensen, "Divided we Fall," *The Family in America*, January 2000.

332 The Effective Dates of No-Fault Divorce Laws in the 50 States http://www3.interscience.wiley.com/journal/118949659/abstract and Divorce Statistics Collection, from Americans for Divorce Reform; http://www.divorcereform.org/why.html.

333 Bryce Christensen, "Deadbeat Dads," *The Family in America*, January 2000, 1–7.

334 *Source: National Committee for the Prevention of Child Abuse*, Child Sexual Abuse Information Sheet, see extensive documentation of child murder by mother's boyfriends, e.g.,: "In 1996, boyfriends were held responsible for 9 of 34 deaths, or 26% of all abuse deaths that year-even more than mothers, who were blamed for 8 of the 34 deaths," Knight Ridder/Tribune News Service; 6/11/2002; Miller, Carol Marbin.

335 See http://www.againstsexualabuse.org/docs/ProtectOurChildren.asp.

336 G. Paveza, Risk factors in father-daughter child sexual abuse. *Journal of Interpersonal Violence*, 3(3), 290–306, 1988 as reported in *The Batterer as Parent* by Lundy Bancroft and Jay G. Silverman, Sage Publications, 2002, 84–85.

337 Lisa Belkin, "The Making of an 8-Year-Old Woman," *The New York Times*, December 24, 2000, Moffitt *et al.* 1992, Ellis and Garber 2000.

338 Eric Fromm, *Values, Psychology, And Human Existence* in Abraham Maslow, *Knew Knowledge in Human Values*, Gateway, New York, 1970, 155.

339 Christopher Lasch, *Haven in a Heartless World, the Family Besieged* (Basic Books, New York, 1979), 135.

340 Christopher Lasch, *Culture of Narcissism* (New York: W.W. Norton, 1991), 164.

341 Ibid. 162.

342 Christopher Lasch, *The Culture of Narcissism* (W.W. Norton, New York, 1991), 164.

343 Ibid., 165.

344 Ibid.

345 Ibid., 162.

346 Ibid., 167.

347 Benjamin Spock, quoted in Lasch, *The Culture of Narcissism*, 163.

348 Lasch, *Haven in a Heartless World*, 135 (emphasis added).

349 Barry Miles, *Hippie* (Sterling Publishing Co, Inc., London, 2004), publisher's review, April 12, 2006.

350 Christopher Lasch, *The Culture of Narcissism* (W.W. Norton, New York, 1991), 165.

351 Cornelia Christenson, *Kinsey: A Biography* (Bloomington: Indiana University Press, 1971), 116.

352 In 1925, the Rockefeller Foundation funded the Kaiser Wilhelm Institute for Psychiatry in Munich, which Dr. Ernst Rudin directed. Additional funding was provided by the Harrimans, the Warburgs and the British Crown. The Rockefeller Foundation continued to sponsor the Institute and its Nazi leader throughout the devastating holocaust of World War II. The Foundation poured money into the occupied German Republic for a medical specialty known as psychiatric eugenics. This field applied to psychiatry the concepts of eugenics, otherwise known as race purification, race hygiene, or race betterment. It was developed in London's Galton Laboratory, and its offshoots, eugenics societies in England and America. In 1925 the Rockefeller Foundation made an initial grant of $2.5 million to the Psychiatric Institute in Munich. It gave it $325,000 for a new building in 1928 and continuously sponsored the Institute and its Nazi Chief Rudin, some data confirm, through all of World War II. http://www.garynull.com/Documents/PathologizingAfricanAmericanPt1.htm

353 Robert Bork, *Slouching Towards Gomorrah (*Regan Books, New York, 1997), 25.

354 Ibid. 25.

355 Lasch, *Haven*, 135.

356 Neil Postman, *The Disappearance of Childhood* (New York: Vintage Books, 1994), 134.

357 Ibid.

358 Ibid.

359 Men line up like train-cars to take turns raping a victim. This was the "joke" among college frat boys at Bucknell University—as I screened child molestation pictures in *Playboy* and *Penthouse*, during a "Free Speech" lecture, April 13, 1987.

360 Ben Shapiro, ibid. *Porn Generation* (Washington, D.C., Regnery Publishing 2005), The author adds, "Levine's boss at Planned Parenthood, Dr. Mary Calderone, would go on to found SIECUS. . . . Calderone's vision was of an open sex education, a sex education that didn't view "sex as a 'problem' to be 'controlled,'" but rather as "a vital life force to be utilized."

[CHAPTER 7]

361 Katharine Hepburn, Interview in *Ladies Home Journal*, January 1984.

362 *Colliers*, "Kinsey: On the Difference Between Men and Women," September 4, 1953, 19–21.

363 Unwin's *Sex and Culture*, Oxford Press, 1934, is reviewed by Raymond Firth in *Reviews of books*, *Africa: Journal of the International African Institute*, Vol. 9, No. 1 Jan., 1936, 126–129: http://www.jstor.org/about/desc.html.

364 Ernest Bell, Ed. *Fighting the Traffic in Young Girls* (Chicago, The Illinois Vigilance Association, 1910), 283–285.

365 Ibid., 287.

366 Wardell Pomeroy, *Boys and Sex* (A Pelican Book, New York, 1981), quotes Kinsey's data in this children's book, reprinted recently and printed seven times prior, and which recommends bestiality, 134–135, also, see *Male*, 667.

367 Edward Morgan, *The 60s Experience: Hard Lessons about Modern America*, Temple University Press, Philadelphia, 1991, 202.

368 Millicent C. McIntosh in Donald Porter Geddes, ed., *An Analysis of the Kinsey Reports on Sexual Behavior in the Human Male and Female* (New York: New American Library, 1954), 141.

369 Ibid.

370 Ibid., 139.

371 Margaret Mead, "An Anthropologist Looks at the Kinsey Report," in *Child and Family*, vol. 18, no. 4, 1979; 294–303.

372 Benjamin C. Gruenberg, M.D., in Geddes, 84. School textbook writer professor, Benjamin C. Gruenberg told parents "children's sex-play . . . which often goes as far as complete coitus or orgasm, is taken too solemnly by parents and teachers; and that the uncompromising and unsympathetic attitude of elders results in fear of sex, and in hostility toward parents, with more or less generalized rebelliousness against the killjoy repressiveness of the adult world." Quite.

373 The American Law Institute, *Model Penal Code, Tentative Draft No. 4*, "207.1" Sex Offenses, April 25, 1955, 206–207.

374 Kinsey has no listing for "adultery" in the *Male* volume. Rather, Kinsey substitutes the non-legal definition of "extra marital coitus" as the first sex "science" setting legal precedent. Lying throughout the *Male* volume about his "correcting" for error based on "the U.S. census for 1940" gave all of Kinsey's fraudulent data weight in the minds and laws of this nation. It is assumed that since Kinsey made no distinction between homosexuals, rapists, pedophiles, and all other men, his analyses of "adultery" would include all of these perverse people as "married" should they be in legal or illegal relations for any period of time. The *Female* volume includes an Index reference to "adultery: legal penalties" and with the reference, "See coitus, extra marital."

375 The American Law Institute, *Model Penal Code,* 208.

376 Phyllis and Eberhard Kronhausen, *Sex Histories of American College Men* (Ballantine Books, New York, 1960).

377 "Sexiles" http://www.alternet.org/health/145094?page=2, and see http://www.getreligion.org/?p=19918, January 30, 2010.

378 The Straight Dope, "What is . . . premarital blood testing," 4/19/1996, http://www.straightdope.com/classics/a5_193.html.

379 Phyllis & Eberhard Kronhausen, *Sex Histories of American College Men* (New York: Ballantine Books, 1960), 219.

380 Ibid., 254.
381 Ibid., 255.
382 Morgan, *The 60s Experience*, 202.
383 Nena and George O'Neill, *Open Marriage* (New York, Avon Publishers, 1972), 28.
384 Ian Kerner, "Women, Regrets & One-Night Stands," July 31, 2006. http://www.ediets.com/news/article.cfm?cmi=839925&cid=4&code=24622.
385 Ibid.
386 Ibid.
387 See http://www.reclaimamerica.org/download/TheTruthAboutAlfredKinsey.pdf.
388 In, *Sex Education in American Schools*, Source, "Youth Indicators 1996; Indicator 7," Concerned Women For America, Washington, D.C., 1996, 11 (from 12.6% in 1950 to 44.6% in 1992).
389 Medical Encyclopedia: Sexually Transmitted Diseases, http://www.answers.com/topic/sexually-transmitted-infection.
390 "The Hidden Epidemic: Confronting Sexually Transmitted Diseases," *Inst. of Medicine* (Washington, D.C.: National Academy Press, 1997).
391 CDC states, http://www.cdc.gov/hiv/topics/surveillance/united_states.htm, November 17, 2009.
392 See http://www.reclaimamerica.org/pages/Petitions.aspx?CID=133.
393 Jay Sekulow, November 6, 2009, in http://blog.beliefnet.com/lynnvsekulow/2009/11/why-push-planned-parenthood.html.
394 Robert Rector, The Case for Abstinence, Education, Grantees Conference, *The Heritage Foundation*, December 7, 2006.
395 See http://www.reclaimamerica.org/Pages/NEWS/newspage.asp?story=2980.
396 Ibid.
397 Stossel, Scott, "The Sexual Counterrevolution," *The American Prospect* no. 33, July–August 1997, 74–82. *The American Prospect* is a monthly magazine "of liberal ideas . . . ." Web site: http://epn.org/prospect/33/33stosfs.html.
398 Ibid.
399 *Male*, 669.
400 Paul Robinson, *The Modernization of Sex* (New York: Harper & Row, 1976), 56.
401 Robinson, ibid.

[CHAPTER 8]

402 Hepburn interview in *Ladies Home Journal*, January 1984.
403 CNN Money, see http://money.cnn.com/magazines/fsb/fsb_archive/2003/09/01/350793/index.htm, June 4, 2009.
404 Thomas Weyr, *Reaching for Paradise* (Times books, New York, 1979), p.11.
405 Hefner on Kinsey, on "Reputations," "Biography," BBC-TV, circa 1989, rebroadcast on the Arts & Entertainment network, 1996.

406 Morris Ploscowe, "Sexual Behavior and the Law," in Morris Ernst and David Loth, ed, *American Sexual Behavior and The Kinsey Report* (Greystone Press, New York, 1948), 128–131.

407 Ploscowe, "Sexual Patterns and the Law," in *Sex Habits of American Men*, supra, n. 125–126, 130.

408 Bill Donovan, "Gender Inequality and Criminal Seduction: Prosecuting Sexual Coercion in the Early-20th Century," 30 *Law & Social Inquiry*, no. 1 (July 2006): 61–88.

409 Maiden issue *Playboy.* December 1953, Hefner's First Editorial Statement.

410 Frankenstein Smith, "'X Virginity' An Important Treatise on a Very Important Subject," *Playboy*, September 1955, 9.

411 Ibid., 50.

412 James K. Beggan, "The *Playboy* Rabbit Is Soft, Furry, and Cute," *Journal of Men's Studies* 9, no. 3. (2001): 341.

413 Daniel Horowitz, "Betty Friedan and the Making of the Feminine Mystique," (Amherst: University of Massachusetts Press, 1998), 206.

414 David Horowitz, *Salon*, January 18, 1999, http://www.writing.upenn.edu/~afilreis/50s/friedan-per-horowitz.html, January 30, 2010.

415 United States Crime Rates 1960–2004, http://www.disastercenter.com/crime/uscrime.htm. "The homicide rate nearly doubled from the mid 1960's to the late 1970s." While the DoJ does not report the 1000s of percent increase in rape, http:/www.ojp.gov/bjs/homicide/hmrt.htm. U.S. Department of Justice Office of Justice Programs Bureau of Justice Statistics, April 1994.

416 Rollo May, *Love and Will* (New York: W.W. Norton, 1969), 58.

417 Ibid., 57. An alleged priest writes to say he "lectures on Hefner's philosophy to audiences of young people and numerous members of the clergy." He says that "true Christian ethics and morality are not incompatible with Hefner's philosophy."

418 Rollo May, *Love and Will*, (W.W. Norton, New York, 1969), 39.

419 Ibid., 39.

420 Ibid., 43.

421 Ibid., 40.

422 Ibid., 57.

423 Masturbation, http://www.healthystrokes.com.

424 Articles about TMS, http://healthystrokes.com/articles.html. Also http://www.menshealth.co.uk/talk/thread.phtml/post744109, 42. Right, now men need lessons in proper masturbation techniques.

425 *Duke L. & Tech. Rev.* 0019; Connie Cass, "20 Charged in Child Porn Ring," *Washington Post*, August 10, 2002, A1.

426 Greg Miller, *Science Magazine*, May 13, 2005, 945–947.

427 Ibid.

428 Ibid.

429 *NeuroImage* (DOI: 10.1016/j.neuroimage.2008.05.051), November 8, 2009.

430 http://scienceblogs.com/cortex/2009/08/porn_and_mirror_neurons.php November 8, 2009.

431 Jason Miller, "Pornification Is A Disease" August 9, 2006, http://www.rense.com/general73/porn.htm.

432 *Financial Times*, March 18–19, 2000, http://www.kenanmalik.com/reviews/thornhill&palmer.html.

433 As noted in by the DoJ/OJJDP NIBRS research team in The U.S. DoJ, National Incident-Based Reporting System, (NIBRS) "Sexual Assault of Young Children as Reported to Law Enforcement: Victim, Incident, and Offender Characteristics," July 2000, 1. While this paper cannot "assess the national representativeness [sic] of . . . the number of sexual assault victimizations" cited to studies like NIBRS, the American Humane Association, Health and Human Services, still "the sample is very large." Especially since no investigator appears to have attempted to identify the failure of those charged with oversight for child protection in past records of child sex abuse, especially of children under age 12, "therefore, accepting the inherent qualifications associated with any analysis" of erratic an often contradictory justice and health service data, "the sheer number of reports and the detailed information available" in this paper should provide "researchers and policymakers with an opportunity to" reassess the past failures of those charged with oversight for child protection.

434 "Index of Crime, United States, 1960–1999: per 100,000 population. Also see "Uniform Crime Reports—1958" Summary 1.

435 Testimony For U. S. Senate Committee On Commerce, Science And Transportation, March 4, 1999.

436 David Shaw, *LATimes.com* essay, May 5, 2003.

437 *Penthouse Forum,* Variations, 1977, at 84.

438 Ibid.

439 Ibid.

440 *Penthouse*, December 1977.

441 *Playboy*, Richard Willis, "Tomeu and His Daughters," December 1977.

442 Judith Reisman, *R.S.V.America* (Crestwood, KY: Institute for Media Education, 1996).

443 *Penthouse*, August 1975, 167.

444 *Playboy*, November 1976.

445 *Playboy*, November 1980, photographer unknown.

446 *Playboy*, August 1971.

447 Graph B53, the Reisman "data book;" *Images of Children, Crime & Violence in Playboy, Penthouse and Hustler* (1989).

448 *Playboy*, November 1971.

449 *Playboy*, May 1987, 46.

450 *Playboy*, April 1980.

451 *Playboy*, March, 1978.

452 *Playboy*, April 1978.

453 "Human Penis Cartoon Ad Campaign Proves Effective in Encouraging Testing for Sexually Transmitted Diseases," International Herald Tribune.htm, December 27, 2006.

454 *Playboy*, August 1954.

455 *Playboy*, November 1968.

456 Judith Reisman, *Soft Porn Plays Hardball* (Lafayette, LA: Huntington House, 1991).

457 Reisman in Bryant, Jennings, & Zillmann, Dolf (eds.), *Media Effects: Advances in Theory and Research*, 2nd ed. (Mahwah, NJ: Lawrence Erlbaum Associates, 2002).

458 Ibid.

459 Ibid.

460 *New York City Tribune*, March 30, 1988.

461 *New York City Tribune*, ibid.

462 Chris Hedges, *Empire of Illusion* (New York: Nation Books, 2009), 87 (emphasis added).

463 *Playboy*, February 1971.

464 *Playboy*, March 1972, 163.

465 *Playboy*, November 1972.

466 *Shields v. Gross*, 58 N.Y.2d 338, 448 N.E.2d 108, 461 N.Y.S.2d 254, 9 Media L. Re1466 (N.Y. 1983 http://jcomm.uoregon.edu/~tgleason/j385/Brooke.htm.

467 *Psychology Today*, http://www.psychologytoday.com/articles/pto-19970701-000027.html, Jul/Aug 97.

468 "Sugar and Spice," *Playboy Press*, 1975, p, 36.

469 Judith Herman, *Father-Daughter Incest* (Cambridge: Harvard University Press, 1981), 16.

470 Jimmy Wales "excised references to soft pornography on a website he ran earlier in his career," http://digg.com/tech_news/Wikipedia_founder_Jimmy_Wales_edits_his_own_biography.

471 Retrieved September 1, 2005, http://en.wikipedia.org/wiki/Incest.

472 Larry L. Constantine and Floyd M. Martinson (eds.), *Children and Sex. New Findings, New Perspectives* (Boston: Little, Brown & Co., 1981).

473 *The International Conference on Love & Attraction*, University College Swansea, Wales, 1977 in Mark Cook and Glenn Wilson Oxford (New York: Pergamon Press, 1979), 490.

474 "Statement of Purpose," *Paidika, The Journal of Paedophilia* (Summer 1987): 2–3.

475 *Playboy*, October 1976, 230.

476 *Time Magazine*, September 7, 1981, also exposed pro-incest propaganda, "Cradle-to-Grave Intimacy," April 14, 1980.

477 Linnea Smith, "*Playboy:* R & R for Pedophiles," *Action Agenda: Challenging Sexist and Violent Media Through Education and Action* 2 (Winter 1996), 11.

478 *Canadian Medical Association Journal* 145, no. 8 (1991), "Incest can have devastating emotional and physical consequences, women physicians told."

479 *Enough Is Enough, Safety 101*, see entire report on http://www.enough.org/inside.php?tag=stat%20archives.

480 *Dangerous Access*, 2001 Edition, David Burt.

481 Protecting the Age of Innocence, http://www.enough.org/inside.php?tag=statistics.

482 NCMEC Child Pornography Possessors Arrested in Internet-Related Crimes: National Juvenile Online Victimization Study, Virginia, 2005.

483 National Center for Missing & Exploited Children. Internet Watch Foundation, United Kingdom.

484 Jerry Ropelato, Top Ten Reviews, Inc. December, 5, 2005. http://internet-filter-review.toptenreviews.com/internet-pornography-statistics.html.

485 National Society for the Prevention of Cruelty to Children, October, 8, 2003, Max Taylor, Combating Pedophile Information Networks in Europe, March 2003.

486 National Criminal Intelligence Service, August 21, 2003.

487 *Red Herring Magazine*, January 18, 2002. The charge by this report is that these are illegal images of children.

488 *Enough Is Enough, Safety 101*, see entire report on, http://www.enough.org/inside.php?tag=stat%20archives.

489 Internet Traders of Child Pornography: Profiling Research, Caroline Sullivan, October 2005. January 10, 2006. http://www.dia.govt.nz/pubform . . . le/Profilingupdate2.pdf.

490 *Enough is Enough, Safety 101*, http://www.enough.org/inside.php?tag=stat%20archives.

491 *Enough is Enough, Safety 101*, see entire report on http://www.enough.org/inside.php?tag=stat%20archives.

492 Global Symposium, http://www.iprc.unc.edu/G8/Hernandez_position_paper_Global_Symposium.pdf, 7.

493 See http://www.kff.org/content/2001/20011211a/GenerationRx.pdf, Kaiser Family Foundation, 2001.

494 Hugh Hefner, "The Legal Enforcement of Morality," 40, *University of Colorado Law Review*, 200 (1967).

495 See The New Jersey Penal Code, Final Report of the New Jersey Criminal Law Revision Commission, October, 1971, x; Morgan S. Bragg, "Victimless Sex Crimes: To the Devil, Not the Dungeon," 25 *University of Florida Law Review* 140 (1973); John S. Eldred, "Classification and Degrees of Offenses—An Approach to Modernity," 57 *Kentucky Law Journal*, 81 (1968–1969); John C. Danforth, "The Modern Criminal Code for Missouri (Tentative Draft)—A Challenge Fulfilled and the Challenge Presented," 38 *Missouri Law Review* 362 (1973); Paul E. Wilson, "New Bottles for Old Wine: Criminal Law Revision in Kansas," 16 *Kansas Law Review* 588 (1968).

496 Michael Goldfarb; http://www.theconnection.org/shows/2000/03/20000314_b_main.aspurged from the Internet by 2010. However, most Hollywood

mavens still casually note "*Hollywood's golden age* (the 1920s through the 1940s)" as just that.

497 http://www.fcc.gov/cgb/consumerfacts/obscene.html, January 26, 2010.

498 http://www.fcc.gov/cgb/consumerfacts/obscene.html, December 13, 2006.

499 Kevin Ring, ed,. *Scalia Dissents* (Washington, D.C.: Regnery Press, 2004), 261.

500 See The Hon. John Harmer and James Smith, *The War We Will Win*, The Lighted Candle Society, Salt Lake City, Utah, 2007.

501 Pornography Statistics. *Family Safe Media*. January 10, 2006. http://www.familysafemedia.com/pornography_statistics.html.

502 *Enough is Enough, Safety 101*, see entire report on http://www.enough.org/inside.php?tag=stat%20archives.

503 http://www.campuskiss.com/defa . . . rvey=show&homepage=true.

504 Jan LaRue, "Obscenity and the First Amendment," Summit on Pornography, Rayburn House Office Building, Room 2322, May 19, 2005.

505 Family Safe Media, December 15, 2005. See http://www.familysafemedia.com/pornography_statistics.html.

506 Robert Weiss, PhD, *Sexual Recovery Institute*, *Washington Times*, January 26, 2000.

507 State of the First Amendment Study, First Amendment Center, Freedom Forum, 2000.

508 Pamela Paul, *Pornified: How Pornography is Transforming Our Lives, Our Relationships, and Our Families* (New York: Henry Holt and Co, 2005).

509 Ibid.

510 MSNBC/Stanford/Duquesne Study, *Washington Times*, January 26, 2000, http://www.afo.net/statistics.htm.

511 Ibid.

512 These data by Shelley Lubben, executive director of *Pink Cross Foundation*, a 501(c)(3) public charity dedicated to reaching out to adult industry workers offering emotional, financial, and transitional support. www.shelleylubben.com and www.thepinkcross.org, are herein corroborated by Judith A Judith Reisman, PhD, former Principal Investigator, Images of Children, Crime & Violence in *Playboy*, *Penthouse*, and *Hustler*, 1989, U.S. Dept. of Justice, Juvenile Justice and Delinquency Prevention, Grant No. 84-JN-AX-K007, November 14, 2009.

513 Based upon in-depth interviews and public testimonies by pornography employees, we estimate 90% are adult survivors of child sexual abuse. These data are considered reasonable based upon the extant data from established governmental statistical findings as follows: 1 in 4 girls is sexually abused before the age of 18. (http://www.cdc.gov/nccdphp/ace/prevalence.htm, *ACE Study—Prevalence—Adverse Childhood Experiences*); 1 in 6 boys is sexually abused before the age of 18. (http://www.cdc.gov/nccdphp/ace/prevalence.htm, *CE Study—Prevalence—Adverse Childhood Experiences*); An estimated 39 million survivors of childhood sexual abuse exist in America today. G. Abel,

J. Becker, M. Mittelman, J. Cunningham-Rathner, J. Rouleau, and W. Murphy, "Self reported sex crimes on non-incarcerated paraphiliacs," *Journal of Interpersonal Violence* 2, no. 1 (1987): 3.

514 The National Center for Missing and Exploited Children now employs a psychologist to aid staff who must view "this work, this objectionable material." (NCMEC Quarterly Progress Report, April 23, 2009). The NCMEC study recommends interventions. "Monitoring employees' well-being" should be proactive to prevent "severe secondary traumatization." Analysts need "support resources . . . safeguard programs, counseling, peer support" to create "awareness of secondary trauma and compassion fatigue." Although the hunt is for child abuse images, an extensive body of work is now emerging on the problems experienced by staff who must view adult pornography to seek criminals and victims. See Judith Reisman, "Picture Poison," SALVO (Autumn 2009), 23–25. http://www.salvomag.com/new/mag/salvo10.ph

515 99% reported by former performers and 66% by Sharon Mitchell, Founder of AIM (Adult Industry Medical Healthcare Foundation at www.aim-med.org).

516 Peter R. Kerndt, MD, MPH Director, Sexually Transmitted Disease Program Los Angeles County Department of Public Health. "Worker Health and Safety in the Adult Film Industry." May 21, 2008. http://bixbyprogram.ph.ucla.edu/lectureslides/Kerndt_5-21-08.ppt.

517 County of Los Angeles Public Health: Adult Film Industry Report. September 17, 2009. http://www.shelleylubben.com/sites/default/files/LA_Public_Health_9-17-09.pdf.

518 Kerndt, "Worker Health and Safety in the Adult Film Industry."

519 Shelley Lubben. Testimony given before Committee on Revenue and Taxation, California State Assembly on AB2914 Taxation: Adult Entertainment Venue Impact Fund. See "Suicide Deaths in the U.S. Porn Industry since 1970." http://www.shelleylubben.com/suicide-deaths-us-porn-industry-1970.

520 Lubben, "Testimony." See also Melissa Farley and Howard Barkan, *Women & Health* 27, no. 3 (1998): 37–49. Inc. http://www.prostitutionresearch.com/prostitution_research/000021.html.

521 Chris Hedges, Pulitzer Prize Winner, *Empire of Illusion* (New York: Nation Books, 2009); see esChapter 2 "The Illusion of Love," re, Lubben, et al. Lubben, "Testimony." See Jan Meza aka Elizabeth Rollings http://www.shelleylubben.com/former-porn-star-elizabeth-rollings-story. See also Anne Bissell, Sex Industry Survivors 12 Step Recovery, author of *Memoirs of a Sex Industry Survivor* at http://www.sexualabusesurvivors.com/SexualIssues.htm.

522 Ibid. Hedges, Lubben, Farley, Bissell as above. See also one site for "porn star" prostitution services at www.bodymiracle.com.

523 Ibid. See also Judith Reisman, "The Science Behind Pornography Addiction," U.S. Senate Testimony on Commerce, Science and Transportation, November 18, 2004.

524 Hedges, *Empire.* See 62–63. Reisman, Lubben, Bissell, Farley et al.

525 Sharon Mitchell, "How to Put Condoms in the Picture," *New York Times*. http://www.nytimes.com/2004/05/02/opinion/02MITC.html. Ms. Mitchell is a former pornographic performer and the founder of AIM (Adult Industry Medical Healthcare Foundation). Mitchell received her PhD from the Institute for the Advanced Study of Human Sexuality in San Francisco, *a non-credentialed agency*, since 1968, that has published and sold child pornography to *Hustler* Magazine (see Reisman, *Kinsey Crimes and Consequences*, 2003 and www.drjudithreisman.com for further information, in Reisman's archives).

526 See employment laws for independent contractor vs. employee at www.irs.gov, http://www.taxes.ca.gov/iCorE.bus.shtml.

527 *Robert Deupree, Petitioner, v. Workers' Compensation Appeals Board* (08–815) March 2, 2009.

528 DOSH, http://www.dir.ca.gov/DOSH/AdultFilmIndustry.html.

529 Shelley Lubben is executive director of *Pink Cross Foundation*, a nonprofit organization that reaches out to pornography employees with aid "as well as helping those who struggle with porn addiction," http://www.shelleylubben.com.

530 See independent contractor vs. employee at, www.edd.ca.gov, http://www.irs.gov/businesses/small/article/0,id=99921,00.html.

531 Allen, M., Emmers, T., Gebhardt, L., & Giery, M.A. (1995). Exposure to pornography and acceptance of rape myths. *Journal of Communication*, 45 (1), 5–26; Saunders, R.M., & Naus, P.J. (1993). The impact of social content and audience factors on responses to sexually explicit videos. *Journal of Sex Education and Therapy*, 19 (2), 117–131.

[CHAPTER 9]

532 Mary Eberstadt, "Pedophile Chic, Part II," *Weekly Standard*, June 17, 1996.

533 ABC News "Primetime Live" interview "Kinsey," October 14, 2004, "Scotland on Sunday," February 27, 2005.

534 Apparently organized by the German, Magnus Hirschfeld, this is the beginning of the search for scientific justification for homosexual conduct; see, among other sources, http://www.etext.org/Politics/MIM/contemp/leftover/germhomophobes.htm.

535 Jack Douglas, *The Family in America*, The Rockford Institute, Mount Morris, Illinois, May 1987, 1–8.

536 Ibid., 2.

537 Jeffrey Masson, *Assault on the Truth* (New York: Farrar, Straus and Giroux, 1984).

538 Ray Abrams, "The Contribution of Sociology to a Course on Marriage and the Family," *M. Fam. Liv.* 2 (1940): 82–83.

539 Christopher Lasch, *Culture of Narcissism* (New York: W.W. Norton, 1991), 167.

540 Ibid. see also Vernon's Annotated Missouri Statutes.

541 Randy Engel, *Sex Education, The Final Plague* (Human Life International, 1989), 48–49.

542 Kronhausen, *Sex History of American College Men*, finding too little promiscuity among college youth who waited for love and romance.

543 Mary Shivanandan, "Childhood and Educational Development," Educational Guidance Institute, Inc. Arlington, 1991.

544 See Kinsey's numerous claims for the value of early sex for children in Chapter 5 in his Male and Female volumes.

545 Charlotte Iserbyt, *The Deliberate Dumbing Down of America* (Ravenna, OH, Conscience Press, 1999), 19–20; cite to William Z. Foster, *Toward A Soviet America*.

546 B.F. Skinner, of the "Skinner box" for childhood rearing, headed the psychology department at Indiana University when Kinsey was there, as did Hermann Muller, discussed in more detail in my book, *Kinsey, Crimes & Consequences* (2003).

547 *Education for All American Youth*, Educational Policies Commission, Washington, D.C., 1944, 118.

548 Iserbyt, *Deliberate Dumbing Down*, 28.

549 Ibid., 29.

550 Ibid., 40.

551 Lawrence Levine, *The Opening of the American Mind* (Boston: Beacon Press, 1996), 6–7.

552 http://www2.hu-berlin.de/sexology/GESUND/ARCHIV/CHR06.HTM.

553 http://health.discovery.com/centers-sex-sexpedia-alfredckinsey.shtml, the Sinclair Institute, a Kinsey-tied pornography site.

554 Lasch, *Culture of Narcissism*, ibid., 161–166.

555 William G. Dyer and Dick Urban, "The Institutionalization of Equalitarian Family Norms," *M. Fam. Liv.* 20 (1958): 53.

556 Sol W. Ginsburg, M.D., in *An Analysis of the Kinsey Reports on Sexual Behavior in the Human Male and Female*, ed., Donald Porter Geddes (New York: New American Library, 1954), 36. Psychiatrist Ginsburg, of New York University, the New York School of Social Work and Columbia College of Physicians and Surgeons, quotes Yale Clinical Professor of Psychiatry, child psychiatrist Lawrence Kubie: "If this report does no more than present us with incontrovertible statistics concerning the incidence of manifest infantile sexuality, and of manifest adult polymorphous sexual tendencies, it will be a major contribution to our understanding of human development. . . . " Kubie: Kinsey "offers valuable guides to child rearing, parent-child relationships, harmonious marriage relations and understanding of many sex problems. It can help strengthen family life in America."

557 Lionel Trilling, "The Kinsey Report," in Donald Porter Geddes, ed., *An Analysis of the Kinsey Reports* (New York: Mentor Books, 1954), 212.

558 Engel, *Sex Education*, 48–49.

559 See Judith Reisman and Cliff Kinkaid, "The *Playboy Foundation*: A Mirror of the Culture?" Capital Research Center, Washington, D.C., 1992.

560 http://www.soulforce.org/article/642, January 30, 2010.

561 Ibid. Reisman, 82, 172–175.

562 James Jones, *Alfred C. Kinsey: A Public/Private Life* (New York: W.W. Norton, New York, 1997); Reisman, *Kinsey, Crimes & Consequences*, Chapter 2.

563 http://www.sfgate.com/c/a/2009/01/04/MN2614SOAT.DTL, January 26, 2010.

564 The "bodywork" certificate now listed online has removed much of the original text: http://www.iashs.edu/cert.html, December 5, 2009.

565 *SIECUS. Report*, January–February 1987, 15.

566 Ibid. Cliff Kinkaid, The *Playboy Foundation*: A Mirror of the Culture?

567 See Reisman, *Kinsey, Crimes & Consequences* and drjudithreisman.com, RSVP America.

568 http://www.esextherapy.com/dissertations/erickson%20dissertation.pdf and see also, http://www2.hu-berlin.de/sexology/Entrance_Page/Free_Online_Courses/free_online_courses.html January 26, 2010.

569 http://www.siecus.org/index.cfm?fuseaction=Page.viewPage&pageId=494&parentID=472.

570 http://www.drjudithreisman.com/childsafe.html, January 26, 2010. Contact author for the original in her archive.

571 http://www.siecus.org/index.cfm?fuseaction=Page.viewPage&pageId=494&parentID=472.

572 http://www.iashs.edu/rights.html.

573 A version of this short time line appeared in SALVO, 2008.

574 Beverly R. Newman, "Should State Funding of the Kinsey Institute's Sexual Research End?" *Insight on the News*, March 30, 1998.

575 Engel, *Sex Education.*

576 Charles Socarides, M.D., NARTH interview, *Homosexuality: A Freedom Too Far*, September 20, 2004.

577 Ibid.

578 Benjamin Shapiro, "Rescuing the PornGeneration," *WorldNetDaily*, June 16, 2005.

579 Fathers, and increasingly mothers abandon their marriage vows (or don't make marriage vows) as well as their children. Child abandonment is seen in the vicious music Mary Eberstat analyzes. It is seen in the films and television shows that exploit pandemic rape, child rape, murder and mutilation—without asking. Why? How did we come to this?

580 For the most recent information see congressional testimony by Joseph Henry, Nikki Craft: "The Nudist Hall of Shame," at http://www.nostatusquo.com/ACLU/NudistHallofShame/index.html.

581 There is a flood now of similar sex training groups, http://www.rense.com/general87/CSC_Strategy_Document.pdf.

582 Typically, the one conference at which I was permitted (inadvertently) to present my Kinsey data, on International Research in Sexology, purged my

two papers from its "Selected Papers from the Fifth World Congress" ("selected" indeed). Harold I. Lief and Zwi Hoch, http://doi.contentdirections.com/mr/greenwood.jsp?doi=10.1336/0275914429.

583 "Statement of purpose," *Paidika: The Journal of Paedophilia* no. 1 (1987): 1–2.

584 Vern L. Bullough, "Alfred Kinsey and the Kinsey Report: Historical Overview and Lasting Contributions," *Journal of Sex Research* 35 (1998): 127.

585 Ibid., 127.

586 Vern and Bonnie Bullough, "Should Sex Have A Different Meaning For Humanists?" *Humanism Today* (1991): 140–141.

587 Ibid., 127.

588 These ACLU Kinsey trainee lawyers would wipe out America's historic religious, moral, and medical sex laws and public policies (see our legal discussion). Even the phallic Freud was too "moral" and "medical" for Kinsey's "scientific" paganistic apprentices.

589 http://www.physiciansforlife.org/content/view/630/27.

590 "The World AIDS Day" brochure recommended in Section IV as "Resources" in the 200-page "Lifetime Wellness Curriculum Framework, Lifetime Wellness Resource Manual" of the Tennessee State Department of Education, taught to Tennessee teachers as a sex education curricula from August 1, 1994 to March 1995. Analyzed by this author, published August 1999, 40.

591 Crooks and Baur, *Our Sexuality*, Perspectives on Sexuality, Chapter 1, 14; 2006. http://64.78.63.75/samples/05PSY0404CrooksBaurrOurSexuality9ch1.pdf.

592 "Doctors Endorse Abstinence Education," http://www.texlife.org/docs/explicit.html, 2008.

593 "Psycho-Sexual Development," quoted in *Planned Parenthood News*, Summer 1953, 10.

594 *Planned Parenthood Federation of America Bulletin* (1996), in http://www.grtl.org/plannedparenthoodquotes.asp##Act1.

595 See http://www.plannedparenthood.org/parents/human-sexuality-what-children-need-know-when-they-need-know-it-4421.htm, November 18, 2009.

596 See, *Margaret Sanger, Founder of Planned Parenthood, In Her Own Words*, http://www.dianedew.com/sanger.htm, November 18, 2009.

597 See http://www.dianedew.com/sanger.htm, Planned Parenthood employee lecturing students of Ramona High School, Riverside, CA, April 21–22, 1986.

598 http://www.fightpp.org/show.cfm?page=leaders teenwire.com (PPFA), 2003, November 18, 2009.

599 *The Great Orgasm Robbery*, Rocky Mountain Planned Parenthood, 1981.

600 Heritage House, http://www.abortionfacts.com/literature/literature_9312ha.asp.

601 http://www.plannedparenthood.org/central-ohio/our-history.htm.

602 http://www.plannedparenthood.org/central-ohio/our-history.htm.

603 See www.teenwire.com, and Ask the Experts, http://www.plannedparenthood.org/teen-talk/ask-experts-25532.htm. Review changed "advice" for altered messages, you be the judge of the "advice."

604 Ibid. www.teenwire.com, November 18, 2009. Emphasis added. Review changed "advice" for altered messages, you be the judge of the "advice."
605 Ibid. www.teenwire.com, November 18, 2009. Review changed "advice" for altered messages, you be the judge of the "advice."
606 Ibid. www.teenwire.com, December 20, 2006. Review changed "advice" for altered messages, you be the judge of the "advice."
607 See http://www.scarleteen.com, November 18, 2009. Review changed "advice" for altered messages, you be the judge of the "advice."
608 Ibid. http://www.scarleteen.com, December 15, 2006. Review changed "advice" for altered messages, you be the judge of the "advice."
609 Ibid. http://www.scarleteen.com, December 15, 2006. Review changed "advice" for altered messages, you be the judge of the "advice."
610 Lee Duigon, Concerned Women for America, http://www.cwfa.org/articles/6122/CFI/family.
611 Ibid.
612 Ibid. 73.
613 Selwyn Duke, http://www.thenewamerican.com/index.php/history/american/1008, April 16, 2009. Masturbation and partner sex alike can cause penile fracture. This painful condition—actually a tear in the tunica albuginea, the whitish tissue surrounding the penis's spongy layers—occurs when an erect penis strikes a hard object or is forced downward. A medical emergency, it often necessitates surgery. http://www.medicinenet.com/script/main/art.asp?articlekey=100371, *David Freeman WebMD Feature.*
614 Thomas Sowell, PhD, "Indoctrinating the Children," *Forbes*, February 1, 1993, 65.
615 John B. Jemmott III, Loretta S. Jemmott, Geoffrey T. Fong, "Efficacy of a Theory-Based Abstinence-Only Intervention Over 24 Months", *Arch. Pediatr. Adolesc. Med.* 164, no. 2 (2010). See also http://www.abstinence.net/pdf/contentmgmt/abstinence.pdf.

[CHAPTER 10]

616 In Robert E. Cooke, ed., *The Terrible Choice: The Abortion Dilemma* (New York: Bantam Books, 1968), ix–xi.
617 James Reed, *From Private Vice to Public Virtue* (New York: Basic Books, 1978), 124.
618 Paul Gebhard, Wardell Pomeroy, Clyde Martin, and Cornelia Christenson, *Pregnancy, Birth and Abortion* (New York: John Wiley & Sons, 1958), 119.
619 Gebhard et al., *Pregnancy, Birth and Abortion*, 65.
620 Vincent Felitti, *The Ace Study*, http://www.cavalcadeproductions.com/ace-study.html.
621 http://www.nrlc.org/abortion/pba/.

622 "Baby Parts for Sale: Fetal Harvesting," http://www.abortiontv.com/Misc/BabyPartsForSale.htm.

623 "Technology a Beacon of Hope to Infertile Couples," *Washington Times*, December 4, 1994, A10. The article finds couples paying up to $10,000 for the woman to be implanted embryonically, suggests a massive industry in embryo farming for sales relating to infertility—or for human harvesting, as in the worst science fiction. Millions of Third World women could be cheaply used in such labor. See cartoon, "Body Parts" in Carr and Meyer's *Celebrate Life* (Brentwood, TN: Wolgemuth and Hyatt, 1990), 148.

624 Right to Life of Greater Cincinnati, August http://www.affirminglife.org/ October 1, 2005.

625 *The Science of Chimeras and Hybrids*, http://www.lifeissues.net/writers/sey/sey_01sciencechimerashyb.html.

626 Ibid.

627 See ad, http://www.all.org/pdf/bloodmoney.pdf.

628 The Ryan Report, http://www.all.org/stopp/rr0404.htm, April, 2004.

629 See http://www.grtl.org/plannedparenthoodquotes.asp, David A. Grimes, Willard Cates, Jr., and Jack C. Smith, APPF, 1976.

630 Gloria Feldt, *INsider* (Spring 1997).

631 "Go ask Alice," "Nutritional value in a serving of sperm," started running October 29, 1999 still running as of February 1, 2010. http://www.goaskalice.columbia.edu/1585.html.

632 George Grant, *Grand Illusions* (Brentwood, TN: Wolgemuth & Hyatt, 1990), 106–108.

633 Ibid., 32–33.

634 Ibid.

635 Ibid., 32.

636 Ibid. See also "Reported and Unreported Teacher-Student Sexual Harassment" *Journal of Ed Research* 3 (1991): 164, 169.

637 Caroline Hendrie, "Sexual Abuse by Educators is Scrutinized," *Education Week*; Charol Shakeshaft, "Educator Sexual Misconduct: A Synthesis of Existing Literature," commissioned by U.S. Department of Education, March 10, 2004.

638 Wishnietsky, "Reported and Unreported Teacher-Student Sexual Harassment," *Journal of Ed. Research*. 3 (1991): 164–169. http://www.sesamenet.org.

639 Greetje Timmerman, "Sexual Harassment of Adolescents Perpetrated By Teachers and By Peers: An Exploration of the Dynamics of Power, Culture, and Gender in Secondary Schools," *Sex Roles: A Journal of Research* (March 2003).

640 SESAME brochure, 1996, Charol Shakeshaft, PhD, Hofstra University, Testimony before the New York State Commission on Children and Families, February 2, 1998, 1, http://www.sesamenet.org.

641 SESAME, 1996; *The Kingston Whig-Standard* [Ontario], September 13, 1997, at. 1.

642 Id., David Finkelhor, "Child Sexual Abuse: New Theory and Research," 1984, at 1.

643 England's Yorkshire television, "SECRETS: Kinsey's Paedophiles," Tim Tate producer, director, interview with Jonathan Gathorne-Hardy, Kinsey biographer, in the author's archive, June 17, 1998, Tape #SP 27 & 28, 46.

644 Judith Reisman, Images of Children, Crime and Violence in *Playboy*, *Penthouse*, and *Hustler*, prepared under Grant No. 84-JN-AX-K007, U.S. Department of Justice, Juvenile Justice and Delinquency Prevention Division, (1984). Reisman directed a two-year content analysis of images of children and crime and violence in *Playboy*, *Penthouse*, and *Hustler* from the years 1953 to 1984. Reisman's study documented that each issue of *Hustler* averaged images of 14.1 children and pseudo-children alongside 47 images of crime and violence. Moreover, 52% of child photos were sexually explicit, and most cartooned children were sexually violated. The Kinseyan sex science leader, John Money of Johns Hopkins was exposed February 11, 2000, on *Dateline*, as well as on *Oprah*, and the *Today Show* as a sadistic, pedophilic-oriented psychopath. See John Colapinto, *As Nature Made Him* (New York: Harper-Collins, 2000), for the story behind Money's sex change operations at Johns Hopkins.

645 See "Cover-Up at American University?" *Accuracy in Academia* 6, no. 11 (November, 1991), at 1, 5, as well as articles on President Richard Barendzen ("Obscene Phone Calls Are Traced to AU President," *Washington Post*, April 25, 1990, A24; "Educator accused of sex abuse" noted AU psychology head, Dr. Elliot McGinnies' turns himself in," [Baltimore] *Evening Sun*, June 19, 1986, D-16 (the story never appeared in the Washington, D.C. papers), and "Nobel Winner Guilty of Abusing Boy," *Washington Post*, February 9, 1997, A–1.

646 See http://www.nostatusquo.com/ACLU/NudistHallofShame/McGinnies.html.

647 See the extensive literature on "sex addiction," e.g., Patrick Carnes, *The Sexual Addiction* (Minneapolis: CompCare Publications, 1983), 51, 95, identifying the link to pornography; see also Reisman, *Soft Porn Plays Hard Ball* (1991), Images of Children, Crime and Violence in *Playboy*, *Penthouse*, and *Hustler* (1986, 1989), *Kinsey, Crimes & Consequences* (1998, 2000), etc.

648 Abraham Lincoln signed off on a statute restricting sexually explicit materials through the mails to the Union soldiers and obviously would argue that widespread access called for by elite "speech" advocates would endanger *children's* health, welfare and liberty.

649 http://www.freerepublic.com/focus/f-news/1506578/posts.

650 Ibid.

651 http://whitetrash.net/bang_that_teacher/coors.beer/1047/|Stephanie+Giam belluca.

652 Teacher's Aide, http://crime.about.com/od/sex/ig/female_pedophiles/Amber-Marshall.htm. About.com Guide.

653 WorldNetDaily, http://www.wnd.com/news/article.asp?ARTICLE_ID=48421.
654 http://badbadteacher.com/angela-comer-pleads-guilty.
655 http://current.com/items/92003338_angela-stellwag-pleads-guilty-to-sex-with-14-year-old-student.htm.
656 http://debra-lafave-news.blogspot.com/2008/08/brandy-lynn-gonzales-pleads-guilty-to.html.
657 http://www.foxnews.com/story/0,2933,241005,00.html.
658 http://pedoteacher.com.
659 http://pedoteacher.com.
660 http://www.teachercrime.com/arizona.html.
661 teachercrime.com/arizona.html.
662 http://badbadteacher.com/heather-chesser/.
663 teachercrime.com/arizona.html.
664 http://crime.about.com/od/sex/ig/female_pedophiles/Carol-Lynn-Flannigan.htm.
665 http://www.thedenverchannel.com/news/13465752/detail.html.
666 http://badbadteacher.com/cathy-heminghaus/.
667 http://badbadteacher.com/christine-scarlett-guilty-plea/.
668 http://badbadteacher.com/darcie-esson/.
669 http://badbreeders.net/2007/12/02/deborah-reeder-pleads-no-contest-to-child-abuse-for-having-sex-with-her-sons-17-year-old-friend/.
670 http://nymag.com/news/features/17064/index2.html, feature story.
671 http://interested-participant.blogspot.com/2005/11/teacher-charged-with-corrupting-boy.html.
672 http://badbadteacher.com/franca-munoz-juvera-charged/.
673 http://www.iwasyouragetwice.com/node/3454.
674 http://www.minthegap.com/culture-in-decline/teacherstudent-sexual-relations/?ln=Bird&fn=Janelle%20Marie.
675 http://www.aboms.com/archives/003922.html.
676 Teacher Kristi Oakes Enters Guilty Plea.
677 http://www.wlwt.com/education/9482415/detail.html.
678 http://www.hottforteacher.com/michelle-kush/.
679 http://interested-participant.blogspot.com/2007/12/teacher-pamela-balogh-guilty-of-sex.html.
680 http://www.statemaster.com/encyclopedia/Pamela-Rogers-Turner.
681 http://www.freerepublic.com/focus/f-news/1610203/posts.
682 http://www.zimbio.com/The+50+Most+Infamous+Female+Teacher+Sex+Scandals/articles/ruzbdpVLO6c/14+Traci+Tapp.
683 Internet site, http://www.masscops.com/idiot-news-stories/2389-women-troubles-january-2010-a.html.
684 These convictions were verified.
685 Associated Press, October 23, 2001.
686 [Fort Lauderdale] *Sun-Sentinel*, July 28, 2001, Broward Metro Edition.
687 Associated Press, October 24, 2001.

688 Associated Press October 26, 2001.
689 Copley News Service Illinois; see also *Peoria Journal Star*, May 31, 2001.
690 [Cleveland] *Plain Dealer*, October 27, 2001 Metro.
691 *Chicago Daily Herald*, November 16, 2001.
692 *Boston Globe*, August 18, 2001.
693 *Baltimore Sun*, August 10, 2001.
694 http://latimesblogs.latimes.com/lanow/2009/12/oc-bus-driver-convicted-of-molesting-three-girls.html.
695 Associated Press, November 13, 2001.
696 *Tulsa World*, October 16, 2001.
697 AP WorldStream, November 29, 2004.
698 Associated Press, August 19, 2004.
699 Associated Press, August 19, 2004.
700 *Daily Press*, December 9, 2004.

[CHAPTER 11]

701 Angie Gaddy, *Spokane Spokesman-Review*, December 29, 2001, B3.
702 See the Supreme Court reversal; http://www.law.umkc.edu/faculty/projects/ftrials/conlaw/usvamerlibassn.html. June 23, 2003.
703 *Playboy* announced its early contributions to the American Library Association. See Cliff Kinkaid, *The Playboy Foundation: A Mirror of the Culture?* (Washington, D.C.: Capital Research Center, 1992), 12, 76, 113, 115.
704 *New York v. Ferber*, 458 U.S. 103 (1982); see http://www.oyez.org/cases/1980-1989/1981/1981_81_55.
705 *American Library Association v. Reno*, No. 92-5271 (1994). http://caselaw.lp.findlaw.com/scripts/getcase.pl?court=us&vol=000&invol=96-511.
706 http://www.qrd.org/qrd/orgs/NAMBLA/1993/nambla.vs.kron.roy.radow, November 8, 1993.
707 NAMBLA/1993, ibid.
708 Kinkaid, "*Playboy* Foundation," 12, 76, 113, 115.
709 945 F. Su772, See also http://www.ala.org/ala/mgrps/affiliates/relatedgroups/freedomtoreadfoundation/ftrfinaction/ftrfnews/vol21no1-2.doc.
710 http://shawnsjames.blogspot.com/2010/01/guide-to-better-experience-at-library.html, January 31, 2010.
711 *Grand Rapids Press*, Grand Rapids, Michigan, July 27, 2001.
712 Associated Press, October 23, 2001.
713 *Chicago Tribune*, January 11, 2002, 4 ("Metro" section).
714 General Internet news, http://www.nbc5.com/news/3985682/detail.html.
715 Examples of Crimes and Filters in Libraries, http://www.plan2succeed.org/examples.html.
716 CBS 2 Investigator Dave Savini, 2006, http://cbs2chicago.com/topstories/local_story_355221218.html.

717 Supreme Court Upholds CIPA; Library Internet Policies under Review, http://www.ala.org/ala/alonline/currentnews/newsarchive/2003/june2003/supremecourtupholds.cfm.
718 Greetje Timmerman, "Sexual Harassment of Adolescents Perpetrated By Teachers and By Peers: An Exploration of the Dynamics of Power, Culture, and Gender in Secondary Schools," *Sex Roles: A Journal of Research* (March 2003).
719 *NewsMax.com*; http://www.newsmax.com/archives/articles/2004/4/5/01552.shtml.
720 Michael Rose, *Goodbye! Good Men* (Cincinnati: Aquinas Publishing, Ltd., 2002), 284, 294.
721 *The Advocate*, April 30, 2002, 30; "Abuse Panel Says It Will Seek Change," *Boston Globe*, March 17, 2002.
722 John Colapinto, *As Nature Made Him: The Boy Who Was Raised as a Girl* (HarperCollins, New York, 2000), 29.
723 *Paidika: The Journal of Paedophilia* (Spring 1991): 12.
724 Ibid.
725 See discussion of the Reinisch-Money connection in Reisman, et al., *Kinsey, Sex & Fraud* (Lafayette, LA, Huntington House, 1990).
726 Thomas Doyle, F. Ray Mouton, and Michael R. Peterson, "The Problem of Sexual Molestation by Roman Catholic Clergy: Meeting the Problem in a Comprehensive and Responsible Manner," (1985), 2.
727 Johns Hopkins University School of Medicine, The Johns Hopkins Clinic, Biosexual Psychohormonal Clinic, patient agreement pages, unpaginated, page 26 of the Doyle-Mouton-Peterson document.
728 Editorial, "Our Say: Stop Shielding Child Molesters," *Capital Gazette*, March 23, 1988, A-18.
729 Ibid.
730 "Doctor Skirts Eeporting Law on Sex Crimes," *Baltimore Sun*, March 4, 1990; see page titled, "attempt to circumvent law on reporting sex crimes."
731 "Founded in 1981 by a priest-psychiatrist who later died of AIDS, St. Luke is one of a handful of" such clinics. Caryle Murphy, "Treating the Priest," *Washington Post*, May 11, 2002, at A1 (Metro ed.).
732 Avram Goldstein, *Washington Post*, June 30, 2002, http://www.snapnetwork.org/legal_courts/maryland_hospital.htm.
733 See *Sex Offender Treatment: Research Results Inconclusive About What Works to Reduce Recidivism*, Government Accounting Office, GGD-96-137, June 21, 1996.
734 *Phyllis Schlafly Report* 40, no. 6 (December 2006), http://www.eagleforum.org/psr/2006/dec06/psrdec06.html.
735 "Ex-Gay Books Banned," http://www.stoptheaclu.com/2009/10/23/ex-gay-books-banned, October 23, 2009.
736 Fathers, and increasingly mothers abandon their marriage vows (or don't make marriage vows) as well as their children. Child abandonment is seen

in the vicious music Eberstat analyzes. It is seen in the films and television shows that exploit pandemic rape, child rape, murder and mutilation—without asking; Why? How did we come to this?

[CHAPTER 12]

737 Hannah Arendt, quoted in Eugene Rostow, *Is Law Dead* (New York: Simon and Schuster, 1971), 221.

738 Kevin Ring, ed,. *Scalia Dissents* (Washington, D.C.: Regnery Press, 2004), 159.

739 René Guyon, *The Ethics of Sexual Acts* (New York: Alfred A. Knopf, 1948, 1958), v–vi.

740 Herbert Wechsler, "Challenge of a Model Penal Code, 65 *Harvard Law Review* at 1103 (1952).

741 The Illinois Commission cites this as a "scientific finding" on 9. See also A.C. Kinsey, W.B. Pomeroy, and C.E. Martin, *Sexual Behavior in the Human Male* (Philadelphia: W. B. Saunders, 1948), 181.

742 Ralph Slovenko & C. Phillips, *Psychosexuality and the Criminal Law*. 15 *Vanderbilt Law Review* 809 (1962).

743 "The term 'sexual psychopath' means a person, not insane, who by a course of repeated misconduct in sexual matters has evidenced such lack of power to control his or her sexual impulses as to be dangerous to other persons because he or she is likely to attack or otherwise inflict injury, loss, pain, or other evil on the objects of his or her desire," 2010. Legal definition supplied by the Metropolitan Police Department Headquarters, see http://mpdc.dc.gov/mpdc/cwp/view,a,1241,q,540375,mpdcNav_GID,1532.asp, January 26.

744 *Sex Offender Treatment: Research Results Inconclusive About What Works to Reduce Recidivism*. Government Accounting Office, GGD-96-137, June 21, 1996. Recent federal health institution studies covering the past half a century of treatment modalities for sex offenders conclude that no form of psychotherapy is shown to arrest sexual predation. This can logically be viewed as a report identifying the failure of the treatment mode of penology.

745 Alan Gregg, *Diary*, July 7, 1950, following his "Visit to Dr. Alfred C. Kinsey," Indiana University, 4, the Rockefeller Archive Center.

746 http://www.obscenitycrimes.org/news/vfrd1206.php, January 31, 2010.

747 Louis B. Schwartz, *Book Reviews: Sexual Behavior in the Human Male*, 96 *University of Pennsylvania Law Review* at 917 (1948).

748 *This is ALI-ABA*. Brochure, unpaginated, The American Law Institute, Philadelphia, October 18, 1995, 1.

749 Ibid.

750 Jonathan Gathorne-Hardy, *Sex, Alfred C. Kinsey, The Measure of All Things* (London: Chatto & Windus, 1998), 449.

751 See the 1955 Draft, n. 4, "Sexual Offenses" Section 207 of the Model Penal Code.
752 http://www.cwfa.org/articledisplay.asp?id=18301&department=FIELD&categoryid=pornography.
753 *Report of the Illinois Commission on Sex Offenders*, March 15, 1953, 9.
754 Pomeroy, Dr. Kinsey and the Institute for Sex Research, 210–211.
755 *Preliminary Report of the Subcommittee on Sex Crimes of the Assembly Interim Committee on Judicial System and Judicial Process*, California Assembly, March 8, 1950, reported in foreword, unnumbered.
756 *Report of the Illinois Commission on Sex Offenders*, March 15, 1953, 9.
757 Herbert Wechsler, *Challenge of a Model Penal Code*, 65 *Harvard Law Review* 1128 (1952).
758 Morris Ploscowe in A. Deutch (ed.), *Sex Habits of American Men* (New York: Prentice Hall, 1948), 125–135.
759 Morris Ploscowe, "Sexual Patterns and the Law," in Deutch *Sex Habits of American Men*, 126.
760 Beryl Levy, "What Is Rape?" *Sexology*, June 1961, 744–748
761 Pomeroy, *Kinsey and the Institute for Sex Research*, 210–211.
762 Kinsey et al, *Sexual Behavior in the Human Male*, 160–161.
763 Paul Gebhard, et al, *Sex Offenders* (New York: Harper and Row, 1965), The Kinsey Institute, Bloomington, IN, 178.
764 Frankenstein Smith, "Virginity" An Important Treatise on a Very Important Subject," *Playboy*, December 1953, 9.
765 See Judith Reisman, *Images of Children, Crime & Violence in Playboy, Penthouse and Hustler*, U.S. Dept. of Justice, Juvenile Justice and Delinquency Prevention, Grant No. 84-JN-AX-K007 1989.
766 Randy Thornhill and Craig Palmer, *A Natural History of Rape*, (Cambridge: MIT Press, 2000); see also Thornhill and Palmer, "Why Men Rape," *The Sciences*, January/February 2000, 30–31.
767 *The Statistical Abstracts of the United States* and the Department of Commerce, Census Bureau data, 1957 to 1997 (even largely ignoring child rape, sodomy, etc.) yield a *326% increase* in violent crime from 1960 to 1999 despite an overall population increase of only 52% from 1960 to 1999 and a decrease of roughly 9.96% in the under-20 population from 1960 to 2000. Note the upsurge in sexual/violent crime over that of property crime post the Kinseyan revolution: 418% more "forcible rape" (17,190 to 89,110); 279% more robbery (to 15,530) (107,840 to 409,670); 168% more aggravated assault (154,320 to 916,380); and 70% more murder (9,110 to 15,530).
768 David Bryden, "Redefining Rape," 3 *Buffalo Criminal Law Review* 317, 318 (2000).
769 Levy, "What Is Rape?" ibid.
770 Susan Estrich, "Rape," 95 *Yale Law Journal* 1087, 1134–1147, 1140 (1986).
771 Ibid.
772 Ibid.
773 Ibid.

774 Ibid.

775 http://www.stateline.org/live/ViewPage.action?siteNodeId=136&language Id=1&contentId=13966, 3/20/2000.

776 Barbara Lindemann, "To Ravish and Carnally Know: Rape in Eighteenth-Century. Massachusetts," in Charles Jackson (ed.), *The Other Americans* (Praeger, Westport, CT, 1996), 27.

777 Ibid.

778 Massachusetts rape data, http://www.mass.gov/Eeops/docs/eops/Publications /082009_violent_crime_v5_jul09.pdf, 7.

779 Morris Ploscowe, Albert Deutsch, *Sex Habits of American Men*, Prentice Hall, New York, 1948, 135.

780 Linda Jeffrey and Ronald Ray, *A History of the American Law Institute's Model Penal Code; 1923–2003.*

781 Linda Jeffrey and Ronald Ray, *The American Law Institute's Model Penal Code & The Kinsey Reports' Influence on "Science-based" Legal Reform 1923–2003* First Principals Press, 2004.

782 Louis B. Schwartz, ALI "Sex Offenses" author, U. Pennsylvania, 1948.

783 University of Pennsylvania, 1952.

784 University of Ohio, 1959.

785 Duke University, 1960.

786 *Playboy's* Hugh Hefner, U. Colorado, 1965.

787 University of South Dakota, 1968.

788 University of Georgia, 1969.

789 Oklahoma University, 1970.

790 Tennessee University, 1965, Missouri University, 1973.

791 University of Maine, 1976.

792 Preliminary Report of the Subcommittee on Sex Crimes of the Assembly Interim Committee on Judicial System and Judicial Process, California Legislative Assembly, 1949 (created by H.R. 232 and H.R. 43), 103, 105, 117.

793 John Gagnon, *Human Sexualities* (Glenview IL: Scott Foreman, & Co., 1977), 303–304.

794 Ibid.

795 Ibid.

796 NIJ Conference, Statement 2009 by Adam Gelbhttp: http//www.ojp.usdoj.gov/nij/multimedia/video-nijconf2009-gelb.htm.

797 National Crime Victims' Right Week, http://thomas.loc.gov/cgi-bin/query/D?c103:1:./temp/~c103YcwSZA:retrieved December 12, 2006.

798 Press release, Senator Howell Heflin, Georgia (deceased), Washington, D.C., June 27, 1996.

799 James Wootton, *Safe Streets*, Washington, D.C. April 14, 1997.

800 Harlem, Wikipedia. See also "244,000 Native Sons," *Look Magazine*, May 21, 1940, 8.

801 New York Crime Rates 1960–2000, http://www.disastercenter.com/crime/nycrime.htm.

802 Ibid.

803 Peggy Sanday, *A Woman Scorned, Acquaintance Rape on Trial* (New York: Doubleday, 1996), 159.

804 Retrieved September 5, 2005, http://www.dcrcc.org/history.htm.

805 *Prevalence, Incidence, and Consequences of Violence Against Women*, U.S. Department of Justice, 1998.

806 May 19 2005 (HealthDay News)—One in six adult men reported being sexually molested as children, Womenshealth.gov, http://www.darkness2-light.org/KnowAbout/articles_men_victims.asp.

807 U.S. Department of Justice, *The National Crime Victimization Survey, 2000.*

808 Judith Reisman, "How the FBI and DoJ Minimize Child Sexual Abuse Reporting," July 2002, http://www.drjudithreisman.com/archives/fbi.pdf.

809 Morris Ploscowe, *Sex and the Law* (New York: Prentice Hall, 1951), 220. *Note* in *Kinsey, Crimes & Consequences* (2003) this is given as Ploscowe as "in *Sex Habits of American Men.* The correct reference is to Ploscowe's 1951 volume cited here.

810 See Factsheets: New York City Statistics: 2004 http://www.svfreenyc.org/research_factsheet_110.html.

811 William Andrews in "The Early Years: The Challenge of Public Order," wrote of "nearly seven million by 1930. The biggest problem in the big city was traffic," confirmed by the official census data above: http://www.nyc.gov/html/nypd/html/3100/retro.html. See as http://www.gothamgazette.com/article/demographics/20060627/5/1894 in "Estimating New York City."

812 Census, http://quickfacts.census.gov/qfd/states/36/3651000.html. Moreover, the skyrocketing crime rate allegedly dropped—murder by 44%—after 1993 when Mayor Rudolph Giuliani took over and began his tough of crime and "broken windows" policing. Always hard to know, however.

813 See http://www.ojp.gov/bjs/pub/pdf/viocrm.pdf: Murder (and also) Forcible Rape, Content Updated, 02/17/06.

814 See http://www.infoplease.com/ipa/A0873729.html, as would be the 4.6 victimization rate during 1950.

815 U.S. Department of Justice, National Institute of Justice Extent, Nature, and Consequences of Rape Victimization: Findings from the National Violence Against Women Survey January 2006, 33.

816 See http://www.fbi.gov/ucr/cius_04/offenses_reported/violent_crime/forcible_rape.html.

817 See http://www.ojp.gov/bjs/pub/pdf/viocrm.pdf: Murder (and also) Forcible Rape, Content, Updated, February 17, 2006.

818 Sexual Assault: The Silent, Violent Epidemic, http://www.infoplease.com/ipa/A0001537.html.Database, 2007.

819 See Judith Reisman in *Destiny*, *The New Black American Mainstream*: "Sex, Lies, Kinsey and Pornography in Black America," September 1993.

820 National Task Force to End Sexual and Domestic Violence Against Women, Vol. III, February 2005.

821 David A. Fahrenthold, "Statistics Show Drop In U.S. Rape Case," *Washington Post*, June 19, 2006; see http://www.washingtonpost.com/wp-dyn/content/article/2006/06/18/AR2006061800610.html?nav=rss_print.

822 http://feministlawprofs.law.sc.edu/?p=694, Porn: Good for America!

823 United States Crime Rates 1960–2008, http://www.disastercenter.com/crime/uscrime.htm.

824 *U.S. News & World Report*, http://www.dppa.com/news/ppan4q05.pdf?step=display&AID=374, December 13, 2006.

825 http://tech.mit.edu/V118/N62/crime.62w.html, *Washington Post* December 1, 1998.

826 Hirsch National Victims Center. 1990 Retrieved August 16, 2000, from the World Wide Web: http://www.ncvc.org/ index.html.

827 Rana Sampson, "The Problem of Acquaintance Rape of College Students," Center for Problem Oriented Policing (2006).

828 http://www.hcs.harvard.edu/~response/statistics.html and the Boston Area Rape Crisis Center, http://barcc.org.

829 U.S. DoJ, ibid., Extent, Nature, and Consequences of Rape Victimization, 35.

830 Chris O'Sullivan, "Fraternities and the Rape Culture," in Emilie Buchwald, Pamela R. Fletcher, and Martha Roth (eds.), *Transforming A Rape Culture* (Minneapolis: Milkweed, 1993).

831 Nancy Knowles, "Instituting a Greek System at EOU," http://www.eou.edu/saffairs/GreekLife3.htm.

832 See "Cover-Up at American University?" *Accuracy in Academia* (1991); "Obscene Phone Calls Are Traced to American University President," *Washington Post*, April 25, 1990, A24; "Educator accused of sex abuse noted AU psychology head, Dr. McGinnies' confession to the crime," *Baltimore Sun*, June 19, 1986, at D16 (the story never appeared in the Washington, D.C. papers; and "Nobel Winner Guilty of Abusing Boy," *Washington Post*, February 9, 1997, A1. For the story behind John Money's sex change operations at John Hopkins see John Colapinto, *As Nature Made Him.* See also *Dateline* (ABC television broadcast, February 11, 2000).

833 Prominent geneticist guilty of molestation http://www.msnbc.msn.com/id/13943102/ MSNBC, July 19, 2006.

834 *Source: National Committee for the Prevention of Child Abuse*, Child Sexual Abuse Information Sheet, see extensive documentation of child murder by mother's boyfriends, e.g.,: "In 1996, boyfriends were held responsible for 9 of 34 deaths, or 26% of all abuse deaths that year—even more than mothers, who were blamed for 8 of the 34 deaths," Knight Ridder/Tribune News Service, June 11, 2002.

835 G. Paveza, "Risk factors in father-daughter child sexual abuse," *Journal of Interpersonal Violence*,3, no. 3 (1988): 290–306, as reported in Lundy Bancroft and Jay G. Silverman, *The Batterer as Parent* (Sage Publications, 2002), 84–85.

836 *Male*, 61.

837 Kinsey Institute, http://kinseyinstitute.org/research/ak-data.html#prostitutes.

838 Council for Prostitution Alternatives http://www.rainn.org and, http://crime.about.com/od/prostitution/a/prostitution.htm, etc.

839 Donald J. West, *Male Prostitution* (Portland, OR: Haworth Press, 1993), 33.

840 Ibid., 34.

841 Ibid.

842 Harry Benjamin, and R.E.L. Masters, *Prostitution and Morality* (New York: Julian Press, 1964), 114.

843 The Institute for Advanced Study of Human Sexuality (IASHS) Mission Statement, http://www.ejhs.org.

844 http://www.iast.net/thefacts.htm; see also Judith Reisman, *Human Events*, "Reisman vs. Rhode Island," August 11, 2009.

845 Ibid. See also http://www.sharedhope.org/involved/documents.

846 See Shelley Lubben, "Pink Cross," http://www.shelleylubben.com, January 31, 2010.

847 Robin Lloyd, *For Money or Love: Boy Prostitution in America* (New York, Vanguard Press, 1976).

848 Ibid., See book cover.

849 Ibid., 17.

850 Judith Reisman, *Crafting Bi/Homosexual Youth, 2002.* 284+ http://www.drjudithreisman.com/archives/regent.pdf.

851 "The NHSLS found that only 0.9% of men and 0.4% of women reported having only same-sex sexual partners since age 18, a figure that would represent a total of only about 1.4 million Americans (men and women combined)." *Composite U.S. Demographics* http://www.adherents.com/adh_dem.html January 26, 2010.

852 E.g., Jim Hopper, PhD, Dept. of Psychology, Harvard Medical School, http://www.jimhopper.com/male-ab.

853 Gene Abel, *Self-Reported Sex Crimes of Nonincarcerated Paraphiliacs*, Emory University School of Medicine 5–25.

854 Ibid., 20–22.

855 Rape Victim Advocates: http://www.rapevictimadvocates.org/children.html.

856 "Attacking the Last Taboo," *Time*, April 14, 1980.

857 See both *Time* magazine articles, written by John Leo, September 7, 1981, and April 14, 1980. *Time* would never again tell the truth about the academic pedophile movement. Mary Calderone, the head of SIECUS. complained to *Time*'s owner, and Leo never again wrote of the sex educators' incest activity. Shortly thereafter Leo fled to *Newsweek.*

858 Jeremy Travis, *Managing Adult Sex Offenders in the Community*. National Institute of Justice, Research in Brief, January 1997.

859 "Sexes: Attacking the Last Taboo," *Time*, April 14, 1980.

860 James Ramey, "Dealing With the Last Taboo," SIECUS. Re7,1979.), 1–2.

861 *Penthouse Forum Variations, November* 1977, 86 (emphasis added).

862 Gebhard letter to Reisman dated March 11, 1981, in the author's archive.

863 March 11, 1981, personal correspondence, in the author's archive.

864 *Male*, 160–161.

865 *Female*, ibid., 118. What did the team mean, sought? How much is "more," what is "less"? On what evidence was the "more" assumption based? Did prosecutors *really* believe such blatant self-interest as fact? Kinsey held that there is no such thing as abnormal sexual activity, since all mammalian sexual conduct is also the norm for humans. In this, Kinsey and the authors of the ALI-MPC appeared in agreement.

866 *Penthouse Forum Variations*, *Incest: A New Look*, November, 1977, at 86–90.

867 Ibid.

868 *Penthouse*, December 1977.

869 Ibid.

870 Wardell Pomeroy, *Girls and Sex* (New York: Penguin, 1978). 133–134 (emphasis added).

871 Wardell Pomeroy, *Boys and Sex* (New York: Delacorte Press, 1968).

872 *Male*, 558.

873 M. Cook and G. Wilson (eds.), *Love and Attraction* (Oxford: Pergamon, 1979).

874 Larry Constantine, in Cook and Wilson, *Love and Attraction*.

875 Judith Herman, *Father-Daughter Incest* (Cambridge: Harvard University Press, 1981), 16.

876 Lloyd DeMause, "The Universality of Incest," *Journal of Psychohistory*, http://www.geocities.com/kidhistory/incestd1.htm.

877 Ibid.

878 The FBI Uniform Crime Reporting Handbook "NIBRS Edition," 1992, 22.

879 Based on this author's several conversations with Giaretto before his death.

880 Personal correspondence with Connie Valentine, director of the California Protective Parents Association, Cppa001aol.com and TaliaCarneraol.com. See www.protect.org for information on the incest exception.

881 Bruce Perry, "Helping Children Heal," http://www.helpmomsprotect.com/id6.html.

882 California Protective Parents (1999), http://www.protectiveparents.com.

883 Jane Ellen Stevens, "Ending an Awful Irony," *Los Angeles Times*, January 25, 2006, http://articles.latimes.com/2006/jan/25/opinion/oe-stevens25/.

884 Gov. Schwarzenegger, http://gov.ca.gov/press-release/13273, September 15, 2009, v/pub/bill/sen/sb_0001-0050/sb_33_bill_20051004_chaptered.html.

885 Susan Martin, "Quasi-governmental Missing Kids Center Enjoys Key Exemptions From Federal Rules," *St. Petersburg Times*, January 25, 2010, Andrew Vachss, see http://vachss.com/updates_page.html, January 31, 2010.

886 http://www.bc.edu/bc_org/avp/cas/comm/free_speech/ferber.html, original ruling in 1981, U.S. Supreme Court ruling on *New York v. Ferber*, 458 U.S. 747 (1982).

887 See "The Child Online Protection Act (COPA)," http://www.epic.org/free_speech/copa/#news.

888 WorldNetDaily.com, September 19, 2005.
889 North American Man/Boy Love Association, "The Case for Abolishing Age Consent Laws," in Daniel Tsang (ed.), *The Age Taboo: Gay Male Sexuality, Power and Consent* (1981), 96.
890 *Capital Letters*, October 19, 2000.
891 STOPP international, http://www.all.org/stopp/st050607.htm, June 7, 2005.
892 Planned Parenthood Sued for Violating Abortion Parental Notification Laws, Cincinnati, Ohio, April 5, 2005, http://www.lifesitenews.com/ldn/2005/apr/05040504.html.
893 Mike Byrne, 866-828-8355, San Diego, Calif., *Christian Newswire*, October 31, 2006.
894 J.T. Finn, jtfinnearthlink.net, "Yes on 73" California campaign. Pro-Life America. http://www.childpredators.com/ReadReport.cfm.
895 *Psychiatrically Deviated Sex Offenders, Report No. 9*, Committee on Forensic Psychiatry of the Group for the Advancement of Psychiatry, February 1950, 2.
896 David Allyn. "Private Acts/Public Policy: Alfred Kinsey, the American Law Institute and the Privatization of American Sexual Morality," *Journal of American Studies* 30 (1996): 3, 405–428.
897 Morris Ploscowe, "Sexual Patterns and the Law," in Albert Deutsch (ed.), *Sex Habits of American Men, A Symposium on the Kinsey Report* (New York: Prentice Hall, 1948), p 137–138.
898 Deutsch, *Sex Habits of American Men*, 29–30.
899 ALI-MPC, 252.
900 Karla Jay and Allen Young (eds.), *Lavender Culture* (New York University Press, New York, 1994), 342–364.
901 Ibid., 364.
902 Ibid.
903 *Diagnostic and Statistical Manual of Mental Disorders, Fourth Edition (DSM-IV)*, 1994, See also http://www.exodusglobalalliance.org/pedophilianolongeradisorderpsychiatricassociationdecidesp38.ph
904 DSM Sadism, http://www.houseofdesade.com/articles/dsm2.htm; see also Masochism file.

[CHAPTER 13]

905 Morris Ernst and David Loth, *American Sexual Behavior and the Kinsey Report*, (New York: Greystone Press, 1948).
906 Ibid., 19, 139.
907 Morris Ploscowe, *Sex and the Law* (New York: Prentice Hall, 1951), 217.
908 In New York, Ploscowe proposed *that all sex offenses* could be processed as "misdemeanor sexual misconduct." Kentucky law once held rape as a capital offense: The law today echoes the New York law: Their sexual misconduct statute states, KRS 510.140, represents the basic crimes of rape and sodomy

and thus includes all of the higher degrees of each of these crimes. "It provides a useful plea-bargaining tool for the prosecutor in certain cases even though some degree of forcible compulsion or incapacity to consent may be present." On December 30, 1979, the *New York Times* described New Jersey as "hung up lately on the subject of sex." During 1979, according to the news report, New Jersey set the age at which teenagers could legally consent to sex; allowed municipalities to establish "zones" for live sex shows and pornography; legalized incest over the age of 16; legalized necrophilia and sodomy; legalized adultery, fornication, promiscuity, and seduction resulting in pregnancy; reduced penalties for the sale of commercial consumer sex (prostitution).

909 Morris Ploscowe, *Sexual Patterns and the Law*, in Albert Deutsch (ed.), *Sex Habits of American Men* (New York: Prentice Hall, 1948), 126.

910 Ibid., 217 (emphasis added).

911 Ralph Slovenko, et al., "Psychosexuality and the Criminal Law," 15 *Vanderbilt Law Review* 809 (1962) (emphasis added).

912 Charles Ashman, *The Finest Judges Money Can Buy* (Los Angeles: Nash Publishing, 1973), 5–6.

913 Linda Jeffrey, *A History of the American Law Institute's Model Penal Code: The Kinsey Reports' Influence on "Science-based" Legal Reform 1923–2003.* Excellent work drawn largely from the Reisman findings, http://www.thewebcottage.com/rsvp/index.php3?pageid=aboutus.htm.

914 E.C.B. Jr., "Pedophilia, Exhibitionism, and Voyeurism: Legal Problems in the Deviant Society," 4 *Georgia Law Review* at 150 (1969) (emphasis added).

915 Ibid.

916 Orville Richardson, "Sexual Offenses under the Proposed Missouri Criminal Code," 38 *Missouri Law Review* 372 (1973) (emphasis added).

917 Vernon's Annotated Missouri Statutes, 2000, 544.040, "Comment to 1973 Proposed Code." 1973 Missouri Symposium, 382 (emphasis added).

918 Judy R. Potter, "Sex Offenses," 28 *Maine Law Review*, 69 (1976) (emphasis added).

919 C. Nemeth, "How New Jersey Prosecutors View the New Sexual Offense Statutes," *New Jersey Law Journal*, May 5, 1983, 6 (emphasis added).

920 Dr. Linda Jeffreys opines citing to, *State v. Collins*, 70 Ga. 42, 508 S.E. 2d 390 (1998).

921 American Bar Association. *The Probation Response to Child Sexual Abuse Offenders: How Is It Working?* Executive Summary. State Justice Institute, Grant, SJI-88-11J-E-015, 1990, 7. Again, despite overwhelming evidence of treatment failure, the *Boston Globe* exposé above reports no prison time was served by the following: 100% of those *convicted* of attempted child molestation; 60% *convicted* of criminally injuring a child; 30% *convicted* of indecent assault/battery of a child; 20% *convicted* of child rape and sodomy.

922 Senate Bill 586, 67th Oregon Legislative Assembly, 1993 Session.

923 Oregon Laws Regarding Grandparent and Psychological Parent Rights, http://www.kramer-associates.com/mkgrandpsycrights.htm#important.

924 Martin Finucane, Associated Press, Boston, May 16, 2000, http://www.gjne.com/hope%20robbins/jeffrey_curley.htm.

925 Deroy Murdock, "No Boy Scouts," *National Review Online*, February 27, 2004.

926 Massachusetts ACLU Press Release, June 9, 2003.

927 ACLU Board Minutes, April 13–14, 1985.

928 ACLU Policy No. 4, cited in William Donohue, "Where Does the ACLU Stand," *Human Events* (1988), 1.

929 See http://info.sen.ca.gov/pub/05-06/bill/asm/ab_2851-2900/ab_2893_cfa_20060810_103655_sen_comm.html.

930 See ACLU, *Kansas v. Matthew Limon*, Case Background. October 21, 2005; http://www.aclu.org/lgbt-rights/limon-v-kansas-case-profile.

931 William H. Masters, Virginia A. Johnson, and Robert C. Kolodny (eds.), *Ethical Issues in Sex Therapy and Research, Reproductive Biology Research Foundation Conference* (Boston: Little, Brown, 1977), 13.

932 Edward Brecher, *The Sex Researchers* (Boston: Little, Brown, 1969), 139.

933 Ibid., 139; and see Rene Wormser, *Foundations* (New York: Devin-Adair Company, 1958), 129–130.

934 See, for example, R.F. Anda, V.J. Felitti, J.D. Bremner, J.D. Walker, C. Whitfield, B.D. Perry, S.R. Dube, W.H. Giles. "The Enduring Effects of Abuse and Related Adverse Experiences in Childhood: A Convergence of Evidence From Neurobiology and Epidemiology," *European Archives of Psychiatry and Clinical Neuroscience* (2005) [Epub ahead of print]; and S.R. Dube, R.F. Anda, C.L. Whitfield, D.W. Brown, V.J .Felitti, M. Dong, and W.H. Giles. "Long-Term Consequences of Childhood Sexual Abuse by Gender of Victim," *American Journal of Preventive Medicine* (2005): 28:430–438.

935 http://jonathanturley.org/2007/08/18/from-adultery-to-polygamy-the-dangers-of-moral-legislation/, November 18, 2009.

936 See Turley in Stephanie Zimdahl, "The Supreme Court and Foreign Sources of Law: Two Hundred Years of Practice and the Juvenile Death Penalty Decision," 47 *William and Mary Law Review* 743 (2005).

937 Judith Reisman, "Sodomy Decision Based On Fraudulent 'Science,'" Part 1 of 3, *Human Events*, August 14, 2005.

938 Roger J. Magnuson, *Are "Gay Rights" Right?: Homosexuality and the Law* 23 (1985); Judith Reisman and Charles Johnson, *Partner Solicitation as a Reflection of Male Sexual Orientation* (1991). Institute for Media Education, Arlington, VA, 1991; George Rekers, "Gender Identity Disorder," 1 *Journal of Human Sexuality* 16 (1996); Marshal Kirk and Hunter Madsen, *After the Ball: How America Will Conquer Its Fear and Hatred of Gays in the 90s* (1989).

939 Those engaged in highly promiscuous sexual conduct are found to have a high propensity for drug and alcohol use, as well as early sexual abuse. As noted in our cites on *The Advocate* self-reports, 21% of their respondents admitted to sex abuse by age 15. Island and Letellier report their findings, that: "[O]nly substance abuse and AIBIDS adversely affect more gay men, making domestic violence the third largest health problem facing gay men

today." Island and Letellier, p 1. These behaviors are regularly Identified in the professional literature, see, e.g., Jeffrey Satinover, *Homosexuality and the Politics of Truth* 44, 97, 105, 106-108 (1996), as reflecting early childhood trauma. Satinover notes the homosexual effort to deny such etymology, seen in the 126 detailed questions asked of lesbians and "gay" men, including self-image and types of and location of sex practices and the like by Jay and Young, in *The Gay Report*, supra note 92. Ten years after Gagnon's warning Jay and Young avoided any questions that might reveal early sexual or other kinds of trauma as causative in the homosexual respondent's conduct. ibid. Holmes and Slap provide further data on the comparatively high rates of dysfunction among homosexualized boys including suicidal ideation, drugs, crimes, sexual and other disorders. W.C. Holmes and G.B. Slap, "Sexual Abuse of Boys: Definition, Prevalence, Correlates, Sequlae, and Management," 280 *JAMA* 1855, 1858–1859 (1998).

940 Kinsey et al., *Sexual Behavior in the Human Male*, 638.

941 *Male*, 1948, 660.

942 Kinsey, et al, *Sexual Behavior in the Human Female*, 643.

943 *Female*, 649

944 *Female*, 648 (emphasis added).

945 *Female*, 646 (emphasis added).

946 *Female*, 645.

947 *Female*, 649.

948 *Female*, 646.

949 Thomas Miconi, *Fitness Transmission: A Simple, Self-Contained, Measure of Evolutionary Activity*, University of Birmingham, UK. http://www.cs.bham.ac.uk.

950 *Female*, 632–636.

951 See papers at the NARTH site on the "Born That Way" issue, http://www.narth.com/menus/born.html.

952 Holmes and Slap, "Sexual Abuse of Boys," 1855–1862.

953 Kirk and Madsen, *After the Ball*, 154 (emphasis added).

954 Ibid., 178.

955 Fifth Column, http://www.britannica.com/eb/article-9034225.

956 Rockefeller Foundation Humanities Fellowships. . . . The Program for the Study of Sexuality, Gender, Health and Human Rights invites applications from post-doctoral scholars, advocates, and activists . . . .on sexuality, gender, health and human rights in U.S. and international contexts. Sexuality Research Fellowship Program from the Social Sciences Research Councill Funds are provided by the Ford Foundation, http://web.gc.cuny.edu/Clags/OtherAwards.htm.

957 *Random House Dictionary*

958 Aleksander Solzhenitsyn, Harvard University Commencement Address, *reprinted in National Review*, July 7, 1978, 838. http://www.americanrhetoric.com/speeches/alexandersolzhenitsynharvard.htm, November 18, 2009.

959 Philip Kotler, *Marketing Management* (New York: Prentice Hall, 1988).

960 Ibid., 345.

961 http://www.washingtonpost.com/wp-dyn/content/article/2005/09/15/AR2005091500915.html.

962 Laura Sessions Stepp, *Washington Post*, September 16, 2005.

963 Wardell Pomeroy, *Dr. Kinsey and the Institute for Sex Research* (New York: Harper and Row, 1972), 207–208, 222.

964 Peggy Sanday, *A Woman Scorned: Acquaintance Rape on Trial* (New York: Doubleday, 1996), 144–145.

965 Pomeroy, *Dr. Kinsey*.

966 Ibid.

967 William H. Masters, Virginia A. Johnson, and Robert C. Kolodny (eds.), *Ethical Issues in Sex Therapy and Research, Reproductive Biology Research Foundation Conference* (Boston: Little, Brown and Company, 1977), 13.

968 Diana Russell, *The Secret Trauma: Incest in the Lives of Girls and Women* (New York: Basic Books, 1999), 75.

969 Gilbert Herdt, "'Coming Out' as a Rite of Passage," in *Gay Culture in America*, 41; "For the first time, an institutionalized process of initiating and socializing youths [into the homosexual movement] emerged." Ibid. 34.

970 *Trends in Child Abuse and Neglect: A National Perspective*, The American Humane Association, Children's Division, Denver, Colorado, 1984, 12.

971 Data collections by the Federal Bureau of Investigation (FBI), the Department of Justice's (DoJ) Office of Juvenile Justice and Delinquency Prevention (OJJDP), the U.S. DoJ National Incident-Based Reporting System (NIBRS), NIBRIS, 2 http://www.missingkids.com/missingkids.

972 NIBRIS, 2.

973 NIBRIS, 2.

974 *Frontline*, http://www.pbs.org/wgbh/pages/frontline/countryboys/readings/stats.html.

975 Ibid.

976 DoJ/OJJDP Fact Sheet, August 1999, 1, #115, see Reisman report, http://www.drjudithreisman.com/archives/fbi.pdf.

977 National Center for Victims of Crime, www.ncvc.org/ncvc/main.aspx?dbName=DocumentViewer&DocumentID=32368.

978 National Runaway Switchboard, http://www.nrscrisisline.org/.

979 http://www.childrenofthenight.org/faq.html and http://www.humantrafficking.org/updates/278.

980 http://www.pcaky.org/advocacy.html, January 31, 2010. See also extensive evidence on rates of abuse. *Time Magazine*, "The Crisis Of Foster Care," Timothy Roche, November 2000, VOL. 156, NO. 20 (emphasis added).

981 http://www.washingtonpost.com/wp-dyn/content/article/2006/06/18/AR2006061800610.html?nav=rss_print, June 19, 2006.

982 United States Crime Rates 1960–2008, http://www.disastercenter.com/crime/uscrime.htm, *(9.6 per 100,000 in 1960 to 31.8 in 2005)*, 2.

983 *Statutory Rape Known to Law Enforcement*, http://www.ncjrs.gov/pdffiles1/ojjdp/208803.pdf. "Statutory rape victims and offenders younger than age 7

were considered data entry errors and were excluded," at 1, without support for said exclusion.

984 1996 and 1999 data, FBI AP report March 14, 2000, in the National Coalition for Protection of Children and Families, Summer 2000.

985 Police Lt James Ponzi in *The American Police Beat* (May 2005).

986 Ibid. See also Lt. Col. David Grossman, PhD, email in the author's archive.

987 Email from Lt. Ponzi to the author, August 25–27, 2006.

988 Ibid.

989 Ibid.

990 See Linda Jeffrey and Ronald D. Ray, *A History of the American Law Institute's Model Penal Code: The Kinsey Reports' Influence on "Science-Based" Legal Reform* (Crestwood, KY: First Principles Press, 2004), especially 27.

991 See also, "Free Them or Freeze Them: In the Crazy World of Canadian Justice, Jailers Rebuke Parole Boards for Being Too Careful," *The Report Newsmagazine*; February 19, 2001.

992 Sex offender registry, News Online December 15, 2004 http://www.cbc.ca/news/background/missingchildren/sexoffenderregistry.html.

993 Jennifer Tang, "Understanding and Managing Sexually Coercive Behavior," Update, *New York Academy of Sciences Magazine*, October, 2002, 2-5.

994 http://www.ojp.usdoj.gov/bjs/crimoff.htm#recidivism,http://www.democratandchronicle.com/assets/pdf/A242954926.PDF.

995 http://www.democratandchronicle.com/assets/pdf/A242954926.PDF, September 5, 2005.

996 Ibid.

997 U.S. Government Accounting Office, *Sex Offender Treatment: Research Results Inconclusive About What Works to Reduce Recidivism*, June 1996.

998 Karl Hanson and Ian Broom, "Evaluating Community Sex Offender Treatment Programs," *Canadian Journal of Behavioral Science* April 1, 2004.

999 Dennis Hollingsworth, California state senator, http://republican.sen.ca.gov/opeds/36/oped1793.aspm, 5/23/2003.

1000 KlaasKids Foundation For Children. http://www.klaaskids.org/pg-legmeg.htm.

1001 *News Tribune*.com, Tacoma, WA, August 21, 2005.

1002 *Ibid.*

1003 Self-Report Data "The Advocate Survey of Sexuality " Reader Admissions of Sadism is Self Abuse, August 23,1994.

1004 U.S. Department of Justice, Office of Justice Programs, Office of Juvenile Justice and Delinquency Prevention, 1999 National Report Series, Juvenile Justice Bulletin: Children as Victims 2 (May, 2000), http://www.ncjrs.org/html/ojjdp/2000_5_2/child_01.html; Stroud and C Pritchard, "Child Homicide," *British Journal of Social Work, 2001*, 31, 249–269.

1005 Ibid.

1006 *Washington Times*, June 14, 1989, F4: in Tacoma, Washington, a paroled child sex offender raped and sexually mutilated and castrated a 7-year-old boy, triggering a "task force on sexual predators" in Washington State. The story was buried by most of the establishment press.

1007 "Officials Cite a Rise in Killers Who Roam U.S. for Victims," *New York Times*, January 21, 1984, A1-7.

1008 Ibid.

1009 http://www.practicalhomicide.com/articles/homoserial.htm; see Vernon J. Geberth, *Sex-Related Homicide and Death Investigation* (New York, CRC Press, 2003), 502–503.

1010 Vernon J. Geberth, *Homosexual Serial Murder Investigation*, http://www.serve.com/PHIHOM/articles/homoserial.htm.

1011 APRI's National Center for Prosecution of Child Abuse brocure announcing their August 20–24 Conference.

1012 http://www.ojp.usdoj.gov/BJA/what/02ajwactcontents.html.

1013 http://www.criminallawlibraryblog.com/CRS_RPT_DomesticViolence_02-05-2008.pdf. January 26, 2010. Order Code RL34353.

[CHAPTER 14]

1014 Lenore Tiefer, "Sexology and the pharmaceutical industry: The threat of co-optation" *Journal of Sex Research* 37 (2000): 273–283.

1015 See Tim Tate's statement, back cover of *Kinsey, Crimes & Consequences*, addressed elsewhere. UNESCO Award-winning director of "Kinsey's Paedophiles" for Britain's celebrated Yorkshire Television.

1016 Gershon Legman, *The Horn Book* (New Hyde Park, NY: University Books, 1964), 125–126.

1017 Paul Robinson, *The Modernization of Sex* (New York, Harper & Row, 1976), 59.

1018 *Obstretical Gynecological News*, December 1, 1980, 10.

1019 *SIECUS Report*, May-July 1983, 9 (emphasis added).

1020 Deposition of June Reinisah at Indiana University, in lawsuit by Judith Reisman, May 7, 1993.

1021 Bruce Perry, et al, "Child Sexual Abuse," in *Encyclopaedia of Crime and Punishment*, vol 1. (David Levinson, ed.) (Thousand Oaks: Sage Publications), 202–207, 2002, http://www.childtrauma.org/CTAMATERIALS/sexual_abuse.asp.

1022 See, for example, Michael Todd Wilson's "Intimacy Counseling Center" and Michael Sytsma's "Building Intimate Marriages" in Georgia as well as similar centers growing nationwide. Unfortunately, unlike Wilson and Sytsma, few Christian counselors understand how Kinsey's manic sexual dogma has impacted their own training.

1023 SASH, The Society for the Advancement of Sexual Health, originally organized by Patrick Carnes to address sexual addiction was co-opted recently by the SIECUS federation, Carnes recently blaming "excessive religion" for sex addiction, as he has joined the SIECUS Kinsey cult.

1024 San Francisco State University, "Kinsey At 50: Reflections," November 6, 1998.

1025 "Sinclair Institute, Professional Advisory Council, 1993-present," Kinsey Institute vitae, listed under "Special National and International Responsibilities."

1026 http://www.washingtonpost.com/ac2/wp-dyn?pagename=article&contentId=A61747-2002Jun28&notFound=true.

1027 Cynthia Gorney, "Designing Women," *Washington Post*, June 30, 2002, W08.

1028 http://www.alternet.org/sex/143682/%22restless_vagina_syndrome%22:_big_pharma%27s_newest_fake_disease.

1029 See Reisman, *Kinsey, Crimes & Consequences* and *Images of Children, Crime & Violence in Playboy, Penthouse and Hustler* for full documentation.

1030 *New York Times*, circa December 2004.

1031 With women "58% of Medicare recipients at age 65 and 71% at age 85" this union seeks the magic female "Viagra" pill.

1032 http://www.pbs.org/wgbh/pages/frontline/shows/porn/special/.

1033 See Sleeper, Woody Allen, http://abcnews.go.com/GMA/story?id=235788&page=1.

1034 Response To Sexology And The Pharmaceutical Industry: The Threat Of Co-Optation—response to L. Tiefer, *Journal of Sex Research* 37 (May 2001): 273, with comments by Tiefer.

1035 http://www.drugintel.com/drugs/viagra.htm: "For men, flagging potency can be a red flag that something's not right in the cardiovascular system. And experts say men who rush to fix the problem with impotence drugs may be ignoring a bigger threat to their health." http://cialis-search.blogspot.com/2004_09_01_cialis-search_archive.html.

1036 Tony Pugh, "Medicare prescription drug plan would cover impotence drugs," *Knight Ridder*, October 12, 2004. A bogus science release cites "Inflexa, another Pfizer product, combines the best of rabbit staying power with the sturdiness of hardened steel," as an animal-human hybrid. Although this is science fiction, the lust for sexual prowess suggests that such studies are doubtless underway and that some number of men would pay for such genetic malformations, given the opportunity.

1037 Mike Adams, http://www.newstarget.com/001668.html, August 06, 2004.

1038 Ibid.

1039 John Bancroft (ed.), *Sexual Development in Childhood* (Bloomington: Indiana University Press, 2003).

1040 http://scienceandreason.blogspot.com/2005_10_01_archive.html, Human papilloma virus vaccine. "First large test shows vaccine prevents cervical cancer," The Associated Press, October 6, 2005.

1041 http://www.cnn.com/2005/HEALTH/conditions/10/06/cancer.vaccine.ap/index.html.

1042 Institute of Science in Society, "The HPV Vaccine Controversy," May 01, 2009.

1043 For basic dossiers on the leaders in this academic child sexual seduction, see drjudithreisman.com and the RSVP America report.

1044 http://www.washingtontimes.com/news/2003/sep/18/20030918-103459-1292r/?page=2; also quoted in the Kinsey Institute Web site, http://www.indiana.edu/~kinsey/publications/PDF/kinseyfall03.pdf.

1045 SexandHealth,http://www.washingtontimes.com/news/2003/sep/18/20030918-103459-1292r/?page=2, September 18, 2003.

1046 Robert Stacy McCain in http://www.washtimes.com/culture/20030918-103459-1292r.htm. September 18, 2003.

1047 Ibid.

1048 Gilbert, *op. cit.* According to the *Chicago Tribune*, Reinisch received a grant of nearly $1 million from the NIH's National Institute of Child Health and Human Development while teaching at Rutgers University, and continued the project when she took over the directorship of the Kinsey Institute in 1982.

1049 Memorandum from Howard Hyatt, Director, Division of Management Survey and Review, OA, Public Health Service, National Institutes of Health, July 17, 1989.

1050 Ibid.

1051 Ibid., 2.

1052 2002 Drug Industry Profits: http://easydiagnosis.com/blog/?cat=41http://www.citizen.org/documents/medicaredrugwarreportrevised72104.pdf.

1053 Beverly Newman, *Insight on the News*, http://findarticles.com/p/articles/mi_m1571/is_n12_v14/ai_20442633/?tag=content;col1 March 30, 1998.

1054 Carroll Quigley, *Tragedy and Hope* (G. S. G. & Associates, 1975), 71–72.

1055 E. Michael Jones, "The Case Against Kinsey," *Fidelity* (April 1989), 22–35.

1056 In 1925, the Rockefeller Foundation funded the Kaiser Wilhelm Institute for Psychiatry in Munich, which Dr. Ernst Rudin directed. Additional funding was provided by the Harrimans, the Warburgs, and the British Crown. The Rockefeller Foundation continued to sponsor the Institute and its Nazi leader throughout the devastating holocaust of World War II. The Foundation poured money into the occupied German Republic for a medical specialty known as psychiatric eugenics. This field applied to psychiatry the concepts of eugenics, otherwise known as race purification, race hygiene, or race betterment. It was developed in London's Galton Laboratory, and its offshoots, eugenics societies in England and America. In 1925 the Rockefeller Foundation made an initial grant of $2.5 million to the Psychiatric Institute in Munich. It gave it $325,000 for a new building in 1928 and continuously sponsored the Institute and its Nazi Chief Rudin, some data confirm, through all of World War II. http://www.garynull.com/Documents/PathologizingAfricanAmericanPt1.htm.

1057 See my recent book, *Kinsey, Crimes & Consequences* (2003), especially chapter 7. Full documentation available upon request. Also see www.blackgenocide.com

1058 Justine Elias in Bloomington, Indiana, "Kinsey's sex revolution is marching on: As a film on Dr Sex arrives, the institute he founded stresses its scholarly role in the straitlaced Midwest," *The Observer* [UK], March 6, 2005. http://observer.guardian.co.uk/international/story.

1059 The Kinsey Institute—Response to Controversy, www.indiana.edu/~kinsey/about/cont-akchild.html.

1060 All of the transcripts from Kinsey's Paedophiles are available in the authors archive.

1061 Tony Pugh, "Medicare prescription drug plan would cover impotence drugs," *Knight Ridder*, October 12, 2004: "675 registered Congressional lobbyists and a 'persuasion' budget of roughly $200 million [1999, 2000]; more than any other industry." June 23, 2003; Drug Industry Employs 675 Washington Lobbyists, Many with Revolving-Door Connections, New Report Finds *Companion Study Shows That Top 10 Drug Companies Made $36 Billion Last Year – More Than Half of All Profits Netted by Fortune 500 Companies.* Public Citizen http://www.citizen.org/pressroom/release.cfm?ID=1469 and see http://www.commondreams.org/headlines04/1020-20.htm.

With women roughly "58% of Medicare recipients at age 65 and 71% at age 85"; this tripartite union seeks the magic female "Viagra" pill.

See Appendix B. See my recent book, *Kinsey, Crimes & Consequences* (1998, 2000, 2003), especially chapter 7. Full documentation available upon request. Full quotes follow throughout this report. KI book contributor Graham "AIDS Prevention Studies" does not appear to offer an abstinence until marriage message for true AIDS prevention or condom failure rates. I was unable to locate information in Bancroft's, Heiman's, or Graham's biographies as to where either of these KI leaders received their "sexuality training."

1062 The SIECUS founding board included Kinsey co-author and sometime lover, Wardell Pomeroy as well as Mary Calderone of Planned Parenthood and John Money (of *Paidika*, the pedophile magazine). Originally funded by *Playboy*, SIECUS' promotion of "sexually explicit material" in the classroom for all age children is in accord with its foundation. A biased, anti–Judeo-Christian philosophy is clear in the Grant Web site, which funds normalization of the unscientific claim that children are genetically born "gay" as in the Long Island Gay-Straight Alliance Network (LI-GSA Network), that "helps high school students start gay-straight alliance clubs," the Youth Enrichment Services (Y.E.S.) that finds "13–15 year old lesbian, gay, bisexual, transgender and questing adolescents" and shapes them in "arts, technology, and peer leadership," and others. W.T. Grant also funded Gilbert Herdt, contributor to the Childhood Sexuality conference and part of the pedophile magazine, *Paidika*, as the Principal Investigator for a "Study of Gay-Straight-Alliances (GSA) in California High Schools." It is fair to say that any examination of the Kinsey Institute "research" will find the results fully support all such leftist political ends. The Kinsey Institute, like its founder, continues to produce unscientific leftist bias in its "sex" research, in its employment and in the "experts" chosen to train

Indiana University students—both at the Institute and at IU. In 2003 the Institute "researched" and taught on alleged "Gay, Lesbian, Bisexual and Transgendered Youth" as though these were genetically based "orientations" as opposed to youngsters experiencing serious experiential, familial, and other trauma. Clinton's former Surgeon General, Joycelyn Elders is a keynoter at the Kinsey Institute. These funds are in keeping with the political requirements as well of the Kinsey Institute funders such as those administering the Ford and Rockefeller Foundations.

1063 B. Rind, P. Tromovitch, and R. Bauserman, "A metal-analytic examination of assumed properties of child sexual abuse using college samples," *Psychological Bulletin* 124 (1998): 22–53.

1064 John Bancroft (ed.), *"Toward a Consensus"* in *Childhood Sexual Development* (Bloomington: Indiana University Press, 2003), 464.

1065 http://www.dailymail.co.uk/news/article-1245697/Boy-16-sex-change-operation-NHS.html, January 28, 2010.

1066 http://www.sinclairinstitute.com/Sites/sinclairinstitute/search/search.asp?keywords=bondage&search.x=10&search.y=2, and http://www.sinclairinstitute.com/Sites/sinclairinstitute/search/search.asp?keywords=anal&search.x=28&search.y=6 Sinclair Institute, Professional Advisory Council, 1993-present http://www.kinseyinstitute.org/about/heiman-cv.html.

1067 Julia R. Heiman, Ph.D. Curriculum Vita, http://www.kinseyinstitute.org/about/heiman-cv.html.

1068 http://www.washtimes.com/culture/20030918-103459-1292r.htm.

1069 Robert Stacy McCain, http://www.washtimes.com/national/20030709-110059-9087r.htm.

1070 Frayser in Bancroft (ed.), 266.

1071 Bancroft, *"Toward a Consensus,"* 14.

1072 *Paidika, The Journal of Paedophilia*, Postbus, 15463, The Netherlands, 1991, 13.

1073 Judith Reisman, "Crafting Bi/Homosexual Youth," *Regent Law Review* (2002): 323.

1074 Robert Stacy McCain http://washingtontimes.com/national/20040129-112152-7324r.htm, January 30, 2004.

1075 Michael Bailey, *Sexual Development* in *Childhood*, p. 424

1076 Erick Janssen, *Sexual Development* in *Childhood*, ibid., 459–460.

1077 Patrick Meehan, in *The Frankenstein Man*, March, 2002, http://www.drjudithreisman.com/meehan.htm, l.

1078 Edward Brecher, *The Sex Researchers*, (New York: New American Library, 1971 edition). 169.

1079 Ibid., 169–170.

1080 Ira Reiss *An End to Shame: Shaping our Next Sexual Revolution* (Buffalo: Prometheus Books, 1990), 41–42.

1081 Larry Constantine, "The Sexual Rights of Children: Implications of a Radical Perspective," in M. Cook and G.D. Wilson (eds.), *Love and Attraction: An International Conference* (Oxford, Pergamon, 1979), 503–507.

1082 Floyd Martinson, "Infant and Child Sexuality: Capacity and Experience. A Conceptual Framework" in *Love and Attraction*, 489–491.

1083 James Kinkaid, *Child Loving* (New York: Routledge, 1992), 21.

1084 Ibid., 185–186.

1085 Lenore Bauth, *How to Talk Confidently to Your Child About Sex* (St. Louis: Concordia, Publishing, 1998), 21–24.

1086 Paul Cameron, *Sexual Gradualism* (Sun Valley: Human Life Publications, 1978, 1981), 7, 24, 32.

1087 Ibid.

1088 Pomeroy, *Kinsey and the Institute for Sex Research*, 173.

1089 *Washington Post*, April 16, 1988. 18 U.S.C. Sections 287, 1001 (1988); *United States v. Breuning*, No. K88-0135 (D. Md., Nov. 10, 1988).

1090 Linda Reichl in R. McDaniel and D. Driebe (eds.), *Uncertainty and Surprise in Complex Systems* (Berlin/Heidelberg: Springer, 2005), 71–76.

[CHAPTER 15]

1091 Sharon Begley, *Train Your Mind, Change Your Brain* (New York: Ballantine Books, 2007).

1092 Norman Doidge, *The Brain That Changes Itself* (New York: Viking, 2007), 102.

1093 Ibid., 108.

1094 Doidge, http://www.normandoidge.com/normandoidge/MAIN.html.

1095 Doidge, *The Brain That Changes Itself*, 107.

1096 Ibid., 108.

1097 Ibid., 105.

1098 *The Qui Tam Information Center*, http://www.quitam.com/quitam3.html. 1099 Government Fraud Whistleblower and Qui Tam Reports, http://www.governmentfraud.us. Government Fraud Whistleblower and Qui Tam Reports.

1100 E. Michael Jones, "The Case Against Kinsey," *Fidelity* (April 1989), 22–35.

1101 Gathorne-Hardy, *Sex, Alfred C. Kinsey, The Measure of All Things*, 356.

1102 James H. Jones, *Alfred C. Kinsey, A Public/Private Life* (New York: W.W. Norton & Company, 1997), 475.

1103 Ibid., 473–474.

INDEX

Note: page numbers followed by "n" refer to endnotes.